T&T CLARK ENQUIRIES IN THEOLOGICAL ETHICS

Series Editors
Brian Brock
Susan F. Parsons

COMMUNITIES OF RESTORATION

Ecclesial Ethics and Restorative Justice

Thomas Noakes-Duncan

Bloomsbury T&T Clark
An imprint of Bloomsbury Publishing Plc

B L O O M S B U R Y
LONDON • OXFORD • NEW YORK • NEW DELHI • SYDNEY

Bloomsbury T&T Clark
An imprint of Bloomsbury Publishing Plc

Imprint previously known as T&T Clark

50 Bedford Square
London
WC1B 3DP
UK

1385 Broadway
New York
NY 10018
USA

www.bloomsbury.com

BLOOMSBURY, T&T CLARK and the Diana logo are trademarks of Bloomsbury Publishing Plc

First published 2017

British Library Cataloguing-in-Publication Data
A catalogue record for this book is available from the British Library.

ISBN: HB: 978-0-5676-7153-0
ePDF: 978-0-5676-7154-7
ePub: 978-0-5676-7155-4

Library of Congress Cataloging-in-Publication Data
LC record available at http://lccn.loc.gov/2015040645.

Series: T&T Clark Enquiries in Theological Ethics

Typeset by Forthcoming Publications (www.forthpub.com)

This book is dedicated to
Cat

Contents

ACKNOWLEDGEMENTS

This book began with a sketchy set of intuitions from a student not yet formed in the craft of distinguishing good ideas from their poor cousins. To reach the point where this body of work stands, hopefully, in a coherent and accessible form, something must have happened along the way. First to be indicted are my doctoral supervisors, Murray Rae and Chris Marshall. Murray has instilled in me the truth that a few words carefully chosen, combined with the persistent pursuit of where theology makes a difference, is sufficient to the task. Chris deserves to be singled out for going far beyond the role of supervisor. Through his friendship, generous support, and rich dialogue, I have been inducted into a world where restorative justice is a way of life. He is a living testimony to the conviction that Christ's restorative Spirit enlarges our human capacity for compassion.

The dissertation upon which this book is based would not have been possible were it not for the financial and institutional support from the University of Otago, the Anglican Dioceses of Wellington and Christchurch, and the wonderful team at the Diana Unwin Chair of Restorative Justice, Victoria University of Wellington. It would not have reached the (e-)printing press were it not for the friendship and connections of people like Mike Mawson, Brian Brock, Susan Parsons, and the encouraging workers at Bloomsbury/T&T Clark. Let us pray that God and others will forgive any transgressions that appear in these pages.

There is an unwritten story that lies behind my exploration of the church as a community of restoration, a story that grounds why I embarked on this journey in the first place. To the people who have constituted that thing we call Urban Vision, whether from the early days or more recently, I hope you might recognize your story inscribed within these pages. Thank you for releasing me to do this work, but, more importantly, thank you for existing as a sign to God's reign of justice producing a people of peace.

Many life changes have occurred over the course of this project, and going through it all has been my family. My formation began under the watchful eyes of my parents, Mick and Ruby Duncan, who unwittingly drafted me into their initiatives for restoration of the other and of the church. No amount of preparation is adequate, however, for becoming a parent and a partner. Tessa, Sammy, and Micah, you are the joy of my life which makes the struggle all the worthwhile. And to Cat, my partner in mission, in love, and in renovation; another chapter added to the book we are writing together with our lives. Who would have thought this 'unlikely romantic pairing', the 'pirate' and the 'school-teacher', could make for such a rich story. I dedicate this book to you.

The final word belongs, however, to Jesus. You brought about a restoring work in my own life, calling me out from that wandering exile and arraigning me with this Christian tribe. Hopefully my attempt to make sense of this community befits your call upon it.

FOREWORD

Esther D. Reed

In 1943 Hannah Arendt published an essay entitled 'We Refugees' which spoke of unpopular facts and recounted the life-stories of people like Mr Cohn who sought refuge in Prague, then Vienna and Paris, and so on. Giorgio Agamben wrote again under the title 'We Refugees' in 1994 and interpreted Arendt's essay as proposing the condition of the refugee as the paradigm of a new historical consciousness. The refugee who has lost all rights is the bare life that now takes center stage on the international political stage. Arendt, says Agamben, saw something significant. The bare life of the refugee is the starting place for European thinking about human rights, the sociopolitical realities of modern nation states, the general corrosion of traditional legal-political categories, and the reconstruction of political philosophy. Leaving aside the old certainties of nationhood and human rights, Agamben builds his political philosophy anew starting from the refugee.

Noakes-Duncan's challenge and Agamben's are analogous. Whereas Agamben's challenge is to think from the refugee, Noakes-Duncan's call is to explicate the meaning of justice as a relational concept defined by God's own self-disclosure in Christ Jesus – who was a prisoner for our sake. The prisoner is the only thinkable figure that lets us see the societies of our time; the only category in which one may see today the forms and limits of our polity, its internal organization and priorities. Jesus is a prisoner. All Christian ethical thinking and reflection on the meaning of justice starts and finishes with him. If Christian ethics wants to engage the demanding social questions of accountability for the state of our prisons, the profit motive underlying incarceration as business, overcrowding, high recidivism rates, the care and resettlement of offenders, and more, our only starting place is Jesus the prisoner whose death and resurrection restored to humankind its vocation of union and communion with God (2 Cor. 3.18; 2 Pet. 1.4), elevating creation to the blessing that was prepared before the fall into sin (Ps. 103.19; Isa. 64.4; Rom. 9.23).

To think from Jesus the prisoner is disquieting but Noakes-Duncan avoids the over-arching problem of objectification, that is, seeing the category 'prisoner' rather than the imprisoned person, by turning the spotlight on ecclesial ethics and meanings of justice in particular. Because of Jesus the prisoner, the link forged by Noakes-Duncan between the criminal justice system and the church is the meaning of justice as restorative. The church learns its commitment to restorative justice from the Eucharist, the internal discipline and integrity of the Christian community, and eschatological hope. Noakes-Duncan applies the demands of restorative justice, learned from the cross and resurrection, as much to the church as to wider society.

Arendt was not optimistic being able to grasp or function with a concept of political responsibility because Jesus' exemplifying of goodness was to be hidden from the world. She cites Tertullian's maxim more than once: *Nec ulla magis res aliena quam publica* – 'no matter is more alien to us than what matters publicly'. For Noakes-Duncan, by contrast, the meaning of justice as restorative includes church and prison, ecclesial and wider societal life, because Jesus Christ is the embodiment of justice. Arendt's essay was entitled 'We Refugees'. The Christian ethicist's topic is 'We Sinners', and must include attention to sinful social structures and how they function. How is a person released from a sixteen-month sentence, with no right to accommodation, very little cash in their pocket, and no prospect of a social security benefit payment for over a month, to restore themselves effectively to society? What about the person who, at the end of their sentence, sat outside the prison and disturbed the peace until arrested again? Structural sin bears negatively upon the choices of conscious agents but Noakes-Duncan's argument in this book precludes the church from separating personal experiences of redemption in Christ from the broken societal relationships that typically make a person's restoration to society after prison so very difficult. 'Let him who is without sin cast the first stone' (John 8.7).

INTRODUCTION

After his retirement as General Secretary of the World Council of Churches, the great twentieth-century missionary theologian and ecumenicist, Lesslie Newbigin, issued a challenge to the WCC's flagship programme, 'Justice, Peace and the Integrity of Creation' (JPIC). While the programme readily affirmed that Christianity is a faith that does justice, Newbigin pointed out that there is nothing specifically Christian about the longing for justice or peace. In fact, it is in 'the name of justice that nations make wars and that oppressed people take to violence', neither of which should be endorsed by the church.[1] The WCC's uncritical adoption of the language of justice and peace could, in Newbigin's opinion, foster a 'web of illusion' whereby each person distorts what is due him or her and so treats their neighbor as a threat.

Newbigin issues an important word of caution to the church if it is to have integrity in its witness to the gospel. The church is not called simply to align itself with the cry for justice, but also to challenge the 'root-paradigms' underlying the dominant conceptions of justice.[2] This is particularly pertinent to the modern era where a specifically individualistic and secular paradigm of justice has obscured from focus any thick conception of the common good. According to Newbigin, there is 'little possibility of achieving an agreed definition of justice within the conceptual framework of secular liberalism'.[3] If the church capitulates to this mode of reasoning, it will eventually find its distinctive contribution eroded and will be viewed as merely one party in an irreconcilable political debate.

1. Lesslie Newbigin, 'Whose Justice?', *The Ecumenical Review* 44, no. 3 (1992): 308.

2. In Newbigin's words, the church is in the 'business of radical conversion', including a conversion of the mind and its perception of what constitutes justice, ibid., 311.

3. Ibid., 310.

According to Newbigin, what is needed in today's world is not just for Christians to add their voice to the wider concern for peace and justice, but rather to ask whether there is a specifically *Christian* way of seeking these goods. He briefly gestures towards a possible answer, suggesting that the church is the bearer of an 'open secret', that the true nature of justice has been decisively revealed in God's justification of the ungodly.[4] Understood in Christian terms, justice has its source in the Triune God and is manifest in the restoring of relationships to rightness, through the acts of repentance and forgiveness. The church has been admitted to this restoration through its participation in Christ. It is to 'embody the justice of God' by welcoming the sinner, standing in solidarity with those on the margins, and continually pointing to 'the One in whom God's justice has been made manifest in the strange victory of the cross'.[5]

Newbigin's brief yet suggestive comments reflect a number of the concerns that will be pursued in this book. His diagnosis of the present situation resonates with the perspective advocated here, as does his suggestion that the greatest need is for local Christian communities to 'embody the justice of God' in their respective contexts. This book is concerned with the ethics of justice, but it seeks to highlight the importance of the embodied reality of the church and the difference this consideration makes to the ethical task.

One of the most significant recent shifts in the discipline of Christian ethics has been the recovery of an appreciation of the centrality of the ecclesia to Christian life. If it was once presumed that general society was more or less Christian and that Christian ethics was more or less concerned with prescribing moral principles for a Christianised society, such a presumption no longer holds true. Not only has society become decidedly less Christian (if it ever were so), the formalistic universalism characteristic of modern ethical thought is now deemed to be insufficient. The ethical task confronting us now is to attend to the character of human life – how it has been formed, its context and history, the language used to express this reality, and so on.

This new appreciation for the contextual particularity of human existence has evoked new directions in ethical inquiry: less prescriptive, more descriptive; less generalised, more particularised; less abstract, more embedded. For Christian ethics, this shift has resulted in a far richer account of how the ecclesia comprises a particular context within which Christian convictions are embodied. The term *ecclesia* denotes both the theological term for 'church' while also pointing to the earliest

4. Ibid.
5. Ibid., 311.

self-understanding of the church as an 'assembly' of citizens within a particular political context. The recent trend towards an ethics of the ecclesia, covered in Chapter 2, is reflective of a broader recovery of the distinctiveness of Christian convictions and of the particularity of the Christian tradition. Theological ethicists are turning their attention to the social and political character of the ecclesia as indispensable to the forming of Christian character and the church's moral vision.

While this shift towards the development of an ecclesial ethic has not met with widespread acceptance, nonetheless it has provided the impetus for some significant reassessments of related disciplines in Christian theology.[6] One such reassessment has been in the field of biblical interpretation, which was one of the first casualties of a distinctly modernist methodology. Rather than individual exegetes approaching the bible with the tools of historical and literary criticism, a new appreciation has arisen of the role of the community in interpreting the bible as Scripture, as it seeks to live faithfully before God in its respective context. The 'theological interpretation of Scripture', as it has come to be known, places an emphasis on how the story of Scripture is being embodied (or *mis*-embodied) by the reading community of faith.[7]

This book is broadly situated within this ecclesial mode of ethical inquiry with respect to the understanding and practice of justice. It asks, 'How does an ecclesial context shape the theological apprehension and praxis of justice?' Its proposition is that the church does not so much possess a *theory* of justice as it understands itself constituted by an *ethos* of justice-making. This is not to say theoretical concepts have no use in the church's thinking. Rather, it means that from an ecclesial perspective justice is better understood in a dynamic sense, as something the church participates in and grasps the meaning of primarily through the *doing* of justice. The church as the Body of Christ inhabits a particular form of justice, a justice sourced in a divine personality. This is what in the biblical and theological traditions is called the 'justice of God', a justice that God both exemplifies in his own being and actions and that God

6. The recent criticisms by Nicholas Healy, surveyed in Chapter 2, stand out as one recent example of how ecclesial ethics is being met within the theological disciplines. His singling out of Stanley Hauerwas is not surprising, as most of the criticisms of ecclesial ethics are directly aimed at Hauerwas or indirectly at his influence over the field of Christian ethics more generally.

7. While many works could be cited here, see especially, Stephen E. Fowl, *Engaging Scripture: A Model for Theological Interpretation* (Oxford: Blackwell, 1998); Stephen E. Fowl and L. Gregory Jones, *Reading in Communion: Scripture and Ethics in Christian Life* (London: SPCK, 1991); Samuel Wells, *Improvisation: The Drama of Christian Ethics* (London: SPCK, 2004).

requires of his people. By exploring the ecclesial context in which the justice of God is understood I hope to spark the contemporary church's imagination as to how it might better embody this justice through its life together and its mission in the world.

The presupposition behind the ecclesial turn in Christian ethics is that there is a significant difference between this way of proceeding and other forms of inquiry. In other words, the church witnesses to the difference God makes by gathering a community around his Son. Just as Christ is different from all creation by virtue of his union with God, so the church that gathers in him is also different from the world: behold a 'new creation' (2 Cor. 5.17). With respect to justice, this difference resides in how the church participates in God's justice-making as embodied in the life, death, and resurrection of Jesus Christ. The pressing challenge for ecclesial ethics is the degree to which the church actually reflects the practices and character of the justice revealed in Christ.

This challenge is especially acute in contemporary society where the understanding of justice is increasingly fragmented. Justice has become a deeply contested concept in the post-modern era. Churches too are increasingly divided between different conceptions of justice. Some churches emphasize the socio-economic ramifications of justice by speaking about 'social justice', with the result that distributive conceptions are at the forefront. Others emphasize the spiritual dimensions of justice by speaking about God's righteousness justifying the ungodly, with the result that individualized and spiritualized conceptions are dominant. Still others emphasize justice as therapy, where inclusion and acceptance are viewed as self-sufficient goods for a just society.

The church's fragmented witness on questions of justice reflects a fragmented and limited understanding of justice itself. Detached from its biblical moorings and ecclesial context, Christian claims about justice can often end up being distorted or truncated as they are captured by or interpreted within categories derived from the human situation. The long history of criminal justice theory and practice, which is briefly surveyed in Chapter 1, reflects such a distorted understanding of justice and, not surprisingly, has deeply shaped how the church's witness to justice has often been perceived. While theologians have been reticent to equate divine justice with human systems of justice, a two-way traffic of ideas has nevertheless flowed between portrayals of God's justice and human systems of law, justice, and punishment. In this flow of ideas, the justice of God has steadily acquired a more abstract and retributive determination by being interpreted in a forensic rather than ecclesial context. This in turn has opened the door to legalistic and punitive practices of justice in general society.

By attending to the connection between the church's understanding of justice and the form of its witness in human affairs, we will be able to show how a more theologically informed understanding of justice has direct implications for the church's witness, not least when responding to conflict and wrongdoing. When its interpretation of justice is grounded in the relational realities implied by the biblical terminology (especially the Hebrew, צדק and משפט, and the Greek, δικαιοσύνη), and interpreted in light of such central biblical categories as covenant and communion, justice acquires a far richer and more dynamic meaning. We will argue that, from a biblical perspective, the justice of God is best understood as a relational and restorative reality that is primarily oriented towards the restoration of right relationships. Such a relational conception allows for a more holistic and fundamentally more compassionate understanding of justice, especially corrective justice.

The traditional justice-related goals of accountability and responsibility not only look different from a relational perspective, they intersect with ideas of resolution, reparation, and transformation – or what the biblical tradition calls repentance and forgiveness. The problem for Christian thought is not the need to reconcile or balance God's love or mercy with God's justice, as has been commonly assumed in the theological tradition; the challenge is to understand God's justice in a way that upholds and includes his mercy. From such a perspective, justice uncoupled from mercy is simply unjust; mercy without justice ceases to be mercy, for mercy is fulfilled in perfect justice. This is the justice the church is called to embody in its collective life, bearing witness to the restorative justice of God.

Understanding God's justice as a restorative justice provides critical insights into the distinctive life of the ecclesia that have remained largely undeveloped within ecclesial ethics. Many ecclesial ethicists have highlighted the visible difference an ecclesial framework makes to notions of peace-making, but little has so far been done on the difference it makes to the pursuit of justice. Where the subject of justice has been raised, it is often to question the church's ready endorsement of justice, as in Newbigin's caution to the WCC.[8] While there are some exceptions to this, none has gone very far in explicating how justice as a *restorative* reality lies at the heart of the church's experience of, and witness to, God's justice.

8. For example, the influential chapter 'The Politics of Justice: Why Justice Is a Bad Idea for Christians', in Stanley Hauerwas, *After Christendom? How the Church Is to Behave If Freedom, Justice, and a Christian Nation Are Bad Ideas* (Nashville, TN: Abingdon Press, 1991), 45–68.

For example, in his book *Good Punishment?* James Logan rightly argues that the United States's propensity for mass imprisonment rests on an understanding of justice as retributive degradation.[9] While Logan offers an alternative to incarceration based on the ecclesial practice of penance, he provides no substantive corrective to the prevailing notion of justice itself. Similarly Daniel Bell Jr. makes what appears to be a significant step in the right direction in his essay, 'Jesus, the Jews, and the Politics of God's Justice', in which he offers a critical reading of how concepts of justice feature in relation to the church's reading of Scripture.[10] Yet Bell's contribution remains suggestive at best. It leaves many unanswered questions about how the church might embody a justice informed by, and given shape through, its particular convictions and practices.

While those associated with the ecclesial turn in ethics have not written extensively about the nature and practice of justice, there are ecclesial traditions that have reflected deeply about what it means to do justice from a restorative angle. In its early inception in the Mennonite-Anabaptist community, restorative justice was understood primarily as a 'peace-making justice', an approach to conflict and wrongdoing that focused on restoration, reconciliation, and reparation of the harm done.[11] In Chapter 3 we will survey how the Anabaptist tradition provided fertile ground for forging connections between peacemaking and the contemporary concerns about the damaging impact of the prevailing criminal justice system. What emerged as the Victim Offender Reconciliation Project (VORP) quickly resonated with churches concerned about the problematic outcomes of the public justice system. It soon became clear that restorative justice practice gave expression to an alternative conception of justice, resembling the biblical concept of *shalom*, a concept that combines justice-making and peace.[12] This holistic conception of

9. James S. Logan, *Good Punishment? Christian Moral Practice and U.S. Imprisonment* (Grand Rapids, MI: Eerdmans, 2008). Logan has in turn drawn on the work of the legal historian James Q. Whitman. See especially his, *Harsh Justice: Criminal Punishment and the Widening Divide Between America and Europe* (New York: Oxford University Press, 2003).

10. Daniel Bell Jr., 'Jesus, the Jews, and the Politics of God's Justice', *Ex Auditu* 22 (2006): 87–112; see also his *Liberation Theology After the End of History: The Refusal to Cease Suffering* (London: Routledge, 2001).

11. See David Cayley, *The Expanding Prison: The Crisis in Crime and Punishment and the Search for Alternatives* (Toronto, ON: Anansi Press, 1998), 11.

12. The seminal text here is Howard Zehr, *Changing Lenses: A New Focus for Crime and Justice* (Scottdale, PA: Herald Press, 1990); Zehr largely drew on P. B.

justice was recovered and given new expression as it was mediated through the ecclesial identity and practices of the Anabaptist peacemaking tradition.

The restorative justice concept has since grown into a field of criminological theory and practice that has far surpassed the expectations of its early church-based practitioners. Over the past four decades, as Van Ness and Strong argue, restorative justice has moved from being a 'community-based alternative' to the criminal justice system, to being both a 'source of public policy' and a 'viable part of the criminal justice system' in many jurisdictions around the world.[13] In the recent four-volume edited work on restorative justice, Carolyn Hoyle rightly states, '...over the last two decades there has been more written about restorative justice than almost any other criminological topic'.[14] But as it has grown to become an accepted component of public justice systems, it has also been adapted to suit the presuppositions and language of the public arena. To a large degree, restorative justice has been secularized and construed as just another option within a justice system it once protested against. While not overtly hostile to a Christian perspective, the restorative justice movement has eschewed its dependence on the theological insights that led to its conception.

This mainstreaming of restorative justice practice within secular discourse has presented new challenges for furthering the church's imagination of justice as a power that restores. On the one hand, the acceptance and spread of a restorative understanding of justice is an occasion for the church to rejoice. While recognising the dangers of co-option and control, the early pioneers of restorative justice saw it as integral to the church's mission to the world, offering a more faithful rendering of justice. On the other hand, the church now has to contend with its own continued relevance to the restorative justice field. What distinctive contribution can the church possibly make to this now complex and increasingly professional body of practice, especially when multiple other identities and interests occupy the restorative justice space?

Yoder, *Shalom: The Bible's Word for Salvation, Justice, and Peace* (Newton, KS: Faith & Life Press, 1987), and Millard C. Lind, *Yahweh Is a Warrior: The Theology of Warfare in Ancient Israel* (Scottdale, PA: Herald Press, 1980).

13. Daniel W. Van Ness and Karen Heetderks Strong, *Restoring Justice: An Introduction to Restorative Justice*, 4th ed. (New Providence, NJ: LexisNexis, 2010), 34.

14. Carolyn Hoyle, 'General Introduction', in *Restorative Justice*. Vol. 1, *The Rise of Restorative Justice* (London: Routledge, 2010), 15.

It is the goal of this book to show that such a contribution does in fact matter and that it must be understood as arising from the church's very *raison d'être*. In other words, the church's distinctive contribution to the wider restorative justice field must be informed by the ways in which the justice of God is taking shape in its own community. I propose that such a contribution might be fruitfully explored by bringing together the insights developed by ecclesial ethics with those of restorative justice practice, which will hopefully be of benefit to both those within the church and those without.

If the burden of proof appears now to lie with the church in explaining its relevance to restorative justice, this is in no small part due to the lack of theological reflection among the early pioneers of the movement. Considering the exponential growth of restorative justice since its inception in the 1960–70s, it is surprising that only a handful of theological thinkers have sought to provide treatments of the subject. Howard Zehr is widely recognized as the grandfather of the restorative justice movement. While not a theologian *per se*, he provided the initial articulation of a theology underlying this conception of justice by drawing on selected Old Testament scholarship.[15] Yet as a criminal justice historian and restorative justice practitioner, Zehr did not view his role as one of broadening or deepening these initial theological soundings. Those with more theological expertise, most notably Christopher Marshall, have contributed significantly to exploring the intersection of restorative justice with biblical, and in particular, New Testament theology and ethics. One of the consequences of this paucity of theological reflection, and something which I intend to address, is the impression that restorative justice is a relatively recent concept, whereas in fact it has precedents stretching back through church tradition to the very texts of the earliest Christian communities.

This book can rightly be seen as building on Marshall's premise that, 'the first Christians experienced in Christ and lived out in their faith communities an understanding of justice as a power that heals, restores, and reconciles rather than hurts, punishes, and kills, and that this reality ought to shape and direct a Christian contribution to the criminal justice debate today'.[16] In the nearly two decades since Marshall put forward this premise, scant attention has been paid to restorative justice by the very

15. See particularly his chapter, 'Covenant Justice: The Biblical Alternative', in Zehr, *Changing Lenses*, 126–57. In terms of theological works, Zehr largely draws on Millard Lind, Perry Yoder and the writings of Reformed criminologist Herman Bianchi.

16. Christopher D. Marshall, *Beyond Retribution: A New Testament Vision for Justice, Crime, and Punishment* (Grand Rapids, MI: Eerdmans, 2001), 33.

community that bequeathed its own conception of justice to the restorative justice movement in the first place. The development of restorative justice theory and practice has far outstripped the level of theological reflection on it, with the result that the theological and ecclesial underpinnings of restorative justice remain obscure.

For example, Anthony Bash in his *Forgiveness and Christian Ethics* fails to see the connection between the biblical understanding of justice, which is concerned with life, community, and relationships, and restorative justice, which, he claims, is more narrowly concerned with criminal justice reform.[17] But, as we will argue, restorative justice emerged precisely as an outworking of the biblical mandate to seek peace and reconciliation between people (and their communities), who have suffered relational injury. On the other hand, there are those like Michael Gorman and Stanley Hauerwas, both of whom describe God's justice as a 'restorative justice', but never acknowledge this concept's indebtedness or connection to the recent field of practice wherein it has gained currency.[18] The adjective 'restorative' becomes merely another qualifier of the noun 'justice', without reference to the distinctive way in which restorative justice was formed as an ecclesial practice, to restore relationships harmed by wrongdoing.

The goal of this book is to address this lack of attention in theological reflection to the ecclesiological dimension and implications of understanding the justice of God as a restorative justice. If the subject of restorative justice requires deeper theological reflection, as I believe it does, and if ecclesial ethics provides a helpful way of furthering such reflection, what might be entailed in such an undertaking? For largely explanatory reasons, I propose that three tasks need to be accomplished, which may be categorized as the descriptive, the prescriptive, and the suggestive tasks. In reality, these may all be present at the same time and should not therefore be treated in isolation from one another.

The *descriptive task* must attend to the context(s) in which the church has understood the justice of God to impinge on the human landscape. As already noted, conceptions of divine justice have not only shaped the church but also had an impact on the enactment of public justice. Without a clear understanding of the way in which justice-related ideas have

17. Anthony Bash, *Forgiveness and Christian Ethics* (Cambridge: Cambridge University Press, 2007), 147.

18. Michael J. Gorman, *Becoming the Gospel: Paul, Participation, and Mission* (Grand Rapids, MI: Eerdmans, 2015), especially 212–60; Stanley Hauerwas, 'Jesus, the Justice of God', in *War and the American Difference* (Grand Rapids, MI: Baker Academic, 2011), 101 nn. 6, 16.

flowed between different spheres of life, any proposal for reform in one area risks making arbitrary changes that have unintended consequences elsewhere. I will attempt to address this descriptive task by offering a critical account of how the ecclesial context in which God's justice has been understood intersects with the criminal justice context, both historically and in the contemporary restorative justice field. This requires uncovering the ecclesiological footprint beneath the various construals of justice, since conceptions of justice are never far removed from their particular social form.

By telling the story of how the Western criminal justice system emerged in relationship to theological convictions about the nature of God's justice, it will become clear how assumptions regarding divine justice always carry social and practical implications. Justice is not a static concept or abstract idea that can be known apart from the various contexts, practices, and relationships that give it concrete form. A besetting problem in the theological tradition is that justice has too often been understood in isolation from its proper biblical and ecclesial context. Theologians have tended to appropriate metaphors of justice drawn from their wider social setting rather than drawing deeply on the biblical witness to God's justice and the lived experience of the community of faith. This has often resulted in highly retributive or non-relational understandings of justice.

The *prescriptive task* concerns the need to clarify what norms ought to guide the church's understanding of the justice of God. While human judgments about the nature of reality are unavoidable, the church has always held that human reason alone is insufficient to determine the truth, both because it is prone to distortion and because God's ways in the world cannot be apprehended by human wisdom alone. For this reason, the church has continually turned to Scripture to form its mind according to divine truth. With respect to its apprehension of justice, it is to the unfolding story of God's justice in the biblical account that the church must look for guidance. In particular, such reflection should center around the story of Jesus, who is presented as the definitive expression of God's saving justice in the world, and of the church, which is understood to be the primary witness to and instrument of the justice of God on earth through its participation in Christ. In Chapters 4 to 6, I will explore the biblical story of God's justice and then focus attention on two passages that exemplify the nature of God's justice – Jesus's parable of the Prodigal Son and Paul's instructions to the church in Corinth. These chapters illustrate what is necessary for re-centring the church's witness on God's restoring justice.

Finally, the *suggestive task* will propose ways in which the church might go about embodying God's justice on earth. I will argue, first, that the church is already engaged in forms of restorative justice within its own liturgical life. By inviting sinners and victims to participate in the liturgical acts of confession, the declaration of forgiveness, passing of the peace, culminating in the Eucharist, the church remembers and proclaims the restoring justice it has received in Christ. At the end of the worship gathering, the church is commissioned to go out into the world to proclaim and embody this same justice of right relationships. This will lead to an examination of how the church might extend its work of restorative justice through its common life and missional life.

Taken together, the descriptive, prescriptive, and suggestive aspects of this book show how the ecclesia is a prime locus for understanding the justice of God, and why the church must continue to find ways of embodying an expression of justice in the world that points to God's restorative and healing purposes. This must always take place in conformity to the way in which the justice of God is disclosed in the biblical story in general and through the story of Jesus in particular.

We noted earlier that contemporary churches all too often reflect a partial and fragmented understanding of justice, which prevents them from bearing witness to a better way of responding to conflict and wrongdoing. Congregations are all too often embroiled in antagonistic relationships, and exhibit a pessimistic attitude that conflict can be managed though rarely repaired. While the presence of conflict is not surprising, the church's inability to respond restoratively to internal conflict is deeply perturbing. By offering an account of how God's justice can be outworked in the life of the church, and by articulating the virtues and practices needed to respond restoratively to conflict, I hope to provide a distinctive contribution to ecclesial ethics, and to the kind of ecclesial witness that is so essential today. Such a witness will testify to how God's justice is at work, restoring the world by bringing peace and healing to all its constitutive relationships.

Chapter 1

Ecclesial Perspectives on Justice in Historical Perspective

What is the relationship between the church's apprehension of the justice of God and other conceptions of justice in the human realm? How has this relationship functioned at different times in church history and what impact has this had on society's response to injustice and wrongdoing? Though such questions are in a sense inexhaustible, they are nevertheless crucial for any exploration of the church's calling to embody God's justice in the world. This chapter has two principal aims. First, to set out how different – and sometimes competing – conceptions of justice have developed and influenced the church's understanding of God's justice over the course of Christian history, and second, to trace the practical and social consequences of this relationship in relation to the adjudication of criminal matters. As will be shown, how the church understands the concept of justice has implications not just for the life of the community of faith but also for the wider social order, and in particular for the way it responds to wrongdoers and their victims.

This ambitious and sweeping task will require attending to the way in which concepts of justice have been shaped by the social settings in which they are forged and practiced, as justice cannot be known apart from the historical contexts, practices, and relationships that give it concrete form. By offering a broad overview of the complex and changing relationship between the church's understanding of justice and its sociological embodiment, we will show how different conceptions of justice owe much more to Greco-Roman antecedents than to the story of God's justice as disclosed in Scripture.

One recurring feature through Christian history that deserves particular note has been the way in which theologians have adopted conceptions and metaphors of justice drawn from their surrounding social world in order to explicate the church's confession of the justice of God. This has created what Timothy Gorringe has aptly called a 'structure of effect' in which there have been consequences both for theology and society.[1] Theologians have usually been reticent, and for good reason, to equate divine and human justice. Even so, there remains a causal connection between them, with understandings of one influencing the other. As will be seen, forensic and juridical notions of justice have had a controlling influence on the church's understanding of divine justice. This has resulted in God's justice acquiring an increasingly retributive and legalistic flavour, as well as in reinforcing retributive practices in the criminal justice system. It is presuppositions such as these that this book is intended to challenge.

The two-way flow of ideas between theological interpretations of justice and societal responses to criminal justice can readily be traced in Western history. Even in contemporary secular societies, the understanding of justice informing practice often rests on unacknowledged theological assumptions about law, punishment, and crime bequeathed to them from the Christian theological tradition. It might even be said that the modern criminal justice system is a secular parody of previous ecclesial notions of justice, sin, and atonement. In order to question the dominant practice of justice in contemporary society, we will need to expose the theological undercurrents that led to the current situation and which continue to exert influence.

Any sweeping historical survey must draw some limits if it is to have any pedagogical use. In what follows we will focus particularly on times of societal upheaval, since it was at these moments that the church's understanding of justice evolved in response to the surrounding societal turmoil. As the church's place in society changed, so did its witness to justice. As a broad generalization, when the church had a more liminal role in society it was more likely to embody a vision of justice that reflected the redemptive and transformative presence of Christ in the community. Where it was perceived to be coterminous with the prevailing social and political order it tended to advocate a view of justice that reinforced the status quo, one that was increasingly abstract and retributive. This in turn opened the door to harsh and punitive practices in wider society.

Our historical survey begins by considering the conception of justice that emerged in Greco-Roman philosophy, where the understanding of justice (δικη) as being immanent in the natural order exerted considerable influence on later theological reflection, even as it came under much-needed critique. This will be followed by a brief consideration of the post-apostolic church's approach to justice-making, where it sought to conform itself to the example of Jesus as the model of God's justice.

1. Timothy Gorringe, *God's Just Vengeance. Crime, Violence, and the Rhetoric of Salvation* (Cambridge: Cambridge University Press, 1996), 8.

Subsequently, in the late fourth century Augustine of Hippo advocated a more stringent penitential interpretation of justice that would profoundly affect both church and society. With the legal revolution of the eleventh and twelfth centuries, the consolidation of papal power created new forms of centralized authority supported by strongly legal conceptions of justice. The theology of Anselm of Canterbury smoothed the way for the triumph of legalistic and retributive interpretations of justice. The sixteenth-century Protestant Reformation saw an increasingly sharp distinction being drawn between the demands of God's law and justice, and the free grace offered in the gospel. This was a distinction that paradoxically reinforced the retributive dimensions of the civil justice system while extending the possibility of evading God's punitive justice through faith and repentance in the practices of the church.

Following the eighteenth-century Enlightenment, as secular modernity took shape, the repressive and retributive conceptions of justice prevailing in the civil order came to be justified on grounds other than theological belief. Immanuel Kant's theory of justice, for example, rests solely on appeals to universal reason and individual autonomy. Closer to our own time, another epochal shift is occurring as modernity enters its twilight. One consequence of late modernity's loss of any unifying narrative is the erosion of any consensus on the meaning of justice. Criminal justice practice is now increasingly subject to political whims and a highly anxious public. This forms the context in which the contemporary church must bear witness to God's justice, which it must do by testing to what degree these different conceptions of justice are reflective of its own biblical and ecclesial convictions.

Concepts of Justice in Historical Perspective

Justice in Greco-Roman Philosophy

In his commentary on the *Laws*, the first-century BCE Roman jurist Cicero declared that justice – *ius* – is encapsulated in the formula *suum ius cuique tribuere*: 'to render to each what is due them'.[2] It was this understanding of justice that governed relations in society. 'There is but one essential justice which cements society, and one law which establishes this justice. This law is right reason, which is the true rule of all commandments and prohibitions. Whoever neglects this law, whether written or unwritten, is

2. Cicero, *De Legibus*, Book I, Chapter XV. This is also the interpretation of justice given in Justinian's law code who drew on Ulpian. 'Justice' (*iustitia*), said Ulpian, is a steady and enduring will to render to each his or her *ius*, Justinian Code, *Digest*, I.1.10, and *Institutes*, I.1.

necessarily unjust and wicked.'[3] Cicero later goes on to stipulate what justice requires when dealing with wrongdoers. He states, 'If a person transgresses any of these rules, the penalty shall fit the crime… In this way each offender is to be paid back in his own coin – violence being punished by death or exile, greed by a fine, improper canvassing by disgrace.'[4] Justice requires that each receive their just desert, to be rewarded or punished according to what they deserve.

Cicero's interpretation of justice relied on a mythology stretching back at least as far as Homer. According to Homer, the universe had a single fundamental order that, while not created by the gods, was nonetheless governed by them. It was Zeus's virgin daughter δικη ('justice') who presided over nature and society by the principle of 'right', ensuring ἐπιείκεια ('fairness' or 'equity') through the balancing of rewards and punishment. For the Greeks, justice was believed to be immanent in the natural order as a principle that ensured order and balance.[5] Human justice thereby required acting in accordance with the immanent order, eventually being regarded as a quality of the virtuous soul. This understanding of justice operated according to what Colin Gunton calls a 'violent grace', as people were fated to receive what was strictly their due.[6] Anything more or less was regarded as an infraction of natural justice.

Socrates and Plato furthered the Greek concept of justice by arguing that justice had a perfect form that could be cultivated by the virtuous soul. According to this conception, as MacIntyre notes, societal rules for ensuring justice were secondary to the 'disposition to give to each person, including oneself, what that person deserves and to treat no one in a way incompatible with their deserts'.[7] Justice moved from being a reciprocal quality to an individual property of the virtuous. According to Plato, those who were just held the *polis* together and therefore deserved positions of authority within it. Those who were judged to be deficient of virtue were to be cured by the discipline of punishment.[8] In Martha Nussbaum's

3. Cicero, *De Legibus*.

4. Ibid., III, 11, 46. Cited in Darrin W. Snyder Belousek, *Atonement, Justice, and Peace: The Message of the Cross and the Mission of the Church* (Grand Rapids, MI: Eerdmans, 2012), 44.

5. Alasdair MacIntyre, *Whose Justice? Which Rationality?* (Notre Dame, IN: University of Notre Dame Press, 1988), 14.

6. Colin E. Gunton, *The Actuality of Atonement: A Study of Metaphor, Rationality and the Christian Tradition* (Edinburgh: T. & T. Clark, 1988), 99.

7. MacIntyre, *Whose Justice?*, 39.

8. It is frequently observed that Socrates viewed punishment as serving the purpose of moral education.

opinion, Plato exemplifies the political embodiment of Homer's theology where 'strict *dike* is a harsh and symmetrical world in which order and design are preserved with exceptionless clarity'.[9]

The understanding of punishment as righting the balance of the moral order finds firm ground in Greek thinking. However, there it is the order of the soul that is paramount. In the *Gorgias*, Plato cites Socrates: 'there is no other possible way to get rid of injustice' than 'by way of pain and suffering'.[10] The imposition of pain was thought to transform an unjust man into a person who is 'either more virtuous or less wicked'.[11] Punishment is here oriented towards the moral reformation of the offender's soul, rather than satisfying a need on behalf of the one offended against.

Plato's conception of justice as an immanent ideal form within the cosmic order continued to influence Greco-Roman philosophy, even if the approach to attaining knowledge of that form would change. Plato's student Aristotle would complete the project of his teacher by providing an account of αρχή (first conceptions and principles) grounded in the imperfect and particular reality of the πόλις (*polis*).[12] The form of justice can only be known, argued Aristotle, by attending to its particular expressions, where it is already embodied and implicitly acknowledged. Working with this model of 'induction', it became clear to Aristotle that retributive exchange is an aspect of justice that is essential for holding society together: 'Men seek to return either evil for evil – and if they cannot do so, think their position mere slavery – or good for good – and if they cannot do so there is no exchange, but it is by exchange that they hold together'.[13]

9. Martha Craven Nussbaum, *Sex and Social Justice* (New York: Oxford University Press, 1999), 159; cited in Richard H. Bell, *Rethinking Justice: Restoring Our Humanity* (Lanham: Lexington Books, 2007), 14.

10. Plato, *Gorgias*, trans. Donald J. Zeyl (Indianapolis: Hackett, 1986), 109 (525b).

11. Plato, *The Laws*, trans. Trevor J. Saunders (Harmondsworth: Penguin, 1970), 854. In Plato's *Laws*, the pseudonymous Athenian specifies extreme punishments for the very hardened criminals, those who are well beyond any thought of cure. The punishments elected for these criminals extend beyond the grave. This feature of Greek thought led Corlett to conclude that, 'If this is not a bold form of retributivism, then there is no such theory as retributivism'; J. Angelo Corlett, 'Punishment and the Socratic Roots of Retributivism', in *Punishment and Ethics: New Perspectives*, ed. Jesper Ryberg and J. Angelo Corlett (New York: Palgrave Macmillan, 2010), 10.

12. MacIntyre, *Whose Justice?*, 81–96.

13. Aristotle, *The Nicomachean Ethics*, trans. David Ross (Oxford: Oxford University Press, 2009), 1132b–33a.

The Greco-Roman philosophical conception of justice would exert considerable influence over the church's later theological categories for understanding justice, even as the concept underwent significant changes. While Christianity remained relatively marginal in society it posed little threat to the Roman commonwealth.[14] Yet as Augustine was later to observe, according to Cicero's own definition of a commonwealth the early church already represented a rival tradition of justice taking root. As Cicero argues in *De Republica*, what defined the Roman people as the true and superior commonwealth was its, 'common acknowledgment of law [i.e., an agreement about right or justice], and by a community of interests'.[15] To the degree that the church acknowledged a different conception of law and justice at work, as it gathered around the interests of God's kingdom, we notice an altogether new commonwealth taking shape.

The Early Church Fathers

We will explore the apostolic church's apprehension of justice as attested in the New Testament at a later point. For now it is enough to note that the church's witness to justice during the first three centuries largely continued the emphasis of the apostolic period in at least two respects. First, when the early church Fathers spoke about justice or righteousness it was often in relationship to God's justice, since all justice was thought to flow from its divine source. Second, the early church's response to wrongdoers was significantly conditioned by its understanding of repentance and the need to restore sinners to the forgiven community. What is not seen in the writings of this period are extensive treatises on justice, nor any overt challenging of the machinations of imperial justice. Instead, the emphasis is on embodying within their own communities an alternative conception of justice grounded in the dawning reality of God's kingdom.

14. Especially considering the propaganda of imperial notions of justice and law. See Simon R. F. Price, *Rituals and Power: The Roman Imperial Cult in Asia Minor* (Cambridge: Cambridge University Press, 1984); and in Pauline studies, Neil Elliot, *Liberating Paul: The Justice of God and the Politics of the Apostle* (Sheffield: Sheffield Academic Press, 1995); Richard Horsley, ed., *Paul and Empire: Religion and Power in Roman Imperial Society* (Harrisburg, PA: Trinity Press International, 1997).

15. Herbert A. Deane, *The Political and Social Ideas of St. Augustine* (New York: Columbia University Press, 1963), 118.

In his only surviving letter, Clement of Rome reflects a typical concern of this period as he writes to the church in Corinth. After a dispute that had resulted in the deposition of the presbyters, Clement instructs the Corinthians that while they are indeed to admonish one another, it should always be for the purpose of restoring the wayward person in love. He quotes from the book of Job, 'Blessed is the man whom the Lord reproveth, and reject not thou the warning of the Almighty. For He causes sorrow, and again restores [to gladness]; He woundeth, and His hands make whole.'[16] Clement reflects the early Christian belief that correction comes from the Lord, and the goal of such chastisement is restoration. In imitation of the Lord's ways, Clement exhorts church members to be exemplary in their love for one another and to banish hostile attitudes contrary to the church's calling.

Clement's exhortation is more than a private word of rebuke; it expresses an alternative understanding of justice. His commendation to imitate the Lord and his justice is already to interpret justice within a framework unknown to Greek thinking. For the Greeks, justice was governed by the gods but it did not reside in them, nor was justice understood in terms of love. For Clement, justice was a quality to be known and imitated through God's self-revelation in Christ as the just One. As Justin Martyr in the second century would later write, the true character of righteousness is found in those who have 'the knowledge of God and of His Christ', for they are proved just in their service by being obedient to the Lord.[17] He writes again in his *Apology*, 'we have been taught, and are convinced, and do believe, that He accepts those only who imitate the excellences which reside in Him, temperance, and justice, and philanthropy, and as many virtues as are peculiar to a God who is called by no proper name'.[18]

It is significant that the early Fathers saw no tension between God's justice and God's other attributes. A contrasting view was advocated by Marcion in the third century, who argued that the Hebrew God could not possibly be the Father of Jesus Christ. Marcion promoted the idea that the 'Father' is without any judicial faculty; he is pure goodness, and as such this Father saves us from the Old Testament God who rebukes and judges humanity. In effect, Marcion attributed to the Old Testament God the unmerciful and harsh reality depicted by the Greek notion of δικη. The orthodox church's rejection of Marcionism was also therefore a rejection of justice so understood.

16. Clement of Rome, 'First Epistle to the Corinthians', in *Ante-Nicene Fathers* (New York: Charles Scribner's Sons, 1907), Chapter LVI, 20.

17. Justin Martyr, 'Dialogue with Trypho', in ibid., Chapter XXVIII, 208.

18. Justin Martyr, 'The First Apology', in ibid., Chapter X, 165.

In his rebuttal of Marcion, Irenaeus argues that the God worshipped by Christians is both just and good and that neither attribute can exist on its own without the other becoming distorted. By splitting God from the Father, Irenaeus believed that Marcion was 'unconsciously taking away the intelligence and justice of both deities'.[19] Rather, the Father is good and wise precisely by exercising his justice in a way that shows his goodness. As Irenaeus puts it,

> [The Father] is Lord, and Judge, and the Just One, and Ruler over all. For He is good, and merciful, and patient, and saves whom He ought: nor does goodness desert Him in the exercise of justice, nor is His wisdom lessened; for He saves those whom He should save, and judges those worthy of judgment. Neither does He show Himself unmercifully just; for His goodness, no doubt, goes on before, and takes precedency.[20]

By upholding God's *saving justice* over against the Father saving us *from* justice, Irenaeus invested the concept of justice with a meaning that was altogether unfamiliar to the Greco-Roman tradition. He conceived of justice as a reality that restores and saves, rather than hurts, punishes, and kills. This was how he understood God's justice at work in Christ.

Early Christendom and Augustine

The ecclesial context in the fourth century was significantly altered by two events. First, beginning with the reign of Emperor Constantine, Christianity began to acquire power and status in the Roman Empire. This meant that official persecution of Christians ended and the church was endowed with the privileges of land, buildings, and authority. Second, by the end of the fourth century the survival of the Empire came under threat, as did the church that enjoyed its protection. In a time of societal turmoil the church needed to show itself as having a status independent of the Empire, while at the same time being no less than a fully political body. To understand how this context shaped the church's understanding of justice we turn to the theologian who would define the terms by which the church's relationship to society was understood, as well as its understanding of juristic norms.

The bishop-theologian, Augustine of Hippo, is widely regarded as being responsible for bequeathing to the Western tradition an understanding of justice that infused classical thinking with the concerns of the New Testament. In the opinion of Belousek, 'Western Christian thinking

19. Irenaeus, 'Against Heresies', in ibid., Book 3, Chapter XXV, 459.
20. Ibid.

concerning justice and peace has been shaped down the centuries by the writings of two great theologians, Augustine and Aquinas. And the thinking of Augustine and Aquinas on justice and peace was influenced substantially by Greco-Roman philosophy, especially Aristotle and Cicero.'[21] Augustine was not the first to attempt a synthesis of Greco-Roman philosophy and Christian theology; Clement of Alexandria and Origen stand out as cases in point. Yet no Christian thinker presented as powerful and enduring a framework for interweaving theological concerns with Roman political philosophy.

Two features of the Augustinian legacy are especially significant for our purposes. First, Augustine enables the repressive function of the governing authorities to be justified by a semblance of justice rather than a full embodiment of justice. This interpretive move opens the door to a two-way flow of ideas between a sphere that practices something less than complete justice and the church's role in endorsing such limited conceptions of justice. Second, in Augustine's schema God's justice suffers from an internalizing drift as it impinges on the human landscape. Justice-making in the context of relationships is largely subordinated to the pursuit of a penitent soul.

According to Robert Dodaro, Augustine's use of the term *iustitia* involves the conflation of three general sets of meaning.[22] The first comes from Greco-Roman philosophy, which regarded justice as 'the habit of the soul or the virtue whereby one gives to each individual his due'. The second derives from the New Testament as understood by Latin patristic writers and equates the virtue with the love (*caritas*) that is due God and neighbor. The third resembles the Pauline notion of righteousness (δικαιοσύνη), understood as the 'condition of the soul whereby it stands in a "right", because properly ordered, relationship with God, its Creator'.[23] This range of meaning Augustine gives to *iustitia* enables him to harmonize the volitional aspect of love and a view of humanity as created for right relationship with an ordered view of nature. For example, Dodaro cites Augustine's definition of justice as 'love serving God alone and thus ruling well those things subject to human beings'.[24] 'Ruling well' means enabling one's neighbors to receive what is their due as prescribed by divine law and by nature.

21. Belousek, *Atonement, Justice, and Peace*, 29.

22. Robert Dodaro, *Christ and the Just Society in the Thought of Augustine* (Cambridge: Cambridge University Press, 2004), 4.

23. Ibid.

24. Ibid., 5.

Augustine's merging of *caritas* and *iustitia* meant that the perfect virtue of justice exists, as Deane puts it, by the 'spontaneous order of love'.[25] Justice describes the condition where all things are in perfect order, specifically the objects of our love, which for Augustine are to be directed towards God and neighbor. This true justice was manifest in only one person according to Augustine, since there has only been one who loved perfectly. Because Christ was without sin, he alone is truly just and has no need of the correction warranted by sin. In other words, justice properly understood has nothing to do with the negative concepts of retribution or coercive punishment, because all things exist in perfect order where God's will is consummate. For Augustine, there is no tension between mercy and justice insofar as they cohere in God's nature.

Augustine clearly shared the early church's concern to establish justice christologically, yet he is far more reticent about where this impinges on the human landscape. The early Fathers generally emphasized Christ's defeat of Satan and vanquishing of sin, thereby construing divine justice in terms of a power that freed the church from the realm of darkness. Augustine, on the other hand, was captivated by the doctrine of universal sinfulness, pervasive even in the church. Consequently, the perfect virtue of justice was unattainable in this earthly existence.[26] Augustine had a rather dark view of the human condition. He writes, 'this moral life itself is wholly one of punishment, for it is all temptation'.[27] He intensifies the conflict between the Adamic condition of sin and the new life in Christ to such an extent that the former overwhelms the present age while the latter can only be anticipated in hope.

To understand Augustine's strict separation between divine and human justice, we must appreciate the changing context within which he understood the outworking of God's justice. Writing in the fourth century, Augustine was under no illusion about the extent to which the church shared many of the same weaknesses prevalent in wider pagan culture. The line that separated the church from the world was becoming increasingly blurred as a consequence of Constantine's adoption of Christianity. There were people in the church who viewed ecclesiastical office as a pathway to worldly status. Accordingly, Augustine argued that God alone was capable of distinguishing between the righteous and those who are

25. Deane, *St. Augustine*, 117.

26. For an overview of this shift, see Adonis Vidu, *Atonement, Law, and Justice: The Cross in Historical and Cultural Contexts* (Grand Rapids, MI: Baker Academic, 2014), esp. 14–28.

27. Augustine, *The City of God Against the Pagans*, trans. R. W. Dyson (Cambridge: Cambridge University Press, 1998), Book XXI, Chapter 14, 1072.

'instruments of unrighteousness'.[28] Thus even as he encourages 'mutual forgiveness' in the company of the faithful, it becomes increasingly difficult to know who this might apply to.

Added to this was the polemical context of Augustine's dispute with Pelagius. According to Dodaro, this significantly coloured Augustine's employment of the term justice.[29] Like Augustine, Pelagius argued that Christ was indeed the 'just man'. However, to this he added that alongside Christ there were others who lived as examples of perfect justice, notably the patriarchs and prophets of the Old Testament. On account of his doctrine of the Trinity and of original sin, Augustine clearly distinguished the justice of God exemplified in Christ and the justice displayed by the faithful before God. Following the Pelagian controversy, Augustine speaks in terms of the gradual growth of justice in the believer as a result of the specific effects of Christ's grace. However, it will never be the complete attainment of justice in its perfect form.

Augustine's impact on the church's conception of justice was considerable. He bequeathed the idea that in order to understand justice, one first had to be just, and the only way to live justly is to have one's soul purified and healed of its ignorance and weakness resulting from sin. Thereafter justice would be understood primarily in a penitential sense. The just would be known by their piety as they practice what Dodaro calls the 'spiritual arts of penitence – self-examination, confession, prayer for pardon, and forgiveness of others'.[30] Only those who knew the depths of their sin and who acknowledged their dependence on the grace and mercy of God were, in Augustine's opinion, fit to rule justly.

Augustine's penitential conception of justice was a powerful heuristic device for distinguishing the just society. This is nowhere more evident than in Augustine's departure from the Ciceronian account of a republic based on justice. With respect to Cicero's notion of a just statesman speaking to the people about justice and so forming a common weal, Augustine writes, 'Rome was never a republic, because true justice had never a place in it'.[31] Not until Christ could a republic exist that might rightly be considered just. It was of this city that Scripture spoke when it said, 'Glorious things are said of thee, O city of God'. It is thus on account of God's justice in Christ that there are 'two kinds of human society', one

28. Ibid., Book XV, Chapter 6, 642.

29. Dodaro, *Christ and the Just Society*, 77.

30. Ibid., 218.

31. Augustine, *City of God*, Book II, Chapter 21, 80. According to Dodaro, Augustine argued that the just society could only exist in Christ, who is the true 'just statesman'.

which exists by the pure grace of God, thereby attaining a higher level of justice, and the other that can only ever reflect a semblance of justice.[32] At present, these two cities are 'commingled...entangled together', which means that citizens of the heavenly city are called to seek after the peace of the earthly city.[33]

Having made clear that the two cities are formed by their respective loves, Augustine resists seeing the earthly city as entirely given over to evil. Self-love, or pride, is the distortion of love as it should be, but there are differing degrees of distortion. The best condition of the earthly city is where it 'desires earthly peace, albeit only for the sake of the lowest kind of goods; and it is that peace which it desires to achieve by waging war'.[34] For Augustine, just as a modicum of peace can be attained by the means of war, so also a modicum of justice can be achieved by the coercive punishments of judgment. Prior to Augustine, there was a far greater reticence about theologically justifying the practice of either soldiery or judging, since both were involved in the shedding of blood.[35] Augustine introduced a dialectic that enabled both these practices to be theologically validated by something less than ideal peace and justice.

After Augustine, both military and judicial vocations were considered exempt from the commandment 'thou shall not kill', so long as a 'just law' authorized them. In his commentary on the Ten Commandments, Augustine develops a formula that would henceforth define judicial procedure: 'When a man is killed justly, it is the law that kills him, not you'.[36] The 'ministry of the laws', as it came to be known, required that a Christian judge or soldier act under a just and lawful authority when he kills.[37]

32. Ibid., Book XIV, Chapter 1.

33. The words of Jeremiah to the exiles in Babylon, 'seek the peace of the city' (Jer. 31), is considered by Luke Bretherton to be the interpretive key to understanding Augustine's *City of God*, Luke Bretherton, *Christianity and Contemporary Politics: The Conditions and Possibilities of Faithful Witness* (West Sussex: Wiley-Blackwell, 2010), esp. 4.

34. Augustine, *City of God*, Book XV, Chapter 4, 639.

35. As Whitman points out, prior to the eighteenth century judges were routinely involved in 'blood punishments', such as execution and mutilation, particularly in the case of low-status persons. 'Like soldiers in a just war, judges took the sword in hand. To serve as a judge was, as it were, to make war on the world'; James Q. Whitman, *The Origins of Reasonable Doubt: Theological Roots of the Criminal Trial* (New Haven, CT: Yale University Press, 2008), 35.

36. Texts are translated and cited by Whitman, ibid., 39.

37. See Augustine, *City of God*, Book I, Chapter 21. Scotnicki points out that the implication of Augustine's conceptuality was that so long as a Christian represents the authority of the state and not their own personal desire they do not break the

The repressive function of the governing authorities was henceforth considered a necessary part of the natural order, since without it sinfulness would overwhelm the peace and justice of the earthly city.

In synthesizing the Ciceronian notion of justice as immanent in the natural order with the New Testament concern for relationships righted by love, Augustine effected change in both conceptions. The imperial justice of the earthly city came to be viewed as a partial reflection of justice properly understood. And yet, it was regarded as no less important for maintaining a rightly ordered society, so long as its earthly magistrates abandoned the pretence of being above the sinners over whom they were ordained to rule. The true church, by contrast, is endowed with the practices needed to achieve true justice, which in this earthly existence can be achieved through the penitential rites that bring healing and purification to the just soul. The church's witness to God's justice turns inward by focusing on the conditions that restrain the sinful desires within. This is at some remove from understanding justice as a quality of human relationships.

Ecclesial and Secular Separation

Just two years before Augustine started writing *The City of God*, the imperial city of Rome had fallen to Alaric and his party of raiding Goths (410 CE). The eventual disintegration of the Empire meant that by the sixth century Roman systems of law and justice no longer exercised any meaningful authority over its citizens. According to legal historian Harold Berman, the institutions for delivering justice ceased functioning as a 'deliberate expression of conscious reason or of will' by those in official authority, and instead were left to the 'common conscience' of local peoples.[38] From the sixth to the tenth centuries, Western Europe operated mostly on the basis of tribal systems of 'community justice' alongside penitential practices that originated in Christian monasteries.

Berman's description of the European attitude to law during this period highlights the uniqueness of this period:

> No one had attempted to organize the prevailing laws and legal institutions into a distinct structure. Very little of the law was in writing. There was no professional judiciary, no professional class of lawyers, no professional legal literature. Law was not consciously systematized. It had not yet been

commandment to not kill when they 'imposed the death penalty on criminals', Andrew Skotnicki, *The Last Judgment: Christian Ethics in a Legal Culture* (Surrey: Ashgate, 2012), 45.

38. Harold J. Berman, *Law and Revolution: The Formation of the Western Legal Tradition* (London: Harvard University Press, 1983), 68, cf. 77.

> 'disembedded' from the whole social matrix of which it was a part. There was no independent, integrated, developing body of legal principles and procedures clearly differentiated from other processes of social organization and consciously articulated by a corps of persons specially trained for that task.[39]

The Germanic tribal legal systems of this period were primarily reparative in nature. The primary context for doing justice was the family or village unit, where the emphasis fell on maintaining community relationships and ensuring victims were compensated, often in the form of financial reparations.[40] Law and judgment were primarily oriented towards holding people together and served more a mediatory or communicative role than a decision-making or rule-making role. There was a feudal system of punishment, although this was viewed as an option of last resort, if a negotiated outcome could not be found.[41] What mattered in the majority of offences, as Zehr puts it, 'was the actual harm done, not the violation of laws or an abstract social or moral order… The feud was one way of resolving such situations, but so was negotiation, restitution, and reconciliation.'[42]

In continuity with Augustine's penitential theology, the concepts of crime and sin were viewed as interchangeable in the feudal context. Both were defined in terms of an offense against actual victims and their kinfolk and, just as importantly, as against God. The conviction that all were sinners, highlighted by Augustine, actually produced a remarkably chastened attitude to the punishment of criminals.[43] The concepts of repentance and forgiveness were an integral part of the understanding of justice, which was further reinforced by the monastic system of penitentials. Penance was viewed as 'medicine for the soul', a preparation for

39. Ibid., 50.

40. For example, the Laws of Ethelbert, which were promulgated by the ruler of Kent in 600 CE, contained detailed schedules of financial reparation for various injuries caused. Each part of the body that was injured carried a price that must be paid to the victim, or in the case of death, the victim's family. See, ibid., 55; Gorringe, *God's Just Vengeance*, cf. 89, 95.

41. In the development of the feudal system of punishment, Gorringe points out, 'all wrongdoing is [perceived as] an attack on the community'. Therefore, the community is compelled to find a way to satisfy all parties through a reconciliatory process, and only if such an outcome cannot be reached the wrongdoer is expelled from the human community; Gorringe, *God's Just Vengeance*, 88.

42. Zehr, *Changing Lenses*, 99.

43. As Whitman argues in his examination of the medieval practice of the juridical ordeal; Whitman, *Origins of Reasonable Doubt*, 53.

reconciliation with the wider community by way of faith and works, so that the 'idea of punishment was subordinated to the idea of cure'.[44] Crime, like sin, was viewed relationally as separation from God and community. This meant that more than punishment, what the offender needed was to be cured of the effects of sin and so be brought back into right relationships.

Yet as the penitentials came to be written down, paradoxically the tendency was to turn morality into a codified system.[45] As such, the penitentials focused less on primary questions about the nature of the moral life and instead concentrated on those actions that ought to be avoided or corrected if one were to aspire to live morally. This led to certain wrongful actions being codified in a way that would later be understood as crimes. Moreover, by viewing actions apart from personal agency, these penitentials were already interpreting wrongdoing at some abstraction from its effect on human relationships.

A significant change occurred with the rediscovery of Roman law in the eleventh century. With this came the mechanism to view the papal church as a juristically distinct institution rather than as part of the *corpus permixtum* of society, in which Augustine's two cities were intertwined. Ironically it was Augustine's two cities model that provided the theological framework for segregating the church from the secular realm, precisely on account of the church's embodiment of a justice distinct from secular justice.

In his magisterial work *A Secular Age*, Charles Taylor argues that the first movement towards secularization began not with society's drift away from religion but rather with the consolidation of the Western church into a distinct entity under the papacy of Gregory VII.[46] Discontent with medieval rulers intruding into ecclesiastical matters led Gregory to push for greater church autonomy. In order to achieve this autonomy, the Western church adopted Roman law as the basis for creating a system of canon law, which then became fundamental to the church's identity. 'Roman law', as Zehr observes, 'was formal, rational, codified law based

44. 'The ultimate penance was excommunication, which signified deprivation of the right to participate in the sacraments of the church (including communion, marriage, burial, and others); this purported to cut off – temporarily – the relationship of the sinner to God and to the church'; Berman, *Law and Revolution*, 71–72.

45. I take these points from two sources: Stanley Hauerwas, 'On Doctrine and Ethics', in *The Cambridge Companion to Christian Doctrine*, ed. Colin Gunton (Cambridge: Cambridge University Press, 1997), 21–40; and Samuel Wells and Ben Quash, *Introducing Christian Ethics* (West Sussex: Wiley-Blackwell, 2010), 44.

46. Charles Taylor, *A Secular Age* (Cambridge: Belknap Press, 2007), 265–66.

on logic and fundamental principles. Instead of being based on custom and history, this law stood alone.'[47] The Latin-speaking papal theologians saw this independent law as a tool for establishing and protecting the church's independence. It should be noted that the Eastern church, which looked to Constantinople rather Rome as its founding city, did not incorporate law as so integral to the church.[48]

Drawing on Augustine, Gregory effectively equated the *civitas Dei* with the church, while placing himself at its head. The Western church thus came to define itself as 'the very embodiment of *justitia*', writes Skotnicki; a divinely ordained juristic institution.[49] It now had the liberty to impose laws and judgments with respect to internal ecclesiastical matters, while other authorities exercised rule over a distinct realm of secular matters. Secular justice systems served as a worldly counterpart to the ecclesiastical justice system.

A number of consequences for the understanding and practice of justice resulted from the splitting of medieval society into ecclesial and secular jurisdictions. First, the system of community justice began to decline as a contest for judicial authority ensued between the medieval church and medieval monarchies. Whitman observes that each party in this contest sought to 'monopolize violence – to take control of the process of justice, forcing Europeans to settle their conflicts in centralized court settings'.[50] In order to impress their new legal authority over the local population, the very notion of law was removed from its communal context. Community-oriented processes that involved people most directly harmed by an offence would eventually give way to outcomes imposed from on high. The legal interests of centralized authorities were increasingly placed above the needs of victims, offenders, and their local relationships.[51]

Second, the separation of ecclesial and secular jurisdictions was paralleled by a separation of the concepts of sin and crime. Canon theologians introduced this sharp distinction by institutionalizing the public litigation

47. Zehr, *Changing Lenses*, 111.

48. The Eastern and Western sections of the Church split in the eleventh century (1054 BCE), and it is possible that the significance given to the concepts of law and justice were a major contributor to this split.

49. Skotnicki, *Last Judgment*, 65. Augustine's differentiation between the city of God and the city of man based respectively on the common object of their love was arguably not intended to harbour ideas of an earthly Christian state, even if he did provide the conceptual framework for such a Christian state.

50. Whitman, *Origins of Reasonable Doubt*, 57.

51. Zehr, *Changing Lenses*, 115.

of ecclesiastical offences under the new inquisitorial judicial method.[52] Yet at the same time as removing jurisdiction over sins from secular authority, they also opened up a new space for any 'act punishable by royal or other "lay" officials [as] henceforth to be punished as a violation of secular law and not as a sin, that is, not as a violation of a law of God'.[53] This move marked the beginning of a trend where the state claimed a monopoly in dealing with matters of criminality.

Third, the very language of 'jurisdiction over sins' signals an even more basic change to the concepts of sin and crime. Both were now defined as against law rather than as against victims and God. The once relational definition of separation from God and neighbor now 'came to be understood in legal terms as specific wrongful acts or desires or thoughts for which various penalties must be paid in temporal suffering, whether in this life or the next'.[54] Offences once deemed a local problem needing to be resolved relationally were now defined as crimes against law. Berman rightly characterizes this definition as 'retributive', since it focuses less on putting right the specific relationships injured by wrongdoing and more on effecting a balance within the legal order.

Fourth, with wrongdoing being interpreted legalistically, both ecclesial and secular authorities came to understand justice as the punishment of lawbreakers. The formalizing of a system of laws greatly extended the role of centralized authorities in handing down sentences. Papal canonists revived the old Augustinian rule that punishments were justified as the 'ministry of the laws', which in Skotnicki's opinion produced a 'theological justification for a harsh justice toward legal infractions'.[55] Justice, as Zehr writes, 'became a matter of applying rules, establishing guilt, and fixing penalties'.[56] And the penalties could be severe. As Gratian in the *Decretum* would later write, 'If holy men and public powers waging wars are not transgressors of that mandate: "Thou shalt not kill", although they kill some criminals worthy of death…if it is not shedding blood to punish murderers and prisoners, but the ministry of laws…' then 'it is obvious that [secular authorities are] permitted not only to whip the evil, but also to kill them'.[57]

52. See Skotnicki, *Last Judgment*, 113–14.

53. Berman, *Law and Revolution*, 185.

54. Ibid., 171.

55. Skotnicki, *Last Judgment*, 73.

56. Zehr, *Changing Lenses*, 113.

57. Skotnicki, *Last Judgment*, 78–79, who is quoting from Stanley Chodorow, *Christian Political Theory and Church Politics in the Mid-Twelfth Century* (Berkeley, CA: University of California Press, 1972), 236.

One further feature of this shifting ecclesial context must be noted, and it relates to the increasingly significant role granted to human authority. Berman writes that the system of law and penalties decreed by the papacy had direct implications on 'the nature and destiny of man, his search for salvation, [and] his moral freedom'.[58] In short, all guilt could be dealt with by human means in this new legal era, which in effect displaced the role of divine agency. Freedom of choice became the determining factor in a person's progress toward salvation. 'The route was charted by a system of punishments and rewards that extended from this world through the next, until the final goal was reached'.[59] While seriously at odds with Augustine's understanding of human freedom, it was his internalizing justice as a condition of the human soul that eventually gave way to a system of justice oriented towards treating human guilt.

Accordingly, it was the separation of church and state on the basis of legal jurisdiction that gave rise to the now basic concepts of the Western criminal justice tradition. These included the institutionalizing of the administration of law, the differentiation of crime and sin, and the justification of punishment as the main currency of justice. Berman goes so far as to state that modern Western law is no more than a 'secular residue of religious attitudes and assumptions which historically found expression first in the liturgy and rituals and doctrine of the church and thereafter in the institutions and concepts and values of the law'.[60] What began in the eleventh and twelfth centuries would not reach full bloom until the nineteenth century. However, the beginnings of the modern criminal justice system can be traced to theological and ecclesiastical developments of this time.

Anselm's Retributive Theology

The concept of justice that evolved during this momentous period found its firmest theological grounding in the work of Anselm of Canterbury.[61] According to Berman, the flow of ideas between theological concepts and notions of law and justice reached a climax in Anselm's doctrine of the

58. Berman, *Law and Revolution*, 184.

59. Ibid., 171–72.

60. Berman goes on to say that '[w]hen these historical roots are not understood, many parts of the law appear to lack any underlying source of validity'; ibid., 166.

61. Anselm's most recent biographer, Richard Southern, writes, 'It can scarcely be too strongly emphasized that the span of Anselm's life covered one of the most momentous periods of change in European history, comparable to the centuries of the Reformation or the Industrial Revolution'; Richard Southern, *Anselm: A Portrait in a Landscape* (Cambridge: Cambridge University Press, 1990), 4.

atonement. It was Anselm who ‘first gave Western theology its distinctive character and its distinctive connection with Western jurisprudence’.[62] According to Gorringe, what Anselm bequeathed to posterity was ‘the insight that atonement and a retributivist view of punishment belong together’. It was his exposition of the death of Christ that ‘pumped retributivism into the legal bloodstream’.[63] In effect, if not by intent, Anselm smoothed the way for the church’s understanding of justice to be removed from its relational context.

In *Cur Deus Homo?*, Anselm sets out his defence of the incarnation against the objection of unbelievers. While the logic of Anselm’s argument has endured in the church’s theology, it is little known that Anselm himself consciously avoided making recourse to Scripture, since he was attempting to refute the objection of unbelievers who did not accept the biblical account.[64] By employing metaphysical categories shared with his surrounding culture, Anselm tried to show that the death of the God-man is a logical necessity. As he states in the preface, his account ‘proves by necessary reasoning that it is impossible for any man to be saved without him’.[65] In his attempt to render Christian faith intelligible to unbelievers, Anselm draws on prevailing feudal concepts of law and justice without them being reworked in light of the biblical account.

In so doing, Anselm unwittingly turned these concepts into universal principles that were then deemed to be an immanent part of reality due to the incarnation. Berman points to the ‘objectification of general categories of thought’ in Anselm’s theology that allowed concepts like sin, crime, humanity, and law to be treated apart from their ‘concrete manifestations’.[66] In making God the upholder and enforcer of an infinite and hypostatized law, the effect was to remove law and justice from being embedded in actual relationships. This opened the way for God’s relationship to humanity to be interpreted in highly abstract and ultimately punitive terms, which in turn lent weight to remotely administered systems of law supplanting local systems of community justice.[67]

62. Berman, *Law and Revolution*, 177.

63. Gorringe, *God’s Just Vengeance*, 224.

64. As McIntyre puts it, ‘the *Cur Deus Homo* is not written in faith, by faith and for faith; it is not faith’s attempt to understand its own inner intellectual structure. It is, rather, faith’s logical refutation of the objections of unbelievers, who maintain its irrationality’, John McIntyre, *St. Anselm and His Critics: A Re-Interpretation of the Cur Deus Homo* (Edinburgh: Oliver & Boyd, 1954), 6.

65. Anselm, *Cur Deus Homo?*, Preface (italics mine).

66. Berman, *Law and Revolution*, 176.

67. It would, however, be incorrect to attribute the title ‘penal substitution’ to Anselm’s doctrine of atonement, or even to describe his theology as legalistic. This

More problematic is the manner in which Anselm incorporates a notion of justice into God's nature that stands in tension with God's forgiveness. Anselm argued that because God's justice cannot allow a world of disorder, the sinfulness of humanity requires either an equivalent punishment or satisfaction.[68] Anselm dismisses out of hand the possibility that God could simply forgive all sinfulness because this would contradict the whole moral order of justice, and so could have nothing to do with God (cf. I.12–13, 24). Justice is thereby considered to be an essential attribute of God, while forgiveness is not, and even when God might be said to forgive it is only after his justice is satisfied.[69] Anselm's diminution of forgiveness and mercy within the outworking of justice is more congruent with Greco-Roman understandings of justice than it is with the biblical tradition.

Finally, Anselm's portrayal of God's justice secured a necessary place for retributive punishment in the church's imagination. Even though Anselm intended his readers to come to an appreciation of how Christ saves humanity from punishment, nevertheless it is still through punishment that the moral order is put right again.

> And if, when wrong-doing strives to disturb the right order of things, Divine wisdom did not annex these conditions, in the very universe which God ought to regulate there would be a certain uncomeliness arising from the beauty of order being violated, and God would seem to fail in His own arrangements. And as both these things are unseemly, they are impossible, so that it is necessary that satisfaction or punishment follow every sin.[70]

can be seen in the distinction made by Dániel Deme, who argues that for Anselm it was not 'divine justice which is deactivated by the sacrifice of the Son, but the punitive will'; Dániel Deme, *The Christology of Anselm of Canterbury* (Hampshire: Ashgate, 2003), 85. One of the shortcomings of McIntyre's otherwise astute reading of Anselm is his relative disinterest in the wider reforms taking place within the fields of law and crime, which he justifies by focusing on Anselm's own intended task of apologetic theology.

68. The punishment, in other words, would have to be as infinite as is God: 'as man, by sinning, steals what is God's [infinite honor], so God, by punishing, takes away what is man's [his very existence]', Anselm, *Cur Deus Homo?*, I.14.

69. Even McIntyre, a sympathetic reader of Anselm, highlights this as a significant lacunae in Anselm's thought which ultimately arises from Anselm's 'theological conception of justice in God' defined in terms of 'bringing punishment upon sin'; McIntyre, *Anselm and His Critics*, 103.

70. Anselm, *Cur Deus Homo?*, I.15.

Here it is evident that Anselm's understanding of justice is as much an aesthetic as a moral concern.[71] The force of Anselm's argument is that any possible infraction of justice, understood legally, necessitates an equal response of punishment or satisfaction.[72] Anselm's theology led to its secular parody, where, as Berman puts it, 'justice in and of itself, justice *an sich*, requires that a violation of a law be paid for by a penalty, and that the penalty should be appropriate to the violation'.[73]

Two Kingdoms, Justice Divided

In the period following the papal and legal revolutions, a great deal of continuity was thought to exist between human conceptions of justice and divine justice, and also between human legal systems and God's law. The church was believed to be instituted by God to formulate laws that reflected the divine will. Confidence in the church as a divinely ordained juristic institution rested on the belief that divine principles of law and justice were immanent in nature and could be apprehended by reason. The close relationship between reason and natural law was especially fostered by the medieval scholastic method, which produced highly elaborate and sophisticated systems for apprehending divine truth. Yet this tradition of natural law had its antecedent as much in Greco-Roman philosophy as in Scripture. It was the rediscovery of Roman law by the canon theologians that initiated the legal revolution in the first place.

By the late medieval era, natural law was all-pervasive in the church's theology. It allowed the church to be construed as a juristic institution with the prerogative to regulate all of human life. God's gift of salvation now came to be mediated by a system of rewards and punishments controlled by ecclesiastical authorities. This was the ecclesial context that gave rise to the sixteenth-century Reformation, which sought to bring about a new vision of the church. Yet in order to reform the church, the prevailing concepts of law and justice also had to be reformulated.

Two generalizations may be made about the new direction given to the concepts of law and justice ventured by the magisterial Reformers.

71. The concept of justice in Anselm's understanding is concerned with 'the importance of fittingness, order and beauty which the social order must exemplify'; Gorringe, *God's Just Vengeance*, 96.

72. 'The new concepts of sin and punishment based on the doctrine of the atonement...given by Anselm and his successors in Western theology was [justified by] the concept of justice itself. Justice required that every sin (crime) be paid for by temporal suffering; that the suffering, the penalty, be appropriate to the sinful act; and that it vindicate ("avenge") the particular law that was violated'; Berman, *Law and Revolution*, 183.

73. Ibid., 194.

First, the justice of God is understood to contradict the operation of justice in the human realm. Luther especially separated divine and human justice by equating the former with God's gratuitous love in justifying humanity, and the latter with the outworking of God's wrath on sinful humanity. Second, the church's witness to justice becomes divided between its testimony to the justice of God outworked in grace and mercy on the one hand, and its duty to societal systems of justice for the repressing of sinfulness on the other. Overall the church's conception of God's justice becomes even more inward, while at the same time it continues to justify a societal system of justice that fails to reflect the reality of God's compassionate mercy.

By his doctrine of *sola fide* Luther attacked the way salvation had been turned into a legalistic operation of human works instead of a divine operation of elected grace.[74] He argued that the church was to be governed solely by the power of the Holy Spirit, not by the juristic categories of law or justice. More so than Calvin, Luther divested law of any positive function within the church. Law was seen as the *alien work* of God, while grace and love were said to be God's proper work. Luther almost views the work of law and the gospel of grace as opposing wills within God, which he portrayed vividly in the image of 'God against God', with 'God's *opus proprium* of grace and mercy overcoming his *opus alienum* of judgment and damnation'.[75] While Luther and Calvin disagreed over whether the proper essence of law belonged to God's nature, both agreed that in response to human sinfulness, law could only ever have a penal or condemnatory function.[76]

It is important to point out that even though Luther divested the law of any positive function within the church, he did not weaken law as the basis for civil society. Both Luther and Calvin inherited from the legal revolution the belief that society depends on centralized systems of law. Their contribution was to formalize the role of law in the relationship

74. Article 76 of Luther's ninety-five theses reads: 'We assert to the contrary, and say that the pope's pardons are not able to remove the least venial of sins as far as their guilt is concerned'. With such statements as these Luther eroded the papacy's claim to have juristic authority over salvation; John Dillenberger, ed., *Martin Luther: Selections from His Writings* (New York: Anchor Books, 1961).

75. Gorringe, *God's Just Vengeance*, 134. In Gorringe's opinion, Luther's radical theology of God's grace overcoming his wrath led him to eschew Anselm's satisfaction theory in favor of a theology of divine exchange where Christ once and for all takes our place.

76. As Vidu cites, 'God reveals himself to us in the law and declares what kind of God he wishes to be towards us, lays down what he demands of us, and, in short, everything necessary to be known'; Vidu, *Atonement, Law, and Justice*, 96.

between the temporal sovereignty of the state and the spiritual authority of the church.[77] Civil authorities were invested with a divinely ordained duty to wrest the world from its squalor of sin by enforcing law. For example, Luther wrote in 1524, 'Let no one dare think that the world can be ruled without blood. The secular [*welltlich*] sword should and must be red and bloody [*blutrustig*], for the world will and must be evil. Thus is the sword God's rod and vengeance on it.'[78] The civil law thus acted as a 'constrained and forced righteousness', as Calvin put it, providing just enough righteousness in civil society to ward off the digressive passions of this sin-ridden world.[79]

The 'forced righteousness' provided by the government's repression of sinfulness was believed by the reformers to create the right social conditions for divine salvation. In other words, the condemning function of the law was thought to act as a mirror to reflect back the sinner's miserable condition and thus bring him to a place of repentance before the grace of God. As John Witte Jr. argues, the civil use of the law was believed to lead naturally to its theological use.[80] The law condemns, but thanks be to God, who in his grace justifies the sinner who repents.

The division that Luther introduces into the concept of law was largely based on a division within his theology of justice. Luther was emphatic that the justice of God is revealed solely in the cross of Jesus Christ and that this meaning can only be contradictory of human conceptions of justice in the earthly city. Having languished under the meritorious and penitential system of justice, Luther felt liberated by the discovery that God's justice is revealed through the grace that justifies in faith.[81]

77. 'The true originality of the Reformational legal philosophy consists in the particular arrangement of the temporal authority in relation to the spiritual authority of the church'; ibid., 91 (original in italics).

78. Brad S. Gregory, *The Unintended Reformation: How a Religious Revolution Secularized Society* (Cambridge, MA: Harvard University Press, 2012), 208–209, citing Luther, *WA*, vol. 15.

79. John Witte Jr., *God's Joust, God's Justice: Law and Religion in the Western Tradition* (Grand Rapids, MI: Eerdmans, 2006), 265.

80. Witte traces the widespread formulation of the reformed doctrine of the law throughout the modern period where it gained special prominence in English and American puritan theology. Witte clearly shows the similarity that exists between the uses of the law as developed by theologians (civil, theological, educational) and their parallel forms among secular jurists (deterrence, retribution, rehabilitation); ibid., 263–94.

81. James D. G. Dunn and Alan M. Suggate, *The Justice of God: A Fresh Look at the Old Doctrine of Justification by Faith* (Grand Rapids, MI: Eerdmans, 1993), 6–8.

It was this discovery that led him to discard the theological presupposition that God's justice supervened on anything in nature, and could thereby be conditioned by nature. In so doing, Luther introduced an even more radical differentiation between the divine and human realms, granting near autonomy to both.

Luther's conception of justice certainly has its strengths, insofar as the justice of God is aligned more closely to the way in which God reveals himself in the crucified Christ. Luther safeguards God's justice from being overly determined by alien concepts of justice. Yet at the same time, Luther continues the Augustinian trajectory of interpreting God's justice in an inward and spiritualized direction. The conception of two contrasting kingdoms, one represented by the physical and material and the other by the inward and spiritual leads to a conception of divine justice that is unconcerned with the concrete material realities of life.[82] Furthermore, by aligning God's justice with his grace while still justifying the repressive system of justice in the civic sphere, Luther opens the way for endorsing a conception of justice that is completely different to the church's apprehension of the justice of God.

The Reformers' understanding of law and justice made sense in a Christianized society where both civil and ecclesiastical domains interacted, to such a degree that even their articulation of moral law was ultimately oriented towards the salvation of the sinner. Yet as Witte points out, secular jurists during this era largely followed this theological framework, except in one significant respect.[83] Instead of subsuming moral law under a general theory of salvation they subsumed law under a theory of government. While structurally and pragmatically similar, secular jurists eschewed the ultimate *telos* of justice by viewing the coercive and repressive functions of government as aimed at nothing more than conformity to a law-abiding morality.[84] As Christianity's influence in society began to wane, this secularist interpretation of justice would gain a much stronger hold.

82. Vidu points out that Luther's theology has not escaped the accusations of Marcionism since 'the style and energy of Lutheran theology to argue away from the body, from the law, from the letter, and toward the spiritual, the inward'; Vidu, *Atonement, Law, and Justice*, 103.

83. Witte, *God's Joust, God's Justice*, 264–85.

84. Witte offers an indictment of the moral collapse of criminal justice theory, but does not go as far as describing the current penitential crisis. For such an indictment see Logan, *Good Punishment?*, esp. 1–142.

The Modern Turn

The shift to a predominantly secular worldview in Western society was neither immediate nor linear. We previously noted its origination in the eleventh century as the papacy sought to consolidate its authority over civil magistrates, and in Luther's 'doctrine of the two kingdoms', which formalized this separation by granting near autonomy to secular and ecclesial authority respectively. In the wake of the Enlightenment this autonomous secular sphere was invested with an importance that would virtually eclipse the ecclesial sphere altogether. Secularism coalesced with the modern turn to the individual and in particular to the capacity of individuals to reason for themselves.

No thinker is more influential in this period with respect to the concept of justice than Immanuel Kant. In his *Rechtslehre*, Kant reframed the concept of justice by aligning it with the post-Enlightenment agenda. Justice is given a rational justification by rooting it in a consensus between autonomous individuals. Kant's starting point is the individual in a state of nature, unencumbered by moral obligations and the bonds of relationality. The individual in this condition is concerned only with their private interests, doing '*what seems good and right in his own eyes*, entirely independent of the opinion of others'.[85] In order to avoid the inevitable violence of this condition, individuals traded their unencumbered freedom in the state of nature for a freedom enshrined in publicly recognized laws, a convention regarded by Kant as the social contract.[86]

Justice is the name given to the conditions of this 'juridical Union'.[87] In this way, Kant equates justice with a publicly recognized system of laws formed to protect individual rights. The institutionalization of law as a rational system is not grounded in nature but rather in the individual's freedom of choice. He justifies the rationality of this system by narrating a creation story in which violence and disorder preceded the emergence of public law and the birth of the nation state. The commutative and reparative justice that prevailed before the legal revolution of the eleventh century appears in Kant's narrative as the 'dark ages'.

85. Immanuel Kant, *The Philosophy of Law: An Exposition of the Fundamental Principles of Jurisprudence as the Science of Right*, trans. W. Hastie (Edinburgh: T&T Clark, 1887), 163, 57.

86. Or as Hegel formulates it: 'Right in itself passes over in civil society into law. My individual right, whose existence has hitherto been immediate and abstract, now acquires the significance of being recognized, of having its existence in the existent will and knowledge of everyone'; Georg Wilhelm Friedrich Hegel, *Outlines of the Philosophy of Right*, trans. Stephen Houlgate (Oxford: Oxford University Press, 2008), 206.

87. Kant, *Law*, 157.

The individualistic orientation of Kant's reasoning serves to obscure from focus any conception of the public good that might stand above the individual. Justice is no longer understood in terms of 'a substantive morality of the good', as Brad Gregory argues, but instead is turned into 'a formal morality of rights'.[88] Justice also loses its teleological dimension, which for previous theologians was preserved by their subsuming justice under an account of salvation history. For Kant, justice is an end in itself and cannot be subject to any other good without compromising the individual's freedom.

The tradition of German idealism that begins with Kant and carried forward by Hegel, intended to depict a coherent and enlightened account of justice in which justice remains dispassionate and objective. Encapsulated within law, justice is transposed into a transcendent principle that is both detached from, and disinterested in, the complex and subjective world of human relationships.[89] This move represented something of a return to the Greek idea of justice as immanent in nature, an immovable form, purified of all passion, desire, and emotion.

When it comes to the justice of punishment, Kant's passion for precision and objectivity is unrelenting. Crime is defined by Kant as the conscious choice of individuals to go against the public order of right, which means that the criminal abdicates his place within the social contract and so renders himself 'incapable of being a Citizen'.[90] Public justice requires that the moral order of 'Right' be restored by the principle and standard of the 'Right of Retaliation'.[91] According to Kant, 'pure and strict Justice' requires that every crime be annulled by retaliation on the criminal, and

88. Gregory notes that this transformation 'constitutes the central change in Western ethics over the past half millennium, in terms of theory, practice, laws, and institutions'; Gregory, *Unintended Reformation*, 184.

89. Hegel, *Philosophy of Right*, 107. Hegel writes elsewhere that retributive punishment in the form of revenge is 'only right *in itself*, not right in the form of what is lawful, i.e., it is not just in its existence' (209).

90. Kant, *Law*, 194.

91. Ibid., 196. To subject punishment to some other good – i.e., utility – would mean that 'Justice would cease to be Justice' (ibid.). Kant is not always so consistent with his own views, as he is not opposed to their being some good either to the individual or to the commonwealth that can come of punishment, even in the case of punishment as deterrence. Jeffrie Murphy points out the inconsistencies in Kant's supposed theory of punishment, notably from his earlier works that include notes like: 'Punishments are, therefore, a means of preventing an evil or of punishing it. Those imposed by governments are always deterrent'; 'Universal Practical Philosophy', in *Lectures on Ethics 55*, ed. L. Infield (1978), cited in Jeffrie G. Murphy, 'Does Kant Have a Theory of Punishment?', *Columbia Law Review* 87, no. 3 (1987): 513.

where this is not achieved society may as well dissolve itself and revert to a violent state of nature.[92]

It needs to be highlighted that this conception of retributive justice operates with a high degree of abstraction. Maintaining the transcendent character of justice, both Kant and Hegel focus on the general justification for justice as punishment but remain uninterested in how this is actually implemented. Hegel openly admits that his conception of justice as retribution is hypothetical. It works better as an 'abstract thought of free will and personality' dealing with the 'inner identity' of crime and its annulment, than it does in its concrete application.[93] Likewise the parties to a crime are treated as an abstraction, since it is the law and the principle of right that needs to be satisfied. Danielle Allen rightly observes that Kant 'effectively purified the concept of retribution of its historical connection to anger, to citizens' wills, to passion and desire'.[94] In this conception, justice has no reference point in the real world of human relationships, which means that wrongdoers and their victims may be treated with dispassionate reason.

The Western theological tradition from Augustine to Luther always relegated the form of justice in the earthly city to a secondary status within the divine order. Human justice was believed to be a parody of true justice, yet this form of justice was still necessary in a world of sinfulness, where digressive passions always threaten to take over. Human justice is therefore necessarily retributive or punitive. Kant's account of justice reflects this same negative determination, yet without its divine counterpart. By eclipsing the divine, Kant's human-centered justice is utterly retributive, driven by a punitive will, and completely divorced from the workings of mercy and a compassionate sentiment.[95]

92. Kant, *Law*, 157, 97.

93. Hegel, *Philosophy of Right*, 99, 104. More recently Dan Markel has similarly argued that retributivism provides the *justification* of the institution of punishment, but does not provide much guidance when it comes to the implications for punishment in individual cases (*sentencing*); Dan Markel, 'Bentham on Stilts: The Bare Relevance of Subjectivity to Retributive Justice', *California Law Review* 98 (2010): 950–51, cited in Michael Tonry, 'Can Twenty-First Century Punishment Policies Be Justified in Principle', in *Retributivism Has a Past: Has It a Future?*, ed. Michael Tonry (Oxford: Oxford University Press, 2011), 21.

94. Danielle S. Allen, 'Democratic Dis-Ease: Of Anger and the Troubling Nature of Punishment', in *The Passions of Law*, ed. Susan A. Bandes (New York: New York University Press, 1999), 203.

95. The characterization Kant makes of Beccaria's utilitarian view of punishment is notable here, since he deplores the latter's reasoning as being motivated by the 'compassionate sentimentality of a humane feeling'; Kant, *Law*, 201.

Interestingly, according to Jeffrie Murphy, the purpose of punishment in Kant's understanding is to root out the 'inner viciousness' of the criminal.[96] Punishment is not only for the wrongdoing done, but is in some sense meant to target human *evil* itself. This accords closely with the purpose of human justice given by the Augustinian tradition.

The real problem, however, is that with the rise of secularism there disappears from view any place for the counter witness of the church to a justice that is primarily restorative or salvific. We are left with a conception of justice that reveals its usefulness through repressing evil but which is incapable of pointing to any positive good beyond this. Such a reductionist account of justice may rest on secular assumptions, yet its emergence owes much to the arrangement between divine and human justice in the theological tradition. The justice of God revealed in Christ and affirmed in the church had become so introverted and spiritualized that it no longer had any currency in a world that deemed theology to be increasingly irrelevant or irrational. The secular conception of justice, therefore, was divested of any connection to grace, mercy, and forgiveness.

Criminal Justice in the Contemporary Context

We come now to our own day, the late modern period, to the secular world come of age. Our particular interest is in understanding how the concept of justice has been construed in response to changing societal attitudes to crime. We have seen how the ecclesial context that shaped earlier conceptions of justice has progressively receded into the background. Today it is no longer the church but the state and society that form the most immediate context for understanding justice and what it requires of citizens. Justice, at least as it pertains to crime, is by and large now viewed as extrinsic to the church and its doctrine.

We have also noted how the modern turn to the individual was driven in part by a confidence in human reason to establish secure foundations for a society come of age. This confidence produced a period of heightened optimism in the human capacity for progress. The late nineteenth and early twentieth centuries were an era of optimism about the ability of socially engineered solutions to address societal ills.[97] Crime control took a

96. Jeffrie G. Murphy, 'Some Second Thoughts on Retributivism', in Tonry, ed., *Retributivism Has a Past*, 96.

97. An early example of this is Arthur MacDonald, *Criminology* (New York: Funk & Wagnalls, 1983). 'The method of the scientific study of criminals' necessitates, according to MacDonald, 'a thorough investigation of the criminal himself, both psychologically and physically, so that the underlying and constant cause of crime

'progressive approach to offending', writes Barbara Hudson. It attempted to 'eradicate the problems of social and environmental deprivation that engendered crime and delinquency, and to seek the rehabilitation of those who nonetheless found themselves on the wrong side of the law'.[98] Crime was viewed as either the result of inadequate provisions or as the product of defective socialization.

This understanding of crime as the outcome of social deficit led to what David Garland has termed an era of 'penal welfarism'. 'The solution for crime', Garland explains, 'lay in individualized correctional treatment, the support and supervision of families and in welfare-enhancing measures of social reform – particularly education and job creation'.[99] The implementation of these correctionalist and welfarist ideals required an ever-expanding body of specialized experts, especially from the medical guild, and it was believed to be the duty of the state to deliver such services. Incarceration was viewed as a measure of last resort, although once incarcerated criminals were often subject to indeterminate behavior modification regimes that were no less torturous than traditional punishments.

There was a clear consensus among criminologists of this era that the retributive rationale for punishment provided by Kant and others was a backward, ignorant, and unscientific response to crime. The sentiment expressed in a 1933 publication captured the general mood well: 'The infliction of pain is never justified merely on the ground that it visits retributive punishment upon the offender. Punitive retribution is never justifiable in itself.'[100] According to Michael Tonry, this consequentialist view of punishment reached its heights in America with the publication of the most influential criminal law document of the twentieth century, the *Moral Penal Code* (1962). Even though it was written by 'the most establishmentarian lawyers midcentury America had to offer', retributivist ideas were almost totally absent in this document.[101]

can be traced out'; ibid., 272, cited in Francis T. Cullen and Paul Gendreau, 'From Nothing Works to What Works: Changing Professional Ideology in the 21st Century', *The Prison Journal* 81, no. 3 (2001): 315–16.

98. Barbara Hudson, *Justice Through Punishment: A Critique of the 'Justice' Model of Corrections* (Hampshire: Macmillan Education, 1987), x.

99. David Garland, *The Culture of Control: Crime and Social Order in Contemporary Society* (New York: Oxford University Press, 2001), 15.

100. Jerome Michael and Mortimer Adler, eds., *Crime, Law, and Social Science* (New York: Harcourt Brace, 1933), 344; cited in Tonry, 'Twenty-First Century Punishment Policies', 8.

101. Tonry, 'Twenty-First Century Punishment Policies', 7.

The rehabilitative idealism of the early twentieth century was subsequently dismantled during the 1970s, although with little thought given to its replacement. The seventies marked what Francis Allen calls 'the decline of the rehabilitative ideal', and what Barbara Hudson terms the rise of the 'justice' model of corrections.[102] In stark contrast to the optimism of the correctional ideals that sought to implement 'what works', the new era was guided by the pessimistic judgment of Robert Martinson that 'nothing works'.[103] Discontent with what was perceived to be an intrusive body of professionals, individualized and disparate sentencing, ineffective treatment programmes, and a loss of the offender's private rights, led to widespread reforms of the criminal justice system.

It is important to point out that this reform agenda was driven not so much by criminologists or correctional experts as by philosophers and jurists seeking to give notions of justice more of a central role. In other words, the character of these reforms was less concerned with reducing crime and its effects as it was with reinvigorating more abstract notions of proportionality in sentencing, punishment as a right, and a more codified system of criminal wrongs. One of the leading proponents behind this shift was Andreas von Hirsch who set out this agenda for reform in the report for the Committee for the Study of Incarceration (1976), published under the title *Doing Justice*.[104] More recently, von Hirsch has argued that the initial attractiveness of remodeling the criminal justice system on retributive theory lay in its 'attempts to give notions of justice a central role'.[105] Justice is achieved, argues von Hirsch, by having a more objective sense of moral censure, something lost in the loftier goals of crime prevention and therapeutic intervention.

102. Francis Allen, *The Decline of the Rehabilitative Ideal* (New Haven, CT: Yale University Press, 1981); Hudson, *Justice Through Punishment*.

103. Robert Martinson, 'What Works? Questions and Answers About Prison Reform', *The Public Interest* 35 (1974): 22–54. In a more recent survey of 'what works', Cullen and Gendreau argue that criminology 'has been dominated by a professional ideology for the past quarter century that is committed to "knowledge destruction"' in which 'scholars have been "raised" within academic criminology to show what doesn't work as opposed to showing what does work. This professional ideology has been important in the creation of knowledge that reveals the foolishness of numerous correctional interventions'; Cullen, 'From Nothing Works to What Works', 314.

104. Hudson, *Justice Through Punishment*, xi, 37; Andreas von Hirsch, *Doing Justice* (New York: Hill & Wang, 1976).

105. Andreas von Hirsch, 'Punishment Futures', in Tonry, ed., *Retributivism Has a Past*, 258.

The conception of justice being advocated, however, was clearly a return to the model of retributive punishment seen in seventeenth- and eighteenth-century moral and political philosophy. It reflected a Hobbesian view of the state, where its duty to citizens was solely that of enforcer-protector. Von Hirsch's report puts it plainly: 'Permeating this report is a determination to do less rather than more… Instead, we have here a crucial shift in perspective from a commitment to do good to a commitment to do as little mischief as possible.'[106] Likewise, there was a return to a Kantian 'free will individual rationality model of human nature', writes Hudson.[107] The criminal was to be punished solely for his choices so that he might 'expiate his guilt and become morally whole again'.[108] Neither the state nor the penal system is under any obligation to correct social injustices or change moral attitudes, which according to Hudson represents a severely reductionist account of justice.[109]

Closer to our own concerns, those who led these penal reforms were committed to a liberal theory that held as one of its premises the interiorization of religious ideas and values. Antony Duff argues that a key feature of this liberal outlook was a separation between the concept of sin and the conception of wrongdoing appropriate to criminal law.[110] This differentiation between sin and crime rested on the presumption that sin was internal and hidden, and therefore of no concern to public society. Crime, on the other hand, was expressly public in nature, which was why criminals ought to be held publicly responsible for their actions.[111] Here we see how the criminal justice debate in the contemporary era consciously avoids any recourse to theological concepts, believing that it belongs to a separate sphere altogether.

Even as an explicit Christian voice receded from public view, there were still some prominent Christian thinkers who added their voice to the criticism of the rehabilitative ideal. Writing in the 1970s, C.S. Lewis deplored the fact that the above 'Humanitarian Theory' had become 'almost universal among [his] fellow-countrymen'.[112] Lewis's objection

106. Hudson, *Justice Through Punishment*, 55, citing von Hirsch, *Doing Justice*, xxxiv.

107. Hudson, *Justice Through Punishment*, 56.

108. Ibid.

109. Ibid., 57.

110. R. A. Duff, 'Penance, Punishment and the Limits of Community', *Punishment and Society* 5, no. 3 (2003): 296.

111. This division between the interiority of sin and crime as external conduct is often cited as the basis for justifying criminal punishment in the public sphere.

112. C. S. Lewis, *God in the Dock: Essays on Theology and Ethics* (Grand Rapids, MI: Eerdmans, 1970), 287.

was directed both at the view of humanity it portrayed and at the absence of any concept of justice. While the 'scientific' approach to criminology appeared progressive and humane, Lewis thought that it was actually a 'dangerous illusion and disguises the possibility of cruelty and injustice without end'.[113] The problem lay in its view of human failure or sinfulness as a disease needing to be cured. This 'simple minded view of fallen human nature' placed corrective justice in the hands of psychotherapists whose concern was with treatment, not justice.[114] Justice, in Lewis's opinion, belonged to the sphere of desert and punishment, not to the medical sphere of healing and treatment. By treating the criminal as a patient needing to be cured, Lewis believed that humanitarians had 'tacitly removed him from the sphere of justice altogether' and no longer saw him 'as a human person made in God's image'.[115] In the interests of the criminal, Lewis urged a 'return to the traditional or Retributive theory' of justice.

The concerns raised by Lewis were mirrored on the other side of the Atlantic in an influential book by Karl Menninger entitled, *Whatever Became of Sin?* Menninger made the historical observation that 'Sins had become crimes', and now in the modern era 'crimes were becoming illnesses'.[116] Criminal justice institutions had become devoid of notions of guilt and moral responsibility. Menninger sought to recapture the language of sin to 'close the moral gap', to proclaim 'what is right from what is wrong', and ultimately to reinvigorate the church's moral leadership.

The concerns of these Christian thinkers reflected a growing sentiment in the church that not only were notions of justice absent in prevailing rehabilitative policies but that church itself had a contribution to make to penal policy. When it came to articulating this contribution, however, these authors simply added their voice to the retributive agenda set forth by their secular counterparts. They did not call to mind the full resources of their own tradition, which might have led them to question some of the presuppositions behind justice understood as purely retributive. In so far as the church endorsed the call for penal reform in a retributive direction, they further eroded whatever alternative contribution they might have had, and they also became complicit in the enormous social cost that resulted from these reforms.

113. Ibid.

114. Ibid., 290.

115. Ibid., 288, 92.

116. Karl Menninger, *Whatever Became of Sin?* (London: Hodder & Stoughton, 1973), 45.

Garland argues that since the 1970s, 'criminal law and penal policy have been working without clear route maps on a terrain that is largely unknown'.[117] This aimlessness coincided with the cultural upheavals of late modernity, the disintegration of Christendom and the rise of neoliberal economic theory. Together they have produced a culture that is insecure in its normative values and more prone to accept repressive controls on those who appear to be a threat to the liberal order.[118] Garland argues that criminal justice policy has become reactive to the social pressures of an

> increasingly insecure economy that marginalizes substantial sections of the population; to a hedonistic consumer culture that combines extensive personal freedoms with relaxed social controls; to a pluralistic moral order that struggles to create trust relations between strangers who have little in common; to a 'sovereign' state that is increasingly incapable of regulating a society of individuated citizens and differentiated social groups; and to chronically high crime rates that co-exist with low levels of family cohesion and community solidarity.[119]

Crime control has shifted from being a relatively small concern on the part of criminological experts to becoming a dominant concern of the general population.

Politicians have capitalized on the ramped-up fear of criminals by promising to 'get tough' on crime and reduce its threat to civil society. In blatant contradiction of expert opinion and evidence-based practice, penal policy has come to be defined by slogans such as, 'Prison works', 'Three-strikes you're out', 'No frills prisons', 'Adult time for adult crime', 'Zero-tolerance', and 'Tough on crime, tough on the causes of crime'.[120] Purporting to be common sense, the voice of the people and a return to basics, such slogans in reality prey on a new era of social insecurity.[121]

Garland argues that prison has undergone a reinvention in this new social landscape. It is 'located precisely at the junction point of two of the most important social and penal dynamics of our time: risk and retribution… With the absolutist logic of a penal sanction, it punishes and

117. Garland, *Culture of Control*, 5.

118. Ibid., 13.

119. Ibid., 194.

120. Ibid., 13.

121. Much of the criminal justice policy that was fueled by this penal populism went far beyond the limits of the retributive justification for punishment, as pointed out by Tonry, 'Twenty-First Century Punishment Policies', 4. Yet these policies would not have been so thoroughly embraced had it not been for the revitalization of retributive theory.

protects, condemns and controls.'[122] Criminals are 'no longer clients in need of support, but risks to be carefully managed', writes Kim Workman.[123] Rates of incarceration have increased sharply where these justice reforms have been embraced. In the United States alone, incarceration rose 500% between 1973 and 1997, even though the crime rate continued to decrease. Some theorists now argue that punishment is justified as an expressive gesture of outrage, and even a desire for revenge.[124]

The social science commentary on the modern-day justice system is extensive. The opinion of Garland and Sparks represents the consensus. Penal policy is no longer based on 'research findings and expert advice, but instead on highly politicized articulations of public sentiment that strike many criminologists as ill-informed, explicitly punitive, and downright anti-modernist in character'.[125] The question that must be asked is whether a different trajectory might have been possible. These reforms were propelled by a theory of justice that has a very mixed theological pedigree, as we have shown, and in the end worked to bracket out theological matters as belonging to another sphere altogether. This resulted in a highly punitive system of mass incarceration with devastating effects. The concern before us now, and what will guide the rest of our exploration, is whether there are resources within the theological tradition that would lead us to question whether the modern-day justice system embodies the best conception of justice after all, and what might such an alternative look like.

This chapter has surveyed historical developments in the theory and practice of justice in order to show, first, that different conceptions of justice exist within the church's tradition, and second, that the church's theological understanding of the justice of God has social and practical ramifications not only for the life of the church but also for the society it

122. Garland, *Culture of Control*, 199.

123. Kim Workman, 'Politics and Punitiveness: Limiting the Rush to Punish', paper presented at *The Rising Punitiveness* conference, Wellington, New Zealand, 17–19 November, 2011, n.p.

124. Terry K. Aladjem, *The Culture of Vengeance and the Fate of American Justice* (New York: Cambridge University Press, 2008); Peter French, *The Virtues of Vengeance* (Lawrence, KS: University Press of Kansas, 2001); on the communicative function of punishment, see R. A. Duff, *Punishment, Communication and Community* (Oxford: Oxford University Press, 2001).

125. David Garland and Richard Sparks, 'Criminology, Social Theory and the Challenge of Our Times', in *Criminology and Social Theory*, ed. David Garland and Richard Sparks (Oxford: Oxford University Press, 2000), 12.

inhabits. It is clear that the church's perspective on the meaning of God's justice spills over into broader social practices, especially relating to how wrongdoers and their victims are dealt with. The secular criminal justice system took shape and developed in direct relationship to ecclesial notions of law, justice, and sin.

By drawing attention to the social outworking of the church's understanding of justice, we have seen how justice is not a static concept or idea that can be known apart from the various contexts, practices, and relationships wherein it is expressed and takes concrete form. It is deeply shaped by the social and relational context within which it is understood and practiced. This is not to suggest that justice has no objective existence; it is rather to say that justice is deeply intertwined with the real concerns of life as it is actually lived, and it is this that gives justice its distinctive dynamic. Justice is not *primarily* or substantively a theoretical concept, despite recent attempts to develop comprehensive theories of justice; it is an experiential reality that bears directly on the stuff of real life.

In considering the fluctuating fortunes of justice through Western Christian history, some recurring themes can be detected. One recurring feature has been the church's conviction that justice is objectively grounded in the divine nature. Justice was thought to be perfect and holy because it coheres in God, and against this divine standard of justice all of its lesser human forms must be weighed. This led to the recognition that the human perception of justice is always distorted, imperfect, and in need of continual correction. This was a particularly strong feature of the Augustinian tradition. It was only in the modern, increasingly secular era, with its confidence in the powers of human reason and the diminution of the traditional theological worldview, that the relative priority of divine and human justice was inverted.

The conviction that God's justice is the standard against which all human forms of justice must be measured is good theology, but this in itself it not impervious to distortion. Our survey has shown how the justice of God has often been defined in terms drawn uncritically from the surrounding social order, such that God's justice and holiness tended to acquire a detached and retributive determination. God has been conceived in terms of a harsh judge exacting his retributive justice on sinful humanity. God's justice has been distanced from the world of human relationships, and the church's emphasis on justice has become more inward, individualized and spiritualized.

While the church's practice of the justice of God became predominantly focused on individual salvation through forensic justification, its theological assumptions and commitments still exerted a formative influence in the secular sphere. The emergence of the modern criminal justice system evolved in relation to theological conceptions about the nature of divine and human justice. These assumptions still exert considerable influence over the meaning and practice of justice in the public sphere today, though they are little acknowledged.

Our present goal is to ask whether the conceptions of justice bequeathed by the church to the modern criminal justice system are actually reflective of the church's own best theology. In particular, is a retributive and ultimately punitive notion of corrective justice the best way to understand the justice of God? I will argue that it is not, for at least two main reasons. Firstly, it interprets God's justice in categories that are neither theologically nor Scripturally warranted and, secondly, it fails to understand the church as a community called to embody true justice in the world through relationships of peace and restoration. As we will see in the next chapter, this is something ecclesial ethicists are drawing attention to in a fresh way.

Chapter 2

THE ECCLESIAL TURN IN CHRISTIAN ETHICS

In the Preface to *A Better Hope*, Stanley Hauerwas dedicates his book to 'The Ekklesia Project'. He explains that those who constitute the Project, 'come from quite different ecclesial backgrounds, some are academics and some are not, and we bring quite different agendas to the work of the group. Yet as the Declaration makes clear, we are united in our commitment to *reclaiming the church as an alternative people for the good of the world*'.[1] According to this group, the witness of the church is under serious threat in the contemporary era. Increasingly eclipsed by forces that seek to conform Christian lives to 'partisan ideologies and identities', the church's witness has been subordinated to the 'imperatives of economic and political power holders and institutions'. The Ekklesia Project provides a forum to unite supporters around the conviction that the church, as God's ἐκκλησία, is 'called out' from the world to be 'an alternative community – a resource of resistance to the social and political structures of the age'.[2]

While it might strike some as unusual to consider the church as a community of resistance witnessing to an alternative mode of life, the Declaration is not meant to be innovative. In fact, the invitation extended by the Ekklesia Project is to engage in a *recovery* of the church, whose allegiance to Jesus as the Lord of life makes this community 'a foretaste of the Kingdom of God'. The resistance advocated by the Project appears to be based on rather traditional practices – the confession of God's Tri-unity, worship under the guidance of the Spirit, furthering the catholicity of the church, a vital prayer life, performing works of mercy, and observing a fast – all of which together constitute 'a form of prayerful resistance to the idolatrous practices of our culture'.

1. Stanley Hauerwas, *A Better Hope: Resources for a Church Confronting Capitalism, Democracy, and Postmodernity* (Grand Rapids, MI: Brazos Press, 2000), 7 (italics mine).

2. References all come from the 'Declaration and Invitation', which appears as an appendix in ibid., 211–15, as well as on the website: http://www.ekklesiaproject.org/about-us/who-we-are/declaration-and-invitation/, accessed 15 June 2015.

Above all else, however, the members of the Ekklesia Project argue that the church loses its proper vocation when it compromises with the world's 'culture of death'. As their Declaration states: 'We believe that the process of renewing the church in our day requires Christians to rethink all those values and practices that presume a smooth fit between killing and discipleship'. Therefore, in addition to being God-centered and church-centered, the Project is committed to being 'Shalom-centered'. For them, peacemaking is the church's central mode of life as an alternative community.

The Ekklesia Project is one example of a trend in recent theological discourse towards a recovery of the empirical church as central to the formation of a distinctively Christian witness. The features highlighted above are largely reflective of this broad trend – a view of the church as an alternative community; resistance to co-option by a worldly wisdom, expressed through liturgical practices; and the singling out of nonviolence as the heart of Christian witness. Leading this recovery has been a cadre of academics writing in the field of Christian ethics who are predominantly, but not exclusively, working in a North American context.

In this chapter we will argue that the emerging discourse of 'ecclesial ethics' provides a productive way of crystallizing the justice dimensions of the church's existence and mission. The reasons for situating the concerns of our topic within ecclesial ethics are multiple. First, ecclesial ethics offers a corrective to the interiorization and spiritualization of theological conceptions of justice discussed in the previous chapter. Ecclesial ethics argues that the church is called to embody a visible witness in the world that is no less than fully social and political in character. Second, ecclesial ethics underscores the problematic consequences of construing God's justice in terms drawn from non-Christian conceptions of justice. It insists that the church's moral reasoning must arise out of its own epistemic base and employ the convictions, grammar, narratives, and vision that are integral to the forming of Christian character. Third, the centrality ecclesial ethics affords to peacemaking as fundamental to the church's witness offers another significant corrective to the traditional theological justification for a harsh and punitive justice system. This peacemaking dimension offers a fresh way of thinking about the difference the church should make to considerations of justice.

While highlighting how the task of Christian ethics might gain from a recovery of the centrality of the church and its grammar of faith, there is still much work to be done in this recovery project. The concept of justice in particular has not received the kind of attention one would expect, especially in connection to the task of peacemaking that features so highly. While this chapter will largely be concerned to chart the direction ecclesial ethics has taken thus far, by the end it will be clear that more consideration is needed as to where this approach still needs to be extended, especially with respect to its understanding and practice of justice-making.

The Emergence of Ecclesial Ethics

The term 'ecclesial ethics' does not denote a discrete theological discipline, nor has any prominent theologian used this designation to describe their work. The term is coined in the book *Introducing Christian Ethics*, by Sam Wells and Ben Quash, to designate an approach to Christian theology, and Christian ethics in particular, that gives priority to the 'life made possible by Christ for Christians'.[3] This simple description captures several ways in which ecclesial ethics differs from other approaches to Christian ethics.

First, ecclesial ethics is unapologetically 'for Christians'. It is not an account of the ethical life that is for anybody or everybody; it does not attempt to develop a 'universal ethics' applicable to all situations.[4] Rather, it gives specific attention to those who are said to be the 'first fruits' of God's transformation of the world in Christ. This is not because their moral behavior is more exemplary than anyone else's, but simply because they are the people God has claimed to bring about his kingdom.

Second, the 'life' made possible in Christ is understood as embodied, situated, and dynamic. In contrast to accounts of the moral life that are decidedly abstract and theoretical, which rest on a static sense of the self that mechanistically applies principles and rules to the external world, the ecclesial approach emphasizes the agency and the ecclesial situatedness of the Christian life. This life has a distinctive character that is formed through the concrete practices of the particular community called the church, which in turn is located in the midst of salvation history – what God is doing in Christ and his church to bring creation to fulfillment.

Third, the distinctive character of this ecclesial life is understood in relation to the person and work of Christ. His death and resurrection make possible a new way of life, to which the practices of the church ought to bear witness. This means that ecclesial ethics is guided by a particular kind of practical reasoning, one that focuses on discerning what obedience to God's saving purposes disclosed in Christ requires, and that is attentive to the divine presence in the community.

3. Wells, *Introducing Christian Ethics*, 180.

4. According to Wells and Quash, 'universal ethics' is the predominant alternative to ecclesial ethics, as will be discussed shortly.

The distinctiveness of this understanding of Christian ethics is also apparent in the sharply polemical tone that marks much of the writing on the subject. For example, Hauerwas, who is one of the leading advocates of this approach, has titled his books in highly oppositional terms: *After Christendom? How the Church Is to Behave if Freedom, Justice, and a Christian Nation Are Bad Ideas*; *Against the Nations: War and Survival in a Liberal Society*; *Unleashing the Scripture: Freeing the Bible from Captivity to America*; *Dispatches from the Front: Theological Engagements with the Secular*; and, jointly published with William Willimon, *Resident Aliens: Life in the Christian Colony, A Provocative Assessment of Culture and Ministry for People Who Know Something Is Wrong*.[5] Many of the key thinkers whose work has influenced ecclesial ethicists have displayed a similar polemical edge. These include Alasdair MacIntyre's piercing assessment of the fragmentation and incoherence of modern ethics,[6] John Milbank's protest against the hegemony of the social sciences,[7] or, going further back, Karl Barth's forthright 'Nein!' to the idea of interpreting God's revelation in light of cultural categories. Basing itself on arguments of such epic proportions, ecclesial ethics is clearly concerned with something far bigger than a minor adjustment in Christian thinking.

The shift that ecclesial ethics is advocating relates primarily to the recovery of the church as the proper context for learning what it means to inhabit the Christian life. It always proposes some form of declension narrative in which the visible difference of the church has been eclipsed, thereby resulting in a distortion of the Christian witness. When exactly this decline started is disputed. Some trace it to the late medieval period, while others go further back to the time of the Emperor Constantine. Whatever its exact details, there is a common narrative trajectory that imagines a time when the communal and institutional life of the church was shaped around particular practices derived from, and dependent on,

5. Hauerwas, *After Christendom?*; idem, *Against the Nations: War and Survival in a Liberal Society* (New York: Harper & Row, 1985); idem, *Unleashing the Scripture: Freeing the Bible from Captivity to America* (Nashville, TN: Abingdon Press, 1993); idem, *Dispatches from the Front: Theological Engagements with the Secular* (Durham: Duke University Press, 1994); Stanley Hauerwas and William H. Willimon, *Resident Aliens: A Provocative Christian Assessment of Culture and Ministry for People Who Know that Something Is Wrong* (Nashville, TN: Abingdon Press, 1989).

6. Alasdair MacIntyre, *After Virtue: A Study in Moral Theory* (Notre Dame, IN: University of Notre Dame Press, 1981).

7. John Milbank, *Theology and Social Theory: Beyond Secular Reason* (Oxford: Basil Blackwell, 1990).

particular perceptions of truth, and looks forward to a time when this will be so again.[8] It should be noted, however, that not all attempts to recover the visibility of the church as an ethically distinctive community have in mind the same church to be recovered.

In describing the eclipse of the church, two different narratives are commonly encountered: one that focuses on relatively recent developments, and another that canvases a much larger historical period. In one, ecclesial ethics tells a story about how ethics in the modern era effectively displaced the church as the constant for ethical inquiry with a new constant, that of the autonomous individual. In the second, ecclesial ethics offers a far-reaching historical narrative about the collapse of the church as an alternative witnessing community largely occasioned by its collusion with earthly rulers and authorities. We will consider each of these accounts in turn before explaining the various correctives offered.

The Eclipse of the Church

Those associated with ecclesial ethics have gathered around the consensus that the general form of ethical inquiry in the modern era, and of Christian ethics in particular, is individualistic, rationalistic, and universalistic. This has resulted in Christian ethics becoming less concerned with the distinctive reasoning of the church as well as losing touch with the importance of the church as the primary site for Christian social practice. Broadly characterized, modern ethics is aimed at everybody and anybody, since it takes for granted the capacity of every individual to be guided by reason. It proceeds on the basis of self-evident principles apprehended by natural reason that must then be put into effect by individual citizens for the guiding of society.

Underlying this approach is the assumption that the institution of the church and the practices of religious faith are an impediment to natural reason. The individual's immanent consciousness is believed to be a more reliable source of truth than the external authority of ecclesiastical dogma. Accordingly, the epistemological framework of modern ethics is essentially individualistic and rationalistic. What is not amenable to reason is considered irrelevant to moral truth, which immediately excludes divine revelation and faithful obedience as a reliable basis for knowledge.

This specifically modern approach has tended to take the form of identifying general principles to guide individuals in moments of decision. It is assumed that individuals act on the basis of self-evident principles, ideals, or rules, and the task of ethics is to prescribe the principles most

8. Wells, *Introducing Christian Ethics*, 181.

accessible to reason. While the various prescriptions might appear to be quite different on the surface, whether it is Kant's more legalistic categorical imperative or Joseph Fletcher's principle of *agapic* love, in both cases the starting point is the individual's freedom to act on the basis of rational principles.[9] When Christianity is accommodated to this approach, it is typically reduced to a series of fundamental principles or values that can serve as the basis for Christianizing wider society.

William Temple's bestseller, *Christianity and Social Order*, typifies this approach.[10] Temple viewed the church as the custodian of social and moral principles for the forming of individual conscience. Yet the church itself disappears into the background when it comes to putting these principles into effect, since this task falls to individual citizens and technical experts.[11] Christian theology more generally mirrors this approach when it proceeds from a separation between doctrine, as an exercise in systematic reason, and ethics, as concerned with right practice.

According to Wells and Quash, the modern account of ethics is characterized by its unacknowledged pretentiousness to speak in universal categories, which in turn serves to erode any sense of a Christian difference. It is universalistic because it is indiscriminate about its subject and therefore about the limits of its perspective.[12] It is an ethic for *anyone*, irrespective of race, history, culture, or personal development, because these situational factors are deemed superfluous to the more important principles that underlie judgments. It is also an ethic for *everyone*, in that it is considered mandatory – on account of its alleged universal foundations. Christian ethics is forced by these parameters to make ethical prescriptions that can reasonably be asked of anyone and everyone, irrespective of their knowledge of, or personal formation in, the Christian story. Christianity is treated like an outer dressing that must be cast aside in order to speak about matters of real substance.

9. Joseph F. Fletcher, *Situation Ethics: The New Morality* (Philadelphia: Westminster Press, 1966). I introduced Kant's approach to ethics in the first chapter.

10. William Temple, *Christianity and Social Order* (London: Penguin Special, 1942).

11. Temple writes, 'The Church must announce Christian principles and point out where the existing social order at any time is in conflict with them. It must then pass on to Christian citizens, acting in their civic capacity, the task of re-shaping the existing order in closer conformity to the principles. For at this point technical knowledge may be required and judgments of practical expediency are always required'; ibid., 58.

12. Wells, *Improvisation*, 28–29.

By suppressing our encumbered nature as socially contingent actors, this approach makes who we are to be of far less ethical significance than what we think. By elevating the role of individual choice, modern ethical theory and its postmodern offspring have deemed 'making the right choice' to be more important than 'making people right'. This represents perhaps the largest shift away from pre-modern (and a specifically Christian) ethics, which focused far more on the formation of moral agents.

The modern turn to the individual subject, in the opinion of ecclesial ethicists, has public implications. When ethical deliberation is centered on the will of the individual, the problem arises as to how to speak about social goods that transcend individual interests. There appears to be little basis for agreement on and working towards the once-traditional goal of a unified common good. Modern societies are no longer viewed as ordered towards some unitive good, since they are but a collection of individuals each seeking their own private good. This is true for the idea of justice, which used to be seen as a unitive force but has since given way to justice as a distributive force, one that, in the opinion of Wells and Quash, 'oversees and regulates the pursuit of private goods and rival interests'.[13] This reordering has also had a devastating impact on the relationship between individuals and the church. The church has increasingly been conformed to the role of catering to individual interests rather than individuals constituting an ecclesial society seeking the eternal good.

Wells describes how two main approaches have tended to dominate ethical discussion in modernity, both of which have their counterparts in Christian ethics. The first focuses on what is *reasonable*, with moral decisions being based on what is intrinsically right or wrong. This approach is *de*-ontological in the sense that judgments are not contingent on the nature of particular beings. It presumes, as Wells notes, that 'there *is* a proper state of things, which *has always been so*, and that departing from it will violate, infringe, or unbalance this proper state'.[14] The value of Christianity, according to this logic, lies in its provision of a strong conception of the moral order, based on the notion of natural law or the law of created order. This is also why the deontological approach has a strongly retrospective or conservative tendency. The second approach focuses more on what appears to be *useful*, with decisions being judged according to their outcomes. In contrast to the deontological emphasis on

13. Wells, *Introducing Christian Ethics*, 224.

14. Wells, *Improvisation*, 28.

the intrinsic value of right, this approach is consequentialist and looks to extrinsic values. Accordingly, Christianity is here judged on the basis of how well it enables individuals to maximize their personal good, even when these goods are external to the church.

Both of these approaches have significantly undermined the epistemological significance of the church by rendering it subservient either to some more basic moral order or to the pursuit of goods external to the church. Conceptions of justice have drifted in both of these directions. When presupposing a strong conception of the moral order, the understanding of justice tends to acquire a legalistic and retributive tone. When presupposing the equitable distribution of goods, in the absence of any unitive description of the common good, justice becomes about the maximization of individual rights.

One further characterization of this period can be observed. Given the concentration on moments of decision, modern ethical deliberation is more concerned with complex quandaries than it is with the ordinary, everyday concerns of citizens.[15] While ethical discussion has always been the domain of philosophers, in the modern period it occurs at an even greater remove from everyday life. For Christian communities, this renders their common concerns ethically uninteresting, especially in comparison to the sort of quandaries faced in bio-ethics, eugenics, population control, and so on.

While no one person is held responsible for all these influences coming to bear on the church, Friedrich Schleiermacher is frequently identified as the chief protagonist in the modern era who sought to marry Christian ethics with the post-Enlightenment intellectual ethos. In his magisterial work *The Christian Faith*, Schleiermacher argued that the essence of the 'Christian Idea' lay within the individual subject, what he described as 'God-consciousness'.[16] This consciousness was already latent in its lower forms within society at large as a 'feeling of absolute dependence', although the awakening of this consciousness depended to a degree on

15. For a description of decisionism as a form of 'Quandry Ethics', see Edmund Pincoffs, 'Quandry Ethics', *Mind* (1971): 552–71. Pincoffs later expanded on his earlier work in, *Quandaries and Virtues: Against Reductivism in Ethics* (Lawrence, KS: University of Kansas Press, 1986). Brock points out how decisionist ethics has gravitated towards complex choices, like those made at the beginning and end of life; Brian Brock, *Christian Ethics in a Technological Age* (Grand Rapids, MI: Eerdmans, 2010).

16. Friedrich Schleiermacher, *The Christian Faith* (Edinburgh: T. & T. Clark, 1976).

the nurturing of church leaders and teachers. For Schleiermacher, the theological task is oriented towards the maturing of humanity, and in particular to the cultivation of civilization and national identity.

Schleiermacher continued the Enlightenment tradition of making the human subject the datum of ethical reflection. He effectively turned Christianity into a principle or feeling that must then be appropriated by the individual subject. He also continued the separation of principle and practice by distinguishing some essence of Christianity that could be known apart from its peripheral characteristics. For ecclesial ethics, the real problem with Schleiermacher's work is how he construes the theological disciplines as in service to some more essential task – civilization, the university, the nation – rather than to their proper role in the church's proclamation of Jesus Christ.[17]

Ecclesial ethics has emerged, then, in response to the damage caused to the gospel by a sharp turn to the individual and the ensuing epistemological upheavals that followed. Yet, in the opinion of some ecclesial ethicists, the era of modern individualism is but the inevitable historical consequence of a more far-reaching error. The eclipse of the church as an alternative visible community with its own distinctive reasoning and social identity occurred, not in the seventeenth and eighteenth centuries, but was occasioned by what has been called the 'Constantinian Shift'.[18] While this assertion features in many of the accounts provided by ecclesial ethicists, it is by no means uncomplicated, either in terms of its historical detail or its theological implications.[19] Even though the shift is identified with the conversion of the Roman Emperor Constantine (312–337 CE), it might just as appropriately be called an ecclesiological shift, given how far the church itself was redefined during this period. John Yoder is typical of those who stress the far-reaching implications of this shift:

17. For an example of how Schleiermacher is regarded in ecclesial ethics, see Hauerwas, 'On Doctrine and Ethics', 30–34.

18. This term was popularized by John H. Yoder, specifically in his essays: 'The Meaning of the Constantinian Shift', in *Christian Attitudes to War, Peace, and Revolution*, ed. Theodore J. Koontz and Andy Alexis-Baker (Grand Rapids, MI: Brazos Press, 2009), 57–74, and 'The Constantinian Sources of Western Social Ethics', in *The Priestly Kingdom: Social Ethics as Gospel* (Notre Dame, IN: University of Notre Dame, 1984), 135–47.

19. One contribution that has intentionally set out to complicate the narrative told by ecclesial ethics in relation to Constantinianism is Peter J. Leithart's *Defending Constantine: The Twilight of an Empire and the Dawn of Christendom* (Downers Grove, IL: InterVarsity Press, 2012).

> [B]efore Constantine, Christians knew as a fact of experience that there was a church, and they had to take it on faith that God governs history. After Constantine, Christians knew for a fact that God governs history (Constantine was one of their number, after all), but they had to take it on faith that there is a church. That is the shift in the meaning of salvation history for which Constantine is the symbol…the eschatology of the New Testament has been turned upside down.[20]

For Yoder, prior to Constantine the church was viewed as the primary arena in which God's eschatological purposes were being fulfilled. The call on Israel long ago to be a 'called out' people that would be a 'light to the nations', was now coming to fulfilment in the church. Accordingly, the early church conceived of itself as an ἐκκλησία, an assembly of citizens called out from among the nations, a proleptic realization of God's 'New Jerusalem' (Rev. 21), a 'chosen race, a royal priesthood, a holy nation, God's own people' (1 Pet. 2.9). After the conversion of Constantine and the progressive Christianization of the Empire, it was the Empire that came to be seen as the primary venue for the realization of God's reign, and demanded the obedience of its Christian subjects. Baptism, which previously expressed loyalty to Christ and his rule, now applied to all citizens. The visible church became co-terminus with general society. As Wells puts it, 'the identity of the church was transformed. Far from being an often-persecuted minority, it became the government… The church became the arbiter of truth and justice for all people, not just those who by commitment and conviction shared its faith. *The [true] church became invisible*.'[21]

One response to this shift is illustrated by Augustine, as discussed in the previous chapter. Augustine did not believe that everyone in the empirical church belonged to God's elect. The church was divided between its visible and invisible aspects. What is most significant, however, is that Augustine equated the 'true Church' with its social invisibility, for only God sees those who are truly his own. Even those holding offices in the church – its priests and bishops – need not be part of the elect in order for their sacraments to be valid for the invisible elect.[22] While Augustine's response is obviously more complex than this, his diminution of the importance of the true church's social visibility had serious consequences.

20. Yoder, *War, Peace, and Revolution*, 63.
21. Wells, *Improvisation*, 25 (italics mine).
22. As Augustine argued forcefully in his response to the Donatist heresy.

Firstly, it accelerated the assimilation of the church to worldly practices, detracting from the first task of the church to be, as Hauerwas argues, a 'contrast model' by which the world may see that all in the world is not yet of God's kingdom and so repent of its destructive ways.[23] Secondly, the focus of God's redemptive work was increasingly turned inward, to become a matter between God and an individual's soul. This anticipates the individualization of ethics in the modern era. Thirdly, Christian ethics became predominantly concerned with what could reasonably be expected of all citizens, regardless of the level of personal piety. Ethics, in other words, became more about social conformity than describing the Christian difference in the world. This paved the way for the emergence of the tradition of universal ethics formulated in conscious detachment from the church's confession of Christ.

The Barthian Revolution

As already noted, ecclesial ethics claims not to be an innovation, but rather a *recovery* of the church as a confessional and ethically distinctive community. Wells and Quash trace the beginning of this recovery to the 'theological revolution' initiated by Karl Barth. Having witnessed the ethical failure of his liberal Protestant teachers in capitulating to the Kaiser's militant policies in Germany during the First World War, Barth came to regard this failure as the result of a 'theological wrong turn'.[24] This wrong turn was related to the tendency to regard some cultural arrangement or moral principle as having an independent and abiding validity, which then serves as the controlling principle for understanding history, identity, and even theology itself.

Barth was convinced that the introduction of such an 'alien element' into theology cannot but lead the entire church astray.[25] Schleiermacher exemplifies the problem by framing Christianity in the terms of his German culture. German liberal Protestantism thereby became synonymous with the fate of German culture, including its understanding of *Volk* and *Reich* that were later exploited by Hitler. We have noted the same problem with respect to justice. By interpreting the justice of God in categories foreign to the biblical testimony, the church promoted an understanding of justice that contradicted its own story, which led to its endorsement of a harsh and punitive justice in the earthly realm.

23. Stanley Hauerwas, *The Peaceable Kingdom: A Primer in Christian Ethics* (Notre Dame, IN: University of Notre Dame, 1983), 100.

24. Wells, *Introducing Christian Ethics*, 182.

25. Karl Barth, *Church Dogmatics*, vol. II, part 2, trans. G. W. Bromiley and T. F. Torrance (Edinburgh: T. & T. Clark, 1957), 523.

According to Barth, Christian theology, if it is to remain true to its subject, begins in the faith that God has decisively spoken in the person of Jesus Christ.[26] This event calls into question every cultural, religious, and epistemological foundation that claims any sense of constancy, including the human subject. By implication, the only constant that matters is God's decision never to be except to be for us in Jesus Christ, which means that Christ is the fundamental ground and norm for ethics. 'The doctrine of God', by which Barth means God's self-communication of his very nature to humanity in Jesus Christ, 'must be expressly defined and developed and interpreted as that which it also is at every point, that is to say, *ethics*'.[27] Ethics begins, in other words, as we are encountered and concretely claimed by the dynamic event of God's speaking, in much the same way as Paul was encountered by the risen Christ on the road to Damascus. This explains why Barth's ethics takes on a decidedly Trinitarian form, because God communicates his very self rather than some good or principle that can be known apart from who the Triune God is in himself.[28]

The distinct features of Barth's ethics are noticeable when he turns to the topic of justice. While we can detect some inherited features of justice early in his career that require closer scrutiny, as his christological approach to ethics matured we notice a gradual redirecting of the meaning of justice. Barth rejects those accounts of justice that are entirely drawn from the human situation, as if sinful humanity has the capacity to judge for itself what is just. Instead, he writes, 'The Judge, the judged, the judgment – the one Jesus Christ who is all these things and in and by Himself does all these things – is the justice or righteousness of God', and this redeems us into an order 'of a world reconciled with God in Him, this One'.[29]

For Barth, Jesus is the justice of God in at least two senses. Firstly, he takes on himself the judgment that is due humanity by placing himself at God's mercy. He became penitent in order to show that God in his justice

26. The formulation I am using here of 'God's speaking' comes from Brian Brock, who interprets *ereignis*, what is often translated in Barth's *Church Dogmatics* (*CD*), as 'moment' or 'concrete event', as a reference to Luther's language of God's speaking. The emphasis on God's speaking is often flatly called 'divine command theory', which in Brock's opinion fails to capture much of the dynamic quality intended; Brock, *Christian Ethics in a Technological Age*, 172.

27. *CD*, II/2, 513.

28. This is why Barth situates his discussion of theological ethics within his Doctrine of God.

29. *CD*, IV/1, 256.

stands in solidarity with sinners. It is not that Christ elects to passively undergo a punishment inflicted by God as satisfaction for his wrath, a theme that the later Barth considered to be very dubious.[30] Rather, Jesus Christ as very God elects to share in the human condition and so suffer the full consequences of our place, including death, all for the purpose of overcoming the chasm that separates us from the love of God, thus freeing us for loving service to God. This points, secondly, to Jesus as the fulfilment of God's justice by restoring a communion of righted relationships effective through grace. We are not saved from God's justice by the divine extension of mercy, rather, we are saved by God's justice active in mercy. Jesus Christ is the justice of God because it is in his person and work that relationships are righted, where the unjust are made just, where enemies are transformed into friends; in short, where God's peace reigns.

According to Wells and Quash, Barth's significance for ecclesial ethics lies primarily in his sweeping rejection of all forms of cultural necessity and moral principle outside the sphere of God's self-communication in Jesus Christ. Yet it is arguably Barth's more positive project that has led to a recovery of confidence in the church as the place where God's concrete claim is made visible. For Barth, the good of humanity is taken up and fulfilled in the life of Christ. This means that humanity's realization of its good must be formed in response to, and participation in, the way that God makes himself present in Jesus Christ.[31] Ethics is primarily concerned, therefore, with the goodness or rightness of certain ways of life as they are exposed to this confrontation by and fellowship with Jesus Christ. The church, as the body of Christ, is singled out as the proper context where this confrontation and fellowship take place, which led Barth to be necessarily concerned with how the church's life is actually lived.

Barth's theological project has numerous implications for ecclesial ethics. His understanding of theology as a practical discipline in service of the church's witness is of particular importance. The decision to name his life-long work *Church Dogmatics* is not incidental. As John Webster explains, theology for Barth is

30. Ibid., 254. A certain form of satisfaction theory is arguably present in Barth's earlier writing. For example, '[T]he righteousness of God which we have offended was really revealed and satisfied… [The wrath of God] was now in our place borne and suffered as though it had smitten us and yet in such a way that it did not smite us and can no more smite us'; *CD*, II/1, 396–97.

31. As Barth writes, '"to become obedient", "to act rightly", "to realise the good", never means anything other than to become obedient to the revelation of the grace of God; to live as a man to whom grace has come in Jesus Christ'; *CD*, II/2, 539.

> primarily devoted to the task of *describing the 'space' which agents occupy*, and gives only low priority to the description of their character and to the analysis of quandary situations in which they find themselves… A Christianly successful moral ontology must be a *depiction of the world of human action* as it is enclosed and governed by the creative, redemptive, and sanctifying work of God in Christ, present in the power of the Holy Spirit.[32]

As this quote suggests, what matters is how human action is described; the performance of a certain action has meaning only insofar as it is inscribed within a certain 'space'. For Schleiermacher that 'space' was the inner experience of the individual, whereas for Barth it is the dynamic event of God's speaking through his Son and Spirit to his church.

For Barth's interpreters this has occasioned an entirely different approach to the relationship between theology and ethics. In particular, it has led to the dissolution of the 'and' that held the two subjects apart throughout the modern era. The distinctions drawn in modernity between doctrine and ethics, belief and behavior, were part of an attempt to rescue Christianity from its antiquated metaphysical beliefs by giving it new relevance as ethical religion.[33] Under Barth's influence, theology is freed from such modern prejudices because, 'dogmatics itself must be ethics and that ethics can be only dogmatics'.[34] Theology describes the 'moral space' wherein human actions become meaningful. Ethics is therefore best understood in relation to the traditional language of the church, such as the doctrine of God, revelation, election, creation, and atonement or reconciliation.[35]

The emphasis on the descriptive task of theology relies, of course, on having a grammar appropriate to the subject under question. George Lindbeck ushered in a more self-conscious beginning to ecclesial ethics by developing Barth's insights with reference to the philosophy of Ludwig Wittgenstein, and in particular his claim that language takes form within

32. John Webster, *Barth's Ethics of Reconciliation* (Cambridge: Cambridge University Press, 1995), 1–2.

33. Hauerwas argues that this same project was continued in the Social Gospel movement, then through the Niebuhr brothers, before finally reaching its end in Paul Ramsey and James Gustafson. He writes, 'Theology, at least Protestant liberal theology, became ethics, but the ethics it became were distinctively Kant's ethics dressed in religious language'; Hauerwas, 'On Doctrine and Ethics', 30.

34. *CD*, I/2, 795.

35. It would be a mistake to isolate any one part of Barth's *Church Dogmatics* as singularly concerned with the ethical; rather, each volume in the *Dogmatics* is treated as another way of speaking about the 'space' in which Christians have their life.

the rules and manners of particular communities.[36] Lindbeck argued that doctrine, in the form Barth understood it, acted as 'communally authoritative rules of discourse, attitude and action'.[37] In other words, theological speech depends upon the practices and grammar of an actual lived community. The church is first of all a community of practice, not an abstract repository of principles or concepts. This means that theological statements always reflect a particular social and political space. Christian concepts of justice, accordingly, ought to be understood in light of the practices and language of the community of faith.

Recognition of the way in which theological language is embodied in communities of faith has given rise to another significant impetus for an ecclesial ethic. While Barth is best remembered as a dogmatician, he was also professor of New Testament exegesis. He thereby brought to the task of dogmatics a rich engagement with the biblical text that would leave a lasting influence on both disciplines.[38] Barth was convinced that the bible is the history of God's speaking to his people and thus provides the Christian community with a grammar and language to live faithfully before God. In that respect his work anticipated what has become known as the 'theological interpretation of Scripture', a development that we will explore more fully in Chapter 4.[39] Barth's distinctive recourse to Scripture was highlighted by Hans Frei in his *The Identity of Jesus Christ*, a work of particular significance for the early post-liberal direction of ecclesial ethics.[40]

The Character of the Christian Community

We have seen how ecclesial ethics has pushed back on the universalizing tendency of modern ethics by recovering the importance of character, tradition, and narrative as indispensable ethical categories.

36. See especially, George Lindbeck, *The Nature of Doctrine* (Philadelphia, PA: Westminster Press, 1984).

37. Cited in Wells, *Introducing Christian Ethics*, 183.

38. Barth's influence over the field of 'biblical theology' can be seen through the work of Gerhard von Rad and Brevard Childs. For a survey and assessment of this influence see the chapter titled 'Reading Doctrinally: The Biblical Theology Solution', in Brian Brock, *Singing the Ethos of God: On the Place of Christian Ethics in Scripture* (Grand Rapids, MI: Eerdmans, 2007), 52–70.

39. This approach to Scripture will be taken up in Chapter 4, for now, see particularly, Fowl, *Engaging Scripture*.

40. Hans Frei, *The Identity of Jesus Christ* (Philadelphia, PA: Fortress Press, 1975). For the influence of postliberal theology on ecclesial ethics, see Paul J. DeHart, *The Trial of the Witnesses: The Rise and Decline of Postliberal Theology* (West Sussex: Wiley-Blackwell, 2006).

More important than helping reasonable individuals make right *decisions* is the need to develop people of *character* who act instinctively rather than out of crisis. This is precisely what the church is called to do.

The main objection to 'decisionism', as McClendon puts it, 'is that it sets out to show *how* to make decisions, but never reckons with *who* it is who makes these decisions'. 'What decisionism lacks, and previous ethical systems so regularly display, is concern with the qualities of human character in the individual and the community.'[41] Even though the concentration on decisions is representative of a turn towards the subject, it turns out that this 'subject' is no one in particular. There is no essential connection made between personal agency and actions. And yet, most people most of the time live by habit rather than by conscious choice. Even when faced with a conscious decision, people tend to rely on their existing commitments or convictions, even to the point where some choices are not choices at all but simply habitual. As creatures of habit, it is our character rather than our choices that is most indicative of how we act. As Wells and Quash point out, 'Character is a kind of power that is developed and strengthened by certain kinds of activities and commitments, and leaves one far from impregnable but certainly not defenseless in the face of inevitable sin, abiding temptation, and agonizing decision'.[42]

This return to an emphasis on character and virtue highlights the impossibility of doing ethics for everyone in a comprehensive way. From the perspective of an ethics of character it becomes important to interpret actions in light of an agent's convictions, history, and hopes, as well as the rituals and practices that have formed him or her. All of these contribute to a much thicker, more complex description of moral agency.

Among ecclesial ethicists, Hauerwas has been at the forefront of using notions of character and virtue for developing a distinctively Christian ethic.[43] As he puts it, he has been particularly concerned to 'provide conceptual categories for understanding and articulating the kind of moral development appropriate' to Christian convictions.[44] Drawing on the notion of virtue developed by Aristotle and Aquinas, he teases out

41. James W. McClendon Jr., *Biography as Theology: How Life Stories Can Remake Today's Theology* (Nashville, TN: Abingdon Press, 1974), 19, previous quote at 21 (italics added).

42. Wells, *Introducing Christian Ethics*, 193.

43. Hauerwas's thesis later came to be published as Stanley Hauerwas, *Character and the Christian Life: A Study in Theological Ethics* (San Antonio, TX: Trinity University Press, 1975).

44. Hauerwas, *A Community of Character: Towards a Constructive Christian Social Ethic* (Notre Dame, IN: Notre Dame University Press, 1981), 131.

the connection between the 'form of an act' and the 'form of the agent'.[45] In the Aristotelian framework, an agent acquires a particular character through habituation to a set of virtues or vices, so that an agent's virtuous action is correlative to how well that virtue has become habit. Good action comes not just from having the right set of ideas, but from being schooled in the right set of virtues, and virtues by their nature require practice. From this perspective, Hauerwas proposes that the church is a 'school for virtue', forming Christians in the particular virtues of patience and hope. Aristotle also argued that it is by external actions that the interior state of a person becomes formed, and that at times an agent may be called upon to act in ways contrary to their interior disposition.[46] The external world where we act and are acted upon is therefore centrally important to the development of our character. This insight, which has no place in the Kantian moral universe, is essential for viewing the church as a site for character formation.

While character has become a central theme in Christian ethics more generally, the validity of virtue theory is more disputed, especially as it is mediated through Alasdair MacIntyre's social theory. MacIntyre's influence on ecclesial ethics is considerable and therefore needs to be considered here, although his polemical tone is perhaps the most sweeping of all. We have noted how virtues are meant to become habits of character through practice. MacIntyre observes how certain traditions elevate some practices while suppressing others. He defines a practice as

> any coherent and complex form of socially established cooperative human activity through which goods internal to that form of activity are realized in the course of trying to achieve those standards of excellence which are appropriate to, and partially definitive of, that form of activity, with the result that human powers to achieve excellence, and human conceptions of the ends and goods involved, are systematically extended.[47]

The practices that are encouraged by a given society, or more specifically, by a *tradition*, are intended to form a character that reflects the convictions of that tradition. Two crucial points are made here – traditions are sustained by their practices, and different traditions order practices differently. A living tradition is one where the practices are practiced and argued over in order that the true *telos* of that tradition may be realized.

45. So Aquinas's contribution, 'the form of an act always follows from a form of the agent', *Summa Theologica* II–II.24.2.

46. Aristotle, *The Nicomachean Ethics*.

47. MacIntyre, *After Virtue*, 187.

Yet it is by a tradition's *telos* that specific practices become ordered, such that some are encouraged while others are suppressed. MacIntyre also makes the point that the *telos* of a tradition has an irreducibly narrative dimension. Action itself has a basically historical character. 'It is because we all live out narratives in our lives and because we understand our own lives in terms of the narratives that we live out that the form of narrative is appropriate for understanding the actions of others'.[48] What all this means for ethics is that an agent's actions must be understood in light of their character, which has been formed in relation to the practices fostered by their community. This in turn is part of a wider tradition with a narrative that explains the purpose of the good life.

In light of this, MacIntyre insists, 'it is no longer possible to speak except out of one particular tradition in a way which will involve conflict with rival traditions'.[49] Since every form of rational inquiry is embodied in a particular tradition, a level of conflict becomes inevitable between members of different traditions. This was, of course, the problem that Kant sought to overcome by proposing a conception of rationality that was independent of all cultural and social traditions. According to MacIntyre, Kant relied on a conception of 'universality and impersonality' that was meant to deliver a 'neutral set of criteria by means of which the claims of rival and contending traditions could be adjudicated'.[50] The problem, however, is that no such criteria have achieved anything resembling a consensus. This has meant that Kant's liberal notion of 'tradition-free individuals' has in itself become a particular tradition, one that is concerned with being free from all external constraints. Liberalism is a tradition because the 'overriding good of liberalism is no more and no less than the continued sustenance of the liberal social and political order'.[51] Debates are not pursued in a neutral way, independent of tradition, but rather always assume a liberal starting point, its own tradition.

Instead of trying to overcome our situated-ness as a means of overcoming conflict, MacIntyre argues that intellectual enquiry between traditions should take place as 'acts of empathetic conceptual imagination'. This involves placing oneself imaginatively within the world as perceived by the alien culture, speaking in a 'secondary mode' from one's first order language.[52] This imaginative act, and the possibility of entering into dialogue with other rationalities, is only possible for the person who

48. Ibid., 197, cited in Hauerwas, *Peaceable Kingdom*, 61.
49. MacIntyre, *Whose Justice?*, 401.
50. Ibid., 334.
51. Ibid., 345.
52. Ibid., 395.

inhabits a 'particular tradition-informed community of discourse'. It is not possible for the person who, claiming to stand above all traditions, expects a standard of rationality that no tradition possesses. Needless to say, MacIntyre's sets the bar high for genuine dialogue between traditions to occur.

Ecclesial ethics is not tied to the kind of sweeping social theory of rival traditions put forward by MacIntyre, but it is sensitive to the difference that tradition, narrative, practice, and language make. Hauerwas in particular argues that the truthfulness of any story, including the Christian story, is dependent on how well it produces people of character. He suggests, 'the church is finally known by the character of the people who constitute it, and if we lack that character, the world rightly draws the conclusion that the God we worship is in fact a false God'.[53] Such claims have led Hauerwas to be accused of 'ecclesiocentrism', that is, of making the truth of the gospel solely dependent on the witness of the church.[54] It is more accurate to say that for ecclesial ethicists like Hauerwas the concrete life of the church is indispensable to its theological truth claims, that they cannot be separated out without significant distortion. For our present purposes, this means that the meaning of the justice of God cannot be abstracted from how it is expressed in the life of the church.

Hauerwas also considers it significant that the Christian claim to truth is not based on abstract principles or ideas, but comes in the form of a narrative. 'Jesus did not have a social ethic', Hauerwas maintains, in the sense of advocating some idea or system beyond himself; rather, 'his story *is* a social ethic'.[55] While MacIntyre pointed to the centrality of narratives more generally, Hauerwas concentrates on the specific story of Jesus as being most vital to the church. Hauerwas has often made the provocative claim that the church's primary task is to be the church. By this he does not mean it should live for its own sake, contra Healy.[56] Quite the opposite. The claim presupposes the idea that 'the church is the place

53. Hauerwas, *Peaceable Kingdom*, 109.

54. This criticism has most forcefully been put forward by Nicholas Healy. He writes, 'There is little sense in Hauerwas's work that thinking carefully through our beliefs or teachings about God has any benefit. It is a redundant exercise, he seems to say, because they are already worked out sufficiently and embodied in the church's practices', Healy, *Hauerwas: A (Very) Critical Introduction* (Grand Rapids, MI: Eerdmans, 2014), 103.

55. Hauerwas, *Community of Character*, 37 (italics mine).

56. According to Healy, Hauerwas's dominant focus is on 'living the Christian life well, and on the benefits of church life over all alternatives'. In Healy's opinion this 'deflects his attention from what we must say about the triune God who makes any of

where the story of God is enacted, told, and heard',[57] which means that the church's first task is to be 'a community capable of hearing the story of God we find in Scripture and living in a manner that is faithful to that story'.[58]

Since it is the story of Jesus that stands at the center of the church, the church ought to become the 'organized form of Jesus's story'.[59] By looking at Jesus's story we ought to discern the vocation of the church, which is to imitate through its practices 'the life of the man whom God made his representative'.[60] The theme of imitation, combined with a focus on narrative and practices, was especially prominent in Hauerwas's earlier work, which was driven by the desire to recover the visible difference the church ought to make to the ethical task.

Another prominent feature of Hauerwas's writing is his disavowal of the individualism that has pervaded modern ethics. This can be observed in the way he treats the subjects of discipleship, salvation, Scripture, and evangelism. The imitation of discipleship is not a matter of isolated individuals copying in an external manner the actions of Jesus. Rather, it involves becoming part of a discipleship community. '[T]o be like Jesus is to join him in the journey through which we are *trained to be a people* capable of claiming citizenship in God's kingdom'.[61] The task of this discipleship community is to initiate others into the story of Jesus, so that this story becomes their own. Salvation, on this account, is understood as individuals relinquishing their own story and moving towards the reinterpretation of who they are, in the light of Jesus's story being made known through the church.[62]

However, the task of being initiated into Jesus's story does not simply happen by retelling the gospel narratives, since this would continue to place the emphasis on individuals. In order to avoid individualistic readings of Scripture, Hauerwas argues that the bible must be reinstated

it possible… Hauerwas's ecclesiocentric thinking distorts to the extent that is fails to be sufficiently theocentric'; Healy, *Hauerwas*, 16.

57. Hauerwas, *Christian Existence Today: Essays on Church, World, and Living in Between* (Grand Rapids, MI: Brazos Press, 1988), 101.

58. Hauerwas, *Community of Character*, 1.

59. Ibid., 50. Hauerwas continues to attract criticism for collapsing Christology into ecclesiology; we will cover some of these criticisms at the end of the chapter.

60. Hauerwas, *Peaceable Kingdom*, 72–73.

61. Ibid., 76 (italics mine).

62. As Hauerwas writes, 'salvation comes only when we cease trying to interpret Jesus' story in light of our history, and instead we interpret ourselves in the light of his'; ibid., 90.

as the sacred text for instructing the gathered community of saints.[63] And when the church gathers, it does not come empty handed but as possessor of a long tradition of learning how to embody the story rightly. For Hauerwas, the practices of the church, baptism and Eucharist in particular, as well as the lives of the saints who inhabit these practices, are of greater significance than either Scripture or the creeds, for understanding the meaning of Jesus's story.[64] They are, in Hauerwas's opinion, 'our most important social witness… They set the standard, as we try to bring every aspect of our lives under their sway.'[65] When these particular practices are marginalized or their meaning is forgotten, the church effectively loses its evangelical identity. If evangelism is solely concerned with individual salvation, fostered by individual testimony, the church cannot but appear as of secondary importance.

Having begun his career with an emphasis on character formation and the role of socially established practices in the performance of a narrative, Hauerwas's more mature work has concentrated more and more on the significance of worship as the activity that combines all of these various threads. This interest in worship led Wells and Hauerwas to co-edit the *Blackwell Companion to Christian Ethics* by arranging each contribution according to its liturgical function.[66] The volume treats the Eucharist and the liturgy as 'an ordered series of specific practices'. By doing so, the editors claim, 'detailed attention may be given to these particular practices, and concentrated emphasis may rest on how the performance of these practices shapes the character of Christians and the mind of the Church as a whole'.[67]

This emphasis on the church's worship as the site for ethical reflection represents the final break from the tradition of modern ethics. The distinctions that prevail in modern ethics – between the immanent world of

63. Hauerwas, *Unleashing the Scripture*, 9.

64. As Richard Hays describes Hauerwas's position, the 'meaning of the text is knowable only for those who participate in a community whose identity is shaped by the story of Jesus and whose practices therefore already embody an ethic specifically determined by that story'; Richard B. Hays, *The Moral Vision of the New Testament: Community, Cross, New Creation: A Contemporary Introduction to New Testament Ethics* (New York: HarperCollins, 1996), 256. Hauerwas's way of stating this is, 'You do not have or need "a meaning" of the text when you understand that Church is more determinative than text'; Hauerwas, *Unleashing the Scripture*, 23.

65. Hauerwas, *Peaceable Kingdom*, 108.

66. Hauerwas had also started developing his course on Christian ethics at Duke University by following the pattern and progress of the liturgy.

67. Stanley Hauerwas and Samuel Wells, *The Blackwell Companion to Christian Ethics* (Chichester: Wiley-Blackwell, 2011), 9.

tangible human experience and the ideal and intangible world of divine aspiration, between a subjective perspective on worth and an objective stance on truth, between private internal activity and public political activity – all such distinctions disappear when worship is viewed as the arena of ethical formation. Worship can no longer be understood as a solitary activity where one leaves the cares of the world behind while being basked in ethereal splendour; it is where people ascribe *worth-ship* to what is true and good. And it is because the church ascribes its worth-ship in a very particular way that ethical deliberation can no longer be done for everybody. For the church, worship is the activity that connects its communal practices to the story of how God meets humanity in Jesus Christ. In doing so, the church forms its character so as to be responsive to how God continues to act in the world.

The Church as Polis

For ecclesial ethics, then, worship is moral formation. Greg Beale makes this point provocatively in the title of his book, *We Become What We Worship*.[68] Beale's thesis is that God has made humans to reflect him, but if they do not commit themselves to him, they will not reflect him but something else in creation. At the core of our beings we are imaging creatures. It is not possible to be neutral on this issue: we either reflect the Creator or something in creation. This has obvious implications for character formation. 'What people revere, they resemble, either for ruin or restoration.'[69] Accordingly, the secular age is not, as William Cavanaugh notes, 'a disenchanted world', a world cleared of God, but is rather 'a world full of idols'.[70] The category of worship is far from being a retreat to a pseudo-private experience, since it evokes a world where spiritual forces compete for human obedience.

Cavanaugh is helpful at this point. He argues that liturgy is a universal category for understanding human participation in political community. 'In a basic sense', Cavanaugh writes, 'liturgy enacts and maintains community by the ritual remembering or re-presentation of foundational narratives, thereby helping to construct the perceived reality in which each member of the community lives'.[71] Here again we see how communities are narrative-dependent, and this is reflected through the visible

68. Greg Beale, *We Become What We Worship: A Biblical Theology of Idolatry* (Downers Grove, IL: InterVarsity Press, 2008).

69. Ibid., 16 (original in italics).

70. William T. Cavanaugh, *Migrations of the Holy: God, State, and the Political Meaning of the Church* (Grand Rapids, MI: Eerdmans, 2011), 120.

71. Ibid., 116.

liturgical practices that sustain communities in their foundational narrative. Cavanaugh also points to how liturgical practices call forth an imagined community. By this he means a community that is no less real yet exists in the imagination of those who live liturgically, as a means of participating in something beyond themselves.[72] In other words, liturgy serves to capture our imagination by evoking a communal reality that gives meaning and order to our individual lives.

Cavanaugh notes how different liturgical forms of life compete for our imaginations, depending upon what political community we see ourselves belonging to. By implication, 'if the Christian liturgy is to reclaim its centrality to the imagination of a redeemed world, we must look with a critical eye on liturgies that compete for allegiance'.[73] Cavanaugh is aware that he is using the term 'liturgy' in a far broader sense than its usual designation as the public worship of the church. His argument might be better served by use of the generic term 'ritual', which is more identifiable with secular political gatherings. However, he is reluctant to limit liturgy to the 'sacred' as opposed to 'secular' spheres. Such an understanding would fail to reckon with the 'eschatological import of the Church's liturgy, because it reinforces the status quo of worldly order'.[74]

Rather than make such categorical distinctions, Cavanaugh thinks it is more helpful to understand the ritualism of politics and of the Eucharistic liturgy as ordered towards the same goal: the organizing of 'bodies in public space' so as to create a 'communal body'.[75] Politics is all about the formation and activity of collective bodies, hence the significance of 'public ritual actions through which the roles and boundaries and goals and allegiances of the body are enacted and reinforced'.[76] None of this

72. Cavanaugh cites in support of his argument the observation of Benedict Anderson that nations are 'imagined political communities', and who goes on to write, 'it is *imagined* because the members of even the smallest nation will never know most of their fellow-members, meet them, or even hear of them, yet in the minds of each lives the image of their communion'; ibid., 117, citing Benedict Anderson, *Imagined Communities: Reflections on the Origin and Spread of Nationalism* (London: Verso, 1991), 6.

73. Cavanaugh, *Migrations of the Holy*, 122.

74. Cavanaugh, 'The Church in the Streets: Eucharist and Politics', *Modern Theology* 30, no. 2 (2014): 388.

75. Cavanaugh uses this definition to refer both to the Eucharist – 'the Eucharist is fundamentally an action that arranges bodies in public space' (ibid., 392) – and to state politics – 'we can see the rituals of the authoritarian state as seeking to organize bodies in space and create a kind of communal body' (389).

76. Ibid., 386.

would happen, according to Cavanaugh, unless individuals subscribe to the given narrative that is told about the body/political community. This way of understanding politics requires moving beyond the usual state-centric models, to include the everyday bodies of civil society.

While Cavanaugh has not developed his argument in relation to the understanding and practice of justice, it is not difficult to see the connections. The context most often associated with the dispensing of justice is the courtroom, and the modern courtroom operates as a public theatre with its own liturgical process. There are carefully scripted roles (judges, lawyers, court staff), each of whom speaks a jurisprudential language that requires moral and technical training. This liturgical process is aimed at construing one body (the offender) in particular ways (as guilty or innocent), so that the norms of the political community might be reinforced. The question, then, is whether this liturgical performance is the best approximation of what Christians learn through the Eucharist, a question that we will take up in the final chapter.

It might be objected that while state politics does use rituals as a way of giving expression to its body, such rituals are merely symbolic and do not have sacral importance. It would be a category mistake to treat statecraft as a religious ritual that exercises liturgical formation over its citizens. Cavanaugh, however, warns against 'the notion that political rituals are made up of mere symbols, as if the symbols could be discarded but the reality would remain. The symbols in fact are part of a larger ritual action that scripts bodies into a performance'.[77] For example, in America,

> Soldiers march in the street while people applaud and wave flags. Elaborate rituals surround the flag as it is saluted and people pledge their allegiance to it. High national holidays (or 'holy days') are observed. Those fallen in battle on behalf of the body politic are commemorated in reverent tones and in monuments that dominate public spaces. Relics of the founding fathers are venerated in temples dedicated to the memory of the republic.[78]

Indeed, it is usually through these ritualistic practices that people become conscious of citizenship. This is exactly the purpose of rituals. According to Cavanaugh, patriotic liturgical practices were invented in the late nineteenth and early twentieth centuries as a means to 'stoke a nascent sense of exclusive national loyalty, supplanting previously diffuse loyalties owed to region, ethnic group, class and church'.[79] The

77. Ibid.
78. Ibid.
79. Cavanaugh, *Migrations of the Holy*, 116.

rise of the nation state should thus be seen not as the overcoming of religious authority in public life but rather as its displacement by a power that trades on all the sacral power of religion while disguising itself as something more than religion.

The Political in Salvation History

By now it should be clear that Cavanaugh's purpose in directing attention to the liturgy is to reinvigorate the sense of the church as a visible political community in its own right. Just as modern ethics suppressed the role of the Christian community in forming people of moral character, so the modern era has also displaced the church as a fully public body that claims our allegiance in matters political as well as personal. Cavanaugh locates the problem in the specifically modern bifurcation of reality into sacred and secular, private and public. Here the church and its liturgy are restricted to the former while politics and public reason are identified with the latter. Cavanaugh, and all those associated with the ecclesial turn, object to both of these claims. They argue that the political bodies usually regarded as secular are no less religious or dependent on the sacred than is the church. Nor are Christians any less concerned with everyday secular matters than are the most political of animals.

Politics does not occupy some autonomous sphere tightly cordoned off from the church, because there can be no sphere that lies outside of God's activity in the world. Ecclesial ethicists are adamant that salvation is not a flight from the world, because salvation in the biblical tradition is a fully public historical event that takes place in the context of kings and empires and before watching nations. It embraces all of creation. This requires that the 'political' be reimagined as a direct response to God's activity in the world. 'Central to this reimagining', Cavanaugh writes, 'is the conviction that the church is at the heart of God's plan of salvation'.[80] The church is directly political because of God's election of a particular people to bear witness to salvation in the world. 'God calls a community of people to be a foretaste of salvation, one concrete community called to live differently so that others may taste and see God's peaceful revolution and be blessed, too.'[81]

Moreover, social actions that take place beyond the altar represent a counter-politics to what is usually thought possible in the world. Such actions are Eucharistic in that those who perform them take 'the social action envisioned in the action of the altar out into the streets and invite

80. Ibid., 137.
81. Ibid., 124.

others to participate'.[82] To participate in the Eucharist is an 'invitation to participate in God's reconciliation of the world', which 'opens up new possibilities undreamed of in a merely worldly politics'.[83]

Such a framework presents a way of imaging the life of the church that involves a much thicker understanding of justice, in several ways. First, it underscores how the human operation of justice ought to be read as a response to how God and his justice are active in human history, as attested in the biblical narrative. The biblical notion of justice is more relational, merciful, and transformative than are more conventional concepts of justice. Second, it also draws attention to how the justice of God is active in the creation of a particular people who bear witness to a redemptive and restorative justice to the world. Third, it enables Christians to see their gatherings, where the peace is shared and reconciliation is practiced in table fellowship, as normative for what it means to extend God's justice in the world.

Cavanaugh points out that while this political understanding of the church may sound novel to modern ears, it was already a view expressed in the nascent church of the New Testament:

> In adopting the term *ekklesia*, the church was making a claim to being more than a mere *koinon*: it was not a mere part of a whole, but was itself a whole, its interests being not particular but catholic, embracing the fate of the entire world. The church saw itself as the eschatological fulfillment of Israel, and hence as the witness and embodiment of salvation to the world. The church was not *polis*, and yet it used the language of the kingdom of God to describe the very concrete and visible fulfillment of Israel that was 'at hand' in the event of Jesus Christ (Mark 1:15). The church was not *polis*, and yet it used the language of citizenship to describe membership in it (Eph 2:19; Phil 3:20). In the church, citizenship was available through baptism to those excluded from such status in the *polis*, namely, women, children, and slaves.[84]

The reason why the early church did not speak of itself as *polis* is because the Greek notion of *polis* involved boundaries that did not apply to the church. Much like the modern nation state, a Greek *polis* was more particularistic than the church, with a more limited vision of who should benefit from the goods inherent to its political community.

82. Cavanaugh, 'Church in the Streets', 391.

83. Ibid., 392. See also Cavanaugh, *Torture and Eucharist: Theology, Politics, and the Body of Christ* (Surrey: Blackwell, 1998).

84. Cavanaugh, *Migrations of the Holy*, 127.

Even so, the church had a political vocation, which incidentally helps to explain the rise of Christendom. As Cavanaugh points out, Christendom was not the

> unfortunate intermingling of two essentially distinct things – theology and politics, church and state – that we enlightened people of modernity have finally managed to sort out and separate. What is lumped together under the term "Christendom" is in fact a very complex series of attempts to take seriously the inherently political nature of the church and its instrumental role in the salvation of the world in Jesus Christ.[85]

While there are many troubling features with Christendom, it is not its political character that is the problem, for the kingdom established by Jesus is no less a political reality than Caesar's *Pax Romana*.

What is disputed, however, is the way in which Jesus's kingship is manifest between the now and the not yet of redemption. Scholars like Oliver O'Donovan place more of an emphasis on the 'already' of Christ's victory, which implies God has made the state subservient to the church.[86] 'If the mission of the church needs a certain social space, for men and women of every nation to be drawn into the governed community of God's Kingdom, then secular authority is authorized to provide and ensure that space'.[87] For O'Donovan, the high point of the church's political theology lies in the period from 1100 to 1650 CE, and is probably best seen through the work of Hugo Grotius. O'Donovan thus tends to privilege the language of rule, judgment, and order in speaking about the church's relationship to the world.

Hauerwas, on the other hand, while no less unequivocal that God's reign will triumph, is wary about equating Christ's lordship with the ways in which the state exercises its rule. According to Hauerwas, Christ's victory is made apparent in the way of the cross, the way of suffering faithfulness that refuses to transform the world through violence and falsehood. The church is the bearer of an alternative politics, a people who cultivate the virtues of patience and hope where injustice and threats of violence seem

85. Ibid., 129.

86. Oliver O'Donovan's major treatment of the church's role in salvation history can be found in his *The Desire of the Nations: Rediscovering the Roots of Political Theology* (Cambridge: Cambridge University Press, 1996). This was followed up by a treatment of political theology throughout church history, see O'Donovan, *The Ways of Judgment, Bampton Lectures 2003* (Grand Rapids, MI: Eerdmans, 2005).

87. O'Donovan, *Desire of the Nations*, 146. Cavanaugh sees this as requiring 'the state to be the police department of the church'; *Migrations of the Holy*, 138

to dominate.[88] The Christian community must not seek to control national or world history, particularly when violence is required to secure justice. It must remain faithful to Jesus's peaceable kingdom without acquiescing to injustice. In speaking of the church's role, Hauerwas prefers the more reticent language of wandering, pilgrimage, exile, and resident alien status, and tends to privilege those times when the church endured martyrdom.

A Community of Peacemakers

According to Wells and Quash, 'perhaps the most significant question posed by ecclesial ethics of other approaches (and of itself) is this. Is Jesus, in the example of his life and death, really the foundation of Christian ethics?'[89] Everything converges on this question. The unique events of Jesus's life, death, and resurrection constitute *the* foundational narrative forming the Christian imagination. This in turn has produced a tradition of communal practices that have been honed through the church's worship. Against the modern tendency in ethical thinking, for Christian ethics there is no getting away from the fact that God became human in Jesus Christ. There is no more basic truth than the one who *is* truth, no religious principle for making decisions other than being encountered by the one who decides to be *for us*. There is no norm or value or sphere of reality, secular or otherwise, that supersedes the church's obedience to the lordship of Jesus, and to the way of the cross in particular.

Expressed this way, ecclesial ethics represents the recovery of the church's distinctiveness as it witnesses to the way of life made possible by Jesus. One feature of this distinctiveness is singled out to be of primary importance. The test of the church's faithfulness to the way of Jesus, and the first casualty when the church's witness is rendered invisible, is its commitment to the nonviolent love of the enemy. For ecclesial ethics, what God has made possible through Jesus is a life of reconciliation, a peacemaking that heals the world of violence.

While there is good reason for ecclesial ethics to see peace as the primary witness of the church, a witness that has suffered as a result of the interiorization and spiritualization of the concept, curiously it has paid little attention to the place of justice in this vocation. Biblically there is a close relationship between the church as the embodiment of God's peace and the embodiment of God's justice. However, this insight has not been prominent in ecclesial ethics. Its treatment of the church's relationship

88. Hauerwas, *Peaceable Kingdom*, 103–104.
89. Wells, *Introducing Christian Ethics*, 204.

to justice has been slim at best, and often written for the purpose of combating problematic conceptions of justice rather than developing the church's own distinctive way of understanding and enacting justice. Our concern in what follows is to address this lacuna by extending the insights of ecclesial ethics into a more theologically rounded understanding of justice. Before this, however, we must consider the way in which peace-making has come to feature so prominently in ecclesial ethics.

It was John H. Yoder who most provocatively asserted the political character of Jesus's life and death as normative for the church's way of life. In his magisterial work, *The Politics of Jesus*, arguably *the* foundational text for ecclesial ethics, Yoder protested against the way Jesus's life and death had been marginalized in Christian social ethics.[90] There were several reasons for this marginalization. Some maintained that Jesus had proclaimed only an 'interim ethic' based on the mistaken belief that the social order would soon pass away. It therefore had little value for guiding society today. Others construed Jesus as a 'simple rural figure' who could not possibly have anything substantive to say to the complex problems of contemporary society. He and his followers did not have to exercise the kind of social responsibility that has since been expected of Christians. Moreover, his teaching dealt with spiritual and existential concerns and had no interest in political matters. As a 'radical monotheist' Jesus directed attention solely to the worship of the one sovereign God, in the light of which all ethical values were relativized. Ultimately he came to deal with the problem of sin and justification that transcends the parameters of ordinary ethics.

Once Jesus has been deemed irrelevant for Christian social ethics, ethical inquiry becomes measured according to what appears as 'realistic' or 'responsible'. This turn is based on an epistemology where the 'natural' – whether as law, as situation, or as nature itself – is directly perceived and understood. Such an epistemological move denies the normativity of Jesus as the basis for the church's ethics, and particularly for the church's witness to Jesus as God's peace. In the previous chapter, we saw this same tendency to focus on the 'realistic' and the 'responsible' as paving the way for the church's witness to God's justice to be controlled by concerns that were in contrast with Jesus's life and ministry.

According to Yoder, underlying the many ways in which Jesus is rendered irrelevant for social ethics is the refusal to take seriously the full implications of either Jesus's humanity or his divinity. Jesus is viewed

90. John H. Yoder, *The Politics of Jesus: Vicit Agnus Noster*, 2nd ed. (Grand Rapids, MI: Eerdmans, 1994), 5–8.

either through ebionitic eyes, as a radical rabbi whose relevance remains firmly fixed in his first-century Palestinian context, or through docetic eyes, as the eternal Word whose relevance is fixed to some truth that transcends his human life. Yoder seeks to avoid reductionist views of Jesus that do not take seriously his relevance to social problems, precisely as the 'Word of the Father, as true God and true Human'.[91]

Yoder singles out one aspect of Jesus's life that rises above all others as normative for discipleship. He writes,

> There is but one realm in which the concept of imitation holds – but there it holds in every strand of the New Testament literature and all the more strikingly by virtue of the absence of parallels in other realms. This is at the point of *the concrete social meaning of the cross in relation to enmity and power.* Servanthood replaces dominion, forgiveness absorbs hostility. Thus – and only thus – are we bound by New Testament thought to 'be like Jesus'.[92]

According to New Testament thought, it is on the cross that Jesus breaks the sovereignty of the 'principalities and powers' by making 'a public example of them', and having 'triumphed over them' he has decisively 'disarmed' them (Col. 2.13-15). The 'powers' here refer to all those features of creaturely existence we cannot live without – the state, family, economy, religion, morality – and yet it is these powers or structures that hold us captive to their totalizing pretentiousness. By living a genuinely human existence, Jesus submitted to the powers while living completely free of their totalizing claims. He was thus able to expose how they keep humanity in slavery. As Yoder puts it,

> his cross is a victory, the confirmation that he was free from the rebellious pretensions of the creaturely condition… His very obedience unto death is in itself not only the sign but also the first fruits of an authentic restored humanity. Here we have for the first time to do with someone who is not the slave of any power, of any law or custom, community or institution, value or theory.[93]

It is by imitating Jesus in the way of his cross that the community of believers lives out a crucified existence, in a freedom that is no longer ruled by the necessities of 'realism' or 'responsibility'. It no longer has to ensure its own survival or the survival of king or country; it is no longer enslaved to categorical imperatives or the imperilled decisions of crisis

91. Ibid., 102.
92. Ibid., 131 (italics mine).
93. Ibid., 145.

moments. This was ‘the original revolution’, as Yoder characterizes it. By living in obedience to the cross, the church is the new humanity set free from the powers and thus able to be ‘the most powerful tool of social change’.[94] It is by reference to this freedom that the Christian community is able to point to where structures in society no longer serve humanity or God, but operate in defiance of their proper created order. ‘The church’s calling is to be the conscience and the servant within society…we are called to contribute to the creation of structures more worthy of human society.’[95] The Christian community is called to exemplify forms of human relating ‘whose only goal is to be faithful to that love which puts one at the mercy of one’s neighbor, which abandons claims to justice for oneself and for one’s own in an overriding concern for the reconciling of the adversary and the estranged’.[96] In so doing, it lives in obedience not to an ideology or set of values but to Jesus as the human embodiment of God’s peace.[97]

Where Yoder becomes more contentious is in his rejection of all forms of strategic or efficacious thinking that would seek to move history and society towards any goal or meaning other than the cross. Yoder detects the desire to ensure that the world comes out right, as lurking behind every kind of reasoning which ends up justifying the use of force, or of sacrificing life to ensure the preservation of some higher good.[98] Against this tendency Yoder writes:

> ‘The lamb that was slain is worthy to receive power!’ John is here saying, not as an inscrutable paradox but as a meaningful affirmation, that the cross and not the sword, suffering and not brute power determines the meaning of history. The key to the obedience of God’s people is not their effectiveness but their patience (13:10). The triumph of the right is assured not by the might that comes to the aid of the right, which is of course the justification

94. John H. Yoder, *The Original Revolution: Essays on Christian Pacifism* (Scottdale, PA: Herald Press, 1971), 31 (italics mine).

95. Yoder, *Politics of Jesus*, 155.

96. Ibid., 236.

97. It is unavoidable given recent revelations to not mention Yoder’s injurious effect and unjust pursuit of relations with women that were characteristically unloving and represented an abuse of power. That Yoder himself did not satisfactorily adhere to his own statements about the character of reconciling relations does not refute what he wrote, but rather highlights the painful consequences of not living in the light of the cross. The concern of the present chapter is not to weigh-in on debates over Yoder’s ongoing relevance but rather to show his influence and theological articulation for an ecclesial ethic of peacemaking.

98. Ibid., 228–29.

> of the use of violence and other kinds of power in every human conflict. The triumph of the right, although it is assured, is sure because of the power of the resurrection and not because of any calculation of causes and effects, nor because of the inherently greater strength of the good guys. The relationship between the obedience of God's people and the triumph of God's cause is not a relationship of cause and effect but one of cross and resurrection.[99]

What Jesus renounced was not violence per se, but all those ways of being the sovereign lord of history that involve sacrificing human life, except his own. He redefined the role of king, judge, and messiah. This was in order that no one would be ruled except through his powerlessness, no one would be judged except through the judgment he took upon himself, and no one would be saved except through his love of the enemy. The implications of this for the Christian community are no less drastic.

Reassessments of Virtue

While Yoder rejects the focus on decisions in modern ethics and its underlying Enlightenment paradigm of the autonomous individual, he would question whether recovery of the virtue tradition can serve as an adequate basis of a Christian alternative. The problem is not just that virtue theory has its origins in the pagan Hellenistic rather than in the Judeo-Christian world. It is that for writers like Aristotle, the paradigm of virtue is the soldier, who is not only courageous in battle but also exercises an indifferent attitude towards those below him.[100] Such a viewpoint cannot comprehend the way of nonresistant love, meekness, humility, and preparedness to sacrifice one's own life rather than wielding the sword in defending a just cause. This begs the question whether the more generic usage of virtue theory, such as that found in MacIntyre's account, actually serves to mask the primacy of the politics of Jesus and his exemplary path of nonviolence.

This highlights the much-needed difference that narrative and community make to the kind of virtues that ought to be formed. In sparking a recovery of virtue ethics, Hauerwas is sometimes mistakenly associated with the republican tradition of civic virtue and of fuelling the hope that the church might acquire public prominence as an exemplary community of virtue.[101] This would be problematic for Hauerwas because civic virtue

99. Ibid., 232.

100. See especially, Aristotle, *Nicomachean Ethics*, 1115a28–5b5.

101. In the early 1990s Hauerwas wrote an article distancing himself from the broader civic virtue advocates such as William Bennett and theological virtue advocates such as Jean Porter and James Keenan; see Stanley Hauerwas, 'The

in the United States is premised on a citizenship that is ready for war and battle.[102] In such a social order, the church is construed as the institution that forms virtuous citizens who are ready to die for the American way of life. The American tradition of civic virtue, in other words, shares in common with Aristotle the presumption that violence is normative and unavoidable in order to maintain a political community.

In place of this presumption, Hauerwas follows Yoder in making non-violence the central presupposition of a specifically Christian ethic. As Wells and Quash explain, 'non-violence requires the kind of disciplined training and constant practice that only a committed community can foster. For Hauerwas and Yoder, pacifism creates politics, because it is constantly shaping and searching for practices that enable the resolution of conflicts that avoid the resort to violence'.[103]

According to Hauerwas, this transformation of violence within virtue theory was already underway when Aquinas made the martyr and not the soldier the paradigm of virtue. By so doing, the virtue of courage was no longer formed in the 'noble acts of war' but required the prior disposition of fortitude and patience to do what is just, even when faced with imminent death.[104] This disposition was believed to be exemplified most perfectly in the martyr. But Hauerwas seeks to go much further than Aquinas by selecting peacemaking rather than justice as the chief virtue of the Christian community.

For both Yoder and Hauerwas, the church is an exemplary community only insofar as it witnesses to Jesus's reign of peace. To render the church invisible, as modern ethics tends to do, or to diminish its exemplary quality, as some Christian ethicists are prone to do, would be to disavow the church's high calling to witness to the gospel of peace. Such a disavowal would be a problem not just for the church but also for wider society. This is because it is through the church that 'the world' can acknowledge itself

Difference of Virtue and the Difference It Makes: Courage Exemplified', *Modern Theology* 9, no. 3 (1993): 249–64. See also the brief introductory comments on the inclusion of this article in John Berkman and Michael Cartwright, ed., *The Hauerwas Reader* (Durham, NC: Duke University Press, 2001), 287.

102. Hauerwas draws this reading from Jean Bethke Elshtain, who writes, 'The problem with the tradition of civic virtue can be stated succinctly: that virtue is *armed*'; Jean Bethke Elshtain, 'Citizenship and Armed Civic Virtue: Some Questions on the Commitment to Public Life', in *Community in America: The Challenges of Habits of the Heart* (Berkeley, CA: University of California Press, 1988), 50.

103. Wells, *Introducing Christian Ethics*, 202.

104. Hauerwas, 'Difference of Virtue', 259.

as such, and so be transformed. This does not depend on the church's moral superiority or sinlessness, but quite the opposite. As a community of forgiven *sinners*, the church is the one place where violence, untruth, and distrust between its members can be openly acknowledged for what it really is: sin. Yet as a community of *forgiven* sinners, such sinfulness can be confronted without threatening to destroy the very fabric of the community, because this community has been formed by the virtue of peacemaking. The visibility of the church is therefore central to the witness of the church, which, as Yoder observes, 'always includes and may sometimes center upon the quality of personal relationships that even the outsider may observe'.[105] Where believers interact with each other in reconciling love, Yoder continues, 'the tool is at hand for changing both societies and personalities'.[106]

An Ecclesial Ethic of Justice-Making?

For ecclesial ethics, the church is called to embody through its teaching and practice the conviction that Jesus is the definitive disclosure of God's very nature. In discharging this call special emphasis falls on the task of peacemaking. This raises the issue of the role of justice and justice-making in the church's vocation. Ecclesial ethicists have given surprisingly little attention to this question, especially compared to the space devoted to the related concerns of peace, nonviolence, and war.

Take, for example, the frequently referenced essay by Daniel Bell Jr. on an ethics of justice. This appears in the edited book on Christian ethics by Hauerwas and Wells, as well as being featured as an example of an ecclesial approach to justice in Wells and Quash's introductory volume.[107] Hauerwas concedes that he himself 'should have written more about justice', but with the appearance of Bell's contribution he no longer needs to because Bell has said everything he would want to say on the subject.[108] What is interesting, however, is that Bell's writing on justice is largely restricted to one essay. Furthermore, this essay is more concerned with

105. John H. Yoder, 'Binding and Loosing', in *Royal Priesthood: Essays Ecclesiological and Ecumenical*, ed. Michael Cartwright (Scottdale, PA: Herald Press, 1998), 352.

106. Ibid., 351.

107. Daniel Bell Jr., 'Deliberating: Justice and Liberation', in Hauerwas and Wells, eds., *The Blackwell Companion to Christian Ethics*, 182–95; Wells, *Introducing Christian Ethics*, 228–30.

108. Hauerwas, 'Jesus, the Justice of God', 99.

how different contexts affect the church's reading of Scripture.[109] As Bell puts it,

> what follows in the broadest strokes is an effort to suggest that the task of reclaiming a properly ecclesial reading of Scripture entails recognizing the way the political context and ends of modernity distort the reading of Scripture. The theological interpretation of Scripture thereby necessitates a recovery of the political vocation of the church. *This broad argument is set within a narrower argument concerning the nature of justice in Scripture*.[110]

This is not to disparage Bell's insights. It is simply to point out that there remains no substantial treatment of justice from the perspective of ecclesial ethics.

It would be a mistake, however, to conclude that ecclesial ethics has no concern for justice-making. Rather, this concern is expressed without explicit use of the vocabulary of justice.[111] The reason for this evasive manoeuvre is the fear that prevailing notions of justice will lead to a distortion of the church's witness. For example, in a provocative essay subtitled, 'Why Justice Is a Bad Idea for Christians', Hauerwas begins by pointing out that the one thing Christians agree about today is that 'our faith is one that does justice'.[112] The extent to which this claim is universally shared is a sign of the extent to which Christians have adopted conceptions of justice that are equally as universal. Yet by adopting universalizing concepts like 'rights' and 'justice', Christians have colluded with an individualistic account of humanity, which has very little to do with the particular truth claims of the Christian faith.

109. I do not include here Bell's analysis of 'social justice' as it has appeared in Catholic social teaching, and in liberation theology in particular; see Bell Jr., *Liberation Theology*. Bell's contribution in this work focuses largely on economic and distributive justice, and while insightful it does not extend to a complete ecclesial perspective on justice as a whole. Bell's essay in the Blackwell Companion is largely reflective of the comments he made in 'Jesus, the Jews, and the Politics of God's Justice'.

110. Bell, 'Politics of God's Justice', 88.

111. Neville agrees with this assessment of Hauerwas, 'it is somewhat surprising that he has devoted *comparatively* little effort to articulating a distinctively Christian conception of justice and the practices that sustain such a conception… My own sense is that although justice per se has not been a major theme in Hauerwas's writings, it has nevertheless been a significant practical concern for him at an existential level'; David J. Neville, 'The Bible, Justice and Public Theology: An Introductory Essay', in *Bible, Justice, and Public Theology*, ed. David J. Neville (Sheffield: Sheffield Phoenix Press, 2014), 17.

112. Hauerwas, *After Christendom?*, 45.

Hauerwas, in particular, has been highly critical of the assumptions behind secular liberal notions of justice. His main concern is that such conceptions fail to have a *telos* beyond that of securing private goods for individuals. By advocating for justice, Christians have the 'ironic effect of reinforcing state power', since in the liberal social order it is the state that distributes society's limited goods amongst its citizens.[113] To the extent that the state's role as the provider of social goods is enlarged, the church's role diminishes. At the same time, it disavows its own particular language with which to challenge such arrangements. Bell's concern is very similar. He thinks Christians too easily adopt conceptions of justice that are extrinsic to the person of Jesus. This contributes to a view of the church that is 'consigned to the role of cultural custodian of values tightly cordoned off from political practice, which finds its highest expression and guarantor in the nation-state'.[114]

Bell is equally critical of more theologically sounding conceptions of justice; what he calls 'justice as justification'. What really matters in this conception is the 'individual entering into a saving relationship with Jesus Christ', which means that justice is ultimately concerned with how individuals are justified.[115] The problem with such an approach is fourfold. First, its focus is distinctly individualistic, which means the church continues to occupy a marginal, and often irrelevant, space. Second, Jesus is rendered instrumental in this account since he is 'cast as the *victim* of divine justice', which means that justice 'remains extrinsic to his being and person'.[116] Bell points out that this conception of justice borrows more from pagan notions of *suum cuique*, which tend to reinforce modern secular accounts that are particularly retributivist. Third, this account is thoroughly ahistorical, as shown by its lack of relation to God's election of Israel and the church. Fourth, it remains atemporal, by focusing on a spiritual victory while handing over temporal matters to the state and its exercise of justice.[117]

Bell's more positive appraisal of justice, and where his account lends itself to ecclesial ethics, follows the now familiar method of a christocentric ecclesiology. He writes,

113. Ibid., 58. Or, as Hauerwas later writes, 'In the interest of working for justice, Christians allow their imaginations to be captured by concepts of justice determined by the presuppositions of liberal societies, and as a result, contribute to the development of societies that make substantive accounts of justice less likely'; ibid., 68.

114. Bell, 'Politics of God's Justice', 90.

115. Ibid., 92.

116. Ibid., 93.

117. Ibid., 94.

> justice is not extrinsic to Christian confessions and practices; it is not extrinsic to Jesus. Justice is not something that happens to Jesus or to which he submits. Jesus does not point to justice nor motivates us to go out and do some version of secular justice. Rather, Jesus in his person *is* the justice of God.[118]

Justice, therefore, is about being incorporated into Christ's body, being made just in the sense of 'being immersed in the life of the ecclesial community; to do justice is to be part of the community whose life is centered in and ordered by Jesus, God's justice'.[119]

In developing the marks of this community in its doing of justice, Bell draws specifically on the church's traditional works of mercy (cf. Matt. 25.31-45). These practices, honed through the church's tradition, encapsulate the ways in which the 'church embodies Jesus as the justice of God':

> The corporal works include feeding the hungry, giving drink to the thirsty, clothing the naked, harboring the stranger, visiting the sick, ministering to prisoners, and burying the dead. The spiritual works include admonishing the sinner, instructing the ignorant, counseling the doubtful, comforting the afflicted, bearing wrongs patiently, forgiving injuries, and praying for the living and the dead.[120]

That these marks do not rest on any particular theory of justice is, for Bell, precisely what makes them conducive to the church's embodiment of God's justice. Or, as Hauerwas remarks, 'Rather than a theory, God has called into the world a people capable of transgressing the borders of the nation-state to seek the welfare of the downtrodden… What we have is a people learning again to live in diaspora…through which it becomes a blessing to all people.'[121]

The way in which Bell draws on ecclesial ethics to highlight the particularity of the church's witness to the justice of God confirms the value of locating our quest to understand the meaning and practice God's justice within this strand of theological discourse. Its emphasis on the visibility of the church as an alternative community of practice and peacemaking provides a natural home for explorations of the church's distinctive apprehension of the justice of God made present in Jesus Christ, as Bell's work

118. Ibid., 97.
119. Ibid.
120. Ibid., 106.
121. Hauerwas, 'Jesus, the Justice of God', 116.

shows. Yet Bell's contribution remains suggestive at best, and its brevity leaves many unanswered questions about how such a justice might be enacted. Much more needs to be said in order to recover the concrete difference that the church's witness to justice might make, especially in view of the wealth of justice-related material in its Scriptures.

In what follows, we will focus attention on one distinctive way in which justice could be developed in the life of the church, namely through the practices of restorative justice. We will consider how restorative justice may function as an ecclesial outworking of the justice of God, in a way that coheres with the church's calling to be a visible sign and instrument of God's redemptive or restorative work in the world.

Chapter 3

THE EMERGENCE OF RESTORATIVE JUSTICE IN ECCLESIAL PRACTICE

We observed in the previous chapter why it is so essential for Christian ethics to recover a vision of the church as an alternative community witnessing to the life made possible in Christ. By virtue of its participation in the story of how God has made known his kingdom of peace and justice through Jesus, the church has been given all that it needs to imagine an alternative to the practices of violence and retribution. However, while ecclesial ethics has had much to say on the subject of peacemaking, its contribution to explicating the church's witness to justice-making remains relatively modest. Our goal is to address this gap.

One ecclesial tradition that has reflected deeply on justice is the Mennonite-Anabaptist tradition, from which the contemporary expression of restorative justice first emerged in the early 1970s. There are a number of reasons why the advent of restorative justice in this tradition is worthy of theological reflection. First, it emerged largely in response to the growing punitiveness of North American penal policy and the damaging effects of its criminal justice system, with its early advocates sharing a similar reading of the problematic features of justice that were discussed in the first chapter. The fresh articulation of a restorative conception of justice was intended to challenge the dominance of competing conceptions of justice that were at play in wider American society.

Second, this response was informed by an ecclesial tradition renowned for its commitment to reconciliation and peacemaking, something ecclesial ethics has singled out as the primary witness of the church. Restorative justice arose out of the peacemaking convictions of the Mennonite tradition as an expression of what Cayley termed a 'peace-making justice'.[1] It is significant that in this articulation justice and reconciliation were both said to be oriented to the same purpose of restoring damaged relationships by incorporating such relationships into a more peaceful sociality.

1. Cayley, *Expanding Prison*, 11.

Third, in its early inception restorative justice was believed to offer a 'contrast model' to the mainstream justice system precisely by being grounded in the particular convictions of the church. Unlike the distinctly modern approach that begins with some universal theory of justice, restorative justice aspired to give expression to a distinctively Christian vision of reality, sustained by a community of discipleship.

Fourth, the way in which the restorative justice vision has been attractive to public justice systems around the world and has become a core element in many of them attests to the social and political relevance of attending to the church's creative witness. At the same time, as the practice of restorative justice has been mainstreamed and reformulated in secular categories, several changes – not all of them positive – have occurred to its ecclesial formation.

There is one further reason why theological attention should be given to restorative justice as an ecclesial expression of justice. Although it was initially advocated as central to the church's ministry of reconciliation, little has been done to extend this restorative vision through the life of the church. While a handful of theological contributions have explored restorative justice in light of the biblical story, none have treated restorative justice expressly from an ecclesiological perspective.[2] This is a serious omission, bearing in mind how important the early pioneers of restorative justice considered the church to be for the continued embodiment of the vision and, arguably, how important the church has been to fostering historical precedents to a more restorative society.[3] Our aim here is to seek to extend the application of restorative justice to the life of the church by drawing on the insights of ecclesial ethics, thereby offering a new perspective for ecclesial ethics itself and for the practice of restorative justice.

The contemporary field of restorative justice scholarship is incredibly diverse, and many of its leading theoreticians and practitioners do not share the theological convictions we will be exploring. As Johnstone and Van Ness observe, restorative justice has become a 'deeply contested concept', no longer sharing a common language or unifying vision.[4] Our

2. We will cover some of these biblical perspectives in the following chapter, and seek to draw out their ecclesiological implications.

3. As Zehr writes in the afterword of his seminal work, 'I continue to have faith the community of God's people can lead in this [restorative] direction. Certainly we will often fail, as those in the biblical record did. But just as certainly God will forgive and restore us'; Zehr, *Changing Lenses*, 228.

4. Gerry Johnstone and Daniel W. Van Ness, 'The Meaning of Restorative Justice', in *Handbook of Restorative Justice*, ed. Gerry Johnstone and Daniel W. Van Ness (Devon, UK: Willan, 2007), 9.

first task then is to give a coherent account of the emergence and early formulation of restorative justice in the Mennonite context. We will see that the practices of a living ecclesial tradition were far from incidental to its origins, even though most of the standard origin stories are much more reticent about probing into the theological and ecclesiological rationale that gave rise to this innovative practice.[5]

Our discussion will be ordered as follows. First, we will connect the emergence of restorative justice to some of the changes occurring in Mennonite theology and ecclesial witness at the time. Second, we will examine the underlying and largely implicit ecclesial identity informing the restorative justice vision. Third, we will track how, as restorative justice became more mainstream, it became progressively more distant from the grammar, practices, and convictions of the ecclesial community that gave it birth. Together, these observations will enable us later to explore how restorative justice might be pursued in ways that are clearly continuous with its early theological vision.

The Roots of Restorative Justice in Christian Praxis

The Kitchener Experiment

On 28 May 1974, two intoxicated teenagers went on a vandalism spree in the small town of Elmira, Ontario, and were charged with 22 counts of willful damage. The 'Elmira Case', as it came to be known, attracted significant attention due to its devastating impact on the close-knit community. Several days before the two young men were due to appear in court, a small group of Mennonite Christians held a meeting. Frustrated by the usual punishment paradigm, they were seeking to develop practices in the criminal justice system more in line with their Christian peace-making tradition. Among their number was Mark Yantzi, a probation officer working in partnership with Mennonite Central Committee (MCC) on exploring community-orientated alternatives. He asked, 'Wouldn't it be neat for these offenders to meet the victims?'[6] Knowing the idea was futile, Yantzi dropped the suggestion, only to be challenged by another person present, Dave Worth, who was the coordinator of Voluntary Service workers for MCC in Kitchener. Despite it having no legal precedent, Yantzi and Worth agreed to look into whether such an alternative might be possible.

5. Examples of the 'standard' account will appear later in the chapter.

6. John Bender, 'Part I: Reconciliation Begins in Canada', *Mennonite Central Committee Peace Section Newsletter* 16, no. 1 (1986): 1.

When Yantzi prepared his pre-sentence report for the presiding judge, Gordon McConnell, he enclosed a letter outlining a proposal for the young offenders to meet and offer reparation to their victims. Unsurprisingly, the judge dismissed their idea as impossible. However, when he came to sentence the young men some time later, with a smile on his face he ordered a one-month remand to allow time for them to meet with their victims and assess their losses, as long as it was done 'with the assistance of Dave Worth and Mark Yantzi'. Everyone in the courtroom was either astonished or confused and, in in the case of Worth and Yantzi, unprepared. With no idea of what they were doing, they accompanied the two young offenders to each of the victims' homes. Of the 22 victims, 20 could be contacted.

As the young men went house-to-house, Worth and Yantzi stood back with notepads in hand. After visiting two churches, a beer store and all the private homes they had vandalized, they tallied up the damage at $2189.04. Over the next three months the young men personally handed cheques to each of the victims for their losses, minus what had been covered by insurance.[7] The victims expressed a wide variety of responses, but in the minds of Worth and Yantzi the experiment had been a success. From this initiative sprung the beginnings of the Victim-Offender-Reconciliation-Project (VORP), which is widely heralded as the beginning of the modern restorative justice movement.

While the Elmira Case is frequently described as the 'origin story' of the modern movement, it contains three theological features that often go unnoticed. The first relates to why Yantzi and his fellow Mennonites were even located in their respective positions. In keeping with their Anabaptist two-kingdoms theology, Mennonites had traditionally maintained a principled separation from political affairs and legal systems.[8] The co-operative arrangement between MCC and the Probation Service in

7. The details of the Kitchener Experiment are recorded in Zehr, *Changing Lenses*, 158–63; Dean E. Peachey, 'The Kitchener Experiment', in *Mediation and Criminal Justice*, ed. Martin and Burt Galaway Wright (London: SAGE, 1989), 14–26.

8. Peachey, 'The Kitchener Experiment', 14. The 1963 Mennonite Confession of Faith stated, 'As nonresistant Christians we cannot serve in any office which employs the use of force', and in the case of working as part of the criminal justice system it was clear, 'In law enforcement the state does not and cannot operate on the nonresistant principles of Christ's kingdom. Therefore, nonresistant Christians cannot undertake any service in the state or in society which would violate the principles of love and holiness as taught by Christ and His inspired apostles'; 'Mennonite Confession of Faith', *Adopted by Mennonite General Conference* (Scottdale, PA: Herald Press, 1963), Article 18 and 19.

Kitchener marked a significant theological shift among Mennonites. This shift heralded a more expansive understanding of Christ's lordship, with the state as much as the church being under the reign of God's justice.[9] Mennonites influenced by this new theology developed a new attentiveness to issues of power and justice in society, and a different understanding of the relationship between the church and the world.

Yantzi's role in the Probation Service was the result of an MCC initiative in 1968 to pursue what it saw as a 'Christian witness to the State'. This involved creating 'listening posts' close to sites of governmental power, like the court services.[10] Yantzi was strategically placed to be a witness to the alternative 'politics of Jesus'. Early drafts of John H. Yoder's *The Politics of Jesus* were appearing as a resource for a generation of Mennonites seeking a biblically informed model of radical political action.[11]

The second feature relates to another theological shift among Mennonites. Not long after Yantzi joined Probation, the Mennonite Church adopted the statement *The Way of Peace*, which included a subsection declaring, 'The Way of Peace is the Way of Justice'.[12] Rather than defining peace as 'nonresistance', which was the conventional Mennonite interpretation, this statement combined what Mennonites had traditionally held apart – peace and justice. There was also a growing sensitivity to 'structural sins', with the statement calling on Christians to 'identify with the oppressed and participate in ministries of love and service in their behalf'.[13]

The Director for MCC Ontario, Ray Schlegel, argued that the calling of the church had to do with applying 'Christian principles to the areas that affect society's weak, broken and maladjusted. In North America, that brokenness shows up in courtrooms and prisons.'[14] Mennonites had a mandate, therefore, to bring the intellectual and practical resources of

9. Dreidger and Kraybill argue that as a consequence of this shift the agencies of the state came to be viewed in a more theological light as agents of the principalities and powers that, while arraigned in opposition to Christ's lordship, were potentially redeemable, Leo Dreidger and Donald B. Kraybill, *Mennonite Peacemaking: From Quietism to Activism* (Scottdale, PA: Herald Press, 1994), 120–24.

10. Ibid., 117–18.

11. The first edition of John H. Yoder's book was published in 1972: *The Politics of Jesus* (Grand Rapids, MI: Eerdmans, 1972), 12.

12. Dreidger, *Mennonite Peacemaking*, 150–51.

13. Ibid., 150.

14. Bender, 'Reconciliation Begins in Canada', 2.

their peace church tradition to bear on criminal justice practice.[15] For Yantzi, the idea of offenders meeting with their victims encapsulated the desire for a better justice to emerge, a justice pursued in the interests of peace. As Bender's record of this experiment explains, Yantzi thought such an idea would only work if it involved a hands-on approach from a church that held together the twin goals of peace and justice.[16]

The third little-acknowledged feature of the Elmira story relates to what in the previous chapter we called the *telos* of justice, which was here identified as *reconciliation*. Unlike similar alternatives being developed within critical criminology, the Kitchener experiment developed out of an intuitive belief in the power of reconciliation, rather than from a 'defined set of objectives'.[17] As Yantzi and Worth explained: 'We see ourselves as being continually involved in a process of refining our purpose and function. The project was not begun with a definitive plan… We are learning by our mistakes and successes…'[18] As a result, the VORP project came to view reconciliation between victims and offenders as the primary goal. Such a goal was not only unusual, it was also in conflict with the dominant retributive goals of the criminal justice system.[19]

By making reconciliation the primary purpose of VORP, its advocates were interpreting crime in light of a more *relational* and *unified* conception of justice. Justice, in other words, was understood in relation to its proper theological purpose as the righting of distorted relationships. McCold puts it succinctly: 'In VORP, reconciliation – the healing of injuries and restoring of right relationship – is the purpose. Direct mediation between victim and offender is the process wherever "relationships have been broken" by the criminal act.'[20]

15. The phrase 'restorative justice' was not widely used of processes like the Kitchener experiment until the 1980s. As McCold rightly points out that in 'the evolution of restorative justice, practice has preceded history'; Paul McCold, 'The Recent History of Restorative Justice: Mediation, Circles, and Conferencing', in Hoyle, ed., *Restorative Justice*, 1:137.

16. Bender, 'Reconciliation Begins in Canada', 1–2.

17. See Peachey, 'The Kitchener Experiment', 17. As we will see below, Scandinavian initiatives in mediation were being experimented following the influence of Nils Christie.

18. Mark Yantzi and Dave Worth, 'The Developmental Steps of the Victim/Offender Reconciliation Project' (unpublished, 1977).

19. Zehr, *Changing Lenses*, 170; Peachey, 'The Kitchener Experiment', 17.

20. McCold, 'Recent History of Restorative Justice', 141.

Such a goal was difficult for others to comprehend, and equally difficult to quantify. Peachey remarks on how, despite the emergence of nearly 20 VORP programmes by the early 1980s, there was still no formal evaluation of the programme because of the continual refrain, 'How do you measure reconciliation?'[21] This resistance to quantify the goal of reconciliation, together with its religious nature, meant the programme received a mixed reception from criminal justice professionals. However, by resisting pressures to secularize and institutionalize it, this experiment in reconciliation yielded many fruitful insights into the many relational dimensions of justice.[22]

As well as growing in conceptual depth, VORP also spawned several other initiatives supported by MCC. For example, Mennonite Conciliation Service was started in 1979 to deal with conflict resolution in the context of social disasters. In 1980, MCC established the Community Mediation Service to deal with neighborhood and interpersonal disputes that could effectively be dealt with outside of the usual legal process. This move to operating outside of the criminal justice system precipitated a number of changes to the early VORP model, particularly with the discontinuation of the co-operative arrangement between MCC and the probation department. When in 1982 Mark Yantzi went on to initiate a programme under MCC for victims of crime, specifically for cases involving sexual offenders, VORP Kitchener established its own operating structure independent of support from MCC.[23] The new organizational name – 'Community Justice Initiatives' – reflected a conscious separation from operating under the auspices of criminal justice services, placing more emphasis on community-led justice initiatives.

In his seminal work, *Changing Lenses*, Howard Zehr describes VORP Kitchener as a 'demonstration plot'. He borrowed this analogy from Clarence Jordan, who had called his racially mixed farm in 1940s' segregated South Georgia a 'demonstration plot for the kingdom of God'.[24] What eventually developed into the Victim-Offender-Reconciliation-Project was birthed as an experiment in enacting God's peaceable kingdom in the midst of the criminal justice system.

21. Peachey, 'The Kitchener Experiment', 20.

22. VORP meetings between offenders and victims focus on the facts that victims need to know, the expression of feelings and personal narratives, and any agreements that will help to restore the relationship to rightness; Zehr, *Changing Lenses*, 161–69. This relational focus also affords victims an insight into the person behind the usual offender stereotype.

23. Peachey, 'The Kitchener Experiment', 21.

24. Zehr, *Changing Lenses*, 173.

In 1976, Mark Yantzi went to the Associated Mennonite Biblical Seminary (AMBS) in Elkhart, Indiana to do further study. There he met Earl Sears, a Mennonite pastor who quickly connected Yantzi with other like-minded Mennonites, like Steve Miller and Edgar Epp. Through such collaborations, VORP Elkhart began in 1978, under the auspices of the Probation Department and staffed by many Mennonites. At the same time, Zehr began reading Yoder's *Original Revolution* while at Talladega College and felt called to move to Elkhart to be part of a more radical Anabaptist ecclesiology. Within a short space of time, Zehr found himself working at both a halfway house sponsored by the Indiana-Michigan Mennonite Conference and as the Director for Offender Ministries responsible for the newly established VORP project.[25]

The appointment of Zehr reflected wider shifts underway in the Mennonite Church. Zehr was specifically charged with engaging the criminal justice system in a more theologically informed way; the abolitionist position was no longer central.[26] Zehr began his involvement with VORP as a self-professed pessimist, believing that most systems-based alternatives to incarceration eventually get co-opted and end up as a new system of punishment.[27] However, once he saw the tangible transformation that could occur when victims and offenders met face-to-face, he was convinced that VORP not only stood for a radically new way of dealing with offenders, it also pointed to a fundamentally different understanding of justice itself.

The Elkhart Initiative

Zehr has earned the title of 'grandfather of restorative justice' due to his visionary leadership and innovative thinking. Soon after taking on the director's role, Zehr led the project through an extensive period of

25. I am indebted to Jackson Beck, a history graduate at Goshen College, for many of these historical details and recordings from personal interviews. This was written up in his senior's thesis project, Jackson Beck, 'The Elkhart County Victim Offender Reconciliation Program: A Story of Witness, 1978–1984' (Goshen College, Indiana, 2013). See also John Bender, 'Part II: Reconciliation Spreads to the U.S.', *Mennonite Central Committee Peace Section Newsletter* 16, no. 1 (1986): 3–5.

26. The position of the Mennonite Church had previously been under the guidance of Edgar Epp, a former prison warden turned abolitionist; see Edgar Epp, 'Why Prisons Fail', *Catalyst* (1982): 15.

27. Zehr had done his doctorate studies on the criminal justice system in France and Germany during the nineteenth century; see Howard Zehr, *Crime and the Development of Modern Society: Patterns of Criminality in Nineteenth Century Germany and France* (London: Croom Helm, 1976).

evaluation, helping to place the intuitive insights of practitioners within a clearer theoretical and theological framework. An internal evaluation highlighted two goals for VORP, both of which matched the three features discussed in relation to the Kitchener experiment, as well as the mission mandate of the Mennonite Church. The first goal was to pursue shalom (שלם) through the work of reconciliation. The second was to provide a prophetic witness to the injustices committed by the rulers and authorities.

In the first edition of *Mediating the Victim–Offender Conflict* (1980), Zehr argues that the rationale behind VORP arises out of the realization that the criminal justice process usually fails to address the real needs of victims, offenders, and the community. It also emerges from the belief that a biblical response to crime points away from retribution and punishment. The key to understanding this biblical response is the Old Testament concept of shalom, which Zehr defines as 'peace combined with justice, harmony, and right relationships'.[28] Hebrew justice had an 'emphasis on making things right, upon doing justice by preserving or restoring right relationships within the community'.[29] The essence of crime is that it upsets shalom; it is the wounding of right relationship. Moreover, the Hebrew word for restitution derives from the same root as shalom, indicating that restitution also has the concrete meaning of 'making peace, "giving back" in order to restore health to persons and relationships'.[30] Justice, in the context of crime, therefore means bringing victims and offenders together with the aim of reconciliation.

Zehr was heavily influenced by the theological ferment in the Mennonite world around the connection between peace, nonviolence, and justice. He drew directly on Perry Yoder's *Shalom: The Bible's Word for Salvation, Justice, and Peace*,[31] Ron Kraybill's *Repairing the Breach: Ministering in Community Conflict*,[32] Millard Lind's *Yahweh Is a Warrior: The Theology of Warfare in Ancient Israel*,[33] and the extensive work of his friend, John H. Yoder.[34] Perry Yoder argued that the English word 'peace' had become narrowly associated with personal opposition

28. Howard Zehr, *Mediating the Victim–Offender Conflict* (Elkhart, IN: Mennonite Central Committee, 1980), 18.

29. Ibid., 6.

30. Ibid., 5.

31. Yoder, *Shalom*.

32. Ronald S. Kraybill, *Repairing the Breach: Ministering in Community Conflict* (Scottdale, PA: Herald Press, 1980).

33. Lind, *Yahweh Is a Warrior*.

34. Further to what has already been mentioned, John H. Yoder, *Nevertheless: A Meditation on the Varieties and Shortcomings of Religious Pacifism* (Scottdale, PA:

to war, which for Mennonites had meant a withdrawal from social responsibility. This needed to be distinguished from the biblical concept of shalom, which possesses a far broader and more positive association with the existence of right relationships.[35] According to Yoder, the presence of shalom within the community is possible only if justice is properly upheld, both judicially and socially. In the bible, it is particularly the duty of kings to uphold this sense of justice. This led Yoder to reach the disturbing conclusion that in the Old Testament the 'state was seen as an instrument of shalom!'[36]

What emerged from this ferment was the development of a biblical theology of shalom, in which the pursuit of justice as shalom was integral to the church's peace witness. The joint statement agreed to by both major Mennonite denominations in 1983, 'Justice and the Christian Witness', called for an enlarged 'understanding of peace with the dimension of biblical justice'.[37] Dreiger and Kraybill sought to show how the shalom concept of peacemaking was not only a significant linguistic tool for uniting Mennonites, it also reflected a major paradigm shift in Mennonite consciousness, towards an activist nonviolent witness that took justice seriously.[38] Biblical peacemaking, therefore, required Mennonites to turn away from their sectarian tendency to withdrawal and begin working as 'shalom agents' by promoting a justice in the world focused on restoring relationships.

For many Mennonites, the relevance of VORP lay in its ability to provide an alternative to the 'tough-on-crime' policies that were producing an exponential rise in incarceration within the United States. In searching for viable alternatives, Zehr invited two figures to a 'palaver' that subsequently formed the original material for the Occasional Paper Series intended to extend the Mennonite Church's imagination in the sphere of criminal justice.[39]

Herald Press, 1971); idem, *Christian Witness to the State* (Newton, KS: Faith & Life Press, 1964).

35. Perry B. Yoder, 'Toward a Shalom Biblical Theology', *Conrad Grebel Review* 1, no. 3 (1983): 46–47.

36. Ibid., 49.

37. 'Justice and the Christian Witness: A Summary Statement', *Adopted by General Conference Mennonite Church and Mennonite Church General Assembly*, (Newtown, KS: Faith & Life Press, 1985).

38. Dreidger, *Mennonite Peacemaking*, 152.

39. 'Palaver' was the name given to the style of open discussions held in early restorative justice meetings.

The first was Herman Bianchi, a criminologist at the Free University of Amsterdam, who delivered a paper to Victim Offender Ministries in 1982 entitled, 'A Biblical Vision of Justice'.[40] Bianchi highlighted the many inadequacies of biblical translation when it came to words like 'peace', 'justice', 'law', and 'repentance'. In addition to a discussion of shalom, Bianchi argued that biblical law ought to be interpreted, not as a list of negative injunctions enforced by the threat of punishment, but rather as 'wise indications' for those who follow God. Drawing on Martin Buber's translation of Hebrew Scripture, Bianchi pointed out that biblical law served to describe how people ought to live in light of the God's promises. Justifying modern criminal law based on the concept of ירה ('*torah*') amounts to a historical and categorical fallacy, Bianchi argued. Criminal law was an invention of the fourteenth century, and should not be read back into the bible. Likewise, Bianchi observed that the concept of צדק, often rendered as righteousness or justice, is not something that is done by applying the rules of law, but is rather a lived commitment to the way of truth. Justice is measured primarily by the fruit it produces – truthfulness – rather than by the Roman measure of following due process.[41]

Zehr would later write that due to this emphasis on procedure over outcome, transfixed in the image of a blindfolded goddess balancing the scales of justice by applying the impartial rule of law, the criminal justice system actually perpetuates inequality and injustice by ignoring the important social and political outcomes of such a system.[42] An 'impartial' justice system aimed at preserving order ends up serving the current order of things, the status quo, however unjust it may be.[43] On the other hand, the justice of צדק looks to the future, and is not content until justice causes all those it affects to flourish. As an attribute of God, the justice of צדק is partial towards addressing those in need, as it seeks their shalom. Bianchi's recommendation to Mennonites was that they call the criminal justice system to נחם, to 'repent' – literally, to stop and turn from its destructive ways.[44]

The second figure Zehr sought out was the Norwegian academic, Nils Christie, who was invited to Conrad Grebel College in Canada the year after Bianchi's visit. Christie provided much needed scrutiny of the language used for describing what usually transpires in criminal justice.

40. Herman Bianchi, 'A Biblical Vision of Justice', *New Perspectives on Crime and Justice: Occasional Papers*, no. 2 (1984): 1–9.

41. Ibid., 7.

42. Zehr, *Changing Lenses*, 78–80.

43. Ibid., 140.

44. Bianchi, 'A Biblical Vision of Justice', 9.

Basic to Christie's argument is that the concept of crime is an abstraction, which oversimplifies complex situational realities, at the same time as creating the need for highly specialized experts to take care of localized conflicts. Christie rejects the basic neo-classicist premise of grading criminal acts according to the evil perpetrated in order that a like evil can be meted out to the criminal. Defining something as a crime so that it can be treated as a commodity, which is then regulated through the infliction of pain, amounts to a moral absurdity.[45]

The idea that punishment is essentially the infliction of intentional pain was particularly influential on Zehr's thinking. Penal law, writes Zehr, should thus be more accurately described as '"pain law"...an elaborate mechanism for administering "just" doses of pain'.[46] Zehr was pushing for society to question the assumption informing the criminal justice system that pain is the antidote to our human conflicts.

Christie proposed that instead of using the abstract category of crime, such events should be defined as *conflicts*. These conflicts, moreover, should be seen as the property of the parties between whom the conflict originated. Christie's aim in defining conflicts as property was to reinvigorate the participation of victims, neighborhoods, and offenders, as agents in their own right. When this happens, a multitude of benefits await: victims are empowered, offenders are given the opportunity to regain responsibility for their actions, neighborhoods once again become sites of political engagement, and society at large has the opportunity to clarify what it considers to be relevant and of value.[47] In addition, Christie postulates that the stereotypes necessary to sustain the abstract category of crime – i.e., a passive victim unable to represent himself or herself and a pitiless criminal resembling a non-human being – will begin to break down in the context of a personal encounter.[48]

While Zehr retained the category of crime, he construed crime as essentially a conflict between persons.[49] Zehr could see that Christian peacemakers offered a more grounded response than Christie's rather abstract and theoretical ideas. Indeed, Christie admitted that a major challenge to his idea of a neighborhood court was the lack of what he called 'healers' – restorative mediators – in society, as well as the dearth

45. Christie's views are expounded in Nils Christie, *Limits to Pain* (Oxford: Martin Robertson, 1982).

46. Zehr, *Changing Lenses*, 75.

47. Nils Christie, 'Conflicts as Property', *British Journal of Criminology* 17, no. 1 (1977): 1–15.

48. Ibid., 8.

49. Zehr, *Mediating the Victim–Offender Conflict*, 6.

of thick communities that could enact such repair.[50] Zehr, however, saw the church as capable of embodying this approach to resolving conflict.

Through the influence of criminologists like Bianchi and Christie, and drawing on his own doctoral work, Zehr began to trace the root problem of the punitive justice system to its underlying concepts of crime and justice. In 1985 he published the article, 'Retributive Justice, Restorative Justice', in which he advanced the thesis that the current retributive paradigm of justice ought to give way to a restorative paradigm.[51] He argued that when a conflict is defined as a crime, as opposed to a civil dispute, a different set of assumptions takes over that shapes our perception of what has transpired and what the appropriate response should be. Under the retributive paradigm, when something is criminalized, the action becomes defined as an offence against the state instead of the victim. It is resolved through punishment instead of restitution, responsibility for the crime is defined as guilt instead of as obligation, and the process for dealing with it is imposed rather than negotiated. In short, the 'retributive paradigm of justice is one particular way of organizing reality'.[52] But it is in perpetual need of reform due to its many inner dysfunctions, and as a way of organizing reality, it has ceased to be viable.[53]

Zehr claimed that prior to the retributive paradigm assuming dominance in the West, there existed a community-based system of justice centered on negotiation and reparation. This system gradually eroded due to the rise of centralized political authorities asserting their power by claiming a legal monopoly over local conflicts.[54] The sovereign supplanted the place of victims, with criminal penalties being prescribed by and owed to the

50. Christie, 'Conflicts as Property', 12. In contrast to lawyers, the 'basic model of healers is not one of opposing parties, but one where one party has to be helped in the direction of one generally accepted goal – the preservation or restoration of health', ibid., 4.

51. Howard Zehr, 'Retributive Justice, Restorative Justice', *New Perspectives on Crime and Justice: Occasional Papers*, no. 4 (1985): n.p.

52. Zehr, *Changing Lenses*, 87, cf. 89.

53. The Enlightenment project attempted to rationalize the retributive paradigm, thought to be scientifically justified by the idea of proportional punishment. The prison institution then became a way of applying proportionality to punishment, and finally the resurgence of just deserts philosophy organized legal structures to deliver retribution in a uniform manner.

54. Zehr, *Changing Lenses*, 97–125. Zehr admits that this era of community justice was not without the retributive or judicial option as means for resolving disputes, however these options were rarely used and often came at some cost to victims in particular. The shift to a retributive paradigm reached its climax at the end of the seventeenth century, yet even then the existence of civil courts still remained.

state. Interestingly, Zehr did not advance a modified form of community justice as an antidote to the contemporary problem. Instead, he advocated for an entirely new paradigm, informed explicitly by the biblical understanding of 'covenant justice'.[55] Zehr's interest was in formulating a way for the church to embody an alternative understanding of justice shaped by its own particular convictions, which he understood as restorative justice.

Focusing almost exclusively on the Old Testament, Zehr argued that the central theme in Scripture is a 'theology of restoration'. God's vision for humankind is encapsulated in the idea of shalom. Covenant justice is primarily about peace, 'making things right, finding a settlement... restoration to right relationships'.[56] While Israel drew on sources of law and justice from surrounding nations, such as the Hammurabi code, these came to be transformed under the covenantal concept.[57] God, not the king, was seen to be the source of all authority, including law and justice, which were focused on his relationship to Israel as the covenant partner. Covenant justice was concerned to preserve or restore relationships, and even punishment was oriented to this restorative goal.[58]

As an aside, the term 'restorative justice' first appeared in the context of criminal justice with Albert Eglash, an American psychologist who was also responsible for developing the notion of creative restitution during 1958 and 1959. Ann Skelton traces Eglash's use of the term to a 1955 English translation of a German book titled *The Biblical Doctrine of Justice and Law*, which describes this 'restorative dimension' as fully disclosed to the church of Jesus Christ:

> Restorative justice alone can do what law as such can never do: it can heal the fundamental wound from which all mankind suffers and which turns the best human justice constantly into injustice, the wound of sin... Restorative justice, as it is revealed in the Bible, alone has positive power for overcoming sin.[59]

55. Zehr, 'Retributive Justice, Restorative Justice'. In his more recent writings Zehr is more reticent about using theological language and thereby refers to his approach to restorative justice as a community-centered approach.

56. Ibid.

57. Zehr, *Changing Lenses*, 135–36.

58. Zehr argues that retributive punishment is present within Hebrew Scripture, although it has a limited and secondary function, which is appreciated when viewed through the covenantal context; ibid., 142, 46.

59. H. Schrey, H. Walz, and W. Whitehouse, *The Biblical Doctrine of Justice and Law* (London: SCM Press, 1955), 183, cited in Van Ness and Strong, *Restoring Justice*, 22. For an exploration of Eglash's significance to the restorative justice

As this quote suggests, the original German term might have been better translated as 'healing justice', but it was the 'restorative' designation that stuck and would later influence the young Zehr.[60] Upon Zehr's use of the term, Eglash once left him a message to say that he did not want to be credited with inventing restorative justice.[61]

Faith and VORP

Through Zehr's efforts, the emerging new paradigm of justice became consolidated around a theology of restoration. In the *VORP Organizers Handbook*, Zehr makes it clear that, 'our program arises directly from a Christian understanding of crime and the role of reconciliation; it draws directly on Biblical models and principles.'[62] For this reason, new VORP programmes predominantly emerged among church congregations, and, revealingly, when non-faith based community groups adopted VORP, they would often leave out words like 'reconciliation'. Yet according to Zehr, the concept of reconciliation 'has a number of important implications for program design and operation: the style of mediation, the way we follow up on cases, even how we define a case, are all shaped by that goal'.[63] At the time Zehr clearly felt that church-based reconciliation was somehow distinct from more secular community-based mediation models, although the difference was potentially difficult for everyone to grasp.

field, see Shadd Maruna, 'The Role of Wounded Healing in Restorative Justice: An Appreciation of Albert Eglash', *Restorative Justice: An International Journal* 2, no. 1 (2014): 9–23.

60. Weitekamp and Parmentier argue that it would be better to return to the concept of 'healing justice' first articulated in the German vernacular. This would avoid some of the potential confusions with the restorative designation, especially the mistaken assumption that restorative justice is about restoring a relationship to its previous state; Elmar G. M. Weitekamp and Stephan Parmetier, 'Restorative Justice as Healing Justice: Looking Back to the Future of the Concept', *Restorative Justice: An International Journal* 4, no. 2 (2016): 141–47. It is just as probable, however, that the designation 'healing justice' would attract a new set of criticisms and confusions. See, for example, Ian M. Borton and Gregory D. Paul, 'Problematizing the Healing Metaphor of Restorative Justice', *Contemporary Justice Review* 18, no. 3 (2015): 257–73.

61. Personal Correspondence with Zehr, October 2014.

62. Howard Zehr, *The VORP Book: An Organizational and Operations Manual* (Valparaiso, IN: Victim Offender Reconciliation Resource Center, 1984), 5.

63. Ibid., 6.

The growing popularity of victim–offender dialogues did, however, lead to the restorative concept being adopted in a more secularized form by other organizations. Paul McCold argues that the 'faith-based concepts underlying VORP were secularized by developing training techniques that encompassed both community mediation and VORP and in recognition of VORP's dependence on secular justice for cases'.[64] McCold is alluding here to the gradual demise of reconciliation as the core goal of restorative justice, which was largely a result of the victim movement having an increased role in the restorative justice movement. Multiple 'humanistic' goals, such as victim satisfaction, offender accountability, and reparation of losses, replaced the single goal of reconciliation.

By the mid-1980s the baton of restorative justice passed from VORP to a more humanistic model of mediation, housed under what was called Victim Offender Mediation (VOM). It was this VOM model that was endorsed by the American Bar Association in 1994, propelling restorative justice into the mainstream. According to Umbreit and Armour, 'VOM was similar to VORP but used language to describe the restorative justice process that was secular and closer to conflict resolution or civil dispute resolution rather than faith-based, for example, shalom, atonement, and forgiveness'.[65]

Another feature that distinguished VOM from the earlier VORP models was the greater emphasis it placed on the role of the neutral facilitator, as opposed to the faith communities. Coming from a 'humanistic social work' perspective, VOM, according to McCold, will 'expect the facilitator to provide active counseling and place great emphasis on the interpersonal skills and training of the facilitator...creating an "expert model" approach'.[66] By contrast, VORP actively promoted the role of church volunteers, because the 'volunteer role gives the community a renewed participation in the criminal justice system. VORP is intended as an attempt not only to empower the offender and the victim, but the entire community as well.'[67]

64. McCold, 'Recent History of Restorative Justice', 141.

65. Mark Umbreit and Marilyn P. Armour, *Restorative Justice Dialogue: An Essential Guide for Research and Practice* (New York: Springer, 2010), 10–11.

66. McCold, 'Recent History of Restorative Justice', 151.

67. Mark Chupp, 'Reconciliation Procedures and Rationale', in Wright and Wright, eds., *Mediation and Criminal Justice*, 58.

While these developments were to some extent welcomed by Mennonites, because they represented a mainstreaming of Christian peacemaking values within the criminal justice system, they also came with the new challenge of relating the church to the VORP initiative. Ron Classen, who started the VORP programme in Fresno, California, wrote to Zehr to ask: 'Is the faith element and church involvement essential to the integrity of VORP?'[68] This issue was at the forefront of many minds during the first annual VORP gathering in 1984. Due to Zehr's busy schedule, the organizing of the conference fell to the Prisoners and Communities Together Institute of Justice, a key partner with VORP since the early eighties. Despite 11 of the 17 VORP programmes being Mennonite sponsored, the formal organizers of the conference failed to provide any space for reflection on church-related or faith-related concerns.

These matters were raised instead at a pre-conference gathering where Zehr articulated his distinction between the retributive and restorative paradigms and led a conversation on viewing VORP from an Anabaptist perspective. Also included was a meditation by Perry Yoder.[69] It is significant to note that Zehr's widely referenced distinction between retributive and restorative justice was first delivered to a small gathering of those who were exploring VORP from an Anabaptist position.[70] Disillusionment was nevertheless beginning to grow among some members of the Mennonite constituency, as they were forced to rethink their relationship to the VORP model, which by this time had begun to spread around the world.[71]

Mark Chupp, who had taken over Zehr's role as Director for Elkhart VORP, acknowledged the growing difficulty facing Christian involvement in VORP. He argued the tension was more a result of resisting the pressure of co-option by the criminal justice system. Mennonites who wanted VORP to retain a strong Christian identity did so because they

68. Cited in Beck, 'Victim Offender Reconciliation Program', 35.

69. Cited in ibid., 37.

70. In the Occasional Papers Series no. 4, it is recorded that Zehr delivered his paper on the day before the 1985 conference, not the previous year's conference. However, it is clear that this paper was presented at the one-day meeting prior to the conference proper, organized to explore issues confronting VORP from a faith-perspective.

71. The VORP model had been exported to the United Kingdom by the early 1980s; cf. McCold, 'Recent History of Restorative Justice'; Marian Liebmann, *Restorative Justice: How It Works* (London: Jessica Kingsley Publishers, 2007), 38–42.

thought this was the only way to protect one of the primary goals of VORP, which was to model a prophetic and humane alternative to the adversarial system.[72] This concern about co-option, notes Chupp, is not unique to the Christian community; it is faced by any initiative seeking a more community-based alternative to state centered models of justice. Chupp issued a challenge to Mennonites to cease characterizing the tension as a Christian/non-Christian tension, and 'affirm that which is of God regardless of its origin and focus less attention on ownership and control of VORP'.[73]

While Chupp was right to suggest that Christians ought not to focus on ownership and control, he minimizes the distinctiveness of the faith dimension. Perhaps for pragmatic and conciliatory reasons, his position risks reducing the church to a mere community organization that, for pragmatic reasons, is opposed to state intervention. Such a perspective, however, fails to account for the recognizably Christian narrative informing the work of VORP. For example, the interest in VORP from non-Christian groups was due in no small part to the growing influence of the victims' rights movement. Yet when Zehr asserted that VORP was a victim-driven process, he did so not for ideological or political reasons, but because he believed God stands in solidarity with victims, by virtue of the Incarnation. Zehr's reasoning is not informed by any community in general but rather by a very particular community constituted by the claim that God has disclosed himself in Jesus.

In 1984 Zehr wrote a brief pamphlet titled *Who Is My Neighbor?*, a resource for churches to support those who have been victims of crime. He points out that Scripture is no less emphatic about the responsibility of 'God's people to care for and identify with the oppressed, the powerless, the wounded – those without support and without a voice' than it is in directing us to minister to those who have wronged us.[74] The church of the New Testament has a special duty not only to support victims in their struggle, but also to understand the very nature of victimization. Central to the New Testament proclamation is that 'God became a victim with us through Christ'.[75] Christians must continually hold out the truth that

72. Mark Chupp, 'Faith and VORP', *Mennonite Central Committee Peace Section Newsletter* 16, no. 1 (1986): 5–6 (6).

73. Ibid.

74. Howard Zehr, *Who Is My Neighbor? Learning to Care for Victims of Crime* (Elkhart, IN: Mennonite Central Committee, 1984), 3.

75. Ibid., 4.

God not only became victorious over all evil, but that God did this by suffering as a victim, and will thereby never abandon victims in their time of greatest need.[76]

In a tone distinctly different from the usual victims' rights message, Zehr speaks openly about the need for victims to experience forgiveness, both of themselves and of their offenders. On the one hand, victims need to be absolved of feelings of blame, whether self-inflicted or based in the belief that God caused their ordeal for some unknown reason.[77] On the other hand, while victims have a need to express strong emotions, including anger, fear, and even revenge, this should not lead them to pursue a course of suffering for their offenders, as this is not 'consistent with God's love'.[78] Forgiveness will likely be difficult and it may take some time for it to be fully expressed, which is why 'real forgiveness is possible only through the work of the Spirit'.[79]

This example makes it clear that while Zehr is not at all opposed to groups practicing community mediation for reasons other than the Christian faith, VORP had been clearly established on the Christian narrative. In 1989 Zehr and Classen published *VORP Organizing: A Foundation in the Church*, partly as a means of addressing the faith-and-VORP question. This publication reiterates that while VORP can be appropriately transplanted across a variety of organizations, the church has a special responsibility to implement VORP as an expression of its 'mission of reconciliation and its mandate to seek justice'.[80] For Zehr, 'VORP not only provides an opportunity for the church to be involved in justice-making outside itself, but also offers a concrete model for addressing conflict within'.[81] Just as the restorative vision of justice is essential to the church's witness, so is the church essential to the integrity of programmes like VORP, which express an alternative to the world's violence.

Given that the central concepts of reconciliation and restoration are not generally valued by the legal system, Zehr argues that the restorative

76. This is made even clearer when Zehr speaks about what victims need to hear from others, especially his section on the 'understanding of God' that Christians need to communicate; ibid., 8.

77. Ibid., 11.

78. Ibid., 9.

79. Ibid.

80. Ron Classen, Howard Zehr and Duane Ruth-Heffelbower, *VORP Organizing: A Foundation in the Church* (Elkhart, IN: MCC U.S., 1989), 3, 6.

81. Ibid., 5–6.

vision is especially prone to the pressures of 'diversion and subversion'.[82] If it is to survive within the precarious environment of the criminal justice system, it will require 'an independent value base and an independent institutional base' from that system, and such a base will need to be genuinely 'committed to the values and vision underlying VORP'.[83] For Zehr and Classen, 'VORP's best hope is a base in the church'.[84] The church is not just any community organization; it is the only community that can lay claim to being the bearer of God's reconciliation in Jesus Christ, which means it is obligated to a mission higher than its own financial or operational survival.[85] Restoration is part of this community's *raison d'être*.[86]

Uncovering the Ecclesial Footprint

So far we have charted the developing rationale and practice of the restorative justice movement as it emerged in the Mennonite peace church tradition. As Tom Yoder Neufeld puts it,

> The paradigm of Restorative Justice took shape within a womb of biblically informed piety and ethics. It emerged in the attempt to answer a biblically informed and urged set of questions: how can persons committed to peace, reconciliation, and restoration, inject that set of convictions and reflexes into the public arena of responses to crime?[87]

More specifically, restorative justice emerged as a vision for how the church could respond to the present criminal justice system, in light of the witness of Scripture and its own peacemaking practices.

It would be easy to overlook the importance of the church for what transpired in the VORP initiative, focusing instead on the individual actors involved and treating their ideas and practices as disembodied

82. Ibid., 6.
83. Ibid., 8.
84. Ibid. Zehr, *Changing Lenses*, 174.
85. Duane Ruth-Heffelbower details the aspects of programme structure, funding sources, and operational delivery that differentiate church-based VORPs from systems-based VORPs; Classen, *VORP Organizing*, 13.
86. Cf. Duane Ruth-Heffelbower, 'Toward a Christian Theology of Church and Society as It Relates to Restorative Justice', paper presented at the *4th Annual Restorative Justice Conference*, Fresno, CA, 25 October, 1996, n.p.
87. Tom Yoder Neufeld, '"In the Middle": Biblical Reflections on Restorative Justice' (Winnipeg, MB: MCC Restorative Justice Network, 2003), 2.

from ecclesial and ethical traditions. Such a reading, however, would be unfaithful to the history of restorative justice as it originated in Christian praxis. The two central goals that animated the work of VORP – the pursuit of shalom through the work of reconciliation and the providing of an alternative prophetic witness to the punitive criminal justice system – were in large part the result of changes in ecclesial practice and identity among North American Mennonites. In this sense, restorative justice depended on the existence of a concrete ecclesial witness seeking to practice an understanding of justice in continuity with its own tradition and convictions.

In the afterword of *Changing Lenses*, Zehr admits his proposal of a restorative vision of justice might well be considered utopian by wider society. Writing in 1990, he did not expect restorative justice to amount to anything other than a modest alternative operating at the margins of the criminal justice system. North American penal policy was fast approaching the nadir of an era of 'populist punitiveness'.[88] Zehr thought it more likely that change would occur through the development of interim strategies and approaches that would seek to embed the 'key elements' of the restorative vision in the hope of sensitizing the criminal justice system of its more punitive tendencies.[89] For this to happen,

> the Church is essential to restorative justice. This is very much the Church's business. Christians are called to be ministers of reconciliation, to help create *shalom*. Victim-offender reconciliation is one of the best opportunities available for the Church to carry out this essential mission in our world today.[90]

In the last few pages of *Changing Lenses* Zehr makes a brief reference to the work of John H. Yoder, who proposed that Jesus's social strategy had been 'to create a new society (the church) with new operating principles and assumptions which would operate in the midst of – and

88. An early termed coined by Sir Antony Bottoms intended to convey the notion of politicians tapping into and using for their own purposes, what Bottoms believed to be the public's generally punitive stance; Antony Bottoms, 'The Philosophy and Politics of Punishment and Sentencing', in *The Politics of Sentencing Reform*, ed. C. Clarkson and R. Morgan (Oxford: Clarendon Press, 1995), 17–50.

89. Zehr, *Changing Lenses*, 226.

90. Howard Zehr, 'Restoring Justice', in *God and the Victim: Theological Reflections on Evil, Victimization, Justice, and Forgiveness*, ed. Lisa Barnes Lampman and Michelle D. Shattuck (Grand Rapids, MI: Eerdmans, 1999), 147.

serve as an example and challenge to – the old'.[91] This new society would exemplify, in its life together and in the giving of its life to the world, a way of dealing with harm and conflict that transcends retributive logic by enacting the healing and restorative justice made possible by Christ. Due to the pervasiveness of the old aeon of retribution, Zehr says this alternative society needs to develop an entirely new 'grammar' and a new 'physics', reflecting the creation of a new politics of peace. These comments are full of promise, but constitute only two brief paragraphs at the very end of the book. However, the importance of Yoder's work on Zehr's thinking should not be underestimated. When it comes to Zehr's vision of the organic connection between church and restorative justice, Yoder looms large.

The Original Revolution

Yoder's influence on Zehr was extensive. Yoder was instrumental in Zehr's move back to Elkhart in the hope of reconnecting with his radical Anabaptist roots and living in a community formed by the vision articulated in Yoder's work.[92] Especially formative on Zehr was one of Yoder's earlier books, *The Original Revolution*, which seeks to connect the shifting social landscape of Mennonites after the Second World War with Jesus's vision of social revolution in the Gospels. The major need of our day to which the gospel must speak, Yoder argues, is the condition of 'unrighteousness, injustice'.[93] The heart of Jesus's message was '*the judgment of God upon the present order and the imminent promise of another one*'.[94] However, Jesus's strategy for social change differed radically from conventional approaches.

On the one hand, Jesus rejected the way of the Herodians, who thought that change could only come through collaboration and compromise with the Establishment. This was hardly an option for Jesus, since it was the Establishment that sought to kill him, first as a baby and then as a messianic pretender. At the other extreme, Jesus also rejected the option of the Zealots, who demanded an 'immediate social remodeling' through violent revolution, but offered little in the way of concrete alternatives to the prevailing system.[95] Infused with the belief in its own righteous cause, this strategy impatiently attempts to achieve a social outcome without the

91. Zehr, *Changing Lenses*, 225.
92. Personal Correspondence with Zehr, October 2014.
93. Yoder, *Original Revolution*, 18.
94. Ibid. (italics original).
95. Ibid., 22.

remaking of a different kind of people. This was the option most readily available to Jesus, but he decisively rejected it because it did not offer enough of an alternative, a social order that is not reliant on violence to achieve its aims.

Tellingly, the VORP model Zehr promoted avoided both of these options. In an article about the 'values and visions in the reform process', Zehr warned against the temptations of 'co-option and diversion' as alternative visions become accommodated to the rationality of the hierarchal and punitive paradigm.[96] If that happened to restorative justice it would then serve to maintain rather than change that which is known to be broken. He cites as an example the Quaker innovation of the penitentiary in which, through reflection and solitude, offenders could become penitent. Despite its good intentions, the penitentiary soon became a tool for institutional and psychological oppression that attempted to make inmates more docile than contemplative.[97]

According to Yoder, two other options were available to Jesus, which more closely resemble approaches taken by the contemporary church in relation to social issues. One was the 'outward emigration' of the Essenes, who withdrew from urban life in order to preserve the purity or faithfulness of a select few. The other option was the 'inward emigration' of the Pharisees, who stressed the rigid observance of ritual law over socio-political involvement. Jesus rejected both these options, seriously challenging the common 'position of noninvolvement'.[98]

The Mennonite world has traditionally favored these latter two options. The Old Order Mennonites, who predominantly live in rural farming communities, had little concern for the punitive direction being taken by criminal justice policy. Their primary concern was to preserve their own separate way of life. Urban Mennonites, on the other hand, tended to exhibit the same dualism between private faith and public life inherent in mainstream American evangelicalism, a dualism that left criminal justice policy unchallenged.

The revolution brought about by Jesus, Yoder argued, differed significantly from all available options – 'the creation of a distinct community with its own deviant set of values and its coherent way of incarnating them'.[99] In other words, Jesus called into existence a new society, a new

96. Howard Zehr, 'Justice Paradigm Shift? Values and Visions in the Reform Process', *Mediation Quarterly* 12, no. 3 (1995): 207–16.

97. Ibid., 207, 15.

98. Yoder, *Original Revolution*, 27.

99. Ibid., 28.

expression of humanity, one which derives its existence, not from the old aeon, where rulers and subversives struggle violently over who will control the path of history, but rather from the new aeon, where God's future kingdom is breaking into the present.

> Jesus did not bring to faithful Israel any corrected ritual or any new theories about the being of God. He brought them a *new peoplehood and a new way of living together*. The very existence of such a group is itself a deep social change. Its very presence was such a threat that He had to be crucified. But such a group is not only by its existence a novelty on the social scene; if it lives faithfully, it is also *the most powerful tool of social change*.[100]

This is the vision that animated the early expression of VORP, and the many other Christian experiments in restorative justice. Restorative justice was viewed as the realization of a new way of relating to one another, a new way of being in the world, which arises from a vision of what human community ought to look like in light of the 'original revolution'. The hope for social change manifest in the restorative vision of justice rests, to a significant degree, on faith that the Spirit of God is continuing to bring into being a human community patterned on Jesus as the justice of God.

Mainstreaming Restorative Justice

The release of *Changing Lenses* in 1990 marked in some sense the beginnings of an international restorative justice *social movement*, and with it the rise of new conceptual challenges.[101] In the ensuing decade, numerous other developments on the edges of the criminal justice system began to coalesce into a concerted move away from reliance on a state-centered, punitive retributive system and towards a more community-centered, informal, and relational approach to justice.[102] While not all were rallying

100. Ibid., 31 (italics mine).

101. After listing the exponential growth in interest in restorative responses, these authors declare, 'Clearly, restorative justice has become *a social movement* that impacts the way we understand and respond to crime and conflict in diverse communities throughout the world'; Mark S. Umbreit, Betty Vos, Robert B. Coates, and Elizabeth Lightfoot, 'Restorative Justice in the Twenty-First Century: A Social Movement Full of Opportunities and Pitfalls', *Marquette Law Review* 89 (2005/2006): 254 (italics mine).

102. Cf. Lode Walgrave, *Restorative Justice, Self-Interest and Responsible Citizenship* (London: Routledge, 2012), 15.

under the banner of restorative justice, Zehr's articulation of a new paradigm, or a new 'lens' for viewing crime and justice, resonated deeply with a broad constituency of criminologists, legal professionals, academics, and community agencies seeking reform.

Alongside the growing critiques of the punitive criminal justice system there also arose a number of experiments that resembled a restorative approach.[103] We have already mentioned the community mediation model developed by VOM. A similar initiative was being experimented within Scandinavian countries influenced by the criminological theories of Christie and Hulsman.[104] In Australia, John Braithwaite published *Crime, Shame and Reintegration* in 1989, which many criminologists herald as *the* key conceptual framework for understanding restorative justice.[105] Braithwaite, however, only made the connection between his idea of 'reintegrative shaming' and restorative justice after later discovering the family group conferencing experiment run by police in Wagga Wagga, New South Wales. The 'Wagga Wagga' initiative was mirrored off the New Zealand conferencing model instituted by the 1989 Child, Young Persons and their Families Act. This is widely regarded as the most comprehensive reform of a juvenile justice system in a restorative direction ever undertaken. Family Group Conferencing was proposed partly as a way of addressing the concerns of New Zealand's indigenous peoples (Maori), who hold to a more collectivist understanding of personal identity. Indigenous people were also responsible for the first use of 'Circle processes' in criminal justice – developed in the Yukon Territory of Canada, and subsequently by the Hollow Water Community in North America.[106]

It should be noted that much of this international spread of restorative justice was as a result of its reception by well-placed Christians. One significant example of this is Aotearoa/New Zealand. Following the advent of Family Group Conferences in 1989, Youth Court Judge Fred McElrea, an Anglican layman, encountered Zehr's book during a period

103. For a summary of these developments, see Van Ness and Strong, *Restoring Justice*, 12–19, 24–33.

104. Walgrave points out that while the North American experience of restorative justice was largely inspired by religious and spiritual motives, in Europe experiments in mediation with victims and offenders were grounded more in the academic critical reflection of Christie and Hulsman, Walgrave, *Restorative Justice*, 33.

105. John Braithwaite, *Crime, Shame and Reintegration* (Cambridge: Cambridge University Press, 1989).

106. See, Kay Pranis, Barry Stuart, and Mark Wedge, *Peacemaking Circles: From Crime to Community* (St. Paul, MN: Living Justice Press, 2003).

of study leave in England. He saw the connection between Zehr's restorative philosophy and independent developments in youth justice in New Zealand. Meanwhile, the New Zealand Christian journal *Stimulus* had published a review of Zehr's book, which led to Zehr being invited in 1994 to speak at a 'Making Crime Pay' conference that involved considerable theological reflection on restorative justice.[107] McElrea frequently referred to Zehr as 'a modern prophet of justice', who was bringing about a 'revolution' in how justice is understood.[108] Many of the leading figures in New Zealand advocating for reform in a restorative direction were people of faith, including prominent figures in the judiciary, politics, academia, the church, prison chaplaincy, and the theological fraternity.[109]

In May 1994, Judge McElrea made a request of Rev. Douglas Mansill, of Saint Giles Presbyterian Church in Auckland, to facilitate the first adult restorative justice conference in New Zealand. The trial was a success in Mansill's opinion, and in order to continue its success he went on to enlist other church ministers who would actively work for the 'reconciliation, restitution and restoration of normal community relationships after these have been broken down through offending'.[110]

McElrea also judged the church's involvement in restorative justice to be an important aspect of this work. Speaking at a conference, he proposed that the involvement of local churches in restorative justice processes provided a 'gospel based ministry', which 'put creative outcomes in the place of punitive ones, consensus in the place of imposed outcomes, inclusiveness and community in the place of professional capture, mutual

107. See the published proceedings of this conference in *Stimulus* vol. 2, no. 3 (1994).

108. See Emily Will, '"Prophet" of Justice Visits New Zealand', *Mennonite Weekly Review* (11 August 1994): 2.

109. To illustrate this shared Christian faith in the promotion of restorative justice, see Douglas Mansill, 'Community Empowerment or Institutional Control: The Development of Restorative Justice in New Zealand's Adult Systems of Social Regulation, Control and Punishment', PhD thesis (New Zealand, Auckland University of Technology, 2013), especially 134–41; also Jim Consedine, *Restorative Justice: Healing the Effects of Crime* (Lyttelton, New Zealand: Ploughshares Publishers, 1995); Judge Fred McElrea, 'A Christian Approach to Conflict Resolution', paper presented at the *Australasian Christian Legal Convention*, Melbourne, Australia, 2001, n.p.; Justice Stan Thorburn, 'Restorative Justice: Some Biblical Perspectives', paper presented at *Prison Fellowship International: Toronto Convocation*, Toronto, Canada, 2003, n.p.

110. Private Correspondence, from Douglas Mansill to Judge F. W. McElrea, 30 June 1994.

obligations in the place of the clash of rights, and cultural sensitivity in the place of mono-cultural rigidity'.[111] In New Zealand, then, as elsewhere in the world, restorative justice was actively promoted by those who saw in it the outworking of Christian notions of repentance, forgiveness, and reconciliation.

Van Ness and Strong observe that by the end of the 1980s and throughout much of the 1990s, restorative justice moved from being a 'community-based alternative' to the criminal justice system, to being not only a 'source of public policy' but also a 'viable part of the criminal justice system'.[112] Accordingly, as Hoyle comments, 'It is certainly the case that over the last two decades there has been more written about restorative justice than almost any other criminological topic'.[113] At the same time, she claims that much of this work has been 'evangelical, rather than academic and critical. Quantity rather than quality has prevailed.' To remedy this problem, several criminologists have sought to provide conceptual categories for explaining the genius behind restorative justice, with John Braithwaite being *the* leading voice in the field.[114] In addition, restorative justice has been scrutinized by theoreticians operating within the frameworks of postmodern theory,[115] political theory,[116] and postcolonial theory,[117] among others.

As it has moved into the twenty-first century, restorative justice has become a 'deeply contested' concept, involving considerably different

111. Cited in Mansill, 'Community Empowerment or Institutional Control', 136.

112. Van Ness and Strong, *Restoring Justice*, 34.

113. Hoyle, 'General Introduction', 15.

114. Ibid., 11. See also John Braithwaite and Philip Pettit, *Not Just Deserts: A Republican Theory of Criminal Justice* (Oxford: Oxford University Press, 1990); J. Braithwaite and H. Strang, *Restorative Justice and Civil Society* (Cambridge: Cambridge University Press, 2001); John Braithwaite, *Restorative Justice and Responsive Regulation* (Oxford: Oxford University Press, 2002).

115. G. Pavlich, *Governing Paradoxes of Restorative Justice* (London: Glasshouse Press, 2005); Walgrave, *Restorative Justice*.

116. Andrew Woolford, *The Politics of Restorative Justice: A Critical Introduction* (Winnipeg, MB: Fernwood, 2010); David J. Cornwell, *Doing Justice Better: The Politics of Restorative Justice* (Hampshire: Waterside Press, 2007).

117. H. Blagg, 'A Just Measure of Shame: Aboriginal Youth and Conferencing in Australia', *British Journal of Criminology* 37, no. 4 (1997); J. Tauri, 'Explaining Recent Innovations in New Zealand's Criminal Justice System: Empowering Maori or Biculturalising the State', *Australian & New Zealand Journal of Criminology* 32, no. 2 (1999); M. Findlay, 'Decolonising Restoration and Justice: Restoration in Transitional Cultures', *Howard Journal of Criminal Justice* 39, no. 4 (2000): 398–411.

conceptions of what constitutes its essence.[118] Walgrave warns of the danger of restorative justice becoming vacuous as it fast becomes 'a label for many different practices, beliefs, values and even states of mind'.[119] It is now commonplace for the first section of any textbook on restorative justice to grapple with matters of definition, as well as with who and what should be included in the restorative justice tent.[120] Gerry Johnstone observes that at its beginning as a social movement, numerous 'internal tensions' stemming from fundamental differences of opinion and worldview were submerged. However, as restorative justice moves from the margins to the mainstream, these internal tensions are fast becoming threats to the coherence and unity of the movement.[121]

Some Ecclesial Implications

Having established the theological and ecclesial wellsprings that helped to feed the emerging conceptuality of restorative justice, it is now time to consider how the church and its language have fared as restorative justice has increasingly migrated to the mainstream. As it has been accommodated to secular modes of thought and practice, to what extent has restorative justice grown distant from its earlier conception as bound up with the practice and reasoning of the church?

The first thing to emphasize is that the mainstreaming of restorative justice, despite all its associated pitfalls, represents precisely what the church is called to do. It is called, as Yoder puts it, 'to contribute to the creation of structures more worthy of human society'.[122] That other constituencies in society have taken up this 'peacemaking' approach to justice is a reason for the church to rejoice, even if the reasoning that informed this understanding of justice is not shared.[123] Even though

118. Johnstone, 'The Meaning of Restorative Justice', 5–23.

119. Walgrave, *Restorative Justice*, 42.

120. For example, the first section of Zehr and Toews' edited book includes sections with the headings: 'How, and in What Terms, Should Restorative Justice Be Conceived?', 'How Large Should the Restorative Justice "Tent" Be?', 'By Whom, and By What Processes, Is Restorative Justice Defined, and What Bias Might this Introduce?'; Howard Zehr and Barb Toews, eds., *Critical Issues in Restorative Justice* (Devon, UK: Willan, 2004).

121. Gerry Johnstone, *Restorative Justice: Ideas, Values, Debates*, 2nd ed. (London: Routledge, 2011), 14.

122. Yoder, *Politics of Jesus*, 155.

123. One such recognition of the peacemaking dimension of restorative justice, and of its early formulation in faith communities, is Jennifer J. Llewellyn and Daniel Philpott, ed., *Restorative Justice, Reconciliation, and Peacebuilding* (New York:

the church has distinctly theological reasons for promoting restorative conceptions of justice in the public sphere, that does not preclude it from continuing to support restorative justice initiatives where that theological reasoning is not present. This does however present new challenges for the church.

One such challenge is the degree to which distinctively Christian approaches will be welcome in the secular public arena. In the previous chapter we saw how modern ethical theory tends to elide the role of local tradition and communities of practice in favor of allegedly universal precepts. As the restorative justice movement has been mainstreamed, it has begun to show this same tendency of displacing particular traditions in place of universal theories. This may be seen, for example, in the four-volume compilation of essays on restorative justice – by far the largest collection to date – edited by Carolyn Hoyle.

In her introduction, Hoyle explains that the aim of the first volume is to acquaint 'the reader to the early development of restorative thinking and the justifications for this new approach, as well as some of the arguments against restorative aims and processes'.[124] One would expect, therefore, some mention of the early pioneering work of Mennonites and of their peace-making approach to crime. Yet, with one exception, this is largely omitted from the discussion.[125] Instead, the origins of restorative justice are made to appear as arising predominantly from criminological academics well accustomed to secular modes of reasoning. Similar omissions are found in other discussions of the early theoretical development of restorative justice.[126] A related tendency is to place the insights of indigenous and religious traditions under the nebulous category of 'spirituality', which makes it possible to avoid attending to the theological reasoning within such traditions.[127]

One disappointing consequence of the recent penchant for a systematic *theory* of restorative justice is that some of those writing in Christian

Oxford University Press, 2014). See also Jennifer J. Llewellyn, 'Integrating Peace, Justice and Development in a Relational Approach to Peacebuilding', *Ethics and Social Welfare* 6, no. 3 (2012): 290–302.

124. Hoyle, 'General Introduction', 3.

125. The only exception is the essay by Peachey, 'The Kitchener Experiment'. Yet, as I showed earlier in the chapter, the key conceptual work was done under Zehr's leadership in Elkhart, Indiana.

126. For example, Elmar G. M. Weitekamp and Hans-Jurgen Kerner, eds., *Restorative Justice: Theoretical Foundations* (Devon, UK: Willan, 2002).

127. Cf. Michael L. Hadley, ed. *The Spiritual Roots of Restorative Justice* (Albany: State University of New York Press, 2001).

ethics no longer see its inherent connection to real relationships in actual communities. For example, Anthony Bash, drawing on the work of restorative justice scholar Gavrielides, mistakenly concludes,

> there is an important difference between the conceptual underpinning of theories of restorative justice and what the New Testament says about justice and restoration: on the whole, secular theories relating to restorative justice confine themselves to being 'theor[ies] of Justice Systems and not… theor[ies] of life' and do 'not imply that we need to take steps towards a transformation of our relationships or lives'.[128]

Bash is right to point out that the biblical understanding of justice calls for 'transformed relationships and lives, and also for transformed communities', and that the 'kingdom of God is about more than transformed systems of criminal justice'.[129] But his characterization of restorative justice as being uninterested in such things shows how easily secular restorative justice theory can be misread. This shows how far recent portrayals of restorative justice have moved away from living traditions and communities, like the church, which helped ground restorative justice as an embodied communal practice.[130]

In 2002, Zehr offered an analogy for understanding the relationship between tradition-dependent reasoning and restorative justice, as a warning against this universalizing tendency. He likened restorative justice to a river that is fed by numerous tributaries, each contributing their own particular cultural and societal traditions for expressing justice in response to wrongdoing.[131] He explained that his own understanding of restorative justice emerged from his belonging to a Mennonite community, but he acknowledged historical antecedents in other religious and cultural traditions as well. By implication, no one tradition should claim to be *the* source of restorative justice, including the modern secular tradition. Restorative justice is made better, not worse, by recognizing its connection to tradition-dependent and context-driven practices.[132]

128. Bash, *Forgiveness and Christian Ethics*, 147.

129. Ibid.

130. As an example of restorative justice retaining its lived dimension, see Zehr's blog on '10 Ways to Live Restoratively', *Restorative Justice blog*, 27 November 2009. Available at http://emu.edu/now/restorative-justice/2009/11/27/10-ways-to-live-restoratively/

131. Howard Zehr, *The Little Book of Restorative Justice* (Intercourse, PA: Good Books, 2002), 62.

132. Ibid., 63.

In its pursuit of a unifying theoretical framework, it is not uncommon today for restorative justice to be conceived in terms that would have made its development within Christian theology virtually impossible. The perspective of Walgrave is typical. In advancing a theory of the 'socio-ethical drive toward restorative justice', he relegates the ethical importance of theological claims to the sphere of individual belief, clearly segregated from the interests of public society:

> Moral judgment is partially a personal affair based on personal criteria. But socially, the only touchstone is common self-interest... [Those who observe religious practices] do so because of personal religious beliefs. A good society must facilitate religious activities out of respect for plurality, but it cannot impose religious obligations on those who do not believe... The public rule is not pleasing God but participating constructively in social life. The quality of social life is the ultimate value in the quest for socio-ethics.[133]

According to Walgrave, it is on the basis of self-interest that individuals invest in society, as anything else threatens their autonomy as citizens. Such a concept of society as an assemblage of individual self-interest bears little resemblance to the Christian understanding of community out of which restorative justice arose.[134] Walgrave's theory fails entirely to comprehend the ecclesial and theological values underlying the early drive towards restorative justice. In stark contrast to Walgrave's theory, Marshall argues, 'restorative justice may be characterized, from a Gospel perspective, as a *compassionate justice*. It is a justice that is enriched, informed, and empowered by the space it gives to compassion.'[135] Defined in this way, restorative justice points to a more relational conception of human personhood, where it is the good of the other and, by extension, of the wider community that orients the practice of justice.

133. Walgrave, *Restorative Justice*, 94–95.

134. 'The others then become allies in a common project for more autonomy and my self-interest is integrated in what I call a common self-interest... It is in my interest to live in peace, to be part of a community that gives me and the others maximum space, based on respect for plurality and solidarity...allowing me to live in peace and to do my own thing. Living in such a community is the common self-interest'; ibid., 80–81.

135. Christopher D. Marshall, *Compassionate Justice: An Interdisciplinary Dialogue with Two Gospel Parables on Law, Crime, and Restorative Justice* (Eugene, OR: Cascade Books, 2012), 252.

Another example of how restorative justice has been redefined in liberal categories is Susan Sharpe's chapter, 'How Large Should the Restorative Justice "Tent" Be?' In her opinion, there is 'little in the restorative justice literature regarding the nature of justice', and where such discussions do occur they usually only cover the historical *context* rather than the *content* of restorative justice.[136] Sharpe includes Zehr's work in this assessment. While this may be true for Zehr's description of community justice, in which he challenges the historical inevitability of a state-centered retributive conception of justice, the same cannot be said of his analysis of covenantal justice. Sharpe fails to see that covenant justice and the pursuit of shalom were essential to Zehr's very definition of restorative justice. Discarding his theological formulation, she turns to social contract theory and Rawls's liberal definition of 'justice as fairness'. Referring to Zehr's definition of crime as a violation of a relationship, which he drew from the biblical narrative of God's covenantal relationship with Israel, Sharpe redefines crime as a violation of a social contract.[137]

The difference, however, between a covenant and a contract is substantial, not least when they are violated. Zehr drew on the biblical tradition, which understands justice as the active upholding of covenantal relationships and as a commitment to restoration when relationships are damaged or under threat. In social contract theory, justice involves adhering to the mutually binding conditions of the contract. If those conditions are violated by crime, on the principle of fairness, the obligation of justice is to punish the violator, not restore him. This explains why Sharpe repeatedly speaks of the need for 'justice to be restored' – i.e., reinstating the conditions of the contract – whereas Zehr speaks of justice-making *as* restoration, due to the unconditional nature of covenant relationships. Moreover, Sharpe unwittingly accepts Rawls' liberal political project that seeks to secure justice by emphasizing procedures that are independent of any 'comprehensive doctrine'.[138] Zehr's approach, by contrast, seeks to go beyond any procedural account of justice and towards a more substantive relational notion of justice.

Perhaps most indicative of the shift away from its ecclesial roots has been the eliding of theologically grounded concepts from the vocabulary of restorative justice. The early vernacular of the VORP initiative

136. Susan Sharpe, 'How Large Should the Restorative Justice "Tent" Be?', in Zehr and Toews, eds., *Critical Issues in Restorative Justice*, 22.

137. Ibid., 23.

138. John Rawls, 'The Idea of Public Reason Revisited', in *The Laws of Peoples* (Cambridge, MA: Harvard University Press, 2001), 172–73.

employed the language of grace, repentance, forgiveness, and love. However, the contemporary secular milieu has developed something of an allergy to such terms. Zehr's language of healing and repair has proved more palatable for secular discourse than has his theological grammar of forgiveness and reconciliation.[139] He has even rescinded on his earlier emphasis by stating that 'forgiveness and reconciliation is not a primary principle or focus of restorative justice', even if it may well provide a context 'where either or both might happen'.[140]

A parallel dynamic can be observed in the field of transitional justice, widely considered to be an application of restorative justice ideas.[141] The most prominent example is the South African Truth and Reconciliation Commission (TRC) which, in the words of its Chairperson, Archbishop Desmond Tutu, tried to forestall 'the cycle of reprisal and counter-reprisal' by going 'beyond retributive justice to restorative justice, to move on to forgiveness, because without [forgiveness] there is no future'.[142] Tutu explicitly framed the work of the Commission in theological terms, placing great emphasis on the theme of reconciliation, which he saw as synonymous with restorative justice.[143] In the words of Antjie Krog, Tutu 'unambiguously mantled the commission in Christian language', leading a procession of rituals of confession and absolution that, in the opinion of Moosa, amounted to a 'secular Eucharist'.[144]

139. Marshall points out that this has further siloed other theologians from engaging with restorative justice; Christopher Marshall, 'A Gracious Legacy', *Restorative Justice: An International Journal* 3, no. 3 (2015): 442–44.

140. Zehr, *The Little Book of Restorative Justice*, 8.

141. On the relationship between transitional justice and restorative justice, see Jennifer J. Llewellyn, 'Truth Commissions and Restorative Justice', in Johnstone and Van Ness, eds., *Handbook of Restorative Justice*, 351–71.

142. Desmond Tutu, *No Future without Forgiveness* (New York: Doubleday, 1999), 260.

143. The motif of reconciliation is ubiquitous with the South African TRC, and the use of restorative justice can be found in the commission's final report, *Truth and Reconciliation Commission of South Africa Report* (Cape Town: Truth and Reconciliation Commission, 1998), 1:125–31.

144. Antjie Krog, *Country of My Skull: Guilt, Sorrow, and the Limits of Forgiveness in the New South Africa* (Johannesburg: Random House, 1998), 202; Ebrahim Moosa, 'Truth and Reconciliation as Performance: Spectres of Eucharistic Redemption', in *Looking Back, Reaching Forward: Reflections on the Truth and Reconciliation Commission of South Africa*, ed. Charles Villa-Vicencio and Wilhelm Verwoerd (Cape Town: University of Cape Town Press, 2000), 117, cited in Jonathan VanAntwerpen, 'Reconciliation as Heterodoxy', in Llewellyn and Philpott, eds., *Restorative Justice, Reconciliation, and Peacebuilding*, 89, 91.

The success of the TRC in avoiding mass bloodshed projected the new field of 'transitional justice' onto the world stage. Yet as it became increasingly institutionalized, the concept of reconciliation – with its intimations of confession and forgiveness – soon became tantamount to what VanAntwerpen calls a 'heresy' within the secular orthodoxy of transitional justice.[145] Tutu's vision of reconciliation, so entwined with his theological reading of a post-apartheid future, never sat comfortably with secularists, who preferred the secular vernacular of human rights and international law. Where the concept of reconciliation remained, it became a secular cipher for civic trust, shorn of its spiritual evocations in the South African experience.[146]

This shift reflects a more chastened attitude toward the potential for the actual *resolution* of conflict, which in turn reflects a considerable flattening of the restorative vision. Conflict, in this account, is something that must be *managed* through careful planning and clear procedures rather than something that can be transcended. This prevailing skepticism reflects, as Brian Brock argues, a flight from living under the certainty that God's Word has decisively spoken into humanity bringing about genuine reconciliation.[147] The preoccupation with the management of conflict rather than its genuine resolution through the practices of repentance and forgiveness reflects a modern narrowing of the possibilities open to humanity, and with it the eclipse of any eschatological horizon infusing the present horizon with hope.

The notion of reconciliation animating the early restorative vision was not just naïve optimism on the part of some enthusiasts; it was integral to the reality of God's future kingdom breaking into present experience.[148] The movement of repentance and forgiveness leading to reconciliation reflected the heart of reality. '[B]y placing a concern for the healing of hurts, the renewal of relationships, and the re-creation of community at the heart of its agenda', Marshall writes, restorative justice 'makes room for the miracle of forgiveness to occur and for a new future to dawn'.[149] It was this eschatological realism of restorative justice that distinguished it from the dominant concerns of the criminal justice system.

145. VanAntwerpen, 'Reconciliation as Heterodoxy', 104, 108.

146. VanAntwerpen places Charles Villa-Vicencio's 'political' conception of reconciliation and Pablo de Greiff's conception of reconciliation as 'civic trust' as secularized examples of this trend; ibid., 106.

147. Brock, *Christian Ethics in a Technological Age*, 173.

148. Marshall, *Beyond Retribution*, 18.

149. Ibid., 284.

A Way Forward for Restorative Justice and the Church

The Mennonite theologian Tom Yoder Neufeld notes that, 'Restorative Justice has become a concept, a paradigm, an identifiable set of principles and practices which can be argued for in the public arena, indeed, which have garnered the adherence of a diverse community of practitioners far greater than the early pioneers could have imagined'.[150] However such developments, he suspects, have 'sometimes outpaced biblical reflection and testing'. The rapid ascendency of restorative justice in mainstream public discourse has been accompanied by a notable lack of continued theological engagement with it in the church. By and large, the church has reneged on the role Zehr called it to, with the result that many of the pressures of 'institutionalization' and 'routinization', along with secularization, have often gone unchallenged from a theological perspective.[151]

While the mainstreaming of a peacemaking approach to justice is desirable and has helped to hold in check the punitive impulses of the dominant system, it has also brought new challenges for Christians seeking to develop restorative justice in a more theological direction. The nature of these challenges are multiple: the contested role of tradition-dependent communities in secular society; the way justice practices are subordinated to political arrangements; the lack of emphasis on the lived reality of people and communities; and the disputed legitimacy of religious convictions and language to sustain a specific social vision.

All this raises the question of how the church might continue to contribute to the rapidly evolving field of restorative justice in ways that are congruent with its own practice and reasoning. There are at least two dimensions to this question: first, how can the distinctly theological reasoning informing restorative justice be safeguarded, and second, how may restorative justice be practiced by the church in ways that are reflective of its own commitments? One way of answering this question is to prioritize the role of particular values. However, while this approach is of some use, it also has significant theological limitations. In what follows, I will outline the weaknesses of a values-based approach to articulating a Christian voice on restorative justice. This will be in order to clarify the need for a more ecclesially based and biblically engaged alternative, as developed in the following chapters.

150. Neufeld, 'In the Middle', 1.

151. Zehr has continually reiterated his concern of the 'soul' of restorative justice being co-opted and serving a purpose other than what it was intended; see Zehr's article, 'Justice Paradigm Shift?'

In her essay titled 'Restorative Values', Kay Pranis makes the observation that restorative justice is a field that 'flows back and forth between practice that informs philosophy and philosophy that informs practice'.[152] This insight confirms what we have been arguing, which is that any concept of justice both emerges from the practices of a community, as well as acts to shape the social form of that community. Theory and practice are not two separate phenomena that can be clearly distinguished from one another; rather, they are mutually interpreting activities. Following this insight, Pranis suggests that restorative justice requires some 'unifying concept' that can ground its theory while guiding its practice.[153]

In restorative justice literature, the language of 'restorative values' is fast becoming the kind of 'unifying concept' that addresses this need. Pranis goes on to list a range of values that are frequently mentioned, such as respect, honesty, accountability, humility, equality, inclusion, and mutual care. She cites Zehr and Toews, who write, 'Restorative values can be distilled to two key underlying values – *humility* and *respect*. Furthermore, we should approach our work with *wonder*.'[154] Pranis suggests that restorative values can be divided into two groups – process values and individual values. Process values, like respect, should encourage and enable individual values to emerge, while it is through individual values, like honesty, that restorative processes can achieve transformative outcomes.

Values are not easily distinguished from principles, ideals, or convictions, but for Pranis restorative *values* are 'those things that feel deeply important to the essence of the restorative impulse and are carried in the spirit of what we do and how we do it'.[155] Drawing on her extensive experience and her beliefs about human nature, Pranis proposes that every person values those qualities that promote good relationships with others and with oneself.[156] 'It appears that awareness of and desire for the values that support healthy relationships are profoundly embedded in human nature. It makes sense; humans are communal. Our DNA should carry the

152. Kay Pranis, 'Restorative Values', in Johnstone and Van Ness, eds., *Handbook of Restorative Justice*, 59.

153. Ibid.

154. Ibid., 62, citing Zehr, *Critical Issues in Restorative Justice*, ix.

155. Pranis, 'Restorative Values', 60.

156. 'The Circle Process is based on a simple notion: Because we all want to be in good relationships with others, when we create a space that is respectful and reflective, people can find their way through anger, pain, and fear to find common ground and take care of one another'; *The Little Book of Circle Processes: A New/Old Approach to Peacemaking* (Intercourse, PA: Good Books, 2005), 62.

information necessary to be successful in community.'[157] It is this interconnected and relational view of human nature that is the 'deep inner truth' behind the restorative values, and the values are one way of describing what it means to live in the light of this truth, especially in situations where relationships have become dismembered and destructive.[158]

As Pranis' comments reveal, the deep inner truth of restorative justice lies not in the values themselves, but in their depiction of how humans *ought* to live in light of reality as it *is* perceived to be. This explains why restorative justice is not a neutral, value-free process, as it privileges those values that point to a worldview characterized by 'wholeness, unity, and connectedness'.[159] This interconnected and relational worldview is not unique to any single cultural perspective, though its features are more noticeable in indigenous and collectivist cultures. Pranis is convinced that there is a significant consensus among humans on what values ought to be affirmed, even when there exists a dissonance between what people value and what they practice.

For Pranis, values function in much the same way that language does for Wittgenstein, except that Pranis gives no account of how the language of values reposes on a particular political community. In her essay, values act in a conciliatory way, bringing about understanding between those held apart by their differences. They help foster practices to resolve difficult problems, often by addressing human needs for acceptance and belonging. In fact, values can provide a way of assessing and guiding practice simply by asking whether existing practices are congruent with the stated values of participants. Values are not static, but instead function in a visionary way to describe where current reality needs to move. Perhaps most importantly, however, is the way in which values emerge from people's core convictions, thus enabling a more integrated and holistic way of uniting the personal and the political.[160]

It is no surprise that values language often features in Christian discourse, especially when speaking in forums where a shared theological reasoning cannot be presumed. For example, Marshall writes, 'what is most crucial as restorative justice continues to grow and diversify, and especially as it becomes more integrated into mainstream justice systems, is that its *undergirding values are safeguarded*'.[161] Values language helps

157. Pranis, 'Restorative Values', 64.
158. Ibid., 73.
159. Pranis, *Peacemaking Circles*, 68.
160. All of these features can be found in Pranis, 'Restorative Values', 66–73.
161. Marshall, *Compassionate Justice*, 6 (italics mine).

to name the fundamental commitments and convictions of a practice like restorative justice, without having to describe where those commitments came from. In a pluralistic context, values help to foster shared agreements that would otherwise prove difficult on account of underlying differences. In this sense, values language functions in much the same way as middle-axioms do in the approach made popular by William Temple. Yet herein lies their limitation for the task we have pursued.[162]

While values language is useful when seeking common ground in a pluralistic context, it is not in itself a sufficient category for describing the particular ways in which ethical commitments are expressed. In other words, for values to have any ethical substance they need to be embodied in the particular practices and character of real people, as they live out their daily existence in real contexts. Marshall recognizes this when he writes, 'Values do not exist in a vacuum, of course; they are held by flesh-and-blood people belonging to particular historical communities'.[163] Pranis indirectly acknowledges it too when she illustrates each of the ten values underlying restorative justice by referring to actual people as they grapple with their professional roles, their history with the criminal justice institution, their commitment to a particular reintegrative programme, their memory of a youth's place in the village culture, and so on.[164] The values that people affirm as important are only understandable within the culture and institutions that give such values their concrete meaning.

Ecclesial ethicists emphasize that the convictions underlying why people do what they do, and even how they do it, are best explored under the rubric of character. Character is a category that connects a person's core convictions with how they live; it also points to the stories and traditions that have formed these convictions and practices. While the language of character avoids the abstract, individualistic, and universalizing mode of inquiry rendering communities like the church invisible in modern ethics, it is not clear whether the same can be said of values language.

At its worst, values language can function as a trope for the same universalizing tendency that displaces the reasoning and practice of particular, tradition-dependent communities. At their best, however, the 'Restorative Values' identified by Pranis encourage recognition of the institutions and traditions within which these values acquire meaning.

162. See Temple, *Christianity and Social Order*.

163. Marshall, *Compassionate Justice*, 7.

164. Pranis, *Peacemaking Circles*, 33–45.

For ecclesial ethics, the most obvious candidate is the church.[165] For the church to continue contributing to the rapidly evolving field of restorative justice, it must recover its identity as a distinctive eschatological community that bears witness to all the ways in which the justice of God impinges on human life, thus opening up new vistas in the theological exploration of restorative justice.

Following the method outlined in the Introduction, we have in this chapter achieved the *descriptive task* by providing a concrete example of one significant way in which the church has sought to embody God's justice, as an outworking of ecclesial ethics. In the chapters that follow, we will turn to the prescriptive and suggestive aspects of our task, beginning with an exploration of a biblical paradigm of restorative justice.

165. Alan Torrance argues that any appeal to derive *ought* from *is*, in the way that Pranis derives certain prescriptive values from a view of reality as relational and interconnected, requires the existence of institutions like the church that can describe what those responsibilities and obligations ought to be. Specifically for the church, it is God's new covenant in Christ that is 'a structured, ecclesially creative and sustaining "institution" which carries definable and specifiable obligations which ecclesial ethics seeks to articulate and to interpret'. It is in the context of certain '*rule-structured, social institutions*' like the church that relational obligations emerge and are given expression; Alan J. Torrance, 'On Deriving "Ought" from "Is": Christology, Covenant and *Koinonia*', in *The Doctrine of God and Theological Ethics*, ed. Alan J. Torrance and Michael Banner (London: T&T Clark International, 2006), 182 and 180, respectively.

Chapter 4

The Theological Interpretation of Scripture and Biblical Justice

We have seen how restorative justice emerged in the context of a living faith community seeking to respond faithfully to the needs of those affected by wrongdoing. This was an attempt by some Christians to bring their ecclesial formation in the Anabaptist-Mennonite tradition in the practices of peacemaking to bear on criminal justice policy and practice. Undergirding it was a way of reading the overarching narrative of Scripture as a 'theology of restoration'.[1] As Tom Yoder Neufeld observes,

> the paradigm of Restorative Justice took shape within the womb of biblically informed piety and ethics. It emerged in the attempt to answer a biblically informed and urged set of questions: how can persons committed to peace, reconciliation, and restoration, inject that set of convictions and reflexes into the public arena of responses to crime?[2]

According to ecclesial ethics, the central task of the church is to be, as Hauerwas puts it, 'a community capable of hearing the story of God we find in the Scripture and living in a manner that is faithful to that story'.[3] The church is not just any community, but one in which the Scriptural story is embodied in the common life of a people. The development of restorative justice reflects this attempt to embody the story of God's justice, which means that in restorative justice the distinctive contours of the church's story may be discerned. Consequently, any attempt to expand the place of restorative justice in the life of the church must begin with a consideration of the church's relationship to Scripture. As Stephen Fowl explains, Scripture 'provides a normative standard for the faith, practice,

1. Zehr, 'Retributive Justice, Restorative Justice'.
2. Neufeld, 'In the Middle', 2.
3. Hauerwas, *Community of Character*, 1.

and worship of Christian communities'.[4] The bible provides the grammar and language for understanding the space within which the church lives faithfully before God. A theological commitment to restorative justice must therefore proceed from bringing the insights of Scripture to bear on this practice. More specifically, this requires a three-way interaction between the convictions, practices, and character of the church, the theological interpretation of Scripture, and the theory and practice of restorative justice.

In this chapter we will begin by clarifying what is meant by the theological interpretation of Scripture, particularly in relation to how two prominent ecclesial ethicists have approached the text of Matt. 18.15-22. This text deals with the restorative justice themes of discipline, confrontation, forgiveness, and reconciliation, all in the presence of wrongdoers and their victims. However, as we will see, there is a striking absence of justice language in the way these two ecclesial scholars deal with the unit, a text that has much to teach the church about the doing of justice. The second part of the chapter will consider how the language of justice in the biblical material has often been misconstrued by interpreters. The trajectory in Christian history towards an abstract, retributive, and interiorized understanding of justice (as discussed earlier), stemmed in part from a problematic interpretation of Scripture, leading to its distorted practice in the church. Instead of viewing justice in a covenantal or christological context, the tendency has been to read it in a more strictly judicial (and Roman) context. This has resulted in a construal of justice in terms of desert, punishment, and abstract law, which has then been read back into the divine nature. The translation of key biblical terms for justice has contributed to this truncated and distorted understanding of biblical justice. The chapter will end with a proposal for conceptualizing God's justice in the biblical story as a predominantly restorative justice, which in turn sets the agenda for the church's embodiment of justice.

The Theological Interpretation of Scripture

Ecclesial ethics represents the attempt to recover the distinctive witness of the ecclesial community as it participates in the life made possible by Jesus Christ. In order to describe the shape of this witness, ecclesial ethicists have repeatedly turned to the concept of character, with a particular emphasis on the way such a character is formed through inhabiting the tradition of the church. While the concept of character may be helpful for

4. Fowl, *Engaging Scripture*, 2.

showing the connections between Christian agency and their formation in community, it is not a self-sufficient category for understanding the vocation of Christians, if for no other reason than that a good tradition or community can still produce bad actions. This is why ecclesial ethicists necessarily turn to the relationship Christians have to Scripture, and in particular to the way their actions might *embody Scripture* in the various contexts in which they find themselves. As the church wrestles with the words of its bible, it discovers what kind of character and actions are appropriate to those who would call themselves disciples of Jesus.

Many of the objections raised by ecclesial ethicists against specifically modern ways of thinking can be detected in their criticism of contemporary biblical scholarship. Indeed, anyone accustomed to the modern conventions of academic inquiry will be all too familiar with the divisions that currently separate biblical scholarship from the concerns of Christian ethicists, and from the concerns of the confessing community in particular.

The interpretation of the bible in the modern period has been dominated by the use of critical methods unrelated to the interests of the confessing community. According to Fowl and Jones, the church has been displaced due to the pursuit of a mode of biblical interpretation that is independent of 'socially-embodied traditions' (i.e., the church) and of context-specific situations (i.e., where the Christian life is actually lived).[5] The characteristic modern emphasis on decisions made by isolated individuals produced a method of interpretation aimed at arriving at the 'objective' meaning of a text by means of universally accepted criteria. Such an approach consciously ignores the role of character, social situation, and circumstance in the interpretive process, while also severely limiting the pedagogic purposes for which interpreters might engage with the text. The church, as a community formed by Scripture for living faithfully before God, has little place in this mode of interpretation.

The preoccupation of the modern approach is with comprehending the *meaning* of the biblical text rather than its *lived* implications.[6] This reflects the subordination of social and relational realities to the assertion of facts and principles believed to be universally true. Even as the modernist

5. Fowl and Jones contend that 'the search for a context-independent ethical method is bound to fail'; see Fowl and Jones, *Reading in Communion*, 13.

6. This produces a rather stifling reading of scripture, as Jim Foder points out: 'Equating reading with the acquisition of information, the distillation of didactic truths from the Bible, simply fails to do justice to the rich, all-encompassing pedagogy that is Scripture reading'; Jim Fodor, 'Reading the Scriptures: Rehearsing Identity, Practicing Character', in Hauerwas and Wells, eds., *The Blackwell Companion to Christian Ethics*, 148.

assumption that a text possesses an objective stable meaning has come under critical scrutiny in the late modern era, it has still not often issued in a renewed interest in the lived application of biblical interpretation. Ecclesial ethicists argue that post-modern 'anti-determinist' readings, as Fowl terms them, are no more helpful for clarifying the church's relationship to Scripture than earlier objectivist readings were. This is because in their effort to expose the colonizing ideology of the text, they further undermine any attempt to shape a common life in obedience to it.[7] Its deep suspicion towards any claim of authority by the text or by any single interpretation of it, ensures the interpreter always stands *over against* the text rather than under its sway. The methodological acceptance of a plurality of interpretations serves to *problematize* and *paralyze* any attempt to derive a common life from the story of Scripture.

While agreeing that hermeneutics is a '"political" discipline'[8] that unavoidably involves bringing convictions, dispositions, and character to the interpretive process, ecclesial ethicists attempt to make 'constructive use of the interaction'.[9] Rather than trying to approach the bible in a neutral or objective way, Christian communities stand in a particular relationship to the bible as Scripture.[10] 'Christian communities interpret Scripture, then, so that believers might live faithfully before God in the light of Jesus Christ'.[11] Scripture, in other words, is to be 'socially embodied in communities of people committed to ordering their worship, their doctrines, and their lives in a manner consistent with faithful interpretation'.[12]

This move to a theological interpretation of Scripture is bound up with the recovery of the centrality of the ecclesia. Ecclesial ethicists point out that it through the preaching and liturgy of the church that Christians have their characters formed and transformed so that they can adequately perform the story of Scripture. As Fodor suggests, 'repeated exposure to and immersion in liturgical readings of the Bible', leads the church

7. As Fowl writes in reference to Derrida's deconstructionist project, 'deconstruction is more like an attitude. It sets out to undermine systems of wholeness, clarity, and closure with the aim of manifesting what is excluded or reduced or obscured within those systems. This subversion is not offered in order to make the system better, but to undermine the very practice of system-making'; Fowl, *Engaging Scripture*, 41–42.

8. Although, not 'restrictively'; see Fowl and Jones, *Reading in Communion*, 16.

9. Fowl, *Engaging Scripture*, 8.

10. Neville concurs, 'the reality is that those whose worldview, moral vision and communal ethos have been shaped by Christian faith relate to the Bible not only as a religious and cultural "classic" but also as a norm for faith and practice'; Neville, 'Justice and Public Theology', 10.

11. Fowl and Jones, *Reading in Communion*, 20.

12. Ibid.

into 'a peculiar kind of scriptural competence, which is but another way of describing "faithful living"'.[13] As well as being formed by the liturgical use of the bible, the church is also engaged in the '*formation of virtuous interpreters* of Scripture', as Fowl argues, so that 'Christian communities can combat the temptation to read Scripture in ways that underwrite sinful practices'.[14] Accordingly, church and Scripture exist in a dynamic relationship, and it is on the grounds of this relationship that the biblical people of God 'stand as an alternative to the world and its values while at the same time living their lives for the sake of that world in its brokenness'.[15]

This way of viewing the relationship between church and Scripture would suggest that some of the problems associated with modern biblical interpretation are as a result of the church's failure to produce virtuous interpreters of Scripture. This can certainly be seen in the work of Fowl and Jones, who criticize contemporary Christianity as being little more than a 'lifestyle enclave' or club in which people gather for reasons other than moral formation. 'For while we *need* to read Scripture in and through the practices of Christian communities, there is a distressing paucity of vital communities in the contemporary contexts of North America and Great Britain. Such common life as we do experience is often impoverished.'[16] They approach the text of Scripture with a particular concern to reinvigorate morally compelling communities while at the same time insisting that Scripture can only be interpreted rightly from within such communities. This has made Fowl and Jones susceptible to charges of methodological inconsistency, which might be responded to by giving greater prominence to the role of the Spirit in effecting a transformation of the church's often feeble readings of the bible.[17]

13. Fodor, 'Reading the Scriptures', 147.

14. Fowl, *Engaging Scripture*, 86–87 (italics mine).

15. To quote in full: 'The church, as those persons who claim to be the covenant people of God and the body of Christ, is shaped continuously by Scripture and its influence in worship, preaching, study, and life together in the community of faith... Here is where Christians receive nourishment in a biblical identity that allows them to stand as an alternative to the world and its values while at the same time living their lives for the sake of that world its brokenness'; Bruce C. Birch, 'The Role of Scripture in Public Theology', *Word and World* 4, no. 3 (1984): 264, cited in Neville, 'Justice and Public Theology', 11.

16. Fowl and Jones, *Reading in Communion*, 64.

17. This response would also address another criticism of Fowl and Jones's approach, which is that it is overly anthropocentric and pneumatologically deficient. See, Brock, *Singing the Ethos of God*, 23–34.

Another clarification deserves mentioning. In viewing biblical interpretation as a performance, ecclesial ethics does not intend to be overly prescriptive about its meaning. What matters is that the church is forming *wise* readers of Scripture so as to embody it in life, rather than prescribing in detail what that embodiment should look like. As Wells argues, Scripture is not so much a 'script' that simply needs rehearsing, it is more like a 'training manual' that schools its members to *improvise* in ever changing situations while taking the right things for granted.[18] Certainly the bible is authoritative, but this authority does not stand in independence of the community that considers it as Scripture. '[A]uthority is not something that has been inserted into the Bible which can then later be found, abstracted, analyzed and either followed or ignored', as Fowl argues.[19] Rather, Scripture has authority in relationship to the ecclesial community that reads and lives out the biblical story in the specific contexts in which it finds itself. This will at times include reading Scripture *over against* the ecclesial community, but never in detachment from it.[20]

It is not the concern of ecclesial ethics to produce another set of methodological criteria that would substitute for the actual task of exegesis. The various ways in which the bible has been rendered more foreign to the church must eventually give way to a fresh engagement with the claims of Scripture on the community of faith. This is the point of theological interpretations which, as Brock suggests, involves understanding 'the *way* we are foreigners in the Bible's world, [and to then] thematize its foreignness in a theologically illuminating fashion'.[21] We now turn to an example of what this looks like in practice, which returns us to our task of discovering how Scripture illumines the meaning of justice as oriented to restored relationships.

18. Wells is wary of notions of 'discipleship as the performance of a script', partly because the church must continue to face new challenges without being locked in the past. He cites Gerard Loughlin as suggesting a better approach, 'When a person enters the scriptural story he or she does so by entering the Church's performance of that story: he or she is baptized into a biblical and ecclesial drama. It is not so much being written into a book as taking part in a play, a play that has to be improvised on the spot'; Wells, *Improvisation*, 65, citing Gerard Loughlin, *Telling God's Story: Bible, Church, and Narrative Theology* (Cambridge: Cambridge University Press, 1996), 20.

19. Fowl, *Engaging Scripture*, 203.

20. This point deserves special emphasis in light of the criticisms levelled at this 'communitarian' method of biblical interpretation. The bible is read to challenge the community of faith, but such challenges are welcomed only because this community regards the bible as the working of God in its midst.

21. Brock, *Singing the Ethos of God*, xii.

Ecclesial Discipline in Matthew 18.15-22

Hauerwas and Yoder both use Matt. 18.15-22 to describe what an ecclesial ethic looks like in practice, albeit in distinctly different ways. Significantly, despite the fact this text deals specifically with wrongdoing and the need for reconciliation, neither author makes any reference to justice, let alone restorative justice. The biblical text reads:

> 'If another member of the church sins against you, go and point out the fault when the two of you are alone. If the member listens to you, you have regained that one. But if you are not listened to, take one or two others along with you, so that every word may be confirmed by the evidence of two or three witnesses. If the member refuses to listen to them, tell it to the church; and if the offender refuses to listen even to the church, let such a one be to you as a Gentile and a tax collector. Truly I tell you, whatever you bind on earth will be bound in heaven, and whatever you loose on earth will be loosed in heaven. Again, truly I tell you, if two of you agree on earth about anything you ask, it will be done for you by my Father in heaven. For where two or three are gathered in my name, I am there among them'. Then Peter came and said to him, 'Lord, if another member of the church sins against me, how often should I forgive? As many as seven times?' Jesus said to him, 'Not seven times, but, I tell you, seventy-seven times'.

What has often been interpreted as a rudimentary process for church discipline, or as an example of the personalism of the primitive church, is interpreted by Yoder and Hauerwas as demonstrative of how the church embodies Jesus's politics of peace.

The process outlined in Matthew 18 for admonishing a wrongdoer is clearly an important feature of what it means to be the church in Matthew's Gospel. It is solely in connection with the function of 'binding and loosing', what Yoder likens to 'conflict resolution', that the word *ekklesia* is mentioned.[22] Both Yoder and Hauerwas make much of this observation, and both draw the same conclusion that peacemaking lies at the heart of what it means to be the church. Yoder offers a fine-grained reading of the relational and sociological dynamics at work in this, while Hauerwas interprets it with his typical language of virtue, habits, narrative, and the grammar of a community, all of which serve as a counter-example to the world's violence.[23] The church serves as a training

22. John H. Yoder, *Body Politics: Five Practices of the Christian Community before the Watching World* (Nashville, TN: Discipleship Resources, 1992), 8–9.

23. Yoder, 'Binding and Loosing', 323–58. Hauerwas's essay is included in his; see Hauerwas, *Christian Existence Today*, 89–97.

ground for the formation of a truthful people who refuse to compromise with the violence of the age.

> We know that as God's creatures we are *not naturally violent* nor are our institutions unavoidably violent. As God's people we have been *created for peace*. Rather, what we must do is to help *the world* find the *habits of peace* whose absence so often makes violence seem like the only alternative. Peacemaking as a virtue is an *act of the imagination* built on long habits of the resolution of differences. The great problem in the world is that our imagination has been stilled, since it has not made a practice of confronting wrongs so that violence might be avoided. In truth, we must say that the church has too often failed the world by its failure to *witness in our own life* the kind of conflict necessary to be a community of peace. Without an *example* of a *peacemaking community*, the *world has no alternative* but to use violence as the means to settle disputes.[24]

The first thing to note about Hauerwas's reading is his avoidance of any technical-exegetical remarks that would situate the church at some critical distance from the text. He simply takes it for granted that Matthew 18 is addressed to the church, although he never makes clear what church he has in mind. By implication, Hauerwas never poses the question of what the church should *do* with this primitive process, as if the problem were with some 'historical discontinuity' that could be answered in relative independence of the text. Rather, his question is with how this text describes the church whose members are capable of confronting one another with their sins. Hauerwas allows the historical distance between the text and the church to be eschewed, supplanted by the greater problem of our contemporary failure to embody faithful living in ongoing Christian communities. That means, as Fowl and Jones argue, 'the discontinuities are not so much historical as *moral* and *theological*'.[25]

The second observation about Hauerwas's reading is the way he allows Matthew 18 to define the distinctive character of the church as *peacemaking*. He draws on an Aristotelian reference, whereby some virtues are 'correlative to certain kinds of relations and cannot exist without those relations being valued by a community'.[26] In particular, relationships based on peace and truth are valued by the church in such a way that peacemaking can rightly be considered an ecclesial virtue. By introducing the language of virtue, Hauerwas makes repeated appeals to the '*habits* of

24. Hauerwas, *Christian Existence Today*, 95 (italics mine).
25. Fowl and Jones, *Reading in Communion*, 57 (italics mine).
26. Hauerwas, *Christian Existence Today*, 90.

peacekeeping' and the *practice* of being 'truthful' so that the church might be *trained* to confront the 'false peace of the world'.[27]

By describing peacemaking as a virtue of the *church*, Hauerwas offers a substantial corrective to traditional understandings of virtue. He moves away from the Aristotelian tendency to speak of 'heroic *individuals*' and instead makes clear that Scripture speaks to a distinctive *community*.[28] According to Wells, whereas writers like Aristotle were primarily concerned to inspire their readers to be heroes, the concern of the biblical writers is to inspire them to be 'saints in communion'. The differences between the two designations are noticeable in the kind of stories they tell. The hero is always at the center of their story, whereas saints remain on the periphery of a story that is really about God. The hero's story is all about their virtuous qualities, whereas the saint has but one quality of faithfulness. The story of the hero presumes a world of violence that sets the stage for a great reckoning, whereas the saint knows that such a reckoning has already been accomplished, setting the stage for great acts of love. The fate of the world lies on the success of heroes, whereas saints are able to rejoice even in their failures; and finally, heroes stand alone, whereas saints 'assume, demand, require…the communion of saints'.[29] This difference in characterisation is noticeable in Hauerwas's approach to Scripture, where he is concerned to produce witnesses ('martyrs') who have been trained to embody the story of Scripture through the life of the church.

This leads to the third observation. Hauerwas makes it clear that only the community that understands its life as defined by Jesus's story can properly interpret and embody this Scripture. 'Our ability to be truthful peacemakers depends on our learning that we owe our lives to God's unrelenting forgiveness.'[30] This requires a church that has been trained to interpret its common life in the light of Jesus's story, and in particular how he is the mediator of God's redemptive forgiveness.[31] In order for the church to confront sin as the forgiven community, it must also 'have a language and correlative habit that makes it possible to know what it is to

27. Ibid., 95–96.

28. Ibid., 96.

29. Wells, *Improvisation*, 43–44.

30. Hauerwas, *Christian Existence Today*, 93.

31. We noted before that this is how Hauerwas understands salvation in narrative terms: 'salvation comes only when we cease trying to interpret Jesus' story in light of our history, and instead we interpret ourselves in the light of his'; Hauerwas, *Peaceable Kingdom*, 90.

be a sinner'.[32] Being formed in the language of Scripture and allowing its life to be interpreted *by* Scripture is indispensable to the church's performance *of* Scripture. This is why those who reject the church's efforts to avoid sin must be treated as 'Gentiles or tax-collectors' – viz., outside the law and grammar of this political community – because they have not learnt to see themselves as those who are sinners in constant need of forgiveness.[33]

The final feature of Hauerwas's reading highlights the polemical edge of ecclesial ethics, as he reads Scripture *over against* the world's violence. Hauerwas frequently describes the mission of the church in terms of how its 'witness' or 'example' serves to 'confront and challenge the false peace of the world'.[34] Accordingly, what the world often calls peace is but a mask for untruth, forgetfulness, and even violence, all of which need to be exposed by the performed practice of truthful peacemaking. Without this witness, the '*world has no alternative* but to use violence as the means to settle disputes', argues Hauerwas.[35] The church's primary social responsibility is therefore to embody texts like Matthew 18 in order to be of service to the world, seeking out the 'development of processes and institutions that make possible confrontation and resolution of differences so that violence can be avoided'.[36]

Hauerwas's theological interpretation of Matt. 18.15-22 offers a specific description of what it means for the church to be the organized form of Jesus's story. 'Peacemaking among Christians', he writes, 'is not simply one activity among others but rather is the very form of the church insofar as the church is the form of the one who "is our peace"'.[37] Hauerwas's reading of this text is specifically concerned with the community of faith, although as a final comment he argues that this peacemaking process points to a way of 'confronting the wrongdoer with the offer of reconciliation' that extends beyond this community.[38] This brings us close to what we have described as restorative justice, although Hauerwas never connects this text with justice-making.

Characteristic of his Anabaptist tradition, Yoder interprets Matt. 18.15-22 as directed to 'the covenant community' that understands discipleship in terms of a lived commitment to mutual correction after the '*rule of*

32. Hauerwas, *Christian Existence Today*, 93.
33. Ibid., 94.
34. Ibid., 95.
35. Ibid., 95 (italics mine).
36. Ibid., 96.
37. Ibid., 95.
38. Ibid., 96.

Christ'.[39] Needless to say, this commitment has not been consistently practiced in the church's history. Yoder is concerned to point to a different way of being church, which is why his interpretation offers both a more careful reading of the context of Matthew 18 as well as challenging the assumptions of other ecclesial traditions.

Yoder initially proceeds from an exposition of the terms 'bind' and 'loose'. These terms were originally at home in rabbinic Judaism, designating the making of interpretive judgments on the Torah. To bind was to 'enjoin, to forbid or make obligatory', even if that meant withholding fellowship, whereas to loose was to 'leave free, to permit', or to forgive.[40] Together these terms formed a moral tradition, what the rabbis called *halakah*, which was intended to guide God's people in faithfulness to the law. In passing the authority to bind and loose to the church, Jesus simultaneously makes two scandalous claims. He indirectly claims for himself the authority to forgive sins – which was the sole prerogative of God – and he claims to be able to pass this authority onto ordinary people, like fishermen and tax gatherers, in a way that binds God to their decisions.

By implication, the church's commission to admonish and forgive sins only makes sense when it confesses Jesus as God's Messiah (in Matt. 16 the power to bind and loose is given to Peter straight after his confession of Jesus as Messiah), and it can only presume to share in the Messiah's authority as it is empowered by his Spirit (Matt. 18.19-20; cf. Deut. 17.6; 19.15).[41] This presents us with the key concepts for understanding Yoder's ecclesial imagination: a messianic community, empowered by Jesus's spirit, a voluntary commitment to the way of Jesus, lived out in the practices of mutual correction and forgiveness of sin. Unlike Hauerwas, Yoder locates the church's distinctiveness not in its exemplary display of some virtue, but rather in the authority that Jesus extends to it.

Yoder is acutely attentive to the practical and relational needs involved when admonishing a wrongdoer. First, steps must be taken to ensure the process is *confidential*, so as to avoid causing any further injury by erroneous and defamatory gossip. Second, the thoroughly *conversational* nature of the process ensures that each party has the opportunity to listen and so become involved in discovering where they have failed one another, and thus also to become involved in each other's recovery. Third, by being bound to its local *communal* context, the process protects the offending party from suffering the consequences of an abstract legalism, as well as protecting the victim from bureaucratic neglect.

39. Yoder, 'Binding and Loosing', 338–39.

40. Ibid., 327.

41. Ibid., 330–32.

The entire process is oriented, in Yoder's assessment, to 'a kind of moral solidarity linking all the members of the body so that if individuals persist in disobedience within the fellowship, their guilt is no longer the moral responsibility of those individuals alone but becomes a kind of collective blame shared by the whole body'.[42] This is what it means concretely to 'bear one another's burdens' (Gal. 6.2). It points to the irreducibly relational nature of human beings in both causing offense and in taking the necessary steps to repair the damage done. As Yoder writes, 'healing, whether from sin or from sickness, is inseparable from the healing of human relationships'.[43] These insights influenced, and were influenced by, the shifts occurring in Mennonite circles during the 1970–80s, which explains the similar-sounding language and reasoning noted in the early restorative justice initiatives.

Yoder expands the implications of this text beyond fraternal forgiveness to describe 'the practical and theological foundation for the centrality of the local congregation'.[44] He claims that with every revival or renewal movement, like those which followed Wesley or Keswick, there was first a 'renewed experience of the gift of openness, the capacity given by grace to be transparent with the brother about one's own sins and the brother's and thereby to make concrete the assurance of forgiveness'.[45] Yoder first illuminates how to 'bind and loose' creates an interrelationship between forgiveness and discernment.[46] To forgive sins requires the prior discernment of some shared moral standards by which sins are knowable, which in turn demands a community that actively fosters relationships where enmity and injury are being reconciled. Yoder goes on to identify three features that distinguish this kind of community, and he does so by blending together Scriptural mandates with his own Believers Church tradition.[47]

42. Ibid., 336.
43. Ibid., 351.
44. Ibid., 352.
45. Ibid., 340.
46. See ibid., 328–30.
47. This study by Yoder first appeared in the *Concern* pamphlet series (February 1967) and it was situated next to Balthasar Hubmaier's 1527 treatise on the subject, which Yoder would later co-edit with H. Wayne Pipkin as part of the collected work *Balthasar Hubmaier: Theologian of Anabaptism* (Scottdale, PA: Herald Press, 1989). See the front matter to Yoder's essay in ibid., 323. However, Yoder intended the revised edition of his essay to be more ecumenical in scope; hence his comments about the mistaken assumptions that different denominational traditions have made in relation to this text.

First, following the few descriptions of congregational decision-making found in the New Testament, especially 1 Corinthians 12–14, it seems clear to Yoder that 'every member has a right, perhaps a duty, to share in the process'.[48] This highly democratic style of meeting is as a result of the Spirit's presence throughout the whole body of believers, bringing them to reach a divinely inspired consensus as they grasp the full implications of Jesus's teaching (John 14.16). Second, the act of binding and loosing gives new significance to the authority of Scripture: its proper context is as it is read and embodied by believers seeking guidance on how to respond to concrete situations in their witness and obedience.[49] Scripture serves the purpose given it by the apostle Paul: 'it is for teaching, reproof, correction, and instruction in right behavior'.[50] Third, in Believers Church congregations, the 'rule of Christ' serves to mark out those who have submitted to the covenant community. Yoder observes that without this voluntary commitment to a community of mutual concern there can be no practice of fraternal admonition.[51]

An important feature of Yoder's essay is the way in which he traces the numerous misunderstandings, diversions, and detours around this text in other ecclesial traditions. The church has constantly reneged on its call to enact processes for confronting wrongdoing, and has also failed to achieve full reconciliation among its members. While Yoder does not mention the criminal justice system, he was surely cognizant of how that system exemplifies the 'unreconciled divisions and conflicts' which have yet to be transformed by the practices of 'openness and forgiveness'.[52] His interpretation beckons for this kind of embodied practice of restorative justice, and he is surely correct that in order for any ecclesial practice to be lasting it must arise from a recovery of the church as a restorative fellowship.

For both Yoder and Hauerwas, Scripture describes the distinctive character of the church, yet it only has authority insofar as the church seeks to embody it in its life before God. The greatest task facing interpreters is

48. Ibid., 342.

49. This sentence is adapted from, ibid., 353.

50. Ibid.

51. As is now well known, Yoder would eventually submit himself to this process of church discipline while being investigated for claims of sexual misconduct. He did so begrudgingly and no final resolution was reached from the process. Only later was the extent of his abuse revealed and so also the failings of the process he himself advocated for. This does not suggest that the text of Matthew 18 is irrelevant, but rather that it is a very difficult process to get right.

52. Ibid., 350.

not the historical distance between the text and its contemporary readers, but the moral and theological distance between how Scripture describes the task of the church and the failure of the empirical church to embody that task – which, according to Matthew 18, entails embodying Jesus's reign of peace. The church is an exemplary community only insofar as it visibly witnesses to Jesus's reign of peace. To fail to do so is a problem not just for the church but also for wider society. This is because it is through the church that 'the world' can acknowledge itself to be such, and so seek to be transformed.

Yoder and Hauerwas show how the importance of recovering the centrality of the church is not because of its superiority or sinlessness, but quite the opposite. The church, as a community of forgiven *sinners*, is the one place where violence, untruth, and distrust between its members can be openly acknowledged for what it really is: sin. Yet as a community of *forgiven* sinners, such sinfulness can be confronted without threatening to destroy the very fabric of this community, because this community has been formed by, and trained in, the virtue of peacemaking. The visibility of the church is therefore central to the 'witness of the church', which, as Yoder writes, 'always includes and may sometimes center upon the quality of personal relationships that even the outsider may observe'.[53]

The Biblical Imagination

We have presented restorative justice as an example of the ecclesiological embodiment of the justice of God, as discerned in Scripture. But this claim can only be substantiated if it can be shown that God's justice in Scripture is, indeed, a restorative justice *par excellence*. But this is not how it has been typically understood in the history of interpretation. It was pointed out in the first chapter that, as a result of how justice has been understood, the church has through the centuries failed to embody consistently the restorative justice of God. Justice was typically understood in a dual sense: in the human realm, it required that evil be repressed through the punishments ordained by the state, and in the divine realm it meant the justification of the penitent so that individual believers might stand acquitted before God. Even in its divine form, justice understood as justification tended to be interpreted in an abstract, individualistic, and retributivist sense, thereby failing to generate the social face of justice in the lives of believers.

53. Ibid., 352.

Such perceptions need to be undone if the church is to recover its mandate to 'become the justice of God' (2 Cor. 5.21). To achieve this requires a brief examination of the presuppositions behind problematic interpretations of justice in Scripture, and a re-reading of how the justice of God operates in the biblical narrative. This groundwork will pave the way in the following chapters for a more extended consideration of how the church might embody the justice of God in light of one of Jesus's parables and one of Paul's letters.

(Mis)Interpreting Justice in Scripture

Why have interpreters been able to reach conclusions about the nature of justice in the bible in ways far removed from those of restorative justice? There are two contributory factors. First, translations of the biblical terms into other languages have made it difficult to detect all the justice-related connections that occur in Scripture. This has resulted in a truncated understanding of justice, limited in the most part to a forensic context that emphasizes the strictly juridical dimensions of justice. Second, there has been a powerful interpretative framework that brings a set of preconceived ideas about the nature of justice to the task. While appearing to be biblically based, this interpretative framework has recast the story of God's justice revealed in Christ's cross and fulfilled at final judgment as essentially retributive. Both these factors have proved disastrous and deserve fuller comment.

English translations of the Bible have tended to divide justice references into two main word groups. First, from the Latin stem *ius* we get 'justice', 'justification', and 'just'; and second, from the Anglo-Saxon *riht* we get 'righteousness', 'righteous', and 'right'. The concept of 'right' has no cognate verb, and it has made little sense to translators to continue with Old English phrases like 'to right' or 'right-wised'.[54] This has resulted in 'righteousness' being understood as a self-contained moral attribute of piety or holiness, lacking any active, relational, or dynamic nuance. This has led translators to make recourse to the 'just' word group for the verbal notions of biblical justice. However, even the words 'justified' and 'justification' fail to convey the social and relational dynamics of their biblical equivalents. This is particularly evident in contemporary treatments of justification, which, despite the obvious linguistic link, fail

54. Although the phrase 'right-wise' does infrequently appear in place of the usual 'justify'; see, for example, Morna D. Hooker, 'On Becoming the Righteousness of God: Another Look at 2 Cor 5:21', *Novum Testamentum* 50 (2008): 358–75.

to observe its connection to justice.[55] In the opinion of N. T. Wright, the 'older English words "righteousness" and "justification" are more or less dead metaphors'.[56] In short, English translations have tended to reinforce a moralistic, static, and individualistic reading of justice in Scripture.

These linguistic problems may have been compounded by the English language, but they did not start there. Translation problems were already evident in the Septuagint, which attempted to carry over the meaning of the Hebrew into the Koiné Greek. The Greek notion of δικαιοσύνη always ran the risk of being understood in a Hellenistic rather than Hebraic sense. The difference, as McGrath points out, is that δικαιοσύνη was originally a 'fundamentally secular concept incapable of assuming the soteriological overtones associated with the Hebrew term'.[57] It tended to be restricted to the sphere of the human *polis*, which meant that justice was thought to be immanent in the natural order, to which even the gods were subject. This immanent understanding of justice made it possible to interpret the δικαιοσύνη of God as some kind of divine regulating force that ensured each person received exactly what he or she was due. This problem was ameliorated by the predominantly Jewish readership of the Septuagint, and in the New Testament writings, by the carefully crafted use of the δικαιο-word group in ways that subverted its Hellenistic meaning.

The real problem arose with the translation of the justice concept into the Latin *ius*, which distanced the concept even further from its original range of meaning. It also upset the careful construction of the δικαιο terms in the New Testament. Justice, translated as *iustitia*, came to be narrowly defined as rendering to another their moral desert, whether as reward or punishment. Within this definition, justice stands opposed to mercy, such that 'mercy involves setting aside the demands of justice and treating persons contrary to what they justly deserve'.[58] Thus, when God

55. For example, in 2005 Douglas Harink reviewed four contemporary books on justification and reached the lamentable conclusion that all treatments remained within a narrow, individualistic mode of interpretation, failing to observe justification's social and political connection to justice; Douglas Harink, 'Setting It Right: Doing Justice to Justification', *Christian Century* (2005): 20–25. See also Harink, 'Romans: A Treatise on Justice?', *Direction: A Mennonite Brethren Forum* 44, no. 1 (2015): 30–42.

56. N. T. Wright, 'Translating δικαιοσύνη: A Response', *The Expository Times* 125, no. 10 (2014): 487.

57. Alister E. McGrath, *Iustitia Dei: A History of the Christian Doctrine of Justification* (Cambridge: Cambridge University Press, 2005), 15.

58. Marshall, *Beyond Retribution*, 44.

is said 'to justify' (*iustificare*), it is not understood as God's prerogative to vindicate those upon whom he chooses to have mercy, but rather to reward the one whose cause is just, while reserving his punishment for the unjust.[59] If God is to remain a God of justice, his mercy must give way to the need to satisfy his prior justice, since the two do not belong together. But this not only disrupts the connections preserved in the Hebrew meaning, it turns the relationship between the justice of God and the human predicament on its head. Sinful humanity is now required to be saved *from* God's justice rather than *by* it.

The context for understanding God's justice was also affected by the Latin translation. As we will see shortly, the biblical context for understanding the justice of God is the covenantal relationship between YHWH and Israel. The Hebrew term for covenant (ברית) was translated by the Latin term *foedus*, which, according to James Torrance, carried a more contractual than covenantal meaning.[60] This opened the door for God's relationship to humanity to be conceived in terms of a juridical contract, with the law (*lex*) spelling out the conditions of this relationship. Within this context, the *iustitia Dei* was understood as God's prerogative to punish those who transgressed against the conditions of the divine human contract.

In the Western tradition the Latinized interpretation of the justice of God helped to foster an image of God as a 'cosmic lawgiver and judge' who upholds strict retributive justice, rewarding the righteous and punishing the guilty according to their deserts.[61] With the spread of natural law thinking, all humanity was thought to be accountable to this God, and especially those who were criminals. Prisons came to be adorned with images of Christ suffering on the cross as an icon of judicial punishment, providing the symbolic logic for a cultural space marked

59. For a description of the distorting effect of *ius*-terms, see McGrath, *Iustitia Dei*, 18.

60. Torrance defines a contract as, 'a *legal* relationship in which two people or two parties bind themselves together on mutual *conditions* to effect some future result'; James B. Torrance, 'Covenant or Contract? A Study of the Theological Background of Worship in Seventeenth-Century Scotland', *Scottish Journal of Theology* 23 (1970): 54. Originating in the Roman classical period there were two forms that this relationship could take: *foedus aequum*, which was a bilateral legal relationship between parties of equal standing; and *foedus iniquum*, whereby one party had supreme sovereignty with the other party(s) expected to render unconditional obedience. The plural form of *foedus* is *foedera*, from which the word for federation is derived.

61. Douglas A. Campbell, *The Deliverance of God: An Apocalyptic Rereading of Justification in Paul* (Grand Rapids, MI: Eerdmans, 2009), 15, 32.

by degradation, pain infliction, and death.[62] Just as Christ was punished according to God's justice for the sins of the world, so criminals were subjected to harsh and degrading punishments for the expiation of their sins. The judgment executed on Christ was re-enacted on prisoners, as exemplary sinners, to wash away their guilt so they could stand ready for God's ultimate judgment.

While translation has contributed to the problem, linguistics alone did not produce the reading of the justice of God as retributive, individualistic, and unmerciful. Interpreters have also brought with them a set of preconceived ideas about the nature of justice that have served as an overarching interpretive grid. For example, one common interpretative framework has recast the story of Scripture around two central axioms: justice as retributive and salvation as individualistic. This framework has recently been described by Douglas Campbell as 'Justification Theory', although it may equally be described as a 'theory of justice' that has informed the reading of justification in the bible.[63]

According to Campbell, this theory of justification arose in the modern era as a result of some distorting dynamics in reading the apostle Paul's δικαιο-texts. These dynamics rest on a foundationalist epistemology that owes more to modern notions of the individual, society, and justice, than to the Scriptural story. The church has, by and large, capitulated to this epistemology whenever it construes salvation in fundamentally conditional and unmerciful terms, directed primarily to individuals.

In Campbell's opinion, 'few discourses are more prone to subliminal cultural projection than judicial ones'.[64] This has presented an acute problem for the Christian understanding of salvation, which in the Western tradition of interpretation has predominantly drawn on Paul's 'forensic' texts (especially, Rom. 1–4; Gal. 3.21-26). According to this tradition, the key problem being addressed in these texts is how sinful individuals might be saved from the retributive justice of God. It is assumed God cannot simply forgive those who have transgressed his law, since that would be contrary to God's nature as just and holy. Paul provides a two-step solution to this predicament. First, God sends forth his Son to satisfy the penalty of sinful humanity by undergoing the punishment of death, thus requiting God's punitive justice. Justification

62. Gorringe, *God's Just Vengeance*, 23.

63. Campbell, *Deliverance of God*, esp. 11–95.

64. Campbell, 'Is Tom Right? An Extended Review of N. T. Wright's *Justification: God's Plan and Paul's Vision*', *Scottish Journal of Theology* 65, no. 3 (2012): 336.

entails 'status declarations', in terms of guilt or acquittal.[65] Second, in order to appropriate the benefits of this saved condition, individuals need to exercise faith, understood as the rational acceptance of what God has done in Christ.[66] The Pauline phrase 'justification by faith' is assumed to be the condensed form of this two-stage salvation scheme.

According to Campbell, this salvation theory begins with a theological interpretation of the biblical material, rather than with what the text itself reveals about the nature of justice and salvation. As a *theory*, it brings to the text a set of preconceived criteria about justice derived from the human situation, which then determines what questions get asked of the text, as well as what counts as an answer. This is what Campbell means by a 'foundationalist epistemology', a problem that has plagued Christian thought from at least the time of Arianism.[67] In particular, this salvation theory begins with fundamental 'commitments to individualism, to consent, and to the practice of regulating human relationships through conditionality and contract'.[68] It analogizes salvation in terms of a contract – or a series of contracts – in a similar way to the sixteenth-century doctrine of the Western *ordo salutis*. This theory provided a reading of the biblical text that owes more to Western notions of the individual, society, and justice, than it does to the categories of Scripture.

Campbell's goal is to expose the master metaphors and analogies shaping this justification discourse. Alongside the analogy of a contract, it presupposes that 'the justice of God that undergirds the created cosmos is…retributive – bound to reward the righteous inevitably and punish the guilty implacably'.[69] This presumption also works in a foundationalist sense. Campbell points out that this presumption has a foundationalist character to it, since God's character as retributive and legislative is known apart from any special revelation. It is solely by our conscience that we know ourselves to be guilty and deserving of God's judgment. 'In a very real sense', as Campbell portrays this theory, '*ethical legislation* based on *retributive justice* is the fundamental structure of the universe, as

65. According to this theory, the meaning of Paul's *δικαιο* terms are concerned with 'status' declarations, whether it is humanity being declared innocent or with God being declared faithful; ibid., 328.

66. Campbell, *Deliverance of God*, 24.

67. Ibid., 30–34; see also, 'An Apocalyptic Rereading of "Justification" in Paul: Or, an Overview of the Argument of Campbell's *The Deliverance of God* – by Douglas Campbell', *The Expository Times* 123, no. 8 (2012): 385.

68. Campbell, *Deliverance of God*, 7.

69. Ibid., 15–16.

well as of the divine nature'.[70] This model of justification offers far more than a reading of Paul's δικαιο-texts; it offers a view of the cosmos and of God's nature understood in fundamentally moralistic and retributive terms.

Clearly then, the terminology used to translate the biblical notion of justice, combined with a set of foundational claims about God and his justice, have produced interpretations of Scripture that are truncated at best, and the antithesis of Paul's gospel of God's saving justice, at worst. These interpretations have had a deleterious impact on the realm of criminal justice. Ecclesial ethics invites a re-reading of Scripture that gives priority to the ecclesial rather than the judicial context for understanding the justice of God. It is to this task we now turn.

Covenantal and Christological Justice

The place to begin is with a fresh consideration of Paul's 'forensic' texts, guided by Campbell's perspective. However, a prior methodological point first needs to be clarified. Even though Campbell identifies 'retributive justice' as the driving presupposition behind 'Justification Theory', he does not propose a more restorative understanding in its place.[71] Instead, he emphasizes the ultimately benevolent character of God: 'Paul's root metaphor of God, then, is benevolent, or merciful. *There is no retributive character to the God revealed to Paul by Christ*'.[72] Campbell still regards God's justice to be a central concern in Paul's theology. However, he is cautious about determining the meaning of this term in advance of its disclosure through the Christ event. This was the mistake of the above theory of justification. It determined the nature of God's justice apart from Christ and then applied this notion to his work, thus producing an image of Christ as falling victim to divine justice.

Campbell pursues what might be called a christocentric approach to δικαιοσύνη Θεοῦ, allowing its meaning to be defined in the light of God's self-disclosure in Jesus Christ. He claims that this was Paul's own

70. Ibid., 17.

71. Michael Gorman notes that his own reading of justification shares much in common with Campbell's, although the parallels may not be obvious given that Campbell identifies 'benevolence' as the antithesis to 'retributive justice', rather than, say, 'restorative justice'; Michael J. Gorman, 'Justification and Justice in Paul, with Special Reference to the Corinthians', *Journal for the Study of Paul and His Letters* 1, no. 1 (2011): 27 n. 19. It is not entirely clear what Gorman intimates by these comments, except that he views his own reading as aligned with a restorative understanding of justice.

72. Campbell, *Deliverance of God*, 706 (italics original).

theological approach, as attested in texts like Rom. 1.17 and 3.21-26.[73] This starting point significantly broadens the content of justice, in that it now incorporates all that is known of Christ, as well as what was achieved through his life, death, and resurrection. Δικαιοσύνη Θεοῦ thus functions as Paul's shorthand for all God has accomplished *through* Christ now being made available for those who are *in* Christ. By implication, Campbell argues that the justice of God is best understood as an event more than an attribute, disclosed through the particular story of Jesus. It is, moreover, a saving or a liberating event, in the sense of being freed from captivity, as well as being brought into a life-giving state. God's justice has a direction, moving away from enslavement to the age of sin and death and towards the eschatological age of resurrection life.[74]

By situating Paul's δικαιο-language within the wider narrative context of Jesus's life, Campbell reveals how limiting it is to read Paul's forensic texts in the modern judicial sense of declaring a verdict. Paul's language is far more flexible than this; it is equally capable of speaking about Christ as the disclosure *of* the justice of God, revealing who God truly is, as well as the justice *from* God, in the sense of pointing us towards God.[75] This is nowhere more clearly demonstrated than in the cross and resurrection of Christ through which the nature *of* God's justice as benevolent is revealed, and the distorted conceptions of justice represented by those who crucified him are overturned.[76] At other times, Paul can use δικαιο-terms in relation to its liberating implications for humanity, since the Spirit is now incorporating people into Christ's death and resurrection as participants in God's δικαιοσύνη.[77] These textual nuances have been obliterated in the translation history noted above.

Campbell proposes that Paul's use of δικαιοσύνη Θεοῦ has deep resonances in the ancient discourse of kingship, and in particular texts like Ps. 98.2-3 that speak of God as king acting to bring about his victory. Paul's purpose in alluding to this kingship discourse is to reinforce what has already been said explicitly: 'In undertaking this act in Christ, God is

73. 'It is clearly one of the central claims of 1:17 and 3:21-26 that the δικαιοσύνη Θεοῦ is disclosed by Christ definitively'; ibid., 683.

74. These designations are spelled out much further in ibid., 684–87.

75. Ibid., 687–88.

76. See Campbell's summary in ibid., 688–99.

77. Ibid., 701. See also Campbell's 'pneumatologically participatory martyrological eschatology' account of Paul's gospel, replete with ethical implications; Douglas Campbell, *The Quest for Paul's Gospel: A Suggested Strategy* (London: T&T Clark International, 2005).

operating as the divine King ought to, delivering his captive creation from its bondage; he is therefore doing the "right" thing, acting as his character and role demand. And δικαιοσύνη Θεοῦ is, as a result and in essence, the deliverance of God.'[78] Paul's justice language is to be understood as deliverance language, deliverance specifically from those powers that are arraigned in opposition to the kingdom inaugurated by Christ and his Spirit.

Paul's understanding of justification, therefore, far from being simply declarative, functions more in a *performative* manner. God justifies in the sense of acting to liberate the captives, which, as Israel's history attests, he does irrespective of whether they deserve that liberation. Paul's justice language 'needs to be read in performative terms as a divine act – a judgment or declaration – that effects release for the captives; it is a command by God in Christ to set the prisoners free!'[79] Jesus's crucifixion does not simply affect a balance on some divine ledger; his entire life is rather the consistent enactment of God's determination to restore humanity to freedom. The benevolent character of God's justice is thus perfectly encapsulated in the claim that 'God justifies the ungodly' – a claim that cannot properly be said of the foundationalist theory of justification, which inserts a prior ethical and penal criterion to which even Christ is subject.[80]

This reading of δικαιοσύνη Θεοῦ in Paul parallels many of the same themes emphasized by those who interpret the justice of God as a restorative justice. For example, Michael Gorman argues that 'the justice of God' has nothing to do with retribution, but must rather be understood as 'God's saving, liberating, and restorative justice'.[81] Paul's justification language is about the restoration and renewal of human relationships made possible by 'practices of justice' that are liberative and transformative.[82] Considering that human dysfunction is profoundly manifest in practices of violence towards others, Gorman argues that justification has the specific determination of creating a people who embody a just peace. 'In Christ, justice and peace embrace, and in Christ God was – and is – making a people into the justice of God'.[83]

78. Campbell, *Deliverance of God*, 702.

79. Ibid., 663.

80. Ibid., 668.

81. Gorman, 'Justification and Justice', 28 n. 20.

82. He writes, 'justification must do something about injustice by making liberation from practices of injustice possible and practices of justice attainable'; ibid., 29.

83. Ibid., 40.

Likewise, Christopher Marshall provides an excellent survey on the biblical notion of justice, concluding that the 'justice of God is not primarily or normatively a retributive justice or a distributive justice but a restorative or reconstructive justice, a saving action by God that recreates *shalom* and makes things right'.[84] Read in this light, Paul's gospel is thoroughly concerned with 'God's definitive eschatological justice-initiative' through the life, death, and resurrection of Jesus Christ. Having entered into the depths of the human condition, Christ absorbed the full punitive power of sin in order that humanity might be absorbed into God's saving justice. This exchange carries with it the implication that believers are to become 'vehicles of restorative justice in God's afflicted world', pursuing the restoration of relationships and the recreation of shalom.[85]

Other examples could be cited, all showing that a better reading of the justice of God is possible.[86] Eschewing the demands of retribution and the vindication of an abstract law, the justice of God is concerned with the liberation/deliverance/restoration of a people from a captive state into a life-giving/restored/peace-orientated state. This is a better reading because it allows justice to be defined by God's self-disclosure in Christ and makes clear that the proper context for the embodiment of God's justice is the church, not the judicial system.

While Paul saw the Christ-event as definitive for understanding the justice of God, he still drew on an existing linguistic stock of biblical terms in order to express the present eschatological reality of Jesus Christ as the justice of God. Some appreciation of the Hebraic background of these terms is therefore essential to understanding his message. The notion of justice in the Hebrew Scriptures is represented primarily by משפט (often translated 'justice') and צדק (often rendered 'righteousness') word groups. These two terms are frequently found together as a hendiadys – 'justice and righteousness' – indicating they are mutually reinforcing.[87] משפט has tended to be translated as 'justice' because of its

84. Marshall, *Beyond Retribution*, 53.

85. Ibid., 69.

86. For example, see Belousek, *Atonement, Justice, and Peace*. At a more popular level see the contributions by Derek Flood, *Healing the Gospel: A Radical Vision for Grace, Justice, and the Cross* (Eugene, OR: Wipf & Stock, 2012); Gordon M. Zerbe, 'From Retributive to Restorative Justice in Romans', *Direction: A Mennonite Brethren Forum* 44, no. 1 (2015): 43–58.

87. Some interpret these two terms together as constituting what in contemporary parlance is meant by 'social justice', or what Swartley describes as the '*social face of righteousness*'; Willard M. Swartley, 'The Relation of Justice/Righteousness to *Shalom/Eirênê*', *Ex Auditu* 22 (2006): 31.

connection to categories of judgment and equity. Temba Mafico suggests that there is 'strong evidence that attests that originally the substantive *mispât* referred to the restoration of a situation or environment which promoted equity and harmony (*sâlôm*) in a community'.[88] The emphasis of משפט is on the re-establishment or restoration of rightness among relationships, an action that takes place in the context of judgment. It was specifically employed in cases where cultural and ritual ordinances were being ignored (Exod. 15.25), or when the unjust treatment of disadvantaged groups prevailed (Deut. 16.18-20; 24.17). This second theme became particularly prominent in the Prophets and the Psalter – especially with respect to the widow, stranger, and orphan – because the existence of the oppressed highlighted the lack of justice in Israel (cf. Pss. 9.7-12; 82.1-8; Amos 5.21-24; Mic. 6.6-8).[89]

The term צדק or 'righteousness' is a much more complex term to define because of the range of other concepts it brings into its service. Interpreters argue over its most fundamental force; some of the candidates are 'justice', 'straightness', 'integrity', 'deliverance', or 'salvation'.[90] What is clear is that the term goes beyond the simple definition of 'not doing wrong' in the sense of transgressing rules and regulations. צדק is '*comprehensively relational*', as Marshall puts it; it is particularly concerned with how one acts towards another for the sake of the relationship.[91] It is not so much an internal disposition or virtue, such that one could possess צדק in isolation from others. As a concept, it is oriented towards the active seeking of relationships that are 'right', in the sense of being whole or at peace.[92]

The relational nature of Hebrew justice explains why it so often appears in connection with the concept of covenant (ברית), understood as

88. Temba L. J. Mafico, 'Just, Justice', in *The Anchor Bible Dictionary*, ed. D. N. Freedman, 6 vols. (New York: Doubleday, 1992), 3:1128.

89. Tanner argues that judgments of mercy in favor of oppressed persons represented 'the highest form of justice that the covenant with Yahweh demands... [R]elations of mercy in which one forfeits what one is owed and gets back what one no longer deserves, what one no longer has a title to, in virtue of debts incurred'; Kathryn Tanner, 'Justification and Justice in a Theology of Grace', *Theology Today* (1999): 516.

90. See, for example, J. J. Scullion, 'Righteousness, Old Testament', in Freedman, ed., *The Anchor Bible Dictionary*, 5:724–26; Nancy Declaissé-Walford, 'Righteousness in the OT', in *The New Interpreters Dictionary of the Bible*, ed. H. R. McMurray (Nashville, TN: Abingdon Press, 2009), 818–19.

91. Marshall, *Beyond Retribution*, 47.

92. Ibid., 36.

a committed relationship. Many biblical interpreters view the covenantal relationship between YHWH and the people of Israel as the primary context for understanding צדק.[93] According to James Torrance, 'a covenant is a promise binding two people or two parties to love one another *unconditionally*'.[94] There were two basic types of covenant: a bilateral covenant between two equals that carried mutual obligations (e.g., a marriage), and a unilateral covenant initiated by one party for the sake of another (e.g., a king to his subjects). It was this latter type that formed the relationship between YHWH and Israel. The covenant was not conditioned by anything YHWH found in Israel, which means that it was freely initiated, an act of grace or love on the part of YHWH. A relationship based on unconditional grace called for an equally unconditional response of devotion to YHWH, on the part of Israel.[95]

Within this covenantal relationship, צדק took the form of faithfulness or loyalty. On Israel's part this meant living in accord with ירה ('law'), understood as God's gift to Israel to conform the people to the ways of God.[96] Faithfulness to law was considered to be liberating, because of its orientation towards shalom, the life-giving peace of God. Law had more of a pedagogical function promoting rightness and peace across all areas of Israelite life, rather than a punitive or prescriptive function.[97] The notion of ירה was not understood as a strictly *legal* obligation in terms of conformity to a rule, but rather as a *filial* obligation to live in a just peace, as YHWH himself is peace and justice.[98] The justice expected of Israel was to be found in faithfulness to YHWH, exhibited in social relationships that were just, caring, and peaceful, as specified in the law.[99]

93. See Ziesler, 1972. Marshall agrees with this '*comprehensively relational*' definition of צדק, ibid., 47.

94. Torrance, 'Covenant or Contract', 54.

95. Torrance thus characterizes this covenant as *unconditioned* and *unconditional*, both free and costly.

96. Vincent E. Bacote, 'Justice', in *Dictionary for Theological Interpretation of the Bible*, ed. Kevin J. Vanhoozer (Grand Rapids, MI: Baker Academic, 2005), 415.

97. 'The law provided a pattern for living in covenant, for living in *shalom*. Specific laws were considered to be just…because they sustained *shalom* within the community'; Marshall, *Beyond Retribution*, 48.

98. As J. B. Torrance puts it, the *torah* spells 'out the unconditional obligations of grace as the Father's loving heart coming out to us in the form of commandments'; 'Introduction', in John McLeod Campbell, *The Nature of Atonement*, 2nd ed. (Grand Rapids, MI: Eerdmans, 1996 [1856]), 1.

99. As Dunn and Suggate put it, Israel were to 'conform social relationships to the model of the caring family'; Dunn and Suggate, *Justice of God*, 42.

The people of Israel repeatedly failed to reflect the righteousness expected of them. They failed, in other words, to be 'image bearers' of God's צדק by being unconditionally faithful to the covenant, and so also to their neighbor as expressed through the law.[100] Israel's failure did not, however, place conditions on God to exact retribution in keeping with his justice. Rather, Israel's failure called forth YHWH's צדק as a *merciful* justice, showing his unconditional faithfulness to Israel by restoring the covenantal relationship. God's justice was satisfied not by the punishment of Israel, though this often occurred, but rather by its rescue and salvation, even when it did not deserve to be rescued. 'For Israel, the justice of God was not an abstract theological or philosophical axiom; it was something about God's being learned from the concrete experience of God's actions of claiming, blessing, and rescuing Israel'. Marshall concludes that, 'Righteousness language in the Hebrew Bible is thus *action* language as well as relational language'.[101] It was an action expressed, moreover, as mercy.

The justice of God filled Israel with hope more than fear. For example, Isaiah prophesies of the day when the 'king will reign in צדק, and princes will rule with משפט', and how on that day 'משפט will dwell in the wilderness, and צדק abide in the fruitful field. The effect of צדק will be peace (שלם), and the result of צדק quietness and trust forever' (Isa. 32.1, 16-17; cf. 9.6; 28.17). This is a vision of justice where the world is restored to rightness or shalom. The justice of God, in essence, is a restorative justice, and one that was to be reflected among God's people. As recipients of God's mercy and faithfulness, Israel was called to be 'image bearers' of God's restorative justice, conforming its communal life to the word of God in ירה.

The LXX translation of משפט and צדק predominantly into δικ-terms introduced the possibility of misconstruing Hebraic justice/righteousness in Hellenistic terms. In Greek thought, justice defined as δικαιοσύνη was originally concerned with a proper distribution in the political and ethical realm, which does have some resonances with the forensic function of משפט. This distribution, however, was in accord with a norm or standard that is more in line with notions of merit and excellence than with the

100. I take this reading of the *imago Dei* from Alan Torrance who argues that Gen. 1.26-28 must be understood in the light of the covenant that frames the entire exposition and redaction of the Pentateuch/Hexateuch. To be 'image bearers' is to reflect, or 'co-respond' as Torrance puts it, the manner of God's faithfulness to the covenant people of Israel; Torrance, '"Ought" from "Is"', 173.

101. Marshall, *Beyond Retribution*, 50.

kinds of relationships specified in the Hebrew covenant. A person was considered *δικαιος* ('just') if he lived in conformity to duty or tradition, which was considered its own reward.[102] Hellenistic *δικαιοσύνη* was not restricted to legal obedience, since it can be found in connection with philanthropy and faithfulness in friendship.[103] Applying *δικαιοσύνη* to God would have been understood more in the sense of God's virtue being displayed in the just distribution of rewards and punishment (verb: *δικαιοω*), whereas the Hebrew sense of God's צדק is of a saving and vindicating action towards God's covenant people.[104]

The difficulties associated with use of the *δικ*-terms in the LXX were ameliorated by its predominantly Jewish audience, which would have transferred Hebraic understandings to the Greek terminology. As a result, the LXX represented a significant broadening of the Greek terminology, mostly due to its being subsumed under the covenantal framework.[105] *Δικαιοσύνη* came to be read in conjunction with God's mercy and faithfulness, active in the vindication of God's covenant partner (cf. Deut. 32.4; Mic. 7.9). In fact, the Hebrew notion of צדק was sometimes translated by ἔλεος-terms ('mercy') or *ὅσιος* ('pious' or 'piety'), in order to retain the strong soteriological overtones. At other times, a new word would be created, *δικαιοκρισία* ('just judgment'), to emphasize the role of God as judge. In other cases *δικαιοσύνη* would be used to translate the Hebrew אמת ('faithfulness' or 'truth'), תמלה ('kindness' or 'mercy'), and משפט.[106]

This variation of terms may, however, have had the negative effect of flattening the meaning of משפט and צדק by sometimes translating them in terms of justice, while at other times construing them as mercy, thus implying a separation between God's justice and his mercy.[107] However

102. A frequent citation is *Letters of Aristotle* 127; see Jutta Leonhardt-Balzer, 'Righteousness in Early Jewish Literature', in Sakenfeld, ed., *The New Interpreters Dictionary of the Bible*, 811.

103. This is especially the case in Aristotle, *The Nicomachean Ethics*, V.

104. John Reumann, 'Righteousness, Greco-Roman World', in Freedman, ed., *The Anchor Bible Dictionary*, 5:745. Some see a much sharper contrast between the Greek notion of *δικαιοσύνη* and the Hebrew צדק, such that the phrase *δικαιοσύνη* Θεοῦ can appear to have 'no immediate practical significance'. *Δικαιοσύνη* was a concept that only had a function in the human *polis*, where gods were not considered members let alone deliverers; see McGrath, *Iustitia Dei*, 15.

105. Leonhardt-Balzer, 'Righteousness in Early Jewish Literature', 808.

106. John Reumann, 'Righteousness, Early Judaism', in Freedman, ed., *The Anchor Bible Dictionary*, 5:737.

107. McGrath argues that this would have been the case for Greek readers who were unfamiliar with the Hebrew original; see McGrath, *Iustitia Dei*, 16.

it was clearly the intention of the Jewish authors to preserve the Hebraic meaning of standing in right relationship, which was the controlling idea of the construction δικαιοσύνη Θεοῦ.

The occurrence of δικ-terms in the New Testament stands in continuity with this early Jewish interpretation, with one significant development: the δικαιοσύνη Θεοῦ is now said to have come to fulfillment in the life, death, and resurrection of Jesus Christ. In the Gospels, the primary theme of Jesus's proclamation and work centered on the arrival of God's kingdom, which according to Richard Hays should be understood as the declaration of 'the radical restoration of God's justice, setting things right but bringing judgment and destruction to those who resist God's will'.[108] It was widely expected that the kingdom would usher in the end-time judgment of those who were ἀδικία and ἁμαρτωλός ('unrighteous' and 'sinners'), while at the same time vindicating those who are δικαιος (cf., Luke 15.7; 25.37, 46; Matt. 13.49; 5.45).

Contrary to popular expectations, however, both in his teaching and through the manner of his life, Jesus was highly critical of those who deemed themselves δικαιος (Matt. 23.28-29; 6.1-3; Luke 18.9-12; 20.20), while choosing himself to associate predominantly with the ἁμαρτωλός (Matt. 9.13; Mark 2.15-17). The meaning of Jesus's commandment to 'strive first for the kingdom of God and his δικαιοσύνη' (Matt. 6.33) must therefore be interpreted by the manner of his life oriented towards the ingathering of those who were deemed outside of the covenant.[109] For this reason, God's justice is 'good news to the poor', 'release to the captives', and 'freedom for the oppressed', as Jesus proclaimed in his inaugural sermon (Luke 4.18). The justice of God's kingdom is concerned, therefore, with the liberation of those who have been oppressed or marginalized, and insofar as Jesus enacted this concern through his life, he '*embodied* biblical justice', as Gorman puts it.[110]

If in the Gospel tradition Jesus is understood as a 'prophet of the justice of the reign of God',[111] as Herzog argues, then it is quite appropriate to

108. Hays, *Moral Vision*, 163; cited in Marshall, *Beyond Retribution*, 71.

109. In Neville's opinion, Jesus' proclamation and embodiment of divine justice entailed a degree of 'interpretive innovation'. While divine judgment retains a retributive dimension according to Neville, Jesus reconstructed the understanding of judgment through his own mission to the degree that it was 'neither purely nor even primarily retributive… [Rather] scriptural justice in its truest and deepest sense may be said to be restorative, rectifying or transformative'; Neville, 'Justice and Public Theology', 8.

110. Gorman, 'Justification and Justice', 24.

111. Herzog, *Jesus, Justice and the Reign of God.*

see his ministry as bringing to fulfillment the covenantal relationship. This can be seen in three movements. First, Jesus re-establishes an even stronger *filial* bond between Israel and YHWH by claiming God as Ἀββᾶ ('Father'). Moreover, Jesus embodies God's healing and forgiving power by making it personally accessible to the paralytic, demon possessed, and ἀδικία.[112] Second, Jesus exemplifies the higher δικαιοσύνη expected of God's covenant people (cf. Matt. 5.20), especially through his teaching and example of non-retaliation, enemy-love, and unlimited forgiveness. Third, Jesus forms a community to be 'living witnesses to the transforming character of God's justice', which it does in part through the practices of peacemaking and reconciliation.[113] Moreover, Jesus ensures that this community is empowered to be δικαιος through his example and Spirit.

In the New Testament, Jesus is consistently portrayed as the embodiment of the restorative justice of God. It is through him that God's deliverance of captive humanity is revealed, and it is in him that humanity is restored to a right relationship with God and to one another. It was on account of this experience of God's justice in Christ that the early church 'lived out in their faith communities an understanding of justice as a power that heals, restores, and reconciles rather than hurts, punishes, and kills', and, as Marshall argues, 'that reality ought to shape and direct a Christian contribution to the criminal justice debate today'.[114] That the early followers of Jesus were known for their forgiveness, fellowship, and relational fidelity, testifies to the restorative and relational character of Jesus's mission. As they reflected on Jesus's story, the church came to regard this prophet from Nazareth as the one in whom the reign of God's justice had been fulfilled.

Our brief survey has confirmed that the justice of God in Scripture is primarily a restorative rather than a retributive or punitive justice. This is not to say that retributive features are entirely absent from the biblical material. However, they are subordinate to the conviction that God's justice is first of all a comprehensively liberative, merciful, and

112. Ibid., 130.

113. Christopher D. Marshall, *The Little Book of Biblical Justice: A Fresh Approach to the Bible's Teachings on Justice* (Intercourse, PA: Good Books, 2005), 64; cf. 53–60. Marshall directly addresses the two themes of forgiveness of offenders and nonretaliatory love as characteristic of how Jesus saw 'the triumph of God's royal justice on earth'; Marshall, *Beyond Retribution*, 72–92.

114. Marshall, *Beyond Retribution*, 33.

redemptive justice.[115] For the biblical people of God, justice is a relational concept defined by God's own self-disclosure through the covenant initiated with Israel, and definitively through his own Son. It is on account of this covenantal and christological qualification that the justice of God can rightly be described as a restorative justice.

The next two chapters will flesh this truth out in relation to one of Jesus's parables and one of Paul's epistles. Focusing attention on two specific texts will complement the broader description of biblical justice presented in this chapter. Before moving on, however, we need to draw together some of the threads that have emerged in this chapter and clarify how the recovery of the theological interpretation of Scripture can help to bring about a better practice of justice in the church.

We began this chapter with the claim that restorative justice is a striking example of the ecclesial embodiment of the justice of God. This claim was substantiated, first, by an exploration of the church's identity as the community that embodies the story of Scripture so as to live faithfully before God, which itself is part of a broader renewal of emphasis on the place of the church as a fully social and political body. A consideration of 'binding and loosing' in Matt. 18.15-22 showed that the distinctive character of this body is formed in the task of peacemaking and communal discernment.

Our overriding concern has been to extend the insights of ecclesial ethics into the realm of justice and justice-making, an undertaking that needs to be grounded in the theological interpretation of Scripture. This involves contending with problematic interpretations that have truncated the meaning of biblical justice and brought a set of preconceived ideas and interpretive frameworks about the meaning of justice to the text. By contrast, ecclesial ethics invites us to give priority to the ecclesial rather than judicial context in the interpretation of the justice of God, which involves interpreting justice in the light of the central biblical categories of *covenant* and *Christ*.

Conceiving of biblical justice as a covenantal and christological reality produces a better reading of Scripture. It is better because it involves a reading that calls for a social and embodied response on the part of the reading community. Interpreting biblical justice in strictly forensic terms has eroded the social face of justice, which has made it increasingly

115. Thus I concur with the assessment of Marshall and Neville, who see a subordination of these retributive features in Scripture to an overarching restorative *telos*; Marshall, *Beyond Retribution*, 33; David J. Neville, 'Justice and Divine Judgment: Scriptural Perspectives for Public Theology', *International Journal of Public Theology* 3 (2009): 339–56.

difficult for the church to give concrete expression to its own distinctive conception of justice. By contrast, a covenantal and christological construal of justice carries definite social obligations. In particular, it requires relational faithfulness, a commitment to restore ruptured relationships to rightness or peace, and a bringing of those who are oppressed or held captive into a life-giving freedom.

In asking how the people of God might collectively embody the liberative justice of God revealed in Scripture, the restorative justice movement has much to offer. This is not to suggest that everything which goes under the banner of restorative justice today is synonymous with God's justice, but there are deep resonances between the two streams. One valuable feature of restorative justice theory and practice is the way it critiques the underlying assumptions of the retributive worldview, including its perspective on God. 'The concept of retribution or punishment as justice', as Zehr and Grimsrud illustrate with reference to the historical roots of criminal justice, 'is an issue shaped decisively by beliefs about God and God's character'.[116] This retributive perspective tends to view all infractions against law as personal violations of God's holiness, which in turn invokes God's righteous anger that needs to be satisfied through some 'violent punishment'.[117] Zehr and Grimsrud argue that this interpretation of the biblical text is untenable; it is the result of a selective reading of Scripture and obsessively committed to a 'basic theology of a retributive God who desires violence'.[118]

After surveying the biblical evidence, Zehr and Grimsrud conclude, 'biblical justice (and the biblical God) places a high priority on restoring relationships and social wholeness in the face of brokenness and alienation (e.g., crime). Hence, we might call it restorative justice'.[119] They go further by explaining how this restorative perspective on God's justice is being lived out in the restorative justice movement. Through practices like Victim Offender Reconciliation, Family Group Conferencing, and Sentencing Circles, a new peacemaking approach to criminal justice is

116. Ted Grimsrud and Howard Zehr, 'Rethinking God, Justice, and Treatment of Offenders', *Journal of Offender Rehabilitation* 35, no. 3–4 (2002): 255.

117. Ibid.

118. Grimsrud and Zehr are aware of some of the interpretive interpolations covered earlier in this chapter: 'A kind of historical short-circuit occurred in which certain concepts were taken from their biblical context, interpreted through the lens of Roman law, then used to interpret the biblical text. The result was an obsession with the retributive themes of the Bible and a neglect of the restorative ones – a basic theology of a retributive God who desires violence'; ibid., 260.

119. Ibid., 267.

taking form that constitutes a vigorous critique of the theological roots of retributivism and shows that 'the *deepest* roots of Western theology, found in the Bible, are indeed fully compatible with new, peacemaking approaches to criminal justice'.[120] With this confidence, we turn now to one of the most potent stories of restorative justice ever told in the Bible.

120. Ibid., 276.

Chapter 5

A Parable of the Justice of God: Luke 15.11-32

The previous chapter established that the justice of God is best understood as a restorative justice, on account of its disclosure in the Christ event as a saving and peacemaking justice. Recognition of this divine justice by the community of faith carries a corresponding obligation to reflect such justice within its own internal life, as well as in the wider world. This in turn requires an ongoing engagement with Scripture. For as ecclesial ethics rightly asserts, the church's primary vocation is to further the story of Scripture by embodying its central convictions and priorities in its own life and witness, especially with respect to peacemaking. Having considered the larger restorative dimensions of biblical justice, in the next two chapters we narrow our focus to two smaller textual units – a Gospel parable and a Pauline epistle – in order to show how a theological reading of Scripture informed by restorative justice can furnish significant insights into the ecclesiological dimensions of God's justice.

First we will focus on one of the best known parables of Jesus, found in the Gospel of Luke – the Parable of the Prodigal Son (Luke 15.11-32). It is a story about a young man who selfishly disregards the livelihood of his father and fellow kin by taking off to a far country with his inheritance. After some time, he 'comes to himself' and returns home, only to be greeted by his father with a compassionate embrace instead of the expected chastisement. This parable provides ample resources for exploring responses to wrongdoing through the numerous characters involved in this story.[1] It throws into relief the difference between a restorative understanding of justice, fulfilled in the reintegration of offenders

1. The parable of the prodigal son is not only one of Jesus's longest parables, it also contains numerous characters: a father, two sons, village people, slaves, gentiles, employers, not to mention the animals or the accusation of prostitutes being involved.

through the practices of repentance and forgiveness, and a justice that prioritizes the law of just deserts through practices of punishment and exclusion.

In exploring this story, I will draw on a recent reading of this parable by Christopher Marshall, one of the foremost theological interpreters of restorative justice. Marshall's reading takes seriously the proper relational context of justice as well as its peaceable ends by bringing a 'restorative justice lens to the task of New Testament interpretation'.[2] His treatment builds on his earlier argument in *Beyond Retribution*, where he argues:

> the first Christians experience in Christ and lived out in their faith communities an understanding of justice as a power that heals, restores, and reconciles rather than hurts, punishes, and kills, and that reality ought to shape and direct a Christian contribution to the criminal justice debate today.[3]

This insight accords closely with the argument proposed here – that just as the early Christian communities embodied a restorative understanding of justice, so Christian communities today should seek to participate in the working out of divine justice, as it is revealed and enacted in Jesus Christ.

Narratives of Restorative Reintegration

One of the downstream consequences of the rush to punish in recent decades, beyond the swelling of the prison population, has been the equally large numbers of those leaving prison to reenter mainstream society. It is now a well-established fact that a significant percentage of these ex-prisoners fail to reintegrate successfully, many of whom return to prison for either breaching their conditions of release or for being convicted of a new crime.[4] Penal policy has now come to target reoffending and the causes of it, such as the Second Chance Act passed in

2. Marshall, *Compassionate Justice*, 3.

3. Marshall, *Beyond Retribution*, 33.

4. Despite the prison muster of New Zealand standing around 10,000 inmates, around 15,000 people are released from prison each year, many for sentences shorter than a year. In a study of 5,000 released prisoners over a 12-month period, it was shown that 52% of those released were convicted of a new offence and returned to prison at least once during the 60-month follow-up period. Over half of those returned to prison for a new offence were re-convicted in their first year of release; New Zealand Department of Corrections, *Reconviction Patterns of Released Prisoners: A 60-Months Follow-up Analysis* (New Zealand: Department of Corrections, 2009).

North America in 2008 and the UK Offender Rehabilitation Act in 2014. These moves reflect a recognition of the support that released prisoners require while also extending the reach of government powers to keep ex-prisoners under surveillance.

With the growth of interest in how successfully to reintegrate prisoners back into society, criminological research has begun to ask a different set of questions. In short, research has shifted from a predominant focus on the criminogenic factors that led to crime to what leads a person away from it. The field of desistance in particular asks the question, 'how and why do people change?'[5] This has proved to be a rather hopeful line of inquiry, since it is now well established that almost all offenders, including persistent offenders, eventually stop offending. This shows that while a person's criminal past is important to their future, they are not necessarily doomed to deviance for the rest of their life. Indeed, desistance theorists like Anthony Bottoms and Joanna Shapland have begun to argue that even persistent offenders can acquire virtue as they become predisposed towards non-criminal ways of relating to others and their objects of desire.[6]

While the majority of those who desist from crime do so for largely passive reasons – getting older being the leading factor – a significant percentage of offenders become active desisters. In other words, this group of people actively resist possibilities for offending and through sustained effort cultivate a life no longer defined by their criminal past. Importantly, research has shown that active desistance is associated with the ability of an offender to make sense of their lives and thereby to reconstruct their identity anew. This 'sense-making', as Shadd Maruna states, 'commonly takes the form of a life story or self-narrative'.[7] In order to desist from crime,

5. For a recent global overview of this literature, see Joanna Shapland, Stephen Farrall, and Anthony Bottoms, eds., *Global Perspectives on Desistance: Reviewing What We Know and Looking to the Future* (London: Routledge, 2016).

6. Anthony Bottoms and Joanna Shapland, 'Can Persistent Offenders Acquire Virtue?', *Studies in Christian Ethics* 27, no. 3 (2014): 318–33. A similar approach can be found in the 'Good Lives Model' advocated, among others, by Tony Ward for rehabilitating sex-offenders through retraining their desires. While his publications are extensive on this matter, see Tony Ward and Mark Brown, 'The Good Lives Model and Conceptual Issues in Offender Rehabilitation', *Psychology, Crime & Law* 10, no. 3 (2004): 243–57.

7. Shadd Maruna, *Making Good: How Ex-Convicts Reform and Rebuild Their Lives* (Washington, DC: American Psychology Association, 2001), 7.

> ex-offenders need to develop a coherent, prosocial identity for themselves. As such, they need to account for and understand their criminal pasts (why they did what they did), and they also need to understand why they are now "not like that anymore." Ex-offenders need a coherent and credible self-story to explain (to themselves and others) how their checkered pasts could have led to their new, reformed identities.[8]

This premise builds on the work of narrative theorists, like Giddens, who wrote that, 'A person's identity is not to be found in behavior, nor – important though this is – in the reactions of others, but in the *capacity to keep a particular narrative going*'.[9]

Desistance theorists point out, however, that there are few stories of radical change available to prisoners. They therefore lack the language and metanarrative to describe the kind of transformation of identity they are seeking. Into this void, religions like Christianity provide 'a new meaning system' replete with a grammar and narrative of redemption; from this material the convert can begin to base their own story of change.[10] Indeed, Maruna argues that prisoners are in need of 'a redemption script'.[11] A story by which they can hope for a future beyond their sinful past and can begin to inhabit a self that has been reformed by embodying this narrative.

One such narrative that might fruitfully be considered a 'redemption script' is Jesus's parable of the Prodigal Son. This parable has long been regarded as one of the most penetrating stories ever told by Jesus, as it cuts directly to the heart of the human experience and exposes it to the love and forgiveness of God. It has also been one of the most explored stories from the perspective of human psychology. As Marshall writes, it deals with 'universal themes of freedom and responsibility, leaving and returning, exile and homecoming, offending and forgiveness, estrangement and reconciliation, honor and shame, generosity and grace-lessness, and of justice, jealousy, and joy. In particular, it explores the anatomy of moral change…'[12]

8. Ibid., 7–8.

9. Anthony Giddens, *Modernity and Self-Identity: Self and Society in the Late Modern Age* (Stanford, CA: Stanford University Press, 1991), 54.

10. Shadd Maruna, Louise Wilson and Kathryn Curran, 'Why God Is Often Found Behind Bars: Prison Conversions and the Crisis of Self-Narrative', *Research in Human Development* 3, no. 2–3 (2006): 167. Maruna et al. also talks about converts adopting a 'new system of rhetoric', whereby 'religious attributions defining and identifying the new self become master attributions, replacing the secular or peripheral religious attributions that existed prior to conversion'.

11. Maruna, *Making Good*, 87.

12. Marshall, *Compassionate Justice*, 187.

Closer still, Marshall argues that Jesus's parables offer the church a unique resource for seeking to promote a vision of restorative justice in secular society, precisely because of their referential or metaphorical function. The parables were intended to 'project an entirely new world of perception and experience, and they invited hearers into that reconfigured world as active participants, both imaginatively and in terms of subsequent behavior'.[13] The reality depicted by these stories invites their audience, both then and now, to participate in this reality by embodying the message of the story in their own lives. For offenders seeking to live crime-free, this parable has even greater pertinence as the story's climax ends with the prodigal son welcomed back into his community as a member restored and honored. A redemption script *par excellence.*

Reading Luke 15.11-32 as a Restorative Parable

Wrongdoing as Relational Rupture

Marshall reads the opening line of Jesus's parable – 'A certain man had two sons' (v. 11) – as an indication that the parable 'is all about interpersonal relationships'.[14] It is a mistake to isolate any individual character in the narrative as *the* central protagonist. Each of the characters in this story plays a representative role – the younger son exemplifying the repentant sinner Jesus came to save, the Father's forgiving embrace personifying the benevolent character of God, and the older son's penchant for legal custom serving as a cipher for the scribes and Pharisees. But the real drama of the parable arises precisely because of the *bonds of relationality* between these characters. As Marshall writes, 'it is simply not possible to appreciate the significance of the actions of any of the characters without taking into account the ties of loyalty and identity that bound them together as a household unit and as a local community'.[15]

This relational context leads Marshall to interpret the actions of the younger son as primarily an offence against his *filial* obligations to his father, and by extension to his fellow kin and community. The boy's thoroughgoing denial of his obligations to family and village make him a potential candidate for the charge of being the 'stubborn and rebellious son' of Deut. 21.18-21, which carried with it the threat of public execution. 'His rebellion', Marshall writes, 'consisted in a thoroughgoing rejection

13. Marshall, 'Parables as Paradigms for Public Theology', in Neville, ed., *Bible, Justice, and Public Theology*, 37.

14. Marshall, *Compassionate Justice*, 185.

15. Ibid., 186.

of his relational connections with, and his responsibilities towards, his father, his brother, and his wider village community'. In short, 'he wrecks bedrock relationships'.[16]

Marshall's emphasis on the prodigal's sin as a matter of relational rupture exposes how deeply ingrained individualism is within the modern liberal psyche and how much it has controlled recent biblical interpretation. The typically modern pursuit of an autonomous and unencumbered self leads many readers to see the younger son as, in the words of Volf, 'breaking out of the confines of a patriarchal home in order to find his authentic self and become an individual'.[17] The failure of the young man is that he 'fails to make something out of himself';[18] he fails to construct his own identity as separate from his culturally imposed identity as a son. Such an understanding of the 'free self' would have been inimical to Jesus's first-century Palestinian hearers, for whom freedom would have been understood in terms of their communal and relational networks.[19] This parable invites its listeners to recognize the fundamentally relational nature of humanity, something that cannot be achieved within the bounds of a Western individualistic worldview.

The relational context of this parable exposes another problematic tendency in modern thought. When the son said to his father, 'give me a share of the property that will belong to me', the seriousness of the wrongdoing is not immediately obvious to modern readers. This is because the son's wrongdoing has meaning only when interpreted within that specific cultural-linguistic world. Within the first-century peasant context, the boy's actions would have provoked extreme outrage. The demand of an inheritance while his father was still in good health would have been considered not only improper – an inheritance can only be given voluntarily, not demanded – it would have also communicated the message that he wished his father were already dead. Indeed, his speedy sale of the inheritance leaving his father with nothing to sustain him in old age would have been seen as a case of the son 'planning metaphorically to kill his father'.[20] In burning all his bridges behind him, the son showed no

16. Ibid., 196.

17. Miroslav Volf, *Exclusion and Embrace: A Theological Exploration of Identity, Otherness, and Reconciliation* (Nashville, TN: Abingdon Press, 1996), 157.

18. Ibid.

19. Christopher D. Marshall, '"I Have Sinned against Heaven and against You": Sin as Relational Rupture in the Teaching of Jesus', in *A Thinker's Guide to Sin: Talking About Wrongdoing Today* (Auckland, NZ: Accent Publications, 2010), 72.

20. Marshall, *Compassionate Justice*, 199. The connection between land, livelihood, and identity in agrarian societies was such that on top of the father losing any

intention of ever returning; he was 'effectively "un-sonning" himself and "de-fathering" his father'.[21]

Having dishonored the head of the family and having let the ancestral estate fall into the hands of outside opportunists, the son had 'set a dangerous precedent that could imperil the welfare of the whole community'.[22] Once resident in foreign lands the boy squandered his inheritance in dissolute living. He was reduced to feeding pigs owned by a Gentile master and on Gentile land – a fate that would 'effectively require him to renounce the regular practice of his religion'.[23] Marshall concludes: 'He is, in short, a serious and serial offender who has so thoroughly covered himself in sin and shame that no place remained for him in regular society. He is utterly unclean, in every sense of the word, and utterly alone.'[24]

By highlighting the relational and culturally specific nature of the son's wrongdoing, Marshall's interpretation shows how important it is to attend to the particular cultural-linguistic world of those relationships. As an ecclesial practice, restorative approaches to wrongdoing require this same attentiveness to relationships and to providing thick descriptions of the culture and context wherein actions have meaning.

The Journey of Repentance

One of the consistent themes in this parable is the importance of viewing wrongdoing in the context of relationship, not just in the context of law. If justice were understood in purely legal terms, given the nature of the younger son's actions within his cultural context, there would be no hope of him being restored without first being publicly condemned and punished for his wrongdoing. This is the perspective of the older brother. Whether or not the punishment of death in Deut. 21.18-21 would have applied, the retributive emphasis of reasserting the priority of law would have left little hope for the son's restoration.

On account of the relational perspective of this parable, a different order of justice is called for, a thicker or relational justice that strives for the younger son's transformation and the healing of the relationships he

sense of security in his old age his very life (*bios*) in the world was prematurely taken from him. Under the law the boy's actions would have been seen as a direct violation of the fifth commandment: 'Honor your father and your mother, *so that your days may be long in the land* that the Lord your God is giving you' (Exod. 20.12, italics mine).

21. Ibid., 200.
22. Ibid., 202.
23. Ibid., 204.
24. Ibid., 205.

has devastated. Without that, the relationships between father and son, brother and brother, village and prodigal, will continue to suffer loss.[25] Whereas a retributive conception of justice would require the wrongdoer to suffer swift retribution, thus upholding the disinterested rules-based nature of this justice, a restorative conception strives for relational repair. It actively involves all the parties to the offence, but with the common determination to heal the harm done and to set a new course where relationships can once again flourish.

For the younger son, his restoration involves a thorough turning around, not only of his moral condition in the far country but also of the relationships he has violated. The biblical word for this 'thorough turning around' is *repentance* (בתשוב, μετάνοια). If, as Marshall argues, the prodigal son serves in Luke as the representative of the 'sinner who repents', then repentance is clearly a costly undertaking that bears witness to a transformation of the whole person. This understanding of repentance involves the distinct practices of contrition, confession, and a restitutive life, that together lead to reconciliation or 'at-one-ment'. Marshall illuminates what is entailed by these distinct practices on the part of the prodigal son.

The first clue that signals the younger son's genuine repentance is in the comment that 'he came to himself' (v. 17). On the edge of starvation, and having discarded every marker of self-respect, the boy has a moment of clarity where he recollects his past and all that he has forfeited. The boy's lament, however, was not simply for his own miserable situation. Marshall points to the boy's repeated reference to 'my father' and argues that his contrition was 'evinced by his remembering the bonds of belonging that grounded him in relationship to his paternal victim, and by his realization of the relational damage his behavior had caused'.[26] The first step in the process of restoration is a truthful assessment of one's life as a social and relational being. Whilst the boy had failed to abide by the law through honoring his parents, at an even deeper level he had failed to abide in the relational bond that made him a son in the first place. It was his 'forfeited

25. Marshall cites Richard H. Bell as one example of this thicker conception of justice who urges for a 'conception of justice as the practice of promoting or restoring human well-being in its totality'; Marshall, *Compassionate Justice*, 218, citing Bell, *Rethinking Justice*.

26. Marshall, *Compassionate Justice*, 208. Volf argues that this 'memory of sonship' is the moment that makes repentance possible, but it is not yet an act of repentance. Yet given that the boy's transgression consisted in un-sonning himself, the turning back to the memory of sonship is already to embody the 'thorough turning about' of repentance; Volf, *Exclusion and Embrace*, 158.

relationship with his father' that truly grieved the son, argues Marshall, and therefore his restoration must be found in the context of a father–son relationship, rather than within the context of law.[27]

If the first step on the path to restoration involves a contrite heart, the second important step is the act of confession. Marshall argues that the younger son's confession involves three distinct features that are crucial to what in restorative justice is described as 'offender accountability'.[28] The son's confession – 'Father I have sinned against heaven and before you; I am no longer worthy to be called your son; treat me as one of your hired servants' – shows, first, an 'acceptance of moral blame', second, a recognition that 'his actions have injured others', and third, an acknowledgment this his wrongdoing has 'changed the nature of his relationship to the victim'.[29] While situational and environmental factors may contribute to an incident of wrongdoing, for an apology to be genuine it must communicate that the offender is now disowning his actions rather than excusing them or justifying what happened.

This highlights an important difference between restorative and retributive notions of accountability. Restorativists share a similar concern for personal responsibility as retributivists, but this is borne out in quite different ways. Responsibility, according to retributivists, is understood as expiation of guilt by means of facing the consequence of deserved punishment. In other words, responsibility is not fully discharged until the punishment has been satisfied, often regardless of whether the offender accepts their guilt or not. So, for example, Antony Duff argues that, 'what punishment requires of the offender is *not actual repentance, but that he undergo the ritual* of apology and moral reparation'.[30] On this account, retributivists are ritualists, in the sense that accountability is

27. Marshall, *Compassionate Justice*, 207.

28. New Zealand's Ministry of Justice defines offender accountability as, 'When a person deliberately inflicts wrong on another, the perpetrator has a moral obligation to accept responsibility for having done so and for mitigating the consequences that have ensued. Offenders demonstrate acceptance of this obligation by expressing remorse for their actions, by making reparation for the losses inflicted, and perhaps by seeking forgiveness from those whom they have treated disrespectfully. This response by the offender may pave the way for reconciliation to occur'; Ministry of Justice, 'Restorative Justice: Best Practice in New Zealand' (Wellington, NZ: Ministry of Justice, 2011), 33.

29. Marshall, *Compassionate Justice*, 208–10.

30. R. A. Duff, 'Responsibility, Restoration, and Retribution', in Tonry, ed., *Retributivism Has a Past*, 79 (italics mine).

communicated to offenders by making them perform the ritual of apology. 'Criminal punishment is', as Duff explains, 'a species of required apology: the offender is required to go through the motions of apology, *even if he does not mean it*'.[31]

Restorativists, on the other hand, view responsibility as part of a dialogical process where all parties of an offence stand in a more truthful relationship to one another. Wenzel et al. argue that a restorative conception of justice is aimed at 'gaining a shared understanding of the harm the offense has done and the values it violated. Justice is restored when the relevant principles and values that have been violated by the offense are re-established and re-validated through social consensus'.[32] It is not enough simply to impose censure on offender *extra nos*. Rather, offenders are encouraged to take an active part in their own self-censure by communicating to their victims an acceptance of responsibility for the harm they have caused and a willingness to re-affirm the values of the relationship they have damaged.

The younger son exemplifies this self-censure by acknowledging his injury to others through his confession, 'I have sinned against heaven and against you' (v. 18). Alongside the boy's father, God is also acknowledged as being injured by the behavior. God's solidarity with victims means that in 'sinning against his father, the boy has spiritually offended against God', and so, as Marshall continues, 'To put things right with God, the boy must also put things right with his father'.[33] The boy's confession acknowledges that he no longer stands in a truthful relationship, either to his natural father or to his heavenly Father. He is no longer worthy to stand as a son or as a child of God, which places him in a position of vulnerability, as his worth must now be conferred upon him rather than claimed as a matter of right. 'Relational renewal', according to Marshall, 'can only ever come as a gift from victim to offender', which, viewed through the lens of this parable, is a divine activity as much as an earthly process.[34]

To depart briefly from Marshall's commentary, we must consider whether the modern mindset would object to the prodigal's confession. On what grounds can God be said to forgive what happens on the horizontal level between humans? According to this mindset, God may be implicated as a secondary victim, at a more abstract level, but God can

31. Ibid.

32. M. Wenzel et al., 'Retributive and Restorative Justice', *Law and Human Behavior* 32 (2008): 378.

33. Marshall, *Compassionate Justice*, 210.

34. Ibid., 211.

never take the place of particular victims and do what only they can do. This dilemma has received considerable attention since the publication of Simon Wiesenthal's book *The Sunflower: On the Possibilities and Limits of Forgiveness*.[35] Subjected to the atrocities of a Nazi concentration camp, Wiesenthal was brought to the bed of a dying SS soldier, who wanted to confess to him, as a Jew, all that he had done, in the hope that Wiesenthal would offer forgiveness. After some deliberation, Wiesenthal left the soldier in silence, since he did not believe he possessed any right to forgive what the soldier had done to victims other than himself. The implication of Wiesenthal's conclusion is that no one, not even God, is in a position to take the place of primary victims by forgiving their transgressors.

The prodigal's confession hints at a possible response to this dilemma by seeing God, not as displacing primary victims and thereby dishonoring them, but as being in ontological union with all victims. Alan Torrance explores this through the doctrine of the vicarious humanity of Christ. As humanity's representative, Christ takes into himself the experience of all victims by identifying *with* and participating *in* each and every pain and suffering by them.[36] Consequently, no victim ever stands alone in their suffering, since they always have with them an advocate and mediator who has absorbed their pain into the very being of God.

Wiesenthal may be right to suggest that he is in no position to forgive what was not done to him, but that does not mean no forgiveness is possible. The God of victims revealed in Christ offers forgiveness where humans cannot.[37] The uncomfortable and costly truth about God's solidarity with humanity is that offenders do not stand alone either, since

35. Simon Wiesenthal, *The Sunflower: On the Possibilities and Limits of Forgiveness* (New York: Schocken Books, 1998).

36. Torrance emphasizes the particularity of Christ's participation in humanity as more central to the Pauline concept than the universalizing of Christ's humanity, which would tend to displace the particular sufferings of particular victims; Alan J. Torrance, 'The Theological Grounds for Advocating Forgiveness and Reconciliation in the Sociopolitical Realm', in *The Politics of Past Evil: Religion, Reconciliation, and the Dilemmas of Transitional Justice*, ed. D. Philpott (Notre Dame, IN: University of Notre Dame, 2006), 75.

37. I am indebted to Murray Rae for this understanding of forgiveness in response to Wiesenthal's dilemma; Rae's views were presented in a paper delivered at *Theology and Church History Seminar*, University of Otago, New Zealand, 2013, n.p. This understanding of divine forgiveness also provides a corrective to Maria Mayo's concern to reserve forgiveness until repentance in wrongdoers is evident; see Maria Mayo, *The Limits of Forgiveness: Case Studies in the Distortion of a Biblical Idea* (Minneapolis: Fortress Press, 2015), 67–96.

God has stooped to become their advocate also. To extend forgiveness therefore, as Torrance points out, 'denotes concrete participation by grace in God's unconditional forgiveness of enemies that, to the extent that they are ours, are also his but whom he also loves and forgives'.[38] It is this reality of God's commitment to both victims *and* offenders that is evoked in the parable.

Returning to Marshall's reading, the acknowledgment by the young man that he has forfeited his right to be a son raises the question of how he is to present himself before his father. He resolves to throw himself on his mercy, asking him to treat him as a 'day labourer', someone who must earn his own place in the household. While Marshall considers it a stretch to interpret this as a means for making full financial restitution to the father, there is still a restitutive quality about the boy's request.[39] Offering to serve as a labourer in service to his father reflects a reversal of his actions in squandering the livelihood his father laboured for. Restitution is a crucial part of the restorative justice process, but more because of its 'symbolic power' than because of the aim of full material compensation. Marshall draws on Zehr's explanation,

> Restitution symbolizes a restoration of equity, and it states implicitly that someone else – not the victim – is responsible. It is a way of denouncing the wrong, absolving the victim, and saying who is responsible. Accordingly, restitution is about responsibility and meaning as much as or more than actual repayment of losses.[40]

Combined with his change of heart and readiness to confess his sins, the boy's willingness to serve as a labourer at his father's service illustrates that repentance involves all of his mental, emotional, spiritual, and physical faculties, as he seeks to be restored. He recognizes that his sin is not merely against law but against relationships; the path back to wholeness is through the difficult and vulnerable process of acknowledging the harm he has caused to those around him, and then placing himself at their mercy.

38. Torrance, 'Forgiveness and Reconciliation', 76.

39. Marshall considers this interpretation as a 'possible inference from the text, not the main point at issue'; Marshall, *Compassionate Justice*, 212; cf. 212 n. 56. Manual workers existed at a subsistence level, and were thus not likely to be in the position of saving the equivalent of what the young son spent on his travels.

40. Zehr, 'Restoring Justice', 145, cited in Marshall, *Compassionate Justice*, 213.

A possible misconception of Marshall's interpretation of this parable needs to be addressed. By emphasizing the relational nature of the son's offending, it does not follow that the parable is concerned only with a private family matter that has little to contribute to public political concerns. This is a common argument against restorative conceptions of justice. According to Duff, for example, criminal punishment has a 'reconciliatory aim', but this is not of the intimate type of restorative justice, which is more 'apt to reconcile spouses, family members, partners, friends, or neighbors, if reconciliation is understood as the restoration of those bonds of affection and close mutual concern by which such relationships are structured'.[41] The criminal law's reconciliatory aim is 'somewhat distant and formal', as it requires solely that 'citizens play their proper part'.[42] But this parable shows that the path of genuine repentance is a thoroughly political process, more so than Duff's compliance-driven understanding of citizenship.

Graham Ward interprets the trajectory of the prodigal son's wrongdoing as leading him into a 'state of depoliticization'.[43] Having alienated himself from the economy and property of his family estate, rebelling against the authority and governance of his elders, and entering into another society where he is no citizen at all, the son has forfeited his place in the *polis*. He had pursued a 'solipsistic freedom, a profound auto-affection' that placed him, in Ward's opinion, 'Outside human society...someone without rights, beyond the law, someone subhuman and therefore to be housed with the animals'.[44] The real political issue, in view of this parable, is how this son might resurrect his citizenship.

The journey of repentance is a political process because it involves restoring the relational bonds that make one a citizen in the first place. Without this relational and political repair, the imposition of any retributive ritual of punishment serves simply to further depoliticize and disenfranchise offenders. It would only thwart the movement detected in this prodigal when he said to himself, 'I will get up' (ἀνίστημι, v. 18). By these words he establishes a future direction for his life, and it moves him to imagine once again a place for himself within the established order of household and economy. The sphere of relationships highlighted by Marshall is no less political because it is relational. Rather, as the

41. Duff, 'Responsibility, Restoration, and Retribution', 80.

42. Ibid.

43. Graham Ward, *The Politics of Discipleship* (Grand Rapids, MI: Baker Academic, 2009), 269.

44. Ibid., 270.

prodigal's words suggest, offenders are in need of resurrection (ἀνάστασις) into a citizenship where their alienation is overcome and they are enabled to contribute their part in the *polis*.[45]

It has been suggested that, for Luke, the prodigal son represents what it means to be a 'sinner who repents'. If this is the case, then the story requires listeners who can also identify themselves as sinners needing to put right their own relationships through practices of contrition, confession, restitution, and atonement. Moreover, as the journey of the prodigal shows, these practices involve the whole person in all their mental, physical, spiritual, and emotional capacities that together point to a consistent way of life. Repentance, in other words, is a life-ethic that requires practice. No community should know this more than the church, where, week after week, these very practices are fostered in response to the call to be renewed in heart, mind, and body. By calling sinners into a communion of repentance, the church embodies the story of the prodigal son as he returns from the far country.

Compassionate Justice, Restoring Belonging

According to Marshall, genuine repentance indicates the presence of a power working to effect change in a person's identity and destiny. This is evident in the life of the prodigal son, who now stands as a markedly different person than the careless and hurtful young man who departed from his father. While the language of justice (δικαιο) is not found in the parable, the narrative depiction of this restorative power point to what we have described as the justice of God – the active liberation of the ungodly to a communion of peace and right relationship. Accordingly, repentance serves as a crucial marker of divine justice at work, enabling sinful offenders to undergo the difficult journey of relational renewal. Repentance, however, represents only one side of the reconciling process – the side of the penitent. Justice awaits the reception of the penitent by their victims, those who have the power to forgive and so confirm their new identity.

This is the real power of the parable, so perfectly captured in the figure of the father embracing his repentant son. The injustice committed by the young son was first and foremost against his father, so it is fitting that this parable of the justice of God reaches its fulfilment as the father restores his lost son as an outworking of compassionate forgiveness. The justice enacted in the parable has the concrete meaning of a 'compassionate commitment to restoration', which means that restorative justice from

45. I take this insight from Ward, ibid.

a Gospel perspective is a *compassionate justice*.[46] 'It is a justice that is enriched, informed, and empowered by the space it gives to compassion.'[47] The divine economy of justice does not operate according to a punitive logic; rather, it employs the logic of compassion, forgiveness, and restorative love, in response to the sinner who repents.[48]

Marshall is right to point out that the pivotal shift in this parable occurs when the father was 'filled with compassion', which then issued in a commitment to the son's restoration. Yet this begs the question of what exactly is being restored? I suggest that the restoration in view in this parable can be understood in terms of *belonging*. The prodigal's actions have placed him in a moral position where he is excommunicated from belonging, and his reintegration is a journey to find how he can belong once again. The father, on the other hand, reflects a concern for human victims who, as a result of experiencing the trauma and fear of being harmed, no longer feel like they can safely belong. Perhaps this is why he throws a public feast and he goes out from the banquet to plead with his older son to join in the celebration. The restoration of victims is ultimately a reinstatement of their belonging, which involves dealing with their trauma, as well as returning to them the respect and dignity that comes with safely belonging.

Marshall's reading draws out numerous features of the father's compassionate attributes as he responds to his younger son, and he contrasts them with the retributive response of the older son. For the purpose of brevity I have grouped Marshall's discussion of these attributes into three categories: the justice of mercy, reintegrative honor, and the building of compassionate community. These three qualities are vital to restorative approaches and each can be extended to show the kind of ecclesial ethic required in the context of conflict and wrongdoing.

The Justice of Mercy

We noted in the previous chapter that the Hebraic notion of צדק understood justice as going hand in hand with mercy. In contrast to this thicker view of justice, the Latin notion of *iustitia* reflected a greater separation between the concepts of justice and mercy, such that the former represented a concern to reward or punish while the later was viewed as a

46. Marshall, *Compassionate Justice*, 249.

47. Ibid., 252.

48. See, however, Jeffrie Murphy's sympathetic embrace of the Christian notion of repentance in Jeffrie G. Murphy, *Punishment and the Moral Emotions: Essays in Law, Morality, and Religion* (New York: Oxford University Press, 2012), 114–28.

denial of the principle of just desert. In the parable it is the older brother who represents this thin understanding of justice when he implicitly accuses his father of behaving unjustly in showing mercy to his prodigal brother (vv. 29-30).[49] The older brother reacts angrily at the news that his younger brother has been received back *without suffering any punishment*, which then leads him to highlight the injustice of his father in *not rewarding* his own virtue as a law-abiding and industrious son.[50] By failing to punish the wrongdoer and by not rewarding upright behavior, the father fails to act justly according to the older son's understanding of justice.

But the justice of the father operates not according to the logic of just deserts but rather according to that 'divine form of justice', as Marshall writes, 'that is committed to reinstating penitent offenders to full participation in the life of the community they have spurned and even bestows honor on them for choosing again the path of freedom and life in place of alienation and death'.[51] The father stands in the biblical tradition of divine righteousness (צדק), a justice that had the distinctive character of restoration. The parable has an unmistakable echo of God's merciful justice in restoring his covenantal partner even after she had squandered her covenantal inheritance (cf. Isa. 42.6; 49.6). This observation only heightens the drama of the parable, since it draws Jesus's listeners to recognize their place in this story and brings them to question their expectations of God and his justice.

Before proceeding, it is important to point out that according to a restorative understanding of justice, the father's merciful actions are an act of justice rather than an act of grace that transcends justice. In this we

49. Ward points out that if it were not for the older brother's questioning, then justice itself would be imperiled by the potentially arbitrary and even tyrannical rule of the father; Ward, *Politics of Discipleship*, 272. In the parable, however, the older brother's first response is not to question his father's decisions and so assess how they uphold a standard of justice, but rather he protested, became angry, and remained petulant before his father. It is doubtful that the older brother provides a check against arbitrariness and tyrannical rule, especially after he exaggerates his own righteousness while labeling his younger brother as an unworthy deviant.

50. Mayo does not read this parable as addressing the matter of justice and forgiveness, as at 'no point does the parable indicate that the father felt wronged by the prodigal son or in any way violated…' She thus concludes that, 'there is no reason to assume the he [the father] forgives his son for anything'; Mayo, *Limits of Forgiveness*, 75. This is a very narrow reading of the text and a complete failure to account for the injustice expressed by the older son in response to the father's forgiving actions towards the younger son.

51. Marshall, *Compassionate Justice*, 217.

are following Marshall's claim that 'there is no justice without mercy and mercy is essential to attaining justice in its thicker or restorative sense'.[52] Justice is not transcended by the virtue of mercy or love; rather, justice is itself configured around the very meaning of mercy. To read this as a story about justice being transcended would be to ignore the biblical and relational framework within which the story is cast and to read it instead in the light of the notion of *iustitia*.[53]

Two striking features of the father's response exemplify merciful justice. First, he never lets go of the filial relationship that the young son had so woefully betrayed, thus showing his commitment to a relationship marked by unconditional love. As Volf recognizes,

> The most significant aspect of the story is, however, that the father who lets the son depart *does not let go of the relationship between them*... Against the force of the wrongdoing suffered and the shame endured that sought to push the son out...he became a father of the 'lost' son, of the 'dead' son (v. 24).[54]

This is a difficult undertaking for the father, because it requires him to renegotiate his own identity as a father in response to the alterity of his son. According to Volf, this is the 'basic thought' behind the parable: 'the will to give ourselves to others and "welcome" them, to readjust our identities to make space for them, is prior to any judgment about others, except that of identifying them in their humanity'.[55]

The merciful justice of the father means that he always keeps in view what Marshall calls the 'true relational identity behind the persona of sinful offender' – 'this son of *mine*' (v. 24). This stands in stark contrast with the older brother, who sees only a criminal who ought not to be trusted and so refuses to affirm his own *fraternal* relationship to his

52. Ibid., 219.

53. This difference in interpretive context creates a great deal of ambiguity, since some read this parable as justice being transcended – literally, 'set aside' – while others read this as a story about justice reconfigured; see Miroslav Volf, 'Against a Pretentious Church: A Rejoinder to Bell's Response', *Modern Theology* 19, no. 2 (2003): 283. See the exchange between Volf and the position of Daniel Bell Jr., who argues for a notion of justice *beyond* the classical notion of dues; see Volf, '*Liberation Theology After the End of History*: An Exchange', *Modern Theology* 19, no. 2 (2003): 261–85; Bell, 'What Gift Is Given? A Response to Volf', *Modern Theology* 19, no. 2 (2003): 271–80.

54. Volf, *Exclusion and Embrace*, 159.

55. Ibid., 29 (original in italics). Volf makes clear, however, that while this 'will to embrace' is a prior commitment, the actual act of embrace must take into account certain judgments.

brother – 'this son of *yours*'.[56] From the perspective of this parable, a restorative conception of justice must entail a steadfast commitment to the relational identity of wrongdoers as the key to their future, rather than maintaining a narrow focus on their past deviant acts as fixing their character and so also their future. Restoration begins in recognition of the fundamentally relational nature of human beings, because what is most in need of repair and healing are the relationships ruptured by wrongdoing.

The second feature of the father's merciful justice is his willingness to take even the smallest sign of repentance as a marker that a hoped-for future is already dawning. Even though the young son had prepared in advance a confession of his guilt and was willing to offer himself as no more than a slave, the father's compassion led him to embrace his son before these words could be uttered. Simply to see his son on the horizon was enough for the father to know that his 'return' was underway, that the transformation in his son had commenced. In fact, the father is so overcome with emotion at the sight of his son that he disregards all sense of decorum by 'hiking up his flowing robes and exposes his legs to public view' as he runs out to greet him, falling on his neck and showering him with kisses.[57]

It is crucial to observe that while the father is exuberant about the return of his son, he still makes room for moral accountability, as Marshall points out.[58] He listens to the boy's confession without challenging its accuracy or denying the reality of his own victimization. There is no attempt to minimize the harm done by the boy, or to excuse what he did. While his relationship to his son does not rest on moral performance, he still leaves room for the son to make a response that would either reinforce or renounce his wrongful past.[59]

56. Marshall, *Compassionate Justice*, 224. The older brother goes so far as to attach further scandal to his sibling's prodigal behavior in v. 30 by mention of prostitution, hitherto not mentioned in the narrative. This is an example of 'deviance labeling', according to Marshall, where criminals are further stigmatized by attaching abnormal labels to their character simply by virtue of being a criminal; ibid., 235–36.

57. Marshall cites many commentators of this parable who point out that according to Eastern custom the father's actions were extremely unconventional.

58. Marshall, *Compassionate Justice*, 226–27.

59. As Volf argues, the final act of an embrace is the opening of the arms again so that the 'alterity of the other may not be neutralized by merging both into an undifferentiated "we"'; Volf, *Exclusion and Embrace*, 144.

What is so overwhelming for the father is not simply the *return* of the son but his *transformation* through repentance into a new creation. The boy has passed through 'death' – his own self-inflicted punishment – and now he is 'alive'; he had been 'lost' but is now 'found' (v. 24). As Marshall notes, 'No injustice transpires when the lost are recovered, when the dead are restored to life, when sinners are forgiven. Justice is vindicated in such transformations'.[60] To celebrate at the first sign of repentance is to rejoice in the reign of God's justice, which brings people from their previously alienated and destructive state into a reality where new forms of relating are made possible. This eschatological dimension to justice calls for a different kind of perception in the midst of conflict, one that is attentive to small signs of reconciliation in the hope of its fuller reality to emerge.

Reintegrative Honor

As noted in Chapter 1, the system of retributive punishment insists that punishment is for the purpose of communicating that some actions are wrong, shameful, and deserving of the inflicted suffering.[61] Offenders have the right to be treated with a dignity that assumes they know right from wrong and are willing to face the consequences of their actions. Even though these claims are made in the name of dignity and so appear to be humane, in practice it is more truthful to say that punishment is for the purpose of imposing shame on offenders. As Whitman points out, the failure of retributive philosophers to account for how degradation occurs in punishment, and what can be done to prevent it, has resulted in a sizable gap between the philosophy of punishment and its actual practice.[62]

60. Marshall, *Compassionate Justice*, 241.

61. On the communicative or expressive value of punishment, see Duff, *Punishment, Communication and Community*; Joel Feinberg, *Doing and Deserving* (Princeton, NJ: Princeton University Press, 1970).

62. Whitman observes, 'the analysis of punishment cannot limit itself to what offenders deserve; the way we punish can have momentous social and interpersonal consequences that have nothing to do with the deserts of the person punished. Most especially, it is wrong to analyze punishment solely by considering its effect on the person punished; acts of punishment can also profoundly affect the person, or the society, doing the punishing. In figuring the equations of punishment, as it were, we cannot hold the punisher constant'; Whitman, *Harsh Justice*, 24.

Public shaming, or what Whitman calls the 'dynamic of degradation', has always been an obvious aspect of punishment. This dynamic often goes unrecognized due to the philosophical concern with the intent or purpose behind punishment, rather than how it functions as an interpersonal and societal dynamic. By attending to the social function of punishment, Whitman observes that degradation is not some 'incidental by-product of punishment', but rather 'punishment only works if it succeeds in making the punished person feel like an inferior'.[63] Criminals are commonly regarded as a public risk to society, and tend to be treated as if they were polluted, which leads punishers to 'ritually degrade them…assigning the offender to the status of an inferior'.[64] This is particularly evident in North American penal practice, where public shaming has become the norm through the use of barred prison doors, day-glo uniforms, chain gangs, indeterminate sentencing, and an institutional culture of violence.

Unlike North America, European penal practice is still influenced by residual notions of mercy and amnesty, which have prevented 'tough-on-crime' practices taking too deep a root.[65] The connection between rituals of shaming and what Whitman calls a 'harsh justice' should make us wary of putting any reliance on shame as a mechanism for restoration. This applies to the restorative justice theory of 'reintegrative shaming' – where the offender is given the opportunity to confess his feelings of shame at his behavior and so be accepted back into the moral community – which, in Marshall's opinion, still relies too heavily on the mechanism of shame to produce comprehensive restoration.[66]

One of Marshall's most significant observations about this parable concerns the way in which the father reverses the effects of shame. Whereas the younger son had prepared himself to accept the consequences of his shameful actions by being disowned as a son and treated as a slave, the father resolves not to treat him as he *deserves* but rather to *deliver* him from the incurred shame. Emulating the pattern of God's

63. Ibid., 20.

64. Ibid., 21.

65. Whitman attributes the Continent's values of mercy to its tradition of state power and relative freedom from 'some distinctively fierce American Christian beliefs'; ibid., 6, 201.

66. Marshall, *Compassionate Justice*, 231. The discussion of shame in restorative justice conferences has been well studied, especially since the seminal work of Braithwaite, *Crime, Shame and Reintegration*. Whitman also notes the dangers of employing shame for reintegrative purposes advocated for by John Braithwaite and Dan Kahan, specifically because shame can quickly turn into a mechanism for public degradation; Whitman, *Harsh Justice*, 24.

justice, the father celebrates his repentance and spares no resource to enact his full return to a place of honor. This is the concrete meaning of the justice of God in response to repentant wrongdoers, a markedly different response from the public shaming rituals enacted through the criminal justice system.

The father's actions are multiple. First, the boy is re-clothed so as to signify his return to *filial* standing (v. 22). Marshall argues that the changing of clothes was a metaphor for moral and spiritual transformation, which once again underscores the boy's entering into a new moral reality. Second, the boy is given a ring to signify that he now shares in the sovereignty of the household (v. 22). This reverses his first shameful act of exacting an inheritance as an affront to the welfare of his family, since he is now bestowed with the family's authority as a gift to acknowledge that he is ready to wield such responsibility. Third, the father throws a lavish feast before the entire village so as to 'lift the cloak of shame from his son's shoulders and underscore his reinstatement as an esteemed member of the family'.[67]

All of these actions signify the irreducible importance of *relationships* as the son is brought from a state of complete alienation to a place of belonging and respect in relationship. It is because wrongdoing is understood in the context of relationships that such importance is given to signs of repentance. Without repentance there are little grounds to hope for a future that includes both the wrongdoer and the one wronged in a relationship of mutual trust and respect.

Nicholas Wolterstorff attempts to give an account of this connection between repentance and relational repair. He suggests that repentance signifies that the moral condition of the penitent is significantly different to that of the wrongdoer on account of their altered stance towards the wrong done. The penitent has moved from a position of standing behind and therefore justifying their actions and has joined the victim in condemning their wrongdoing as wrong. When a 'wrongdoer *offers* the victim his repentance', Wolterstorff notes, he does so 'in the *hope* that the victim will regard him in a new moral light, treat him as having a new moral identity'.[68] Repentance signifies a moral solidarity with victims, and it is on account of this moral solidarity that a different relationship can emerge. To the extent that this moral solidarity is met with forgiveness by victims, there can emerge a 'new insight into the moral character of

67. Marshall, *Compassionate Justice*, 232.

68. Nicholas Wolterstorff, *Justice in Love* (Grand Rapids, MI: Eerdmans, 2011), 188; cf. 72.

the other; thereby they open up the possibility of a renewed relationship'. Wolterstorff goes on to note that 'Punishment of the wrongdoer achieves neither of these; it neither liberates the parties from the moral pit in which they find themselves nor does it enable reconciliation'.[69]

This celebration of repentance is what differentiates the father's response from that of classic retributivism. He honors the change that has occurred in his son, evident in his return and confession. Retributivists, on the other hand, prioritize procedural uniformity and an external rules-based notion of justice that offers little space for the moral and relational position of wrongdoers. In the narrative, it is the older brother who expresses such distrust of judicial leniency. He seems to prefer, in Marshall's words, 'the simplicity of punitive ostracism to the complexity of wrestling with the ambiguities that always surround situations of human offending and the corresponding obligation to employ Brien's "gentle virtue of mercy" in the interest of achieving moral outcomes'.[70] Furthermore, by honoring the repentant wrongdoer, the older brother believes that the honor due him as a law-abiding individual has been usurped.[71] Honoring law-breakers is equivalent to dishonoring law-keepers, according to the retributive logic of the older brother; the inclusion of one constitutes the exclusion of the other.

The older brother's polarized thinking illustrates a core presupposition behind legal responses to wrongdoing, and this returns us to where we began this section. The primary objective of the law is to judge between the guilty and the innocent, the wrongdoers and the wronged, law-keepers and law-breakers. While such absolute polarities rarely correspond with reality, the apparatus of legal judgment still functions against the background of an adversarial and bipolar system of justice.[72] The older brother embodies this adversarial approach when, in order to make the accusation of injustice stick, he portrays his younger brother

69. Ibid., 189–90.

70. Marshall, *Compassionate Justice*, 241.

71. Marshall argues that behind this 'distrust of judicial leniency' lies a character trait of 'embittered victimhood… His sense of victimhood', writes Marshall, 'runs so deep that he assumes that the celebration thrown for his brother somehow detracts from his own virtue and devalues his standing in his father's eyes'; ibid., 239.

72. The two dominant systems of legal judgment are adversarial, where a judge or jury judges in favor of either the prosecution or the defense after the two sides have contested their case, and inquisitorial, where a judge or panel investigates a case to determine if any charges should be brought; cf. Peter J. Van Koppen and Steven D. Penrod, ed., *Adversarial Versus Inquisitorial Justice: Psychological Perspectives on Criminal Justice Systems* (London: Springer Limited, 2012).

in the worst possible light, while presenting himself as a paragon of righteousness (vv. 29-30).[73] Degrading wrongdoers or exacerbating their shame helps maintain a status differentiation between the righteous and the unrighteous. In the thinking of the older brother, this status differentiation should result in his receiving more of his own share, and providing him with more privilege (v. 23). The father, on the other hand, exhibits the radical and unbounded generosity of God's own forgiveness and the depth of solidarity with sinners and wrongdoers that were embodied in Jesus's own life and ministry.

The father's actions unequivocally proclaim the restoration of his son to a place of belonging, and so also affirm the new commitment of his son to right living. Yet in order for such a transformation to be lasting the father must enlist the commitment of the wider community, which is the third restorative feature of this parable on justice.

Building a Compassionate Community

Before the establishment of a centralized system of laws, our historical survey noted that there existed a period of community justice whereby wrongdoing was primarily conceived as an offence against the entire community. The social fabric of the local community was endangered whenever the values of that community were flagrantly disregarded, not least the value of trust upon which any notion of civic order is based.[74] In the parable, the younger son provoked the outrage of the village community in at least three ways: he allowed the ancestral ownership of the land to fall into the hands of outside opportunists, he publicly shamed his father who, due to his wealth, was also a village patriarch, and he became unclean by his association with pigs and Gentile outsiders. It is significant, therefore, that the father's actions seem to have taken place in public before a watching community, and that the father eventually enlists this community to participate in his son's full restoration by the throwing of a feast.

73. Volf writes that the older brother 'encourages self-righteousness and the demonization of others'; Volf, *Exclusion and Embrace*, 162–63.

74. Ross London argues that in the context of wrongdoing our sense of injury primarily centers on an abuse of trust; Ross London, *Crime, Punishment, and Restorative Justice: From the Margins to the Mainstream* (Boulder, CO: Lynne Rienner Publishers, 2010). I am indebted to Marshall's extensive engagement with London's notion of trust in his inaugural address; Christopher Marshall, 'Restoring What? The Practice, Promise, and Perils of Restorative Justice in New Zealand', paper presented at Rutherford House, Victoria University of Wellington, New Zealand, 25 March 2014.

Through his actions, the father did not simply intend to placate the village's urge for vengeance. Instead, as Marshall points out, the father models 'the restoring love of God'. This parable is intended,

> to furnish a model for how believers are to treat those whom the wider community judges to be treacherous offenders worthy only of punishment. They are to emulate the graciousness of God toward them – which means inviting their repentance, receiving their confession without objection, and restoring them to full participation in community.[75]

The father furnishes a restorative communal response towards penitent wrongdoers in at least two respects: by a public display of forgiveness and, second, by an act of hospitality. While the word 'forgiveness' is never used in the parable, it occupies a crucial place in the overall narrative. In the Mediterranean social order, where honor and shame played a central role in public life, forgiveness 'was as much about restoring honor as assuaging guilt'.[76] Marshall argues that the father's restorative actions were an 'outworking of the discipline of forgiveness', which in the case of his son meant his reintegration to a place of belonging in the community.[77] Through his public actions the father acts in a representative fashion on behalf of the community to forgive his son.

This parable clearly demonstrates a privileging of the needs and voice of primary victims over any secondary concerns. While the village members may have had their communal ethic threatened by the prodigal's actions, no one has been more shamed or injured than the father. He is the primary victim. At the very least this means that the father's forgiveness is considered to be final, that the village members have no right of redress that supersedes that of the father. Moreover, if we take in full seriousness the boy's confession – 'I have sinned against heaven and you' – then he represents God's forgiveness of this son as well, which is likewise final. The restorative power of primary victims is evident in the father's response when he takes upon himself the collective injury caused by the wrongdoer and releases him from his bondage of guilt by an act of forgiveness. The resonance with how God in Christ acts to forgive his wayward creation by bearing their transgression is all too evident.

75. Marshall, *Compassionate Justice*, 233.

76. Ibid., 229.

77. Ibid., 245; contra Mayo, *Limits of Forgiveness*, 75–76.

Forgiveness is neither easy nor cheap, which is why Marshall stresses that forgiveness takes place within the 'moral space created by remorse, repentance, confession, and accountability, and demands moral effort on the part of both giver and receiver'.[78] For the father to forgive, he must first judge his son as having done wrong, otherwise there would be nothing to forgive. Forgiveness is inescapably a form of judgment, which is why receiving forgiveness is often as difficult as the giving of forgiveness.[79] Yet in the same instance, by forgiving the father relinquishes any right of redress, otherwise he would be exercising a conditional forgiveness that is no forgiveness at all. A forgiveness that first awaits the redress of retributive justice is not forgiveness; it is simply the refusal to act vindictively.[80] A forgiveness patterned after this restorative response is an active rather than passive action. It enlists both the victim and the offender in a relationship whereby the actions of the past are *healed* and *repaired*, rather than allowing old wounds to fester and destroy.

We noted earlier that the language of forgiveness and reconciliation no longer features as prominently in the restorative justice vocabulary as it once did. The more secular-sounding language of healing and repair is now preferred, though not without some of the same criticism.[81] However, this lexical shift is misleading, since both sets of words describe the same relational process and the same hoped-for outcome. Forgiveness is embodied as healing, and to experience emotional healing is to be, at some level, in the grip of forgiveness.

78. Marshall, *Compassionate Justice*, 243.

79. As Wolterstorff argues against Nygren's *Agape and Eros*: the 'concept of forgiveness incorporates the concept of being wronged. It follows that if we never employ the concept of being wronged in our engagements with our fellow human beings, the concept of justice being violated, we cannot understand ourselves as forgiving them'; Nicholas Wolterstorff, *Justice: Rights and Wrongs* (Princeton, NJ: Princeton University Press, 2008), 105.

80. Some have criticized the *Kairos Document* written before the dismantling of apartheid South Africa as advocating this notion of justice before forgiveness, even if it was written in the sincere attempt to pursue genuine rather than cheap reconciliation. See *The Kairos Document, Challenge to the Church: A Theological Comment on the Political Crisis in South Africa* (Grand Rapids, MI: Eerdmans, 1986), cf. Article 3.1.

81. Borton and Paul, 'Problematizing the Healing Metaphor of Restorative Justice'. See also Kathleen Daly, 'A Tale of Two Studies: Restorative Justice from a Victims' Perspective', in *New Directions in Restorative Justice: Issues, Practice, Evaluation*, ed. Elizabeth Elliot and Robert M. Gordon (Cullompton, UK: Willan, 2005), 153–74; idem, 'Restorative Justice – the Real Story', *Punishment and Society* 4 (2002): 55–79; Heather Strang, *Repair or Revenge: Victims and Restorative Justice* (Oxford: Clarendon Press, 2002).

Marshall describes the ensuing feast as a 'feast of forgiveness' because of the costly and transformative work that has made this renewal of relationship possible. The father's acknowledgment of the boy's repentance and his response of compassionate forgiveness models a better system of justice to the rest of the community. This is a justice that, taking into account 'the ontological reality of human relatedness', is fulfilled in 'the making right of relationships'.[82]

The second way in which the father exhibits a communal ethic of restoration is through an act of hospitality. The throwing of a feast to mark the celebrated return of his repentant son is an invitation for others to participate in the restoration of the 'lost' and 'dead' son (v. 24). Feasting takes on even greater significance within its Lukan context, where it symbolically represents the dawning eschatological age of God's salvation being made available to all. The metaphor of a feast echoes God's election and deliverance of Israel in the Jewish Passover, and looks forward to the Last Supper where God gathers the new Israel to participate in his heavenly banqueting. The restoration in view of God's justice is 'liturgically enshrined in eating', as Ward argues.[83] Lending further weight to this eschatological allusion is the father's emphatic 'must' to celebrating in the presence of 'life', thus pointing to the signs of resurrection present in the son's return.

Acting as the host to this banquet, the father extends his invitation in the expectant hope that others will join him. This is, however, a vulnerable act by the father. It opens him up to the possibility of rejection if his invitation be declined, which would only compound his humiliation and loss of status within the communal order. Hospitality is often a risky enterprise, but no risk was considered too great so as to outweigh the enjoyment of receiving a lost son back into full communion.

It is this risky hospitality in search of a fully restored relationship that embodies the way of God's justice in the world. Hans Boersma rightly points out that in order to draw humanity into a pure unconditional hospitality, God had to step into 'a world that is already beset by violence, injustice, and inhospitality… [I]ncarnation and crucifixion mean getting involved and getting "messed up" in the quirks and quarks of a thoroughly inhospitable situation'.[84] In the midst of the world's injustice

82. Marshall, *Compassionate Justice*, 243.

83. Ward confirms this theme of eschatological feasting in Ward, *Politics of Discipleship*, 273.

84. Hans Boersma, *Violence, Hospitality, and the Cross: Reappropriating the Atonement Tradition* (Grand Rapids, MI: Baker Academic, 2004), 36–37. Boersma's reference to 'undeconstructible justice' comes from Derrida, who argues for a strong

and inhospitality, God establishes a place of pure hospitality through the cross of Christ, which has also been shown to be the site of God's restorative justice.

Significantly, the older son refuses to participate in the feast of forgiveness. This refusal indicates not only a judgment against his younger brother but also a failure of perception, as 'he feels no need of forgiveness himself'.[85] The older brother's legalism and penchant for just deserts leads him to be outraged by his father's compassionate forgiveness, which he considers to be a flagrant denial of justice. Were he to take up his place alongside his father in this practice of 'open-handed hospitality', he would not only be endorsing the ritual of forgiveness, but he would also be extending the offer of livelihood to his empty-handed brother. According to this parable, the practice of restorative hospitality has the concrete definition, in the words of Marshall, of being ready to share our '"living" (*bios*) and "substance" (*ousia*), so that they [offenders] may again participate as equals in the social and economic life of society. Nothing less than this qualifies, finally, as restorative justice.'[86]

To conclude this discussion, we return to Broughton's comments about what Marshall brings to the interpretation of Scripture. According to Broughton, Marshall's reading is distinguished by being prescient, peaceable, and performable.[87] A *prescient* reading engages with the historical context of the text, while bringing contemporary concerns to the interpretive task. By following Marshall's reading of this parable, we have been able to address contemporary justice concerns, like, for example, the role of shame in modern penal practice. A *peaceable* reading fosters reconciliation between divisive identities or cultures, which in this parable has been evident in the restored relationship between father and son, victim and wrongdoer, village and prodigal. A *performable* reading brings the theological-imaginative thrust of the narrative together with its concrete enactment in relationships and community. The reading of

differentiation between justice and law, with the former always deconstructing the latter. The result, however, is that justice remains the only thing that is undeconstructible; Jacques Derrida, 'Force of Law: The "Mystical Foundation of Authority"', in *Deconstruction and the Possibility of Justice*, ed. Drucilla Cornell, Michael Rosenfeld, and David Gray Carlson (London: Routledge, 1992), 3–67.

85. Marshall, *Compassionate Justice*, 239.

86. Ibid., 245.

87. Geoff Broughton, 'Making Public Theology More Biblical or Biblical Theology More Public? Christopher Marshall's Interpretation of the Parable of the Prodigal Son in Luke 15', in Neville, ed., *The Bible, Justice and Public Theology*, 74.

this parable has given insight not just to some generic truth about wrongdoing, repentance, or compassion. Rather, we have described in concrete detail the relational nature of wrongdoing, the stages on the journey of repentance, and the ways in which compassion has been enacted through embrace, honoring, and feasting.

We have seen that Marshall's approach of bringing a 'restorative justice lens' to the interpretation of Scripture opens up a fruitful perspective for furthering restorative justice in a more theological direction through engagement with Scripture. While not suggesting that restorative justice should be used as a master metaphor for interpreting all Scripture, or suggesting that all Scripture points unambiguously to a restorative understanding of justice, Marshall *has* nevertheless shown that restorative justice provides fresh insight into texts that do have a clear justice dimension. This is especially true with texts that point to the justice of God's kingdom as embodied in the life, death, and resurrection of Jesus. A restorative conception of justice makes for a better reading of Scripture than do readings that presuppose a purely legalistic or retributive conception of justice.

It would be expected that the community that has grappled with this story generation after generation should appreciate the difference between a retributive conception of justice and justice understood as a restorative and relational reality. Unfortunately this has not always been the case. For this reason, Marshall believes

> part of the mission of the restorative justice movement is to remind the Christian community of what it supposedly believes and ought to practice more consistently, to call the church's attention back to what Jesus himself expounded in his teaching and embodied in his life.[88]

In the next chapter, I will follow Marshall's lead by bringing a restorative justice lens to the interpretation of one of Paul's epistles to a church struggling to live out its faith in God's saving justice in a pagan environment. We will investigate the extent to which Paul reflects a similar theological imagination about the nature of God's justice that we see reflected in the teaching of Jesus.

88. Marshall, *Compassionate Justice*, 7.

Chapter 6

The Restorative Spirit in Christian Community: A Reading of First Corinthians

I have argued that the justice of God is best understood as a liberative, salvific and restorative justice, rather than a retributive or retaliatory justice. As such it is inherently relational, concerned primarily with the righting of relationships that have been distorted and conflicted. Such an understanding of the justice of God constitutes a better reading of Scripture and also results in a better performance of Scripture. That is to say, it summons the people of God to respond to God's justice by embodying this same kind of restoring justice in its life together.

The goal in this chapter, as it was in the previous one, is to extend the church's imagination as to how it might bring about the kind of restoration and healing we have been describing. As the body of Christ, the church has been given everything it needs to witness to the justice of God. The intention, then, is not to import a series of restorative practices from elsewhere to enable the church to be more restorative. Instead, it is to search for clues from the church's own theological and Scriptural sources that help direct us to a form of restorative justice germane to the life of the ecclesia. This has already done this in the analysis of Jesus's parable of the 'Tender-Hearted Father and His Two Difficult Sons', as Marshall calls it.[1] I now turn to some selected features of Paul's great epistle to the church in Corinth. The aim is not to provide a detailed exegetical treatment of 1 Corinthians, but to identify theological themes that can help guide the church to better enact God's restorative justice in the world.

In what follows I will first explain why the Corinthian correspondence is a good choice for probing into how Paul understood the justice of God taking form in the church. We will then draw out a number of features that together show what it means for the church to 'become the justice of God' (2 Cor. 5.21). In particular, I will trace how Paul calls on the Corinthians to practice relationships formed after the way of the cross,

1. Ibid., 186.

where God's justice was decisively revealed. Their fractious and conflict-ridden relationships (1 Cor. 1–4; 12–14) were evidence that they were *mis*-embodying God's justice, and therefore were in need of new justice practices such as caring for the least, seeking unity, exhibiting relationships that are *fraternal* and *koinōnial* (κοινωνία), and listening for the Spirit. It is through such practices that the church lives out the 'ministry of reconciliation' (2 Cor. 5.20) by localizing its experience of reconciliation with God in particular contexts. We will see that the church has uniquely *theological* reasons for why its 'doing of justice' ought to take the form of restorative justice. We begin, however, with a word about the context in which Paul pens his letter to the Corinthians.

Reading First Corinthians

The Setting of the Letter

The authorship, chronology, and sequence of the Pauline corpus have long been a matter of intense debate in Pauline scholarship. Rather than rehearsing that debate here, which would distract us from our chief interest, it will be enough to draw on Douglas Campbell's recent work to locate 1 Corinthians in its historical context.[2] Less than two years before writing the letter, Paul was involved in a serious conflict in Antioch with Cephas, one of the leaders of the Jerusalem church. After resolving this conflict through a conciliatory, though confrontational, process, Paul was incarcerated somewhere close by the Lycus valley, on his way back from Syrian Antioch, as he was heading towards the Aegean. During his imprisonment, Paul wrote a cluster of letters to fledging communities and households in the Lycus valley (Ephesians, Colossians, and Philemon).[3] No doubt his prison-time would have clarified a number of matters, not least his understanding of the place of the church within the economy of God's justice.[4]

2. See the recent treatment of Paul's epistolary chronology, Douglas A. Campbell, *Framing Paul: An Epistolary Biography* (Grand Rapids, MI: Eerdmans, 2014), especially 404–11.

3. The inclusion of Ephesians and Colossians in the Pauline corpus diverges from the long-held view that these were written by a latter devotee of Paul. Campbell offers a robust rebuttal to this earlier proposal that is likely to reshape the presuppositions that have heretofore divided up the Pauline material.

4. Paul's productive letter writing from prison is not an unlikely phenomenon. Campbell notes that throughout human history incarceration has shown to be a 'fertile space for reflection and literary work, especially by (literate) activists. This space affords them time like no other to reflect, think, and compose. The result can then be

In Ephesians, Paul writes, 'I therefore, a *prisoner* in the Lord, beg you to lead a life worthy of the *calling* to which you have been called… making every effort to maintain the unity of the Spirit in the bond of *peace*' (4.1-3). He summons his readers to be 'renewed in the spirit of your minds, and to clothe yourselves with the new self, created *according to the likeness of God in true justice* (κατὰ Θεὸν κτισθέντα ἐν δικαιοσύνῃ) and holiness' (4.23-24). The church is renewed in the likeness of God's justice by sustaining its relationships in the bond of peace. The purpose of this calling is that, 'through the church the wisdom of God in its rich variety might now be made known to the rulers and authorities' (3.10). Included in these 'rulers and authorities' would be those representing Roman justice currently holding Paul captive. Paul was no stranger to Roman justice, yet the call to justice he urges the church to pursue is to be found in the bond of a *liberating peace*, which is wholly unlike the incarcerating 'justice' he is currently experiencing.[5]

After his release from prison, Paul experienced a range of setbacks. In an unpreserved letter to the Corinthians, he outlined his plans to take up a collection for the poor in Jerusalem. This collection would not simply convey economic help, it would also serve to promote peace between Jewish and Gentile believers (cf. 2 Cor. 8–9). The collection would be an occasion for ethnically diverse communities to testify to the peace they now share in Christ. Evidently the Corinthians responded to this proposal somewhat assertively, and it became clear to Paul that the congregation was divided in its loyalty to him. The church was also splintered into factions along social and economic lines, and relationships within the church had become abusive, disempowering, and outright antagonistic. It is at this point that Paul writes his 'Letter of Tears' from Ephesus (2 Cor. 2.4), which could well be our 1 Corinthians.[6]

This background shows that 1 Corinthians was written in order to address multiple failures in this community's witness to the saving justice of God. The actions of the Corinthians testify to their *mis*-embodiment of the gospel of God's justice, and Paul's efforts to rectify this situation

work of a truly definitive nature, provided that the material can be written down in some way and retrieved from the prison'; ibid., 269.

5. For a reading of Ephesians that highlights this ecclesial peace-making and justice-making, see Christopher D. Marshall, '"Making Every Effort": Peacemaking and Ecclesiology in Ephesians 4:1-6', in *Struggles for Shalom: Peace and Violence across the Testaments*, ed. Laura L. Brenneman and Brad D. Schantz (Eugene, OR: Pickwick Publications, 2014), 256–66.

6. See Campbell's argument for 1 Corinthians as Paul's 'letter of tears'; Campbell, *Framing Paul*, 61–74.

afford us great insight into what a true embodiment should look like.[7] Paul thought the Christians in Corinth had capitulated to a conception of justice drawn from their surrounding cultural context rather than the form of justice revealed in the crucified Messiah (1.18-31). In reply, he describes practices that reflect what it means to be in Christ, 'who became for us wisdom from God, and righteousness and sanctification and redemption' (1.30).

In spelling this out, Paul's argument moves through four main phases. First, he reiterates the nature and calling of the Christian community by emphasizing its obligation to embody the gospel of Christ crucified (chs. 1–4). This entails relationships that are *fraternal* and *koinōnial*, grounded in the relationship God has extended to them through Christ's cross. Second, Paul addresses certain practices that reflect a failure to embody their call (chs. 5–11). These include sexual licentiousness, taking fellow believers to court, and abuses at the Lord's Supper. Third, Paul suggests how the church might healthily confront practices of injustice by employing a restorative ethic (chs. 12–14). This involves the recognition of unity in diversity, the obligation to show mutual care, training in how to love well, and encouraging intelligible speech and consensual decision-making. Finally, Paul restates the gospel of Christ's death and resurrection that is at the core of the Christian life yet which has been called into question by the Corinthians. Paul thus bookends his letter with the hope to which the church is called, sharing in the *koinōnia* of Christ's suffering community in the present while steadfastly awaiting the glory of Christ's victory over the sting of death.

Remember Your Call (Chapters 1–4)

At the beginning of his letter, Paul is quick to explain his reason for writing. Those simply identified as 'Chloe's people' have reported to him that there is 'quarrelling' in the church (1 Cor. 1.11).[8] This was no small squabble; it was a major dispute about 'who belongs to whom'. Most commentators agree that the factionalism was a result of the Corinthians's enthusiasm for a style of sophist rhetoric, with its resultant arrogance and competitiveness.[9] Rather than understanding that all believers belong to

7. Citing Yung Suk Kim, Gorman argues that Paul's letter was written to address 'the Corinthians' failure to embody Christ crucified', which this chapter will show to be a failure of their embodiment of God's justice; Gorman, *Becoming the Gospel*, 234.

8. Hereafter all citations will be from 1 Corinthians unless otherwise stated.

9. So Richard B. Hays, *The Conversion of the Imagination: Paul as Interpreter of Israel's Scripture* (Grand Rapids, MI: Eerdmans, 2005); idem, *First Corinthians*

One alone, they had displaced Christ with favored human heroes and so were forming the church after 'human inclinations' (3.3-4). The result was a community suffering rampant sexual immorality, court action between members, elitist attitudes, disregard for the faith and conscience of new believers, drunkenness and abuses at the Lord's Table, and allowing the poor to go hungry while the rich got fat.

Paul considers each of these issues to be symptomatic of a deeper malaise – absconding from the call to participate in God's redemption of the world through relationships that are *fraternal* and *koinōnial.* The problems in Corinth require a theological as much as a pastoral response if there is to be an end to the selfish and antagonistic spirit rife in the congregation. Paul does this by redefining their identity as a people 'called out' from the world and into the communion God has established in Christ.

Paul employs the language of 'calling' no fewer than five times in the opening chapter. He starts by referring to himself as one 'called to be an apostle of Christ Jesus' (1.1), and describes the Corinthians as 'called to be saints' (1.2) and 'called into the fellowship (κοινωνία) of his Son, Jesus Christ our Lord' (1.9). The language of 'calling' here echoes the call of Israel to be God's covenantal partner: 'The Lord spoke to Moses, saying: "Speak to all the congregation of the people of Israel and say to them: You shall be holy, for I the Lord your God am holy"' (Lev. 19.1-2).[10] By referring to the Corinthians as 'called', Paul is saying that, like Israel, they too have been addressed by God and called to be a holy people. Their reply involves them in 'calling on the name of our Lord Jesus Christ' (1.2), which shows how 'God's free Self-identification and Self-presentation to humanity in Christ' is a relational reality.[11] It is 'an event of communion' between persons, and all those who are called in Christ must now understand their being in relation to this event of communion.[12]

Paul's reference to the Corinthians being 'called into the κοινωνία of his Son' is ambiguous, perhaps intentionally so. It can refer both to the communion the Corinthians share *with* Christ, as well as to the communal relations with one another that the Corinthians exhibit *in* Christ. As Torrance observes, 'God's Self-communication also must be

(Louisville: John Knox Press, 1997); Ben W. Witherington III, *Conflict and Community in Corinth: A Socio-Rhetorical Commentary on 1 and 2 Corinthians* (Grand Rapids, MI: Eerdmans, 1995); S. M. Pogoloff, *Logos and Sophia: The Rhetorical Situation of 1 Corinthians* (Atlanta, GA: Scholars Press, 1992).

10. Cited from Hays, *First Corinthians*, 16.

11. Torrance, '"Ought" from "Is"', 168 (italics added).

12. Ibid., 169.

understood as a *generative* event of communion. Through the presence of the Spirit, the *koinōnia* or communion that God establishes with humanity engenders communion at the "horizontal" level.'[13] The church is thereby called into a communion of *fraternal* relationships – 'brothers and sisters' (1.10) – as it shares in the *filial* status of being God's children in Christ. The church is to reflect the communion God has established with humanity by bringing that humanity to participate in κοινωνία with his Son, and it does this by exhibiting relationships that are intimate, life-sharing, and sacrificial.[14]

By drawing attention to this *koinōnial* context, Paul is at the same time hinting at the weakness of the Corinthians in sustaining the kind of relationships that really matter. This offers a crucial insight into Paul's understanding of the church – it is to be known by the quality and character of its relationships. Throughout the letter Paul expends considerable effort in re-orienting the nature of relationships in the ecclesia. Fundamentally they are to be conformed to the message of 'Christ crucified' (1.22), an event that is incomprehensible when judged according to human standards, yet for 'us who are *being* saved (viz., the church), it is the *power* of God' (1.18). Salvation comprises an event of liberating power that progressively unfolds in the corporate life of believers. Paul is effectively arguing that Jesus's cross defines for the church the very shape and character of God's restoring justice in the world. To be saved is to be transformed by a power that is re-creating relationships in a way that is marked by the cross.

That the Corinthian church is full of quarrelling and divisions is a sign they have failed to comprehend the nature of God's saving justice. This would suggest that their own salvation is in question, for, as Gorman points out,

> justification means a *transfer* from the realm of the unjust/unjustified into the realm of the just/justified, which simultaneously means a *transformation, a conversion* from being unjust people to being just people and thus a *transition* from practices of injustice to practices of Christologically shaped justice.[15]

13. Torrance, 'Forgiveness and Reconciliation', 47.

14. Gorman writes, 'the Pauline language of *koinōnia* indicates a deep participation in Christ, especially in his death, that is shared with other believers and that comes to fruition in concrete practices of sacrificial, generous, self-giving love and even suffering'; Gorman, *Becoming the Gospel*, 31.

15. Ibid., 237.

Paul addresses the root of the matter by asking the Corinthians to consider their own 'call' (1.26), which was itself a testament to the restorative and benevolent nature of divine justice. He reminds them that, 'not many of you were wise by human standards, not many were powerful, not many were of noble birth'. Most were from the ranks of 'the low and despised in the world' (1.26-31). And yet they were called to live in communion with God, who showers them with every gift of 'speech and knowledge of every kind', and ensures they have everything they need (1.4-7). Their elevation from a state of social marginalization to a place of covenantal communion was itself a demonstration of God's liberating, saving justice at work. Now, as a just/justified people, they must embody that same justice in their life together. This requires their recognition of how the worldly markers of status – wisdom, power, wealth, and nobility – were reduced to nothing in the light of how God had revealed himself in the cross (1.28).

Paul's argument is that the cross of Christ empties the powerful of their power and the wise of their wisdom, so that power and wisdom may be conceived anew through him. Justice too – the justice of the 'the rulers of this age' who crucified the Lord of Glory (2.8-9) – must also be reconceived, since, for the church, the Crucified One is both the 'wisdom of God and the *justice of God* (δικαιοσύνη Θεοῦ)' (1.30).[16] The Corinthians must consider whether the character of their relationships testifies to the wisdom and justice of the present age, where the powerful dominate the low and despised (1.29; 2.6, 8), or to the new age, inaugurated by the life, death, and resurrection of God's Messiah. Paul calls them, as Hays argues, to a 'conversion of the imagination', whereby they might find their 'primary identification with fellow believers rather than seeking legitimacy according to the status-defining standards of their native civic culture'.[17]

Paul illustrates what it means to live under the sign of the cross by contrasting the Corinthians's attitude towards leadership with his own example of apostolic suffering (3.4–4.13). The factionalism in the church stemmed from their elevation of human leaders to a position whereby

16. So Gorman, 'we should read 1:30 not merely as a description of what Christ *provides* but primarily of what Christ *is*, that is, the divine attributes he embodies as the crucified one'; ibid., 230.

17. Hays, *Conversion of the Imagination*, 13, see especially 12–21. Hays convincingly argues that Paul was teaching the Corinthians to see their identity in eschatological terms in order to counteract the noneschatological ideas indigenous to their culture.

the body of Christ 'belongs' to them. This not only displaced Christ; it reflected the prevailing practices of wider society (3.4, 20; cf. Matt. 20.25-28). The cross inverts social reality and reflects the wisdom of a different kind of justice, one that relinquishes power over others and suffers on their behalf. This wisdom, Paul argues, is made known through those who participate in the age of the Spirit (2.10-13). Having received the Spirit of the new age, the Corinthians must disown the patronage of and rivalry between leaders, instead recognizing their 'common purpose' as they 'work together' in building up God's church (3.5-9). Instead of boasting in what human leaders confer on them, they must recognize that all things are theirs in Christ (3.21-23). Leaders are re-schematized as 'servants' (3.5), 'stewards' (4.1), and 'labourers' in the construction of a building belonging to the one Master of the house (3.9). To this end, Paul appeals to the Corinthians to 'imitate me' and 'my ways in Christ Jesus, as I teach them everywhere in every church' (4.16-17).

Paul's apostolic 'ways in Christ Jesus' are synonymous with the inverted reality of the cross, the way of non-retributive love: 'When reviled, we bless; when persecuted, we endure; when slandered, we speak kindly' (4.12-13). Paul is sustained in this non-retaliatory stance by his belief that this is the very nature of God as revealed in the cross. Having crucified the axioms of 'this age', Paul considers his life to be transformed by the light of the cross, which brings light to the darkness and discloses the purposes of the heart (4.4-5). Paul expects this same transformation to be evident in the practices and character of the church. This is what it concretely means for the church to embody the justice of God as disclosed in the cross.

Practicing Just Relationships (Chapters 5–11)

Having laid out the foundation for what it means to live united in Christ, Paul builds on this foundation by further explicating what it means to live as Christ's sanctified community with respect to some of the issues that have come to his attention. Of the many issues traversed in chs. 5–11, here we will focus on three issues with a clear justice-dimension that illustrate how the Corinthian Church was failing to embody the justice of God. The first involves an incident of sexual licentiousness in the church, the second is a chronic matter of litigiousness between church members, and the third relates to practices associated with the Lord's Supper. Each of these issues employs forensic categories – 'pronouncing judgment' (5.3), 'appointing judges' (6.2-4), and 'eating and drinking judgment' (11.22, 27-31) – though in an ecclesial context and with a strong orientation towards the reintegration or restoration of the wrongdoers.

Before addressing these specific issues, an important reminder is in order. It might be tempting to treat these texts as illustrating a conventional morality; for example, a 'sexual ethics' or 'marital ethics'. Such an approach, however, would fail to keep in mind Paul's overarching concern of re-centering this community's ethos on the *κοινωνία* of God. Paul does not use these specific incidents as an occasion to reprimand individual sinners, even though he believes they should be so chastised, but rather to lead the church into an understanding of its own call to practice relationships that are holy and just. By keeping this in view at all times, we can avoid the separation that often occurs in modern readings of Paul between his theology and his ethics.

Sexual Holiness

Paul brings the Corinthians's attention to the matter of one of their members having sexual relations with his father's wife (5.1-8). It is assumed that the woman in question is not a member of the church, since she is never addressed. Such sexual licentiousness (πορνεία), Paul says, was abhorrent even in 'pagan' culture. In fact, if the woman were indeed married to the man's father and not his concubine (presuming he is still alive), it would have been a breach of pagan law as well.[18] The apostle is dismayed at not only the Corinthians's toleration of this incestuous practice, but also at their celebration and sense of pride in the man's freedom – 'you are arrogant!' (5.2). They probably saw him as an exemplar of the motto that 'all things are lawful to me' (6.12; 10.23), which in this case meant flouting even pagan law. Paul calls the Corinthian church to view their conduct no longer in terms of their native pagan culture, but rather according to their new covenantal status.

According to Paul, the Corinthians's attitude stands in stark conflict with their call to embody Christ crucified by exhibiting relationships that are humble, holy, and just. Justice and holiness are two sides of the same coin. As a people called out from the world to share in communion (κοινωνία) with God's Son, the church embodies the justice of God through relationships patterned after the way of the cross. This was the whole logic of the first four chapters of his letter. This transformation takes the form, Paul argues, of being 'called to be holy' (κλητοῖς ἁγίοις, 1.2). This is why holiness or sanctification (ἁγιασμός), as Gorman argues, 'is not an addition to justification but its actualization'.[19] The church's

18. See the discussion in Marshall, *Beyond Retribution*, 152 n. 19.

19. Michael J. Gorman, *Inhabiting the Cruciform God: Kenosis, Justification, and Theosis in Paul's Narrative Soteriology* (Grand Rapids, MI: Eerdmans, 2009), 111 (original in italics)

commitment to holiness in all of its respective relationships is how it lives out the justifying justice of God. For Paul, sexual libertinism is a denial of the transformation of relationships into the form of the cross and, as Hays points out, is also a denial of their call to live as the covenant community of the new Israel.[20]

A notable feature of Paul's response is how he directs a sense of shame, not at the individual culprit, but at the whole community. The responsibility for the wrongful relation is held collectively. Paul calls the entire community to account, not because they are all involved in similar sins, but because, as Yoder aptly puts it,

> there is a kind of moral solidarity linking all the members of the body so that if individuals persist in disobedience within the fellowship, their guilt is no longer the moral responsibility of those individuals alone but becomes a kind of collective blame shared by the whole body…unless I am the agent of that person's sharing in restoration, he or she is the agent of my sharing guilt.[21]

Hence, the appropriate posture of this community in the face of wrongdoing ought to be of 'mourning' (1.2); collectively grieving over the loss that is suffered by the community as a whole. This sense of corporate guilt is undoubtedly difficult for the post-Enlightenment psyche to comprehend, but it would not have been lost on Paul's listeners. Just as they are 'puffed up' by sharing in their members' defying of moral norms, so Paul chides them for not sharing in the shame that attaches to such behavior. Paul will shortly expand on why this is so in his metaphor of the body: 'If one member suffers, all suffer together with it; if one member is honored, all rejoice together' (12.26).

The metaphor that Paul uses here is that of 'leaven', which has the effect of shaping the 'whole batch of dough' – for better or worse. The implication is clear enough. If the Corinthians leave this man's action unaddressed, then a certain contamination will spread, resulting in this community being inedible, to extend the metaphor. Paul associates this contaminating leaven, which in this case is sexual in nature, with 'malice and evil' (v. 8), thus exposing this action as coterminous with the destructive ways of sin. Whether consenting or not, sexual relationships are

20. Hays argues that in this passage Paul is 'trying to reshape their consciousness so that they take corporate responsibility for the holiness of their community; he does this by using Scripture to address them as Israel'; Hays, *Conversion of the Imagination*, 23.

21. Yoder, 'Binding and Loosing', 336.

never without consequence. To remain unleavened, as Paul puts it, the Corinthians must clear out this leftover from their previous life outside of Christ. If they do not, they risk the destruction that inevitably follows, and which the wrongdoer has already exposed himself to.

The church must respond collectively to the wrongdoing because they have a special responsibility to be a community sanctified in 'sincerity and truth' (5.8). Were the church to endorse or even tolerate those who unremittingly engage in wrongdoing, it would cease to bear witness to its participation in 'the kingdom of God' (6.9), and would instead inherit the fate of their previous life outside of Christ. By holding the entire church to account, Paul hopes to bring about a collective repentance that will issue in the disciplining of the offender (5.13) and the restoration of right relationships throughout the whole community.[22]

It is important to note that Paul does not single himself out from the burden of responsibility held by this community. He considers himself bound, if not in body, then at least in spirit, whereupon he pronounces his judgment on the wrongdoing (v. 3). In some proleptic sense, mystical even, Paul saw his spirit being present with the Lord's power when the Corinthians assemble to deal with this matter. Not unlike what we mentioned in relation to Matt. 18.15-20, Jesus is present with the community of saints when community discipline is being exercised.[23] This provides both authority and protection to the church's disciplinary process; authority to 'bind' and 'loose' as the body of Christ and the salutatory reminder that Jesus calls on the church to protect both victim and offender from abuses of power.

The expulsion of one of its members does not mean the community is to have no concern for the recalcitrant offender. Paul encourages the Corinthian community to pass judgment on the wrongdoer by handing 'this man over to Satan for the destruction of the flesh' (5.5). This text has created much confusion in the history of interpretation, even leading some to take this as a sign that the church should endorse capital punishment.[24] This is strongly refuted in Marshall's treatment of the passage,

22. This is the view expressed by both South and Marshall; see J. T. South, 'A Critique of the "Curse/Death" Interpretation of 1 Corinthians 5:1-8', *New Testament Studies* 39, no. 4 (1993): 539–61; Marshall, *Beyond Retribution*, 154–55.

23. Hays notes this connection also in his commentary; Hays, *First Corinthians*, 84.

24. Havener argues that 'capital punishment [is] required by Paul' as part of a 'curse for salvation'; I. Havener, 'A Curse for Salvation – 1 Corinthians 5:1-5', in *Sin, Salvation and the Spirit*, ed. D. Durken (Collegeville, MN: The Liturgical Press, 1979), 341.

which argues that the penalty was a temporary excommunication in the interests of ultimate restoration.[25] By 'turning over' the man to the realm of Satan through expulsion from the worshipping community, the Corinthians would communicate to this man that his actions belonged to the world over which Satan ruled. The decision to excommunicate follows that which is already true for the wrongdoer; it enacts at a corporate level what has already subjectively taken place in the individual. This would mean that the individual would no longer enjoy the protection of participating in the gathered community of believers.[26] Yet the ultimate purpose in withholding full communion was to 'encourage repentance and restoration of the obstinate sinner', writes Marshall.[27]

In the very act of holding the wrongdoer to account the church was extending to him the possibility of being restored to the community by turning away from an unholy sexual union and embracing the holiness of communion in Christ. As Paul wrote to the Galatians, 'Those who belong to Christ Jesus have crucified the flesh with its passions and desires' (Gal. 5.24), so in this instance, 'Paul hopes that the community's censure and expulsion of the incestuous man will lead to this result'.[28] As we noted previously, church discipline is oriented by the ultimate goal of forgiveness and reconciliation, which is precisely what the Corinthians would be expected to offer were the wrongdoer to repent. This offers a salient lesson for the church today. A commitment to restorative justice by the church flows from its own internal discipline and integrity to be a community that counters the many forms of wrongdoing in the world.

Communal Conciliation

Another matter that Paul singles out for comment is the practice of bringing disputes between members in the ecclesia to be tried before the secular courts (6.1-11). Paul expresses his deep dismay over this situation,

25. See Marshall, *Beyond Retribution*, 153.

26. This concurs with Fee's reading, 'In contrast to the gathered community of believers who experience the Spirit and power of the Lord Jesus in edifying gifts and loving concern for one another, this man is to be put back out into the world, where Satan and his "principalities and powers" still hold sway over people's lives to destroy them'; Gordon D. Fee, *The First Epistle to the Corinthians* (Grand Rapids, MI: Eerdmans, 1987), 209.

27. Marshall, *Beyond Retribution*, 155. Marshall's reading concurs with Fee, who argues that it would be 'out of character with Paul's theology as we meet it elsewhere that one who sins within the Christian community should be so punished in the present age that he lies beyond the redemptive, restorative love of that community'; Fee, *Corinthians*, 212.

28. Hays, *First Corinthians*, 86.

indicated by his moving the Corinthians to feel shame about what they are doing. As we will see, he is not alarmed at the existence of grievances or conflict in the church per se, but he is deeply concerned with how they are resolved. Paul's concern is for the church to embody God's justice-*making* and peace-*making* as an alternative to the injustice and violence of the world, which in this case puts the spotlight on how disputes are to be settled within the ecclesia itself.[29]

The practice of taking fellow believers to court over 'trivial' and 'ordinary' matters – literally the stuff of everyday life (6.2-3) – reflects a failure by the Corinthians to embody God's justice in at least two ways. First, Paul considers the courts to be part of the realm of the unjust (ἄδικος, 6.1), certainly not reflective of the reality that is being transformed by God's cruciform justice. Marshall points out that civil litigation in first-century Roman Corinth often favored those with greater status and wealth. One's case was greatly enhanced by showing up the inferiority of the other party or by tarnishing their character.[30] Sampley writes, for example, 'civil courts were not to be trusted for justice. Even Roman citizens did not have equal opportunity before the law. Wealth, position, and standing…were the best assurance of favorable judgment in the courts.'[31]

By dragging their disputes before the court, the Corinthians were emulating the ways of 'the unrighteous', reflecting the priorities and practices of this age rather than the new age. Practically, this would have resulted in the weaker members of the church suffering injustice at the hands of their fellow believers. This is reflected in Thiselton's apt title in his commentary, 'Legal Action by the Socially Influential as an Abuse of Power'.[32] Far from being a peripheral matter, this pattern of the stronger or wealthier members of the church dominating the weaker or poorer members is repeated throughout the letter (especially, 11.17-34). For

29. Or, as Hauerwas puts it, 'Christians are called to live nonviolently, not because we think nonviolence is a strategy to rid the world of war, but rather because as faithful followers of Christ in a world of war we cannot imagine not living non-violently'; Hauerwas, *War and the American Difference*, xii.

30. Marshall, *Beyond Retribution*, 150–51.

31. J. Paul Sampley, *Pauline Partnership in Christ: Christian Commitment and Community in Light of Roman Law* (Philadelphia, PA: Fortress Press, 1980), 3, cited in Edward M. Keazirian, *Peace and Peacemaking in Paul and the Greco-Roman World* (New York: Peter Lang, 2014), 166.

32. As Thiselton titles this section in his commentary, 'Legal Action by the Socially Influential as an Abuse of Power'; Anthony C. Thiselton, *The First Epistle to the Corinthians: A Commentary on the Greek Text* (Grand Rapids, MI: Eerdmans, 2000), 420.

this reason Paul retorts, 'Why not rather be wronged? Why not rather be defrauded than to wrong or defraud fellow members of Christ?' (vv. 7-8).

As an alternative to this deplorable situation, Paul advocates an extra-judicial procedure of something resembling private arbitration between members of the church, a procedure that reflects their standing as 'saints' or holy ones who will one day 'judge the world' and 'judge angels' (vv. 2-5).[33] The reference to judging angels serves to highlight the ridiculousness of their present situation when viewed from their eschatological destiny of having to judge the entire world. Hence, lawsuits in court are 'already a defeat' for believers, regardless of the outcome. The Corinthians are, in Hays's words, 'failing to act as a community, failing to take responsibility for one another', and thus failing to be a people called to enact justice in all respective parts of their life together.[34]

The reference to a form of ecclesial arbitration suggests a second way in which Paul considers the Corinthians to have failed in their calling. Paul opposes civil litigation because it was a forum not at all conducive to reconciliation, and as such it fails to reflect the form of justice they have experienced in Christ (6.7, 11). As opposed to civil litigation, Paul's suggestion of an internal process of mediation has a focus on restoring to rightness relationships between 'one brother and another' within the community of faith (6.5). In other words, this process is concerned with the familial bonds within God's family; this is this community's structure of belonging. It is this bond that suffers injury when disputes occur, and it is this that needs to be restored. The failure of the Corinthians to see their disputes in this way is highlighted by their choosing a form of litigation that prioritizes a contrary set of values.

It is likely that Paul was drawing on texts like Deut. 1.9-17 and Exod. 18.13-26 in calling the Corinthians to appoint judges over their internal affairs. In Deuteronomy, Moses is instructed to appoint wise and reputable persons to share in the burdens of judging Israel: 'Give the members of your community a fair hearing, and judge rightly between one person and another, whether citizen or resident alien. You must not be partial in judging' (Deut. 1.16). Such persons would act, as Thiselton rightly points out, as a *tribunal* attempting mediation or conciliation rather than issuing legal pronouncements.[35] It would be fair to assume that the success

33. See Marshall, who says that Paul 'advocates private arbitration, an extra-judicial procedure available under Graeco-Roman law and supported by Scripture (Deut. 16.18-20), wherein a community member is selected to mediate between the disputing parties'; Marshall, *Beyond Retribution*, 151.

34. Hays, *First Corinthians*, 93.

35. Thiselton, *Corinthians*, 428–30.

of such a tribunal to resolve disputes is dependent on the community's acceding authority to it – such authority cannot be claimed as a matter of right. Paul adds another essential criterion to the appointment of judges in this passage: that they shun the vices that characterized their former life before Christ (vv. 9-11).

Paul ends his instruction on this matter with another reminder to the Corinthians of their new identity in Christ: 'this is what some of you used to be. But you were washed, you were sanctified, you were justified in the name of the Lord Jesus Christ and in the Spirit of God' (6.11). The 'deft wordplay' of this passage is often lost in English translations, but Hays underscores its justice dimension by translating it, 'You used to be unjust (*adikoi*)...but you were justified (*edikaiōthēte*)'.[36] In other words, you used to practice injustice but having been washed and sanctified and justified in Christ, you must no longer practice injustice, especially within the community of faith. This is also, as Gorman points out, an issue of the church's witness. For by bringing their matters before the courts of the unjust, they are implicitly communicating to their pagan neighbors that the church is not a place where reconciling love is practiced.[37] By their actions they testify to a counter-gospel rather than the gospel of God's restorative justice.

Table Manners

Our third example relates to one of the central practices of the Christian community, the Lord's Supper (11.17-34). The Corinthian practice of this meal appears to have been hosted by one of the wealthier members of the congregation and involved a substantial feast to which individual guests contributed their own offerings.[38] The host in this instance was failing to delay the serving of the meal until all were present, which meant that the food was not being evenly distributed between rich and poor, some were going away drunk, while others left hungry (11.21). Paul castigates the Corinthians for allowing their factionalism and divisions to become a source of injustice towards the poor and weak (11.18-19). In so doing they had allowed what was meant to be a radically counter-cultural practice to become a tool for reinforcing cultural norms.

36. Hays, *First Corinthians*, 98.

37. 'When members of the community of the just take their matters to the courts of the unjust, they are obviously saying something to those courts and to all who are aware of their actions'; Gorman, *Becoming the Gospel*, 239.

38. As surmised by Paul F. Bradshaw and Maxwell E. Johnson, *The Eucharistic Liturgies: Their Evolution and Interpretation* (Collegeville, MN: Liturgical Press, 2012), 10.

The origins of the Christian meal, of course, lay in the meals that featured regularly in Jesus's ministry, particularly the Last Supper. Crossan describes the original character of these meals:

> The table companionship practiced by Jesus thus recreated the world, redrew all of society's maps and flow charts. Instead of symbolizing social rank and order, it blurred the distinctions between hosts and guests, need and plenty. Instead of reinforcing rules of etiquette, it subverted them, making the last first and the first last.[39]

This was not the practice of the Corinthians, which is why Paul tells them that their gatherings are 'not really the Lord's supper they eat' (v. 20). In fact, insofar as they continue in their unjust practices they 'eat and drink judgment against themselves' (v. 29). An important clue lies in Paul's reminder to the Corinthians about the proper performance of this meal.[40] When the meal is practiced in a way that Jesus is 'remembered', the gathered community 'proclaims' Christ crucified (vv. 25-26). This meal was meant to be both a remembrance (ἀνάμνησις) and a proclamation (καταγγέλλω) of the event that decisively revealed the character of God's liberating justice, especially towards the weak and vulnerable. Just as God had chosen the weak of the world to shame the strong (1.27), so the church was called through its liturgical life to enact this same reality. The Corinthians's disregard of the poor was a direct refutation of God's justice, and it reflected, as Hays writes, 'an odd amnesia about Jesus' death'.[41]

Paul calls on the community to transform its practice, so that it 'may not be condemned along with the world' (v. 32). The divisions in the community need to be healed, and their gatherings must not be allowed to degenerate into private dinner parties, otherwise they will incur the same fate as those who stand outside of Christ. Interestingly, Paul's final words on this matter stop short of calling for a more radical economic equality among the Corinthians. In the opinion of Gerd Theissen, this is a compromise for Paul: 'Within their own four walls they are to behave according

39. John Dominic Crossan, *The Historical Jesus: The Life of a Mediterranean Jewish Peasant* (San Francisco, CA: HarperCollins, 1991), 344; cited in Bradshaw, *Eucharistic Liturgies*, 9.

40. By 'proper performance', I do not mean the right liturgical pattern for administering the Eucharist, which is arguably not Paul's intent in this passage. Rather, Paul is concerned with the enactment of this meal in a way that points towards the life and death of Jesus.

41. Hays, *First Corinthians*, 199.

to the norms of their social status, while at the Lord's Supper the norms of the congregation have absolute priority. Clearly this is a compromise.'[42] At the same time, we must not underestimate the revolutionary potential of a dissident community truly living as the ecclesia of Christ, especially when the social norms that apply in the church are understood to be the first installment of an eschatological transformation that will soon affect the whole world.

It is clear, then, that the Corinthians had allowed their distinct call to become severely compromised. Rather than embodying Christ crucified in a lifestyle that is holy, reconciled, and liberating, they were mirroring the priorities and norms of the surrounding culture. By their sexual immorality, litigiousness, and general disregard for the weak and poor, this community was contradicting what Gorman describes as God's gift of justification – 'to be part of a new creation, to participate in the very purpose of God for humanity: becoming the embodiment of God's saving, reconciling, restorative justice in the world'.[43]

Practicing a Justice that Restores (Chapters 12–14)

This section brings to a head Paul's understanding of what it means to be 'spiritual', which, in contradistinction to the Corinthian 'pneumatics', is defined in terms of the mutual edifying of relationships in the Spirit-filled community. One of the striking realities experienced by the Corinthians on entering into κοινωνία with Christ was the gifts of the Spirit and the new reality of inspired speech (cf. 1.4-8). In their previous life as pagans ('Gentiles'), they were guided by idols that 'could not speak' (12.2), that is, by non-communication.[44] Idols that cannot speak will fail to be heard and will in turn fail to generate genuine communion, both vertically and horizontally.[45] The new era, by contrast, is one of inspired speech brought about by the Spirit. It is, however, also open

42. Gerd Theissen, *The Social Setting of Pauline Christianity: Essays on Corinth* (Philadelphia, PA: Fortress Press, 1982), 164, cited in Hays, *First Corinthians*, 203.

43. Gorman, *Becoming the Gospel*, 249.

44. This insight is corroborated by Zizioulas, who argues persuasively that both historically and existentially the concept of the *person* and with it the concept of *communion* is 'indissolubly bound up with theology'; John D. Zizioulas, *Being as Communion: Studies in Personhood and the Church* (Crestwood, NY: St Vladimir's Seminary Press, 1985), 27.

45. This explains why non-speaking pagan idols have the capacity to evoke obeisance but not obedience, as only the God who speaks can issue forth words – commands – that can be heard and heeded (cf. 1 Cor. 14.37).

to any number of abuses, as readily attested by the Corinthians. Most notable is their tendency to situate the various manifestations of spiritual gifts within a context of selfish and prideful individualism.

The individualism of the Corinthian community had a particularly libertarian shape. Several times Paul quotes what appears to be a slogan of some in the church, 'All things are lawful to me' (6.12; 10.23; cf. 8.9). Each time Paul limits the application of the motto by confronting it with a concern for the other as well as for self: 'Not all things are beneficial' (6.12); 'Do not seek your own advantage, but that of the other' (10.24); 'take care that this liberty of yours does not somehow become a stumbling block to the weak' (8.9). Some Corinthians had allowed their inspired speech to heighten their singularity and exceptional role in the church. Such spiritual elitism led to a hierarchy in which some members were no longer being valued on account of their unimpressive spiritual prowess.

Paul confronts this individualism at its theological root by insisting that those ruled by the Spirit must think in terms of the 'common good' (12.7) rather than individual competitiveness. Those who regard themselves as 'spiritual' must see themselves as persons-in-relation with Christ and his body. Hence, Paul's language subtly shifts from 'spiritual gifts' (πνευματικός) to 'gifts of grace' (χάρισμα). The first term was a favorite of the Corinthians and emphasizes the *experience* of spiritual energy; the second was Paul's preference and emphasizes the *gift* nature of the experience. Accordingly, the attention shifts away from the gift to the giver of the gift, who gives these gifts for the common good.[46]

While the χάρισμα created problems for the Corinthians, Paul never repudiates the belief that the new aeon is one of inspired speech and knowledge (1.5-7). Brock contrasts this with the modern era, which has become supremely skeptical towards any claim to having heard the word of God. This is especially so when it fosters certainty and banishes the fear of others, both of which are considered fuel for the fire of religious war. Modern humanity has replaced dependence on divine leading with the 'safer language of decision making and planning'.[47] If Christian theology were to succumb to such skepticism, it would soon lose all certainty about ever having heard God's Word and would be severed from its source.

46. On this interpretation of Paul's usage of πνευματικός and χάρισμα, see Jr. C. M. Robeck, 'Prophecy, Prophesying', in *Dictionary of Paul and His Letters*, in Gerald F. Hawthorne and Ralph P. Martin (Downers Grove, IL: InterVarsity Press, 1993), 758.

47. Brock, *Christian Ethics in a Technological Age*, 173.

Moreover, it is only the inspired speech of the Spirit that makes possible proper self-criticism. Only the interruptive Word that comes from 'outside the thought and habits of our age is able to take seriously the depth of our embedding in those very ways of life'.[48] It is the rule of the Spirit that empowers the church to exhibit relationships that are restorative.

Diversity in Triune Unity

One significant feature of Paul's response is the way he draws together the diversity of expressions in the church into a more profound unity. He does this by locating the variety of gifts, services, and activities in the one mission of God. There is an unmistakable Trinitarian structure here: 'there is a variety of gifts but one *Spirit*, a variety of services but one *Lord*, a variety of activities but one *God* who activates them all in all' (12.4-7). Paul urges the Corinthians to recognize both the diversity within the church's life, as well as the grounds for its unity in the nature of the triune God. A favoring of certain gifts over others distorts the character of the church because it fails to see the many gifts in the ecclesia and how they cohere in the nature of the one God. This is an important observation. Paul values the diversity of people and gifts within the church on account of the more profound unity they share in communion with God.

This thoroughly theological grounding of 'diversity in unity' has been particularly highlighted in the contentious work of John Zizioulas, who argues that the distinct notion of humans having a *person*ality arose within the patristic debates about the triune persons.[49] Personhood, with all its corresponding uniqueness, is only explicable within the communion generated by the triune life of God.[50] Zizioulas goes further in arguing that within the church the notion of the 'individual' must, of necessity, give way to personhood as conceived in communion. There are certainly resonances here with Paul's instructions to the Corinthians. The apostle is urging his readers in Corinth to recognize that the diversity of functions within the church, as well as the diversity of persons, are affirmed on the grounds of their more profound unity in the Spirit, as they share together in the life of God.

For Paul, the church's unity was constitutive of its sharing in the life of Christ. The Corinthians were expected to embody this unity by valuing each person equally, in the light of the Spirit's presence in their

48. Ibid., 174.

49. For an argument against Zizioulas, see Stephen R. Holmes, *The Holy Trinity: Understanding God's Life* (Milton Keynes: Paternoster Press, 2012).

50. Zizioulas, *Being as Communion*, esp. 27–65.

life (12.8-10). The church, as it participates in God's restoration of the world, must be committed to the good of all persons through fostering an awareness of, and respect for, the deeper unity that exists between them. Living restoratively flows from this commitment to value the gifts and personality of each person on account of the deep reality that unites all.

Mutual Care of One Another

In the second half of ch. 12, Paul employs his distinctive metaphor of the church as the *body of Christ*. For our purposes, three observations are pertinent. First, Paul reminds the Corinthians that they share in Christ's reconciled body through the practices of baptism and Eucharistic celebration (v. 13). Second, their reconciled form of life extends to the division between weak and strong, honorable and less respected, such that dissension along these lines is tantamount to a rejection of Christ himself (vv. 22-24). Third, as the church lives out this reconciled life it testifies to a mutuality of care such that solidarity in suffering and rejoicing become the *telos* of this community's life together (vv. 25-26).

Paul's description of the church's 'body politics' enables us to see how the church embodies God's restorative justice by working to reconcile vast social, economic, and ethnic divisions; by cultivating practices that localize this reconciliation in a form of life, and by nurturing a common life grounded in relationships of mutual care, to the extent that suffering and celebration become communal experiences. In all these ways the church's reconciled life is governed by the rule of the Spirit (12.8-11, 28-30); it is the Spirit's ordering of this community according to different gifts that makes possible its reconciled form of life.

In v. 13, Paul urges the Corinthians to recognize their common reconciliation, conveyed in the acts of baptism and Eucharistic fellowship. It is notable that Paul does not urge the Corinthians to realize the *ideal* of reconciliation through practicing the sacraments, which would suggest that reconciliation is a goal attained via the church's perfection of certain habits. Rather, as Wannenwetsch suggests, Paul's appeal is to a '*given reality*', a reality all participate in, as detected by the corporate 'we'.[51] The reconciled reality in which the church participates is a common experience – 'we were all, Jews or Greeks, slaves or free'. The issue for the Corinthians is whether or not they are living in a way that is consistent with this eschatological reconciliation.

51. Bernd Wannenwetsch, '"Members of One Another": *Charis*, Ministry and Representation: A Politico-Ecclesial Reading of Romans 12', in *A Royal Priesthood? The Use of the Bible Ethically and Politically: A Dialogue with Oliver O'Donovan*, ed. Craig Bartholomew et al. (Grand Rapids, MI: Paternoster Press, 2002), 200.

The church's continual practice of Eucharistic fellowship and shared citizenship through one baptism is the church's attempt to localize its experience of God's reconciling justice in the world. It is through these practices that the church enacts the proclamation that the world is no longer to be divided along social, economic, and ethnic lines. As Wannenwetsch points out, the church's worship represents a conscious restructuring of the *polis* whereby wider social divisions are giving way to a new, more fruitful ordering of political society.[52] It is in the church's 'political worship', which Wannenwetsch describes as the Christian 'form of life',[53] that the Spirit gathers the many into the one body. This is in order to 'proclaim the Lord's death until he comes' (11.26), a death that has decisively disclosed God's redemptive justice upending the present unjust social order.

In a clear targeting of the spiritual elitists in Corinth, Paul employs the body metaphor to argue that those who appear weak or inferior are indispensable to the proper working of the body and that in their absence the body would become deformed or dismembered (12.22-24). Indeed the presence of these 'inferiors' in the church is an occasion for the church to show what it already enjoys, the reconciling power of God's justice. Conferring honor and respect on those who are weak, poor, isolated, suffering, and marginalized, marks the erasure of those features of human existence that divide, isolate, and ruin.

Paul then brings his discussion of the body to its striking conclusion. God has so arranged the body so that there might be an equality of care among the different members. This tangibly means that what happens to one is experienced in solidarity by all (12.26). A *koinōnial* fellowship in both suffering and joy is meant to characterize Christian community. By participating in Christ's body, the church exists in the form of a '*being there for others*', a formula that Bonhoeffer used to refer to the vicarious solidarity of Christ with humanity. Just as Jesus exists only as a 'man for others', so also 'the church is only the church when it exists for others'.[54] This is the form of 'true transcendence', according to Bonhoeffer, the genuine encounter with the neighbor in need. Paul's view of the church certainly presses in this direction, as he suggests that within the Corinthian

52. Bernd Wannenwetsch, *Political Worship: Ethics for Christian Citizens* (Oxford: Oxford University Press, 2004), 146–54.

53. 'Political worship is a form of life – nothing more and nothing less. As a form of *life*, it embraces the life of believers as a whole, not just certain parts of it, be it the political sphere'; ibid., 32.

54. Dietrich Bonhoeffer, *Letters and Papers from Prison* (Minneapolis, MN: Fortress Press, 2010), especially 361–67.

church there is to be a vicarious sharing in the suffering or joy of each and every member. As members bound together in the one body by the Spirit, there exists the foundation for an equal commitment to the wellbeing and flourishing of every other member. This means an equal commitment to seeing God's restoring justice experienced by all.

Trained to Love

Paul's instruction to the Corinthian community on what it means to be governed by the Spirit contains an interlude in ch. 13. This chapter is well known for its exposition of the meaning of love, and is frequently the reading of choice at ceremonial occasions to describe the affective feeling between two parties. But Paul's exposition of love must be understood within the ecclesial context in which it occurs. Love is the appropriate disposition of those who live under the rule of the Spirit; it is the fulfilling of the 'law of Christ' (Gal. 6.2), and as such it describes the character of the community that lives under God's reign of justice. According to Paul, those who strive after the 'greater gifts' of the Spirit, which no doubt would appeal to the Corinthians, must seek to inhabit the 'more excellent way' of love (1 Cor. 12.31). Without love, no gift, nor understanding, nor boasting, has any value, and as such nothing can be gained without love (13.1-3).

Elsewhere Paul speaks of love as the 'fruit of the Spirit' (Gal. 5.22), which seeks to work for 'the good of all, and especially those of the family of faith' (6.10). Here he describes what this looks like practically: love is patient, kind, generous, humble, and polite (1 Cor. 13.4-5a). Instead of being insistent, irritable or resentful, it is open, flexible, and contented (v. 5b). More than anything, it rejoices not in wrongdoing (ἀδικία), corruption or falsity, but in truthfulness, where people are genuine and honest (v. 6). These qualities of love are all ways of being in relationship, of inhabiting a character and lifestyle that is restorative towards others. As Marshall writes in relation to the command to love one's neighbor, 'neighbors are not simply created by legal fiat; they are discovered through love, and love is a quality of human relationships before it is a category of law'.[55] The things that Paul says love is *not* are the attributes that feed conflict and reproduce antagonisms; the things he says love is are the qualities that make the restoration of peaceful relations possible. Those who are trained to love do not display the combative mode of self-assertion but instead strive to restore relationships to wholeness.

55. Marshall, *Compassionate Justice*, 78.

Paul is under no illusion that human love, like human knowledge, will always remain partial this side of the eschaton (vv. 8-12). But even now we are 'fully known' (and fully loved) by God (v. 12). This may be an allusion to the cross, where humanity is known in its completeness – 'in our transgressions' – it is where God makes room for the sinful other. Miroslav Volf argues that this 'knowing' or 'enlarged thinking' reflects what he calls 'double vision';[56] where the will to embrace the other – even the unjust other – precedes the rightness of one's cause. This requires the reversing of perspectives, genuinely seeing things from the perspective of the other, and making space within ourselves for the viewpoint of the other. This protects us from 'blind justice', as Volf writes: 'We need to see our judgments about justice and our struggle against injustice through the eyes of the other – even the manifestly "unjust other" – and be willing to readjust our understanding of justice and repent of acts of injustice'.[57] Abiding in the justice of love as revealed in the cross, the church becomes practiced in attending to the experience of others. Love in this sense is extremely costly, since it involves laying aside judgments about the other, who may well happen to be 'the enemy'.

Encouraging Intelligible Speech

While Paul recognizes a diversity of gifts within the church, he nevertheless singles out one gift in particular as essential for the church to be 'united in the same mind and the same purpose' (1.10). Some of the Corinthians had elevated the gift of tongues as the quality that distinguished this new aeon of inspired-speech, but Paul is quick to point out the limited nature of this form of speaking. It is the gift of prophecy that has greater import on account of its intelligibility. Prophecy connects the gathered community to the God who speaks by opening up new forms of dialogue within the community. Those who speak in tongues, on the other hand, unless attended by interpretation, fail to generate genuine dialogue because 'nobody understands them' (14.2). Prophecy, by contrast, builds the community's capacity to communicate meaningful words to one another and therefore to generate unity (v. 11).

As a spiritual gift, prophecy assumes a God who not only speaks but who continues to speak and act in the worshipping community, thus bringing believers to share in *koinōnial* fellowship with God's Son. The close connection between prophecy and revelation is attested by Paul's

56. Volf, *Exclusion and Embrace*, 213–15.
57. Ibid., 218.

linking of the two terms (14.6, 30-31; cf. v. 26). According to Robeck, it is 'revelation when spoken [that] forms the basis of the prophecy', and both come by means of the Spirit.[58] Hence, while the edification of fellow believers is the outcome of prophetic speech, the source of this edification is the God who has revealed himself to be *for us* in Jesus, by continuing to be *with us* through his Spirit. Prophecy is not viewed as the exercise of individual prowess or status. Rather, it is the divinely gifted form of speech that is given for the good of the community in establishing κοινωνία.

The primacy Paul gives to the gifts of speech, and of prophecy in particular (12.28), suggests that the church is to cultivate forms of dialogue that build up the community. Every feature of the church's life must be disciplined by the gifts that declare, expound, and apply revealed truth.[59] It is significant that Paul speaks of the church as gifted not with a set of skills to perform ethical action in some remarkable way, but rather with a new language and grammar in order to discern in what ways her actions are ethical. The gift of prophecy in particular serves the gathered community with this purpose in mind. Yoder describes the function of prophecy as a 'kind of discourse' that 'states and reenforces [*sic*] a vision of the place of the believing community in history, which vision locates moral reasoning'.[60] According to Yoder, prophecy serves to direct the gathered community by communicating words that situate the life of the church under the leading of the Spirit. The community of faith recognizes this gift to the extent that it lives in expectation that the Spirit is at work, shaping a community that speaks and listens to one another.

Paul is clearly aware that words have the power both to build-up and to tear down, which is why he provides a number of guidelines to the exercising of this gift. First, prophecy must be conformed to the way of love described in ch. 13 (14.1). The non-retaliatory and peacemaking disposition of love must be detectable in those who would prophesy, which means that even prophets must not 'insist on their own way' when they have some revelation (13.2, 5; cf. 14.30). Second, those who prophesy should speak words that build up, encourage, and console the

58. Robeck, 'Prophecy, Prophesying', 759.

59. Marshall opines that perhaps this 'primacy of the oral gifts is because teaching and prophecy are the gifts that declare, expound and apply revealed truth, and thus provide the context in which the other gifts may be profitably exercised'; Christopher D. Marshall, 'Pauline Pneumatology', unpublished paper, Auckland, 23.

60. John H. Yoder, 'The Hermeneutics of Peoplehood: A Protestant Perspective on Practical Moral Reasoning', *The Journal of Religious Ethics* 10, no. 1 (1982): 52.

church (vv. 3, 5, 12, 26). Prophecy is not directed primarily to individuals but to the empowering of the collective gifts in the church. Third, prophecy must be recognizable as a disciplined form of human discourse that requires the 'weighing' of other members (v. 29). Prophecy does not communicate a vision that is entirely unverifiable or which depends on completely trusting one individual's vision alone. Nor is the responsibility for judging prophecy the domain of a certain office of prophets (vv. 30-31; cf. 1 John 4.1; 1 Thess. 5.19-21). Prophecy is given for the entire church, as it discerns together the things that make for peace (cf. v. 33; cf. 1.10; 1 Thess. 5.12-22). Fourth, prophecy also has a role in calling unbelievers to repentance. When unbelievers hear prophetic utterances in the church they are 'reproved', or 'called to account', having the secrets of their hearts 'disclosed', which leads to submission to God and the worship of him (vv. 24-25).

One further feature deserves highlighting, which we might call the *mindful* character of prophetic speaking. I have already referenced numerous times Paul's appeal for the Corinthians to be 'united in the same mind' (1.10), which is a matter of being attuned to the Spirit who gives believers 'the mind of Christ' (2.16). Having this 'mind' requires that no one be excluded on the basis of being of 'lesser' value (12.12). On the contrary, it means rejoicing in the reordering of the church's body politics, such that every voice is heard and contributes to the church's discernment. It is against this background that we must read Paul's repeated appeal to the character of the church's worship. Nothing is more effective for building the church up in unity than fostering the mind of Christ as the church gathers to pray, to praise, or to instruct (14.15-19).

Prophecy is a gift exercised within a 'pneumatic democracy', as J. C. Beker puts it, a community committed to fostering the equality of all members, not least in its pursuit of arriving at shared convictions.[61] The church is to foster this unity in the Spirit through forms of dialogue guided both by meaningful words and mindfulness in its discernment. When Paul writes in Ephesians that the church is 'to maintain the unity of the Spirit in the bond of peace' (4.1-6), he is affirming that, in the words of Marshall, 'a commitment to peace-building is a necessary corollary of the church being the body of Christ'.[62] The church lives restoratively by fostering peace and justice through mutual dialogue guided by the Spirit.

61. See Johan Christiaan Beker, *Suffering and Hope: The Biblical Vision and the Human Predicament* (Grand Rapids, MI: Eerdmans, 1994), 84.

62. Marshall, 'Making Every Effort', 256.

The goal of this chapter has been to extend the church's imagination as to how it might embody the kind of restoration and healing that the bible attributes to the justice of God. I have highlighted selected features in Paul's letter to the Corinthians in an attempt to help guide the church today to better embody God's restorative justice. The epistle has proven to be a rich resource for achieving this goal, on account of the extent to which the Corinthians failed to embody God's restoring justice. This failure occasioned Paul's writing of the epistle – to remind the church of its calling. He sought to correct the unjust practices of the Corinthians by providing an account of how God's justice had been revealed in the cross of Jesus, a justice the church must embody through cruciform practices of justice-making and peace-making.

The failure of the Corinthians to enact Christ crucified through practices of justice can largely be attributed to their lack of theological discernment. They had allowed the priorities and values of their surrounding culture to go unchallenged by the gospel. Their unconverted notions of wisdom, power, nobility, and justice had produced a factionalized church where the weak, poor, and unimpressive were being treated unjustly. Paul's resolve to know nothing but 'Christ crucified' was a direct challenge to the Corinthian Christians and to the pagan culture they inhabited. Paul's letter must be read in the light of what it would mean for the Corinthians to embody this cruciform reality in their context, to assess their life in the light of the one who became the power, the wisdom, and the justice of God (1.18-30). In him, the church too is beckoned to 'become the justice of God' (2 Cor. 5.21).

In the final chapter I will turn to what this means for the contemporary church. The prescriptive or normative task drawn from the theological interpretation of Scripture will give way to the more suggestive task. Here I will plot practical ways in which the church might embody its understanding of the restorative justice of God.

Chapter 7

Ecclesial Embodiments of Restorative Justice Practice

The previous chapters have outlined a theological account of restorative justice that draws on the church's own sources of faith, especially its reading of Scripture. To complete our task, we now need to ask what positive difference this account makes to the church's practice of restorative justice? This chapter will examine three aspects of the church's life with respect to this question. First, I will suggest some of the ways in which the church is already engaged in forms of restorative justice within its own liturgical life. Second, I will suggest how restorative justice offers a way of strengthening the church's common life of decision-making, planning, and relational disputes. Third, I will look to one specific instance of where the church's missional life has extended restorative justice through an in-prison programme called the Sycamore Tree Project. While not exhaustive, the suggestions offered here will hopefully stimulate the church's imagination as to how it might further embody the justice of God in the world.

Before embarking on this task, however, we need to address some of the criticisms made of ecclesial ethics – specifically, whether the church should be the primary locus of an alternative praxis of justice-making. These criticisms serve to highlight a core presupposition behind the work of ecclesial ethics. This is that the church, as a community of readers of Scripture, is best placed to embody God's justice as it is disclosed in the biblical narrative. Insofar as it is a community formed in the practices of forgiveness, repentance, and reconciliation, it is ideally placed to develop ways of responding to wrongdoing that do not rely on harsh and violent punishment. One reason why the church often fails to live out more fully its own vision for justice is that it lacks concrete mechanisms that connect ecclesial practice with restorative justice.

The order of this chapter is intended to reflect the way in which the church is a locus for restorative justice. By inviting sinners and victims to participate in the liturgical acts of confession, the declaration of forgiveness, passing of the peace, culminating in the Eucharist as the celebration of its reconciliation, the church remembers and proclaims the restoring justice it has received in Christ. At the end of the worship gathering, the church is commissioned to go out into the world to proclaim and embody this same justice of right relationships. This chapter follows this movement from worship to witness, beginning with what happens within the church through its liturgy and common life and moving onto initiatives that bring restorative justice to bear on the world. These examples show that by displaying embodied practices of restorative justice that are theologically informed, the church *as church* may still be a catalyst of the restorative justice vision, as hoped for by its early pioneers.

Ecclesial Ethics: Sectarianism, Idealism, or Not?

From its inception, ecclesial ethics has been plagued by the criticism that an excessive focus on the distinctive life of the church issues in a sectarian, fideistic, and tribalistic account of Christianity. The phrase 'sectarian temptation' was coined by James Gustafson in 1985 and has been reiterated in more sophisticated forms ever since.[1] Theological sectarianism, argues Gustafson, 'isolate[s] Christianity from taking seriously the wider world of science and culture and limits the participation of Christians in the ambiguities of moral and social life in the patterns of independence in the world'.[2] It insulates Christian theology and ethics from the critical assessments and correction of 'other modes of construing reality',[3] all 'in order to maintain the uniqueness or historic identity of Christianity'.[4]

While the occasion for Gustafson's comments can be attributed to the growing influence of Stanley Hauerwas in the field of Christian ethics, he does not limit his comments to Hauerwas's work. He directs the charge of sectarianism against those he terms 'Wittgensteinian fideists' like D. Z. Phillips and Paul Holmer, the 'cultural linguistic' approach to doctrine of Lindbeck, those engaged in a hermeneutically enclosed fideism associated with 'narrative theology', and not least those 'Anabaptist

1. To his credit, even at this early stage Gustafson was able to articulate many of the primary criticisms that would repeatedly emerge as ecclesial ethics gained increased recognition.

2. James Gustafson, 'The Sectarian Temptation: Reflections on Theology, the Church and the University', *Proceedings of the Catholic Theological Society of America* 40 (1985): 84.

3. Ibid., 86.

4. See ibid., 83.

ecclesiologies' that construe God as the tribal deity of Christians rather than the Creator of the world.[5] This suggests that Gustafson's understanding of sectarianism is broad enough to encapsulate a number of different developments in contemporary Christian theology. Sectarianism is no longer a peripheral concern directed at a few errant groups of unorthodox Christians.[6]

According to Gustafson, those associated with the ecclesial turn falsely assume that 'there is, or can be, a kind of Christian tribe living in a kind of ghetto whose members are (or can be) shaped in their inner dispositions, their religious passions and their moral outlooks almost exclusively by the biblical or Christian language or narratives'.[7] The root of this error apparently lies in a problematic dependence on the teaching and example of Jesus for the church's ethical thinking, as well as an inadequate doctrine of creation.[8] Gustafson's counsel to Christians is to participate responsibly in the 'patterns and processes of interdependence of life' on account of how 'God orders life through nature'.[9]

This criticism of ecclesial ethics betrays the widely held assumption that the church is a subset of a more comprehensive reality (nature, civil society, the world). The implications of this for Christian socio-political responsibility is that theology and ethics ought to be done in the service of something other than what Christians do within the confines of the church. This explains the criticism of those, like Jeffrey Stout, who argue that if ecclesial ethicists like Hauerwas 'were to stop thrashing his liberal

5. See ibid., 85–88, 91–92.

6. Cavanaugh observes that unlike the theological usage of the term 'sect', where a group placed itself outside of the authority of the church, a 'relatively novel sociological use of the term', has emerged with writers like Gustafson. The definition of a sect now seems to 'indicate a group whose practices put it at odds with the dominant culture and political elites of the nation-state. The underlying assumption is that it is not the church but the nation-state that is "catholic"; the church, insofar as it is a political actor, is a particular association of civil society that is encompassed by the larger universal political sphere of the nation-state'; Cavanaugh, *Migrations of the* Holy, 139.

7. Gustafson, 'Sectarian Temptation', 90.

8. Gustafson's appeal to the doctrines of creation and revelation are curiously augmented in a way that dismisses any central role for Jesus in Christian ethics. They seem to imply that, (1) God as Creator can be known apart from how God is at work to redeem creation in and through Jesus, (2) knowledge of nature must be allowed to correct knowledge gained through the reading of Scripture and discipleship to Jesus, and (3) participation in society is premised on the acceptance of political and moral pluralism rather than fidelity to the one who incarnates God's way with the world.

9. Ibid., 92, 83.

straw man, rediscover the language of justice, and put that language to use in prophetic works of social criticism, his reviewers would surely stop charging him of sectarianism'.[10] From this perspective, if ecclesial ethics wants to show a commitment to social engagement, then it must do so within the order of state and society rather than within its own ecclesial community.

Underlying the perspective of critics like Gustafson and Stout is the belief that the church as described by ecclesial ethicists does not, in fact, exist. They claim that descriptions of the church as a community of virtue is illusory and, to some degree, conceited.[11] Concentrating too much on the church diverts energies that could be spent on the more general task of forming democratic citizens, they would counsel. As this study has shown, however, it is for *theological* reasons that ecclesial ethicists are attempting to recover the resources needed to form Christian character, including the resources of a church that has been trained to resist the vices of individualism and violence.[12] This is not to say that ecclesial ethics is uninterested in 'the activities and institutions that constitute our common life together', as Stout alleges; it means rather that engaged Christians need to first grasp their own grammar and practice, their own place to stand.[13]

10. Jeffrey Stout, *Democracy and Tradition* (Princeton: Princeton University Press, 2004), 160.

11. 'In its Hauerwasian form, virtue's rejection of the way of the world leads to an unpleasant dilemma. On the one hand, the stronger its claim to represent virtue as distinct from the way of the world, the more quickly it degenerates into a form of "conceit" that cannot honestly be sustained. The actual church does not look very much like a community of virtue... This is why Hauerwas has difficulty in articulating the "for" of his position as clearly as he articulates the "against"'; ibid., 161.

12. Hauerwas's position is not always helpful in clarifying this goal. He writes, for example, 'My own theological convictions will not let me escape by distinguishing between visible or invisible churches, or by suggesting that I am recommending ideals to be realized, or by claiming that the theologian's task is to say what the church ought to be, not what it is'; Hauerwas, *Dispatches from the* Front, 18. Such statements make it appear that Hauerwas is arguing that the church is already a community of virtue, when he is in fact calling on the church to recognize what is has already received in Christ so as to live in virtue.

13. Stout, *Democracy and Tradition*, 152. Hauerwas writes elsewhere that he is not advocating for Christians to withdraw from social engagements. Rather, 'I just want them to be engaged as Christians. [Moreover, the] image of retreat is all wrong. The problem is not that Christians, to be faithful, must withdraw. The problem is that Christians, particularly in liberal social orders like that of the United States, have so identified with those orders that they no longer are able to see what difference being

Ecclesial ethics is concerned first and foremost with the formation of Christians according to the grammar and practices that are constitutive of the church's worship of God. It is wrongly assumed that given this focus ecclesial ethics is commending an inward-looking church, where Christians cannot develop friendship or find co-operative endeavours with those outside the church. Nor does this focus commit Christians to shun those who, by their example, testify to the peace and justice Christians have learnt to recognize in Christ. All of these assumptions fail to appreciate the kind of formation of Christian character being advocated. For example, it is in worship that Christians are formed to welcome the stranger and be reconciled to their enemies just as they have been received and reconciled by God in Christ. Friendship and hospitality are frequent themes in ecclesial ethics, and are never simply constrained to those relationships inside the church.[14]

The point to remember is that ecclesial ethics calls for an engagement with the world in a way that *does not render the church invisible.* The church is to be engaged *as church*, not allowing the world to dictate the terms of reference or language upon which engagement should happen. This requires Christians to be trained to recognize where the surrounding culture is no longer hospitable to the church. It is not a question of '*complete* involvement in culture or *complete* withdrawal', as Gustafson presumes, but rather one of selective participation. The pressing issue is for Christians to work for justice in a way that reclaims the visibility of the church in recognition of the dawning of God's eschatological justice in the midst of history.

According to Hauerwas, the point at which Christians must withdraw from involvement with the state, culture, or society, is when

> government and society resorts to violence in order to maintain internal order and external security… Such an admission, however, hardly commits me to a sectarian stance, unless one assumes, as some do, that every function of the state depends on its penchant for violence. Indeed, *I believe it to be the responsibility of Christians to work to make their societies less prone to resort to violence*. Surely one of the ways they can do that is by using the law as a means to settle disagreements short of violence.[15]

Christian makes. I am not trying to force Christians to withdraw but to recognize that they are surrounded. There is no question of withdrawing, as all lines of retreat have been cut off'; Hauerwas, *Dispatches from the Front*, 18.

14. While many examples could be illustrated here, a simple reference to the edited volume of Christian ethics from this ecclesial perspective will make the point; see Hauerwas and Wells, *The Blackwell Companion to Christian Ethics*.

15. Hauerwas, *Dispatches from the Front*, 15 (italics mine).

The commitment to nonviolent peacemaking espoused by ecclesial ethics is not a symptom of sectarianism, as it 'demands strenuous political engagement, because such a commitment forces us to expand our social and political imaginations'.[16] This is why the approach taken here aligns with the concerns of ecclesial ethics. The forerunner of the restorative justice movement emerged as a result of the recovery of a radical Anabaptist ecclesiology that emphasized the peacemaking witness of the church in sites of power exercised by the state. Mennonites, often accused of being sectarian and withdrawn, began to develop alternative processes for resolving conflict and the harm caused by crime as an embodiment of Jesus's politics.

While not entirely *of* the justice system, the Victim Offender Reconciliation Program nevertheless existed *within* this system to provide an alternative (nonviolent) option for responding to wrongdoers and victims. The point at which restorative justice was reticent to participate fully in the justice system was when it might collude with the violent, punitive impulse that seeks justice by inflicting pain on offenders.[17] This required Christians to be directly engaged with wrongdoers, victims, the judiciary, policy makers, community members, and correctional officers, all of which testifies to the non-sectarianism of this ecclesially formed approach to justice-making.

16. Ibid., 15. Hauerwas is serious about the law being used as a means to settle disputes nonviolently, which is why he has long held a concern for the work done by Christian lawyers. He writes, 'For the law to be part of the way of life that helps us serve one another it must draw its rationale from practices that are more determinative than the law itself. That is, it must acknowledge that the law is always in service to a politics – a politics, that to be sure involves power, but not as an end in itself but rather in service to goods such as marriage or the peaceable resolution of conflicts'; Hauerwas, 'Christian Practice of the Practice of Law in a World without Foundations', *Mercer Law Review* 44 (1992): 748. See also the law journal volume devoted to Hauerwas's theological work, *Law and Contemporary Problems* 75, no. 4 (2012).

17. These claims about restorative justice are not shared among all practitioners and theorists, some of whom would contend that restorative justice should be fully incorporated into the justice system, while others would argue that restorative justice is viable only as it relies on the coercive stick of retributive punishment. See, for example, London, *Crime, Punishment, and Restorative Justice*; Kathleen Daly, 'Revisiting the Relationship between Retributive and Restorative Justice', in *Restorative Justice: Philosophy to Practice*, in John Braithwaite and Heather Strang (Aldershot: Ashgate, 2000), 33–54; L. Zedner, 'Reparation and Retribution: Are they Reconcilable?', *Modern Law Review* 57 (1994): 228–50.

Nor was the restorative vision of justice solely tied to this one ecclesial tradition. From its beginnings as a distinct approach to resolving the harm of crime, it quickly resonated with a number of Christians from denominations that had little interaction with a specifically Anabaptist theology. One could fruitfully trace the many antecedents to the modern form of restorative justice in respective ecclesial traditions. But the point that has been made in this book is that the understanding of justice as a restorative and liberative action is ultimately grounded, for all Christians, in the story of what God was doing with Israel, in Christ, and now through the church. Were the church to lose sight of this, it would squander not only its own inheritance, but would fail to serve the world.

This explains why the account of restorative justice I have developed here is one that springs from the life of the church. It is therefore important to draw attention to the ways in which the church is already engaged in forms of restorative justice within itself. In other words, before examining instances of restorative justice beyond the church, we need to consider the restorative dimensions of what takes place in the weekly life of the congregation and the difference it makes to its members.

Worship as the Ecclesial Context for Restorative Justice

One of the principal aims of ecclesial ethics has been to reclaim the importance of the liturgical life of the church. In its liturgical performance, the church orders itself by a series of specific acts that are intended to shape the character and imagination of its members. This section will explore how these liturgical acts – which involve an invitation, story-telling, confession, declaration of forgiveness, acts of reconciliation, and commissioning – are all ways that the church lives out a justice that restores. We must first address, however, why worship features so prominently in the church's life.

Worship occupies a special place in the church's life because this is where the core principle of the Christian life is discovered: God is to be worshipped. It is in worship that the church proclaims that the God who has revealed himself, in his person and in what he has done, is doing, and will do, is a God that is worthy and deserving of praise. Worship takes the form of our response to God, which means that it is God who both initiates and perfects our worship. God initiates worship by revealing his nature and deeds as worthy, but also by gathering a community that exists for the purpose of worshipping him. As Peter writes, 'you are a chosen people, a royal priesthood, a holy nation, God's own people, *that you may declare the praises of him* who called you out of darkness into his wonderful light' (1 Pet. 2.9, NIV).

Our worship all too often fails to reflect the worth of the one being worshipped and it is rarely offered with wholehearted devotion. Jesus's criticism of the Pharisees applies to the church also, 'This people honors me with their lips, but their hearts are far from me; in vain do they worship me, teaching human precepts as doctrines' (Matt. 15.8-9). The church responds to this failure as it does with any failure, by pointing to Jesus. By offering in our place the response required of us, Jesus completes our worship. It is on account of his perfect sacrifice and devotion that the church is able to worship in 'spirit and truth' (cf. John 4.22-24), sharing in Jesus's spirit as it proclaims the truth of the gospel.

It is the dynamic interaction between the worshipping community and the God who is worshiped that gives this activity such a unique character. Worship is a 'form of *life*', Wannenwetsch argues, since it 'embraces the life of believers as a whole, not just certain parts of it, be it the political sphere [*sic*]'.[18] Wannenwetsch has in mind here the way in which Christians bring their everyday concerns into the worshipping community, thereby constituting each worship service as a fresh encounter between the community and the God being worshipped.[19] The performance of the liturgy is not simply a ritualistic rehearsal. More importantly, it is the way in which the congregation is formed through word and sacrament, as it remains attuned to the needs and concerns of its members. Included in this is the concern for a justice that can restore people and relationships to rightness.

Turning our attention to the specific actions of the Eucharistic liturgy, we notice how a number of these actions enact a concern for a restorative justice. The first act in this liturgical drama is the invitation of sinners to gather together for worship. Through the call to worship God welcomes into his presence people who are carrying disappointments, struggles, and hurts, as well as those who carry the guilt and shame of having done wrong to others and to themselves. Because all are gathered into one body, this invitation brings together both victims *and* offenders, often in the same person. If this is not to be done naïvely, then some care and thought must be given to preparing the space where this encounter takes place. This may involve attention to the physical layout of the congregation or

18. Wannenwetsch, *Political Worship*, 32 (italics original).

19. The primary task of theology is therefore to identify the 'activity of critical reflection on the "change" wrought in the worshipping community as it goes from one liturgical act, one service of worship, to the next, and of the "adjustment" of each new act of worship to that change… [I]t is the intellectual stock-taking of the change which each encounter of the community with God brings with it'; ibid., 81–82.

to ensuring that those entering this space are met with the simple gesture of a welcoming face.

It should be emphasized that this invitation has an active rather than a passive orientation. The church that gathers to celebrate the Eucharist recalls the meals Jesus shared in his earthly ministry as a sign that God's kingdom exists for the lost and the least. Jesus demonstrated the message of the kingdom through the forgiveness of sins, which he enacted parabolically by eating with tax-collectors and sinners: 'This man receives sinners and eats with them' (Luke 15.2). These common meals were turned into liberative and redeeming events that gathered in the unrighteous to feast with the Righteous One, thereby exhibiting the restorative character of God's justice. The congregation is likewise commissioned to go out to the highways and the byways in order to gather in the wrongdoer and the wronged, the good and the bad, so that they may taste the banquet of the Lord (Matt. 22.1-10; Luke 14.15-24).

The second liturgical act that enacts the church's work of restorative justice is the confession. We have already discussed the significance of confessing sin in relation to Matt. 18.15-22 and the parable of the Prodigal Son, but we reiterate those points here. First, the presence of concealed sin is a problem for the congregation as a whole, not least because it can become a source for untruth, revictimization, and even violence. Confession of sin frees the church to become a community of truthful peacemakers by confronting wrongdoing and conflict in a way that prevents the sin from causing further harm. Second, because sin has an irreducibly relational nature, confession opens up the possibility for ruptured relationships to be repaired. As Yoder writes, 'healing, whether from sin or from sickness, is inseparable from the healing of human relationships'.[20] Without genuine repentance, which includes the act of confession, there is little hope for reconciliation.

Finally, confession of sin reminds us that we owe our lives to God's unrelenting forgiveness. We need to keep in mind the voluntary nature of this process. The congregation openly confesses that it is a community of sinners because it has learnt to acknowledge itself as those who Christ came to forgive. Unlike the prodigal's confession in the far country, the sons and daughters of the church are made aware of their sin in the embrace of the father, who has borne their wrongdoing and already declared his forgiveness upon it. This is why the act of confession is a liberating event, because it enables wrongdoing to be brought into the open without threatening to destroy the fabric of this community.

20. Yoder, 'Binding and Loosing', 351.

This takes us into the third liturgical act, the declaration of forgiveness. Through the cross of Christ, God has disclosed his gift of forgiveness for the sake of the world's restoration. For those who have suffered harm or who are experiencing the shame of having harmed others, they are invited to receive the life of Christ poured out in grace and forgiveness. Through participating in Christ's self-emptying gift of forgiveness, as David Power writes, 'we might well enlarge our capacity to ask, give, and receive forgiveness'.[21] This has important implications for both sinners and victims. By virtue of Christ's vicarious solidarity with all victims, his declaration on the cross, 'Father, forgive them…' (Luke 23.34), opens the way for victims to be released from their enmity while extending to offenders the offer of divine forgiveness. The congregation thus provides a place where those who may have once been at enmity with one another can be made one in the body of Christ.

In any restorative justice encounter there arise a number of strong emotions that need to be expressed, and this often takes place through stories. The fourth liturgical act is what I am calling story-telling, which involves individuals in the congregation learning to identify their own story in the stories told about God and his people. The inclusion of Scripture readings and the sermon in the liturgy is for the purpose of re-encountering the story of how God is bringing salvation to his people. 'Scripture renders a "world"', according to Hays, a symbolic universe that is undergirded by a 'grand story of election and promise, the story of δικαιοσύνη Θεοῦ, God's covenant faithfulness reaching out to reclaim a fallen and broken humanity'.[22] By inscribing listeners within the world of the biblical story, it becomes possible to see how Scripture is being fulfilled in the life of the church. According to Richard Hays, the church is called to engage in 'metaphor-making, placing our community's life imaginatively within the world articulated by the texts', so that the community might be transformed as it 'embodies the meaning of the text'.[23]

Concretely, this means that the present realities and situations facing the congregation and its members are to be reinterpreted through the lens of the biblical drama. It is here that the liturgical act of telling stories from Scripture can become a restorative justice event. Scripture contains texts that speak of bringing comfort to the downtrodden, rebuilding lives and livelihoods, stories of contrition, repentance, and vindication, as well as

21. David N. Power, 'Eucharistic Justice', *Theological Studies* 67 (2006): 877.

22. Hays, *Conversion of the Imagination*, 146–47.

23. Hays, *Moral Vision*, 299, 304.

songs of lament. These are all important for responding to those affected by conflict. There are also texts that express a desire for vengeance, what is known as the imprecatory psalms:

> O God, break the teeth [of the wicked] in their mouths; tear out the fangs of the young lions, O Lord! Let them vanish like water that runs away; like grass let them be trodden down and wither… The righteous will rejoice when they see vengeance done; they will bathe their feet in the blood of the wicked. (Ps. 58.6-7, 10)

> O daughter Babylon, you devastator! Happy shall they be who pay you back what you have done to us! Happy shall they be who take your little ones and dash them against the rock! (Ps. 137.8-9)

What possible place could these prayers have in the church's worship? While they may evoke great discomfort, they nevertheless express some of the most visceral emotions experienced by those who have suffered injustice, violation, and abuse. Scripture does not offer a sanitized piety, yet neither does it leave victims alone in their anguish. Murray Rae offers two further comments about the use of these prayers in worship. First, whoever prays to God for vengeance waives the right to seek vengeance themselves. The words in these prayers give voice to the wrath of God in the face of human atrocity, but at the same time God removes the prerogative to seek vengeance from the one who would pray them. 'Vengeance is mine, I will repay, says the Lord' (Rom. 12.19; cf. Deut. 32.35). 'Giving up all claim to seek vengeance themselves', Rae writes, 'those who pray the psalm place the ultimate fate of their enemies into the hands of God and learn, in the meantime, that they are to feed their enemies if they are hungry and give them water if they thirst'.[24]

Second, as a prayer to God, those who desire vengeance are directed to the way in which God answers this prayer. They look, in other words, to the one in whom the 'whole of Scripture' and the 'Word of the one God' is fulfilled, namely, to Jesus as the Word made flesh.[25] The vengeance of God, where his wrath is visited upon the world's sin and evil, is exercised in the cross of Christ. If the wickedness of humanity is intensified in this single event, then those who would pray these words

24. Murray Rae, 'Christ in/and the Old Testament', *Journal of Theological Interpretation* 2, no. 1 (2008): 5. Rae is drawing upon the discussion of Bonhoeffer in Martin Kuske, *The Old Testament as the Book of Christ: An Appraisal of Bonhoeffer's Interpretation* (Philadelphia, PA: Westminster, 1976), 85–92.

25. Rae, 'Christ in/and the Old Testament', 5.

are taught to see in Christ's sacrifice the way that God responds to his enemies: by transforming them through his declaration of forgiveness. Once again, by inhabiting the story of Scripture, the church embodies the way of God's justice at work to restore victims and offenders to right relationship.

The church's liturgical performance reaches its climax in the celebration of the Eucharist, what might appropriately be called the act of reconciliation. In the Christian tradition, the Eucharist has been conceived of as a sacramental enactment of the reconciliation brought about in and through Christ. Its character as an event where relationships are restored to rightness is drawn from the presence of Christ becoming, in some way, real in the breaking of bread. In partaking of this meal, the church does not simply recall a past event locked away in history. Rather, Christ's once and for all reconciliation is sacramentally *re-membered* in the body of Christ, where the presence of the risen Lord is acknowledged. This gives the Eucharist an eschatological character in which, in Moltmann's words, 'Christ's redeeming future is anticipated and this hope celebrated in remembrance of his passion. *In this meal his past and his future are simultaneously made present*.'[26]

The church has not always taken seriously its performance of the Eucharist as an invitation to embody God's restoring justice. In the post-apostolic church, admission to the Eucharist was reserved for committed believers alone, and then only after months, sometimes years, of preparation and self-reflection. The rigour with which the Eucharist was taken reflected the eschatology of the time. Commenting on the eschatological significance of the Eucharist, Cavanaugh writes, 'At the Eucharist the feast of the last day irrupts into earthly time, and the future breaks into the present. The *ekklesia* or church…is not merely the church in its flawed earthly manifestation but the church in its full and proper sense, the eternal gathering of all creation by Christ into the Father's Kingdom.'[27] This purportedly lies behind Paul's warning to the Corinthians to 'discern the body' when eating the bread and drinking from the cup, lest they 'eat and drink judgment against themselves' (1 Cor. 11.29). The Eucharist is an event that is set against the horizon of the eschatological judgment of God on the world, which is why the church must be prepared for final judgment by practicing God's restorative justice in a manner worthy of the Lord.

26. Jürgen Moltmann, *The Church in the Power of the Spirit: A Contribution to Messianic Ecclesiology*, trans. Margaret Kohl (London: SCM Press, 1977), 243 (italics mine).

27. Cavanaugh, *Torture and Eucharist*, 224.

Adding further weight to the pursuit of reconciliation as a presupposition for partaking of this meal was Jesus's instructions in Matt. 5.23-24. These words are often read in association with the 'altar' of the Eucharistic table: 'So when you are offering your gift at the altar, if you remember that your brother or sister has something against you, leave your gift there before the altar and go; first be reconciled to your brother or sister, and then come and offer your gift'. This injunction contains several important features. First, it fosters self-reflection on the nature of one's relationships, whether or not they exhibit the reconciliation expected of those who have a share in Christ. Second, leaving a gift at an altar temporarily hastens the need to reconcile, adding an incentive to complete this work quickly. Finally, returning to the altar signifies the inseparability between human and divine reconciliation, that both are essential for the church to worship rightly. It is likely that Jesus's words were originally an allusion to Lev. 6.1-7, where restitution to and reconciliation with those who one had harmed was a prerequisite to reconciliation with God.

The post-apostolic church developed two practices in particular that expressed this work of restoring relationships. First, as a prelude to the Eucharist, members would embrace each other with a 'Holy Kiss', as a testament to the peace and reconciliation at work in their relationships within the ecclesia.[28] Second, bishops were urged to mediate and settle disputes between church members on the second day of the week, giving ample time to establish peace by the day of the Eucharist.

The practice of the Eucharist is a remembrance of one meal in particular, the night of Jesus's betrayal leading to his sacrifice on the cross (Luke 22.17-20). The breaking of bread symbolizes the suffering body of Christ, the body that was tortured and sacrificed in solidarity with all other victims.[29] The church becomes the body of Christ when it 'performs an *anamnesis* of Christ's sacrifice', as Cavanaugh argues, 'suffering in its

28. Eleanor Kreider provides an excellent summary of the practice of the Holy Kiss. The teaching on this practice in the first four centuries of the church is clear: 'The "greater sacrifice" is reconciled relationships. The acceptable gift is prayer offered in peace, in brotherly concord. Pure worship required "mutually pledged unreserved forgiveness". And all of these were symbolized by the kiss'; Eleanor Kreider, 'Let the Faithful Greet Each Other: The Kiss of Peace', *The Conrad Grebel Review* 5 (1987): 37.

29. Cavanaugh particularly draws out this feature of the Eucharist in his discussion of torture under the reign of General Pinochet in Chile. He writes, 'the Eucharist conforms the followers of Christ to the true body of Christ, a body able to provide a counter-discipline to state terror. If torture is the imagination of the state, the Eucharist is the imagination of the church'; Cavanaugh, *Torture and Eucharist*, 229.

own flesh the afflictions taken on by Christ'.[30] This joins the church to the cause of all those who have been victims at the hands of others, seeing in their plight, the agony that was suffered by Christ. The pouring of the wine symbolizes the new covenant, where sinners are washed clean by the blood of Christ. The church as the body of Christ is the one place where the fate of wrongdoers is determined not by their past but by the new life promised in Christ's resurrection.

Finally, the Eucharist is also where ecclesial discipline takes place. In the previous chapter, we discussed Paul's urging of the Corinthians to 'excommunicate' an unrepentant offender, a practice that continued to develop in the early church and acquired increasing theological gravity. As the body of Christ, the church understood its call to exemplify God's reconciliation in its own life, which sometimes involved withdrawing communion from wrongdoers until they had repented. Hein elaborates, 'Since the early Church made no adequate distinction between ecclesiology and soteriology – the Church being identical with those who were to be saved and were therefore already saved – the ecclesiological motives for eucharistic excommunication were often equally soteriological'.[31]

The Eucharist was reserved, in other words, for those who were open to being disciplined by it and so standing against the forces of a world mired in violence and division. The motive for excommunication was not so much to punish offenders, but rather to communicate that sin that has not been repented has no place in the Eucharist. The offender excommunicates himself or herself by failing to be penitent. The congregation, however, extends to them the possibility of restoration by inducing them to change their conduct. 'As an invitation to reconciliation', as Cavanaugh argues, 'excommunication done well is an act of *hospitality*, in which the church does not expel the sinner, but says to her, "You are already outside our communion. Here is what you need to do to come back in."'[32]

The final liturgical act is the commissioning of the congregation. Having enacted the work of restorative justice through the liturgical event that culminated in the Eucharist, Christians have also become practiced in the work of restorative justice, which they are now to proclaim and embody in the world. Just as the Eucharistic life of the church does not end at the altar, so too the church must take its performance of restorative justice beyond the confines of the congregation in order to invite others to participate in the restoring justice of God.

30. Ibid., 267.

31. Kenneth Hein, *Eucharist and Excommunication: A Study in Early Christian Doctrine and Discipline* (Bern: Herbert Lang, 1973), 439.

32. Cavanaugh, *Torture and Eucharist*, 243.

The inseparability between the church's worship and its commissioning to serve others was given special emphasis in the apostolic church. This is especially clear in Acts 2.42-47, where mention of the breaking of bread is placed side-by-side with the sharing of material resources as summary descriptions of the church's daily existence. One of the earliest ministries recognized in the church was that of διάκονος (Acts 6.1-6), from which we get 'deacons', whose task evidently included gathering the contributions to the common meal and distributing what was not eaten among the poor and widows.[33] The implications for the contemporary church are spelled out by Moltmann: 'As the supper with Jesus and his disciples demonstrates fellowship with his mission to the poor, the imprisoned, the sick and the despised, so in the same way the Lord's supper leads to mission and missionary tasks for the conquest of need, the liberation of prisoners and the acceptance of the despised'.[34]

The church's liturgical performance, then, is a prime example of where restorative justice is already embedded in the life of the church. It is through these practices that the church reveals its solidarity with victims *and* offenders, receives reconciliation in and through Christ, and disciplines its members to be restored to right relationship. It may be tempting to suppose that Christian expression of worship and so also of restorative justice concludes at the end of the liturgy, but liturgy and worship are to be the work of our whole lives. The commissioning given at the end of a service of worship indicates that the gestures of forgiveness and reconciliation learned and practiced in the Eucharist are to be enacted throughout the week that follows. This is what Christian life consists in. In what follows, I want to explore how this restorative ethos may be carried through to the church's common life and missional life. Specifically, how might the church continue to express its core commitment to a restorative conception of justice as it engages in decision-making or deals with relational disputes, right through to its ministry to prisoners and victims of crime?

The Church's Restorative Witness in the World

We mentioned earlier the criticism of ecclesial ethics that argues the church, as advocated by scholars like Hauerwas, does not exist. As Healy succinctly puts it, 'Hauerwas's church is the one he worships in, but he

33. Wannenwetsch highlights through examples like this that the New Testament never sets worship and the active life of mission against each other; Wannenwetsch, *Political Worship*, 80.

34. Moltmann, *Church in the Power of the Spirit*, 258.

seems to prefer, and talk more about, the one he constructs for himself'.[35] This is evident in presentations of the church's life that are idealized or romanticized, and which fail to account for most people's experience of the church as a messy, confused, and confusing body. In response, Hauerwas has argued,

> The people of God are no less an empirical reality than the crucifixion of Christ. The church is as real as his cross. There is no 'ideal church', no 'invisible church', no 'mystically existing universal church' more real than the concrete church with parking lots and potluck dinners. It is the church of parking lots and potluck dinners that comprises the sanctified ones formed by and forming the continuing story of Jesus Christ in the world.[36]

If ecclesial ethics is concerned with the church of parking lots and potluck dinners, and many other features in between, then how might the common life of the congregation better express its commitment to peacemaking and restorative justice? With this question in mind I want to explore the work of Thomas Porter, a lawyer and minister in the United Methodist Church, who advocates for the creation of a culture of what he calls 'JustPeace'.[37]

A Restorative Common Life: Peacemaking Circles

In his 23 years as a lawyer for his denomination, Porter participated in several church trials. He noted that the way churches deal with conflict or theological differences is often no different from the adversarial retributive model of the courts, where he worked as a trial lawyer. It is no better at the level of local congregations. Due to a severe lack of relational and conflict-resolution skills, many congregations struggle to discuss difficult issues and employ healthy decision-making processes. After experiencing the restorative and spiritual process of the South African Truth and Reconciliation Commission, he sought to develop a more constructive, and biblical, way of dealing with conflict within churches.

As a lawyer and mediator, Porter realized early on the significance of getting people to a table where they could engage each other and work together to address the issues, the harms, and the problems that divide them. He noticed the many connections between this work of conflict transformation and what happens at the 'Table of Holy Communion'.

35. Healy, *Hauerwas*, 10.

36. Berkman, *Hauerwas Reader*, 382–83.

37. Thomas Porter, ed., *The Spirit and Art of Conflict Transformation: Creating a Culture of Justpeace* (Nashville, TN: Upper Room Books, 2010).

'The Table is a place of accountability to God, to each other, to the cosmos. It is a Table of restorative justice, of healing. The Table is a banquet table placed in the presence of our enemies.'[38] Porter became convinced that it was at this table, where the Eucharistic liturgy is practiced, that Christians are formed to be peacemakers and ministers of reconciliation. It is in here that Christians find the '*place*, the *time*, the *ritual*, and the *spiritual power* for healing relationships and doing the work of reconciliation in this world'.[39] Porter's observations reinforce the perspective we have been developing in this chapter.

Yet Porter also highlights how at this table Christians call to mind the conflict that surrounds them, whether present in other places or within the church itself. Indeed, the very practice of the Eucharist has historically created great divisions within the church, not all of which have been healed. This is why Porter raises the question, 'how does conflict inform Holy Communion and how does Holy Communion transform conflict?'[40] He identifies several features of conflict-transformation processes that are consistent with the biblical story and the practice of Holy Communion. In essence it involves providing a sacred space where people can recognize their interdependence and connection, with a sense of equality and respect, so that all voices can be heard, which requires deep listening and respectful speaking, where all feel responsible and accountable for outcomes, so that problems can be solved and relationships healed.[41]

Porter's description of healthy congregational processes bears many similarities with Paul's commendation to the Corinthian church in 1 Cor. 12, discussed in the previous chapter. To be 'spiritual', as Paul conceived it, was to participate in relationships that were mutually edifying in recognition of how each person carried gifts that were essential for the common good (v. 7). Within the body of Christ, there are no autonomous individuals, since all are members of one another through baptism into the one body (vv. 12-13). Practically, this required honor and respect to be shown to those who were 'inferiors' according to this world – the weak, the poor, the isolated, suffering, and marginalized (vv. 22-24). The reconciling power of God's justice, manifest in the cross of Christ,

38. Thomas Porter, ed., *Conflict and Communion: Reconciliation and Restorative Justice at Christ's Table* (US: Discipleship Resources, 2006), 11.

39. Ibid., 10.

40. Ibid., 13 (original in italics).

41. These elements are discussed more fully in Porter, *Culture of Justpeace*, 19–72.

has inaugurated a new order. The church is to witness to this new reality, expressed through a mutuality of care such that solidarity in suffering and rejoicing becomes the *telos* of the community's life together (vv. 25-26).

As Porter sought out processes for embedding what he calls 'JustPeace' within the church, he was drawn to the power of Peacemaking Circles. 'The circle is a vessel for grieving together, for healing, for talking through an issue, for making decisions, for working through difficult conversations, for dealing with conflicted situations, for developing a team, and for celebrating together.'[42] He concludes from his experience of using them,

> I found the circle process a great gift to the church and the world... Sitting in circle expresses in a physical and symbolic way the interconnectedness, interdependence, and unity of all life as found in God... In fact, circle process calls the church back from doing business like the Chamber of Commerce, to doing '*worshipful work*', and seeing its task to *discern in and through community* the will of God.[43]

The connection between Peacemaking Circles, worshipful work, and community building brings together the strands that we have been exploring.[44]

Modern Peacemaking Circles did not emerge from the same Christian epistemic base we have pursued in this study, though as the resonances with 1 Corinthians show they are deeply congruent with Christian conviction. Influenced in part by the indigenous tradition of Talking Circles, they began in the Minnesota criminal justice system as a form of restorative justice that focused on the harm caused by crime and devising strategies for repairing the harm through a dialogical process.[45] Early on they focused on the sentencing process, yet it was not long before they were applied to other parts of the criminal justice system. Some courts began operating in the format of a Circle, probation programmes for

42. Ibid., 85.

43. Ibid., 81 (italics mine).

44. Porter also uses the Circle process in connection with the church's gathering at Table in the pursuit of community building, see especially Porter's contributions titled 'The Last Supper: Naming the Conflicts and Giving Bread and Wine' and 'The Practice of Reconciliation at the Table', in Porter, ed., *Conflict and Communion*, 17–24, 79–90.

45. While beyond our present purpose, the degree to which modern Peacemaking Circles are a reflection of indigenous justice practices is highly debatable.

reintegrating prisoners employed the use of Circles, and some innovative practitioners began taking Circles into contexts beyond the justice system.[46] Circles are now used in schools, workplaces, social services, churches, neighborhood groups, and families.[47]

The authors of *Peacemaking Circles* describe Circles as having both an inner and outer frame. The outer frame designates the visible structural elements of Circle processes.[48] *Ceremony* or rituals are used to mark out the Circle time as 'sacred space', leading participants into a different way of relating and being present to one another. The *talking piece* is used as a symbolic tool for regulating the tone, pace, and purpose of dialogue. The *keeper* maintains the space of the dialogue, ensuring that participants remain attentive to the established guidelines. The *guidelines* describe the behaviors and commitments expected of one another in order to speak openly and truthfully. *Consensus making* involves exploring what decisions can be supported by all participants without the use of coerced obligation.

The inner frame is concerned with the underlying philosophy or view of reality that underpins Circles. They are not a neutral, value-free process. The 'underlying worldview', the 'view of the cosmos', as the authors of *Peacemaking Circles* put it, is 'one that sees the universe as characterized by wholeness, unity, and connectedness'.[49] Grounded in this conviction about reality, the Circle process is based on a fairly simple notion: 'Because we all want to be in good relationships with others, when we create a space that is respectful and reflective, people can find their way through anger, pain, and fear to find common ground and take care of one another'.[50] While presenting a rather idealized version of humanity, it is nevertheless clear that Circles exist to strengthen relationships by building on people's latent desire for connectedness.

46. A brief history of Circle processes can be found in Pranis, *The Little Book of Circle Processes*; and Pranis et al., *Peacemaking Circles*.

47. There have also emerged Talking Circles, Circles of Understanding, Healing Circles, Sentencing Circles, Support Circles, Community-Building Circles, Conflict Circles, Reintegration Circles, and Celebration or Honoring Circles. In a recent publication on the application of Circles in schools, Boyes-Watson and Pranis provide what they call a 'cookbook' containing dozens of variations on the Circle process, Carolyn Boyes-Wilson and Kay Pranis, *Circle Forward: Building a Restorative School Community* (St Paul, MN: Living Justice Press, 2015).

48. See Chapters 2 and 3 of Pranis, *Peacemaking Circles*.

49. Ibid., 68. See also Pranis, 'Restorative Values', 59–74.

50. Pranis, *Little Book of Circle Processes*, 62.

This overview of Peacemaking Circles certainly does not exhaust the depth of insight often experienced by its practitioners. Pranis, for example, speaks of Circles as creating, 'possibilities for freedom: freedom to speak our truth, freedom to drop masks and protections, freedom to be present as a whole human being, freedom to reveal our deepest longings, freedom to acknowledge mistakes and fears, freedom to act in accord with our core values'.[51] This perspective is often contrasted with processes in Western society that are characteristically rigid, conformist, and devoid of emotion.

Their power to transform conflicts has convinced many practitioners that Circles provide a way through contemporary society's most intransigent problems. 'With Circles, the center of conflict can become the center for practicing democracy to a degree that few of us have experienced anywhere else before.'[52] Circles could purportedly offer a way of practicing democracy that overcomes the many shortfalls of majority rule. Agreeing on the values that guide decision making, including all voices, seeking common ground, and building relatedness are just some features of the 'radical democracy' to be found in Circles.[53]

Porter describes his use of Circles within the church as a ritual that facilitates good listening, truthful speech, and peaceable outcomes. These are the elements essential to building a healthy common life within the church. Given his particular theological commitments, Porter adapts the format and language of Circles to fit the ecclesial context. He urges congregations to develop 'relational covenants':

> Relational covenants emphasize the relational nature of our understanding of how we should be treated in community, and recognize that this relationship with each other is embedded in the covenant God has made with God's creation. The covenant expresses our greatest values and give us a structure in which we can address relational brokenness. As people called to imitate God, the covenant is one that we continually and lovingly work to restore when it is broken. This understanding significantly affects how we react to breaches of the covenant.[54]

51. Ibid., 11.
52. Jennifer Ball, Wayne Caldwell, and Kay Pranis, *Doing Democracy with Circles: Engaging Communities in Public Planning* (St Paul, MN: Living Justice Press, 2010), 12.
53. Ibid., 163–70.
54. Porter, *Culture of Justpeace*, 97.

A relational covenant communicates the shared expectations and aspirations of the community regarding how each member wants to be treated. It outlines a set of promises to one another and to the community as a whole. It is specifically focused on the practices of listening and speaking, and the level of confidentiality expected. It is not intended to be a list of rules about negative conduct or how deviant conduct should be brought back into line. It is instead an affirmation of the vision and character of the community, and gives expression to the kind of conduct that expresses that vision.

Following the formation of a relational covenant, Porter leads the community or group into a 'facilitated conversation'.[55] Circles are essentially a structured form of dialogue oriented towards making connections and building understanding between people, on the basis of which more difficult conversations and conflicts can take place. These dialogical practices ensure that people are listened to, that they are given a chance to tell their story, and that decisions are made in a consensual way. Each of these three elements – listening, story-telling, and consensus – is essential for restoration to occur.

To help to facilitate listening, a talking piece is passed around the Circle. This practice serves two purposes. At a basic level, it regulates dialogue to ensure that each person has the opportunity to contribute. Since no one speaks unless holding the piece, interruptions and disruptive speech are minimized. An added benefit, as Pranis points out, is that it slows the pace of conversation and encourages thoughtful and reflective interactions among participants.[56] At a more profound level, the talking piece focuses everyone's attention on the person holding it, which in turn may become a healing moment as the holder experiences 'being heard'.[57] In most group processes, people compete with each other to be heard, which often leaves people with the feeling that they have been talked to but rarely heard. The talking piece shifts participants

55. Porter uses the term 'facilitated conversation' instead of a 'Circle process' partly to avoid creating an expert-model approach as well as to communicate that these kinds of conversations can occur in any place at any time; ibid., 76–77.

56. Pranis, *Little Book of Circle Processes*, 35.

57. Pranis et al., *Peacemaking Circles*, 95. These authors quote Margaret J. Wheatley, 'Why is being heard so healing? I don't know the full answer to that question, but I do know it has something to do with the fact that listening creates relationship…'; Margaret J. Wheatley, *Turning to One Another: Simple Conversations to Restore Hope to the Future* (Los Angeles, CA: Berrett-Koehler Publishers, 2002), 94.

from a position of 'adding their bit' to a disposition of respectful and genuine listening. Circle dialogues also foster the practices of silence and patience as essential features for cultivating attentive listeners. This challenges dominant attitudes towards time, which is often viewed as a limited resource that must be used efficiently and resourcefully.

'The Circle Process is a story-telling process', explains Pranis. 'Every person has a story, and every story has a lesson to offer. In the Circle, people touch one another's lives by sharing stories that have meaning to them'.[58] While advice and information can contribute to a conversation, listeners more readily absorb stories than subscribe to another's advice. It is often through the wisdom of stories that dialogue is guided towards a deeper apprehension of truth. Umbreit describes the difference between conventional approaches to dialogue, which are highly cognitive and oriented towards problem-solving, and restorative dialogues that focus on 'honoring the enormous healing power' of stories.[59] The power of storytelling lies in its self-revealing nature. 'In telling our stories we articulate how we understand what has happened to us, why and how it has impacted us, and how we see ourselves and others. Our way of constructing our stories, which shapes our view of reality, becomes more transparent to us [and others] when we speak the story out loud to others.'[60]

Stories invite people to venture to the root of the conflict, helping others understand its impact on people. They provide an opportunity to give voice to the grief, trauma, and enslavement the conflict has caused. Stories call others to participate in the healing or change that needs to take place. This is evident in 1 Corinthians, where Paul retells the story of Jesus's Last Supper as the basis for challenging abusive practices in the church's life (1 Cor. 11.17-34).

Porter uses a story to illustrate how Circles can be used to affirm the kind of work churches are called to do:

> Two churches were at war with each other. One church had been in existence for over one hundred years. Behind this church was a large cemetery. The church had membership of a few hundred. This old country church found the city spreading out and around it. Another United Methodist church bought land a mile away. This church already had several thousand members and was growing. The old country church was deeply threatened.

58. Pranis, *Little Book of Circle Processes*, 4.

59. Mark Umbreit, Jennifer Blevins, and Ted Lewis, *The Energy of Forgiveness: Lessons from Those in Restorative Dialogue* (Eugene, OR: Cascade Books, 2015), 14.

60. Pranis, *Little Book of Circle Processes*, 40.

> A war developed between these two congregations to the point where they were sending e-mail viruses to each other. I spent time with each congregation, listening to their concerns and hopes. We then gathered a circle of five representatives from each church, surrounded by the members of both churches, about four hundred people whose only job was to listen. We decided that all ten people would bring something to share in the circle that symbolized why they loved their church…
>
> One member of the 'country church' brought an electrical plug. I was eager to hear why! When it was his turn to describe what he had brought and its importance to him, he explained, 'When I joined this church, I was asked to help one of the senior members of the church rewire the church. From him, I learned all I know about electrical wiring, but, more importantly, I learned what it meant to be church.' This plug and all the other objects on the table in the center of the circle became a ritual affirmation of each church and reminded everyone throughout the evening what was best about these churches that they were trying to affirm together.[61]

It is significant that Porter concludes his study with a discussion on the Eucharist as the place where Christians become practiced in the kind of peacemaking and justice-making he associates with Circles. We may take from this that, at least for Christians, Circles must be understood, communicated, and practiced in the light of worship – not the other way around. How congregations navigate their common life, with all its decision-making, planning, and relational disputes, must be done in a way that reflects what has been learned in the liturgy. While Peacemaking Circles may help congregations in cultivating the kinds of relationships and dialogues that are essential for restoration to occur, it should not be forgotten that the church pursues restorative justice on account of its theological commitment to God's restoring justice.

A Restorative Missional Life: The Sycamore Tree Project

Designed by Daniel Van Ness and facilitated by Lisa Rea, the Sycamore Tree Project was pioneered in 1998 at a Texas medium-security prison. It was replicated soon after in New Zealand and the United Kingdom, and has since spread to over thirty-four countries. The Sycamore Tree Project is an initiative of Prison Fellowship. According to the organisation's mission statement, its goal is to be, 'Engaging the Christian community to pursue justice and healing in response to crime to the end that offenders are transformed, relationships are reconciled, and communities are restored'.[62] Prison Fellowship also pioneered 'Communities of

61. Porter, *Culture of Justpeace*, 92.
62. This is the mission statement of Prison Fellowship International.

Restoration' – an intensive 'character-focused, faith-based' programme where prisoners learn to live, serve, and work alongside others in a supportive environment, with the aim of transforming attitudes and behaviors in prisoners. They also advocate for justice reform in a restorative justice direction. This includes legislative change, promoting healing dialogues between community members and prisoners, and lobbying organisations, like the United Nations, to foster the use of restorative justice in criminal justice systems around the world.[63]

In this section we will focus on the Sycamore Tree Project as one specific instance of where the church's missional life has extended its work of restorative justice through an in-prison programme. This programme takes its name from the New Testament story of Jesus's encounter with the despised tax collector Zacchaeus (Luke 19.1-10). According to Van Ness, this narrative contains many of the features of a restorative justice encounter, with the unique addition of Jesus facilitating this encounter through to its restorative end. We will briefly summarize the restorative features of this narrative before exploring how the Sycamore Tree Projects brings this restorative reality to bear on its work in prisons.[64]

Van Ness first points out that it is Jesus that sets up this restorative justice encounter. Zacchaeus, on account of his short stature, had climbed a sycamore tree in the hope of seeing Jesus, who was expected to pass by that way (Luke 19.2-4). 'When Jesus came to the place, he looked up and said to him, "Zacchaeus, hurry and come down; for I must stay at your house today"' (v. 5). All we know of Zacchaeus at this point is that he is a chief tax-collector, who is very rich, and yet the crowds had not given him the space to see Jesus as he processed through their town. Given his profession, it is likely his fellow countrymen despised him. Tax-collectors were profiteering opportunists, Jewish collaborators with the colonizing Roman Empire who extorted payment from the already oppressed Jewish people.

Jesus's summoning of this 'white-collar offender' to leave the security of the tree and enter into the crowd brought together an offender with his victims. Van Ness surmises that Zacchaeus and his victims had become accustomed to separation. It may have been the case that Zacchaeus, like many others who commit crime, felt no empathy for those he had

63. See these initiatives on the Prison Fellowship International website, https://pfi.org/how-we-make-a-difference/restoring-justice/, accessed 10 September 2015.

64. I will be following Van Ness's sermon, 'Today Salvation Has Come', delivered at Wesley Church, Perth, Australia, 2 December, 2001. Downloaded from http://restorativejustice.org/restorative-justice/rj-library/today-salvation-has-come/2430/, 12 October 2015.

defrauded. Whatever the case, in this narrative it is the distance between the crowd and Zacchaeus that defines their relationship. This separation is overcome, first, through the presence of Jesus's person and, second, as Jesus calls down this wrongdoer to meet his victims. The first important step towards a restorative encounter happens through an encounter with Jesus.

By announcing his wish to feast at the house of Zacchaeus, Jesus provoked a strong reaction from the crowd. His words were intentionally provocative according to Van Ness, for they 'began a dialogue that was ultimately redemptive'. The crowd is the first to speak, grumbling together, 'He has gone to be the guest of one who is a sinner' (v. 7). Behind these words Van Ness detects the deep pain and disappointment from those who were seeing their hoped-for Messiah choosing to side with their abuser. Jesus's actions had prompted these victims to express their deep hurt. In response, it appears that Jesus simply listened. He created a space where victims would be heard, and then he waited to see what would happen next.

Zacchaeus had also been listening. Turning to Jesus he said, 'Look, half of my possessions, Lord, I will give to the poor; and if I have defrauded anyone of anything, I will pay back four times as much' (v. 8). Van Ness regards this as a confession, an acceptance of responsibility that he is the one who needs to make things right. In the presence of Jesus, Zacchaeus realises that 'truth is not something for others to discover and prove [as in a criminal trial]; truth is something to acknowledge and disclose'. Recognizing the intangible harm he has caused the town and its citizens, Zacchaeus elects to undergo a 'kind of community service', or at least a self-imposed fine of giving money to charity. More importantly, he promises to make full restitution to those he has directly harmed. These are the signs of a repentant sinner according to Van Ness: confession, acceptance of responsibility, facing the truth, and making restitution.

This brings us to the final part of the dialogue, and this time it is Jesus who speaks. It was Jesus who set up this encounter, who brought Zacchaeus the offender together with his victims, and now having heard from both parties, Jesus declares the purpose of this encounter. 'Today salvation has come to this house, because he too is a son of Abraham. For the Son of Man came to seek out and to save the lost' (vv. 9-10). Jesus wanted to 'bring salvation into this conflict', argues Van Ness, which tangibly means the restoration of offenders through repentance and their reintegration by a community that acknowledges this son of theirs. Jesus came to inaugurate a justice that restores and, through the lens of this narrative, this restorative justice happens through being encountered by Jesus.

The story finishes here, and yet the reality remains. The next day Jesus was already on his way, leaving behind him Zacchaeus and the crowd. Van Ness highlights the need for binding commitments following a restorative justice encounter. In order to fulfill his promises, Zacchaeus would need to list his victims and begin paying back his debts. He would need to live on less money, and change his tax-collecting practices or abandon them completely. As for the crowd, they would need to decide how they might treat Zacchaeus. Would they remain hostile towards him or extend an offer of forgiveness? While this narrative remains silent on these matters, this is the kind of hard work that needs to follow a restorative justice encounter.

The Sycamore Tree Project invites a group of prison inmates and victim surrogates to explore together the themes of repentance, confession, forgiveness, and reconciliation in the hope that offenders will commit to a life of restitution and victims can begin the journey of healing. While variations of the programme structure exist, it is common to include a panel of six victims and six prison inmates. The group meets over eight sessions to share their own personal experiences of crime through the use of small group discussions, role-plays, and readings. Towards the end of the course, those imprisoned are encouraged to formulate a 'covenant' outlining the commitments they will make on leaving the programme. In the final session there is an opportunity to celebrate those who have graduated, and notable dignitaries from the wider community are invited.

Despite being identified as a faith-based, restorative justice initiative, to my knowledge no *theological* treatment of the Sycamore Tree Project exists. This attests, once again, to the paucity of attention given to restorative justice by those working in theological ethics.[65] This inattention has contributed to some confusion about the programme's purpose. Not understanding the theological ethos behind restorative justice, some Christians have interpreted the purpose of Sycamore Tree as primarily an avenue for getting inmates 'saved' without the attendant emphasis on reconciliation or on attending to the needs of victims.[66] As the Zacchaeus

65. Two recent theological treatments of mass incarceration in the United States point to the use of restorative justice, but neither of these treatments explores how restorative justice is actually practiced within the prison environment; see Amy Levad, *Redeeming a Prison Society: A Liturgical and Sacramental Response to Mass Incarceration* (Minneapolis, MN: Fortress Press, 2014), 112–26; Logan, *Good Punishment?*, 128–33.

66. John Sage, one of the first volunteers for the Texas-based Sycamore Tree Project, objected to the proselytizing nature of the programme and eventually established another similar programme titled 'Bridges to Life'. Based on anecdotal

narrative showed, however, salvation describes the entire process of restoring relationships to rightness as mediated through an encounter with Jesus. An individualistic understanding of salvation that leaves people and relationships unchanged is not the salvation brought by Jesus.

One of the challenges facing the Sycamore Tree Project is its ability to challenge the understanding of justice that undergirds the prison setting in which it operates. Most restorative justice programmes operate in diversionary or pre-sentence settings rather than in post-sentence or correctional settings. This is because restorative justice emerged initially as an *alternative* to the expanded use of imprisonment by directing attention to the resources available in local communities, like the church, for dealing with wrongdoing. Early advocates of restorative justice often drew a sharp contrast between the restorative conception of justice underpinning community responses to crime and the retributive impulses that shape criminal justice institutions. As Russ Immarigeon, one of the early pioneers, writes, 'Incarceration is the institutional manifestation of the punitive impulse that restorative justice is designed and intended to challenge'.[67]

The prison regime and environment present numerous challenges for embedding an alternative practice like restorative justice. At its best, Sycamore Tree creates a space where prison staff, inmates, policy makers and community members are invited to rethink the purpose of imprisonment.[68] Do prisons exist only for the purpose of punishment, or can they exist to foster restoration and healing as well? Operating within what already exists, initiatives like Sycamore Tree invite those within the system to see beyond the dominant rationale informing the institutionalised forms of the justice system.

evidence, Sage's experience of Sycamore Tree being used as a means for 'conversions' is not uncommon. This influence can be attributed in part to the founder of Prison Fellowship, the politician-turned-inmate Chuck Colson, who believed that transformation of prisoners must come through conversion to Christ.

67. Russ Immarigeon, 'What Is the Place of Punishment and Imprisonment in Restorative Justice?', in Zehr and Toews, ed., *Critical Issues in Restorative Justice* (Devon, UK: Willan, 2004), 150.

68. Tim Newell, a former governor of Grendon and Spring Hill Prison, argues that what a restorative justice philosophy brings to the correctional system is not so much a 'once-for-all paradigm shift' but rather an 'evolutionary development' in how a society's justice systems respond to crime and its effects; see Kimmett Edgar and Tim Newell, *Restorative Justice in Prisons: A Guide to Making It Happen* (Hampshire: Waterside Press, 2006), 37.

One way in which Sycamore Tree fulfills this task is by raising awareness that crime is a matter of relational injury. Prisoners often display low levels of empathy and an awareness of the human impact of their offences, an issue that is further compounded by being separated from healthy examples of empathy and remorse while incarcerated. Alongside prisoners, the prison regime and the offender-focused role of correctional staff generally fail to accommodate the experience and needs of victims. The Sycamore Tree Project unsettles this neglectful complacency by providing a space where actual victims are enabled to tell their story of victimization, to explain through the use of personal narratives the relational and human impact of crime. Like the crowd in the Zacchaeus narrative, this fosters victim awareness in offenders as well as providing an opportunity for victims to experience the healing effects of giving voice to their story.[69]

Participants often recount how their attitude towards others changes as a result of exchanging stories of wrongdoing and victimisation. Victims no longer feel afraid of prisoners, prisoners express a hope that change and forgiveness are possible, and unlikely friendships begin to form between both. As Van Ness writes, 'in the context of shared emotions, victim and offender achieve a sort of empathy. This may not make the victim feel particularly positive about the offender but it does make the offender seem more normal, less malevolent.'[70] This observation suggests a unique facet about justice from a restorative perspective. When justice is understood as that which restores relationships, it becomes vitally important to attend to the way in which people express meaningful experiences and events – including traumatic or shameful events – through the use of personal and collective narratives. Justice is experienced in the listening and telling of stories, especially when they open up ways of healing the memory of the past.

The power of restorative justice initiatives like the Sycamore Tree Project lies in their ability to foster truthful and healing exchanges between those who have experienced trauma, shame, hurt, and distrust. People are invited through these encounters to participate vicariously

69. Victims are open to restorative justice because, as Lisa Rea puts it, 'the current system does not adequately acknowledge the impact violent crime has on victims, or hold offenders accountable to their victims in meaningful ways'; Lisa M. Rea, 'Restorative Justice: The New Way Forward', *Christian Reflection: A Series in Faith and Ethics: Prison*, Journal of The Center for Christian Ethics, Baylor University (2012): 33.

70. Van Ness and Strong, *Restoring Justice*, 72, citing David Moore, 'Evaluating Family Group Conferences'.

in the experience of others and so become participants in their recovery also. Even though in-prison programmes like Sycamore Tree bring together unrelated or 'surrogate' victims and offenders, the effects of these exchanges are no less tangible.[71]

Building awareness of the relational realities of crime and justice is one reason why the church ought to lend support to initiatives like the Sycamore Tree Project. Recognition of the relational injury of crime is of pivotal importance in seeking the restoration and reintegration of offenders.[72] Zacchaeus was presumably moved to repentance upon hearing the pain he had caused to his fellow countrymen. This was even more noticeable in Jesus's parable of the Prodigal Son, where the repentance displayed by the younger son was brought about by remembering the relational bond to his paternal victim and by his realization of how his behavior had caused injury to this relationship. This suggests that the first step in repentance involves wrongdoers in undertaking a truthful assessment of their life as relational and social beings.

The Sycamore Tree Project attempts to embed this same movement in its programme, albeit without identifying repentance as the overarching reality. In the curriculum, repentance is expressed as one theme alongside 'confession' and 'restitution', with perhaps the greatest emphasis given to the session on 'taking responsibility'.[73] It would, however, be more conducive to a theological conception of restorative reintegration if these movements were situated within the overarching reality of repentance, as this would more clearly communicate the vertical as well as horizontal

71. For an understanding of the use of 'surrogates' in restorative justice, see ibid., 69. Barb Toews calls the use of unrelated victims and offenders, *Dialogue Groups*: 'This practice is most commonly used in prison…[as] a way to meet justice participant needs. Participants talk about their crime stories and, in return, receive validation for their experiences and feelings. Offending participants talk of their remorse and responsibility, offering symbolic vindication to victim participants. They learn about crime's impacts and causes. Participants receive many of the same benefits of face-to-face meetings'; Barb Toews, *The Little Book of Restorative Justice for People in Prison: Rebuilding the Web of Relationships* (Intercourse, PA: Good Books, 2006), 67–68.

72. According to Van Ness, 'The purpose of these meetings is to help victims find resolution and to expose offenders to the damage caused to others by their crime, thereby producing a change in the offender's attitudes and behaviors'; Van Ness and Strong, *Restoring Justice*, 69.

73. The usual eight week curriculum is structured as follows: (1) Introduction, (2) What is Crime?, (3) Responsibility, (4) Confession and Repentance, (5) Forgiveness, (6) Restitution, (7) Toward Reconciliation, (8) Final Celebration.

dimension involved. In a Christian sense, repentance is not a journey taken alone. It requires learning to see oneself as dependent on the mercy of others and of God, which is arguably the key insight imparted to participants in the Sycamore Tree Project.

This raises the question on the extent to which the success of Sycamore Tree is dependent on participants being encountered by something beyond themselves. In the Zacchaeus narrative it was clear that the encounter between the crowd and Zacchaeus would not have taken place were it not for Jesus's presence. He not only brought about the encounter, he started a dialogue between the two parties, and finally moved the dialogue towards a more restorative outcome. If the Sycamore Tree Project is genuinely patterned on the reality of Jesus's reconciling presence, then it must find ways of acknowledging its dependence on this spiritual dimension. It might do this through prayer or other gestures that communicate how, through the Spirit, God's gift of reconciliation is made available to those who ask and seek after it.

Perhaps the most controversial aspect of the Sycamore Tree Project is the way it opens up a space for offenders to experience forgiveness and reconciliation with those who are not their direct victims. While repentance is the means by which wrongdoers adopt a different relationship to their crime, it is not until the penitent have been conferred with forgiveness that restoration can be fully achieved. However, can those who are not primary victims offer such forgiveness? This matter was left unanswered in response to Zacchaeus's repentance. Yet in Jesus's parable of the Prodigal Son, it was the principal victim of the offence that conferred forgiveness. Without the father's generous pardoning of his prodigal son the parable's potency would be lost and its legacy stilled.

By bringing together a group of unrelated victims and offenders in a carefully planned and facilitated format, I suggest that Sycamore Tree acts as a rehearsal of the movements hoped for in a fully restorative response to wrongdoing: repentant offenders, forgiving and compassionate victims, and reconciliation outcomes. It guides people through a restorative justice process not unlike what the church does through its liturgical performance. What might take months or years in a fully restorative justice process, the programme offers in a condensed format each of the steps that need to be present in order to repair the effects of crime. As a rehearsal, there is no expectation that all situations of wrongdoing will progress in this way, but this is no reason to forego learning what it means to respond out of a restorative sense of justice. In order to be successful, however, this requires at least some participants who have learnt to recognize the signs of genuine repentance and the way to restoration. This is where the church could continue to extend or enrich the programme.

The church should be an ideal place to find participants for the Sycamore Tree Project who have been formed in the kind of restorative liturgy enacted in the Eucharist. To 'participate in the Eucharist', as Cavanaugh writes, is an 'invitation to participate in God's reconciliation of the world', which 'opens up new possibilities undreamed of in a merely worldly politics'.[74] Sycamore Tree might rightly be considered an extension of the church's Eucharistic life according to this description. It needs to be emphasized, however, that this does not involve leaving the church behind but rather taking the social actions performed in the Eucharist beyond the altar and into the prison environment. Restorative agents are sent out into the world to embody the sacramental life of the church, bringing others into the knowledge of God's reconciling justice as they share about the ways in which God's forgiveness and grace has been tangibly experienced.

It is through the church's liturgy that Christians learn to speak the language of the biblical narrative. Through the very same process, they are being formed as persons and learn the gestures of restorative, reconciliatory practice for responding to conflict. When done thoughtfully, worship is the context wherein Christians develop the sensitivity to recognize the movements so essential to human interaction, especially when strong emotions are present, and to perceive when and how intervention or silence is most appropriate.[75] By bringing their ecclesial formation to bear on the Sycamore Tree process, Christians can provide a language, an understanding, and set of skills that can help guide others to experience the transformative effects of a restorative encounter.

The perspective of those who have survived terrible abuse and harm at the hands of others and who have learned to forgive is an invaluable feature of any restorative justice encounter. The church has something unique to offer here too. While sensitive to the needs of victims, the church attests to the power of forgiveness made available in and through Christ. Christians who have joined their agony with this offer of forgiveness become a living testimony to the message that transformation through forgiveness is possible. This is a much-needed message within today's prisons where hope is in such short supply. Even for those who have not been victimized, learning to be in solidarity with the pain and suffering of others provides a valuable perspective on the human effects of wrongdoing.

74. Cavanaugh, 'The Church in the Streets', 392.

75. Brock in particular gives worship methodological pride of place as the context wherein Christians develop a renewed attentiveness and perception, first of all to how God is present in worship and through this to God's love for concrete neighbors; Brock, *Christian Ethics in a Technological Age*, see especially, 167–86.

We have argued that the church is already embedded in its own form of restorative justice, which it rehearses week after week as it embodies the story of God's justice through its liturgical practices. What the Sycamore Tree Project condenses into just eight sessions on a programmatic basis, often under budgetary constraints and the pressures of the prison regime, the church could offer through being a place where the same movements of repentance, confession, forgiveness, and restitution are practiced on a free and regular basis. This is crucial for at least two reasons.

First, Sycamore Tree is just a starting point for exploring the significance of restorative justice, and there is a need for places where these initial insights can be deepened. Participants often enter the programme with a great deal of hesitancy and guardedness, yet this changes as they progress and by the final session they commonly express a desire to begin again in light of their changed attitude. For offenders who are not able to meet their own victims, or victims their assailants, the healing effects of this programme are nevertheless significant. The church is ideally situated to be a place where people can regularly encounter the ethos of restorative justice as it is recapitulated through the church's liturgy, and thereby deepen what they have begun to experience through Sycamore Tree.

Second, one of the downstream effects of high incarceration rates is an equally high percentage of prisoners being released back into communities, and often without adequate support.[76] The programmatic basis of Sycamore Tree is incapable of embedding restorative justice across the many communities where ex-inmates are being relocated. Churches might extend to released wrongdoers a community where restorative justice is a way of life, not just a one-off programme. By bringing people into relationships that practice accountability, honesty, and respect, the church demonstrates a concern for restorative reintegration.[77]

This points to a final reason why the church's witness to restorative justice might extend to the Sycamore Tree Project – the celebration ceremony that completes this programme anticipates the acceptance of the repentant wrongdoer back into the community. While valuable as a single event, the real need is to have communities where the covenantal

76. This does not imply a reduction in incarceration rates, but rather a heavy reliance on imprisonment for more minor offences that carry shorter prison sentences.

77. Kathy Fox points to how restorative reintegration relies on the existence of hospitable communities, like the church, that can induct released offenders into pro-social and supportive relationships; Kathryn J. Fox, 'Restoring the Social: Offender Reintegration in a Risky World', *International Journal of Comparative and Applied Criminal Justice* 38, no. 3 (2013): 235–56.

promises made can be lived out. Just as importantly, the offender's restoration relies on the existence of communities where the shame of their offending can be lifted and their honor restored. We noted the importance of bestowing honor on repentant wrongdoers in Jesus's parable. The church has the opportunity to embody this same response by extending its own resources and relationships towards those being released. It might be an agent in the restoration of offenders by inviting them to participate in God's restoring of the world through the life of the church.

One misconception of ecclesial ethics is that it is uninterested in making a positive difference in the world, choosing to focus instead on buttressing a Christian culture against the travails of wider society. By contrast, we have shown that a recovery of the sources internal to the church, like its performance of the Eucharist or its reading of Scripture (cf. 1 Cor. 12; Luke 19.1-10), actually encourages engagement with forms of restorative justice beyond the boundaries of the church and provides impetus for the task. In the Eucharist, the church recollects the reconciliation it has received in and through Christ, and the social actions performed in this practice can be emulated in other contexts, like the prison. Having been formed liturgically in the practices of repentance, confession, absolution, and reconciliation, Christians extend the work of restorative justice to initiatives like the Sycamore Tree Project. In doing so, they are not leaving the church behind, but are bringing the practices and formation developed in the ecclesia into the arena of criminal justice so that through repentance, confession, absolution, and reconciliation, the well-being of both perpetrators and victims might be restored.

The examples of the Sycamore Tree Project and Porter's use of Peacemaking Circles illustrate a number of elements that are crucial to the success of restorative justice. First, these processes reflect a fundamentally relational understanding of humanity. Wrongdoing is conceived of as a relational injury, and justice is about restoring those relationships to a healthy condition. Second, healing happens when people are able to tell their story in a context of truthful and attentive listening. Victims and offenders need places where they can share their stories of trauma and shame, and so invite others to participate in their recovery. Third, restorative justice is about cultivating forms of dialogue where people are honest, respectful, and can begin to trust. In such dialogues, strong emotions may emerge and need to be mediated in a way that people feel safe, while still being heard.

Each of these elements is crucial to the success of restorative justice practice. Yet through the theological lens of this study, another dimension has also been necessary. On account of how God's restoring justice is manifest in the cross and resurrection of Christ, it is vital to acknowledge the ways in which restorative justice happens through an encounter with Jesus Christ. This is the entire logic of the Eucharist, where victims experience the comfort and solidarity of the crucified one and where offenders experience the forgiveness and new life made possible by his resurrection. This reality of encountering the crucified yet risen Christ is also present in programmes like the Sycamore Tree, and needs to be acknowledged as such. Likewise in the congregation's practice of Circles, the transformative effects of genuine dialogue happen on account of the work of the Spirit in community, bringing together the many gifts for the sake of building up the body of Christ.

I have suggested that the church has its own reasons and context for exhibiting these restorative practices in its life together. Yet it also has much to gain through participating in restorative justice initiatives that take place in the world, not only as a way of sharing its own practices but also as a way of more faithfully embodying God's restoring justice in the world he has redeemed.

Conclusion

At a colloquium held to mark his retirement as founder and director of the world's first Center for Theology and Public Issues, Duncan Forrester addressed the subject of a public theology for the twenty-first century. He highlighted several key elements that should be included in the general field of public theology. First, it needs to engage with the world in a way that respects rather than disparages the distinction between Christian discourse and a secular discourse. This requires attending to the academic and practical issues that are pertinent to public debate on any given issue. Second, he urged theology to make a 'modest but truthful, constructive and challenging contribution to public debate', while always having as its ultimate aim the pursuit of 'human flourishing in community'.[1] He believed that the theological disciplines ought to make a difference in a way that 'heals, reconciles, helps, challenges'.[2] Finally, public theology must necessarily be '*ecclesial* theology', that is, it must be able to speak of the church as the (albeit imperfect) embodiment of the Gospel it proclaims.[3]

We began this exploration by asking the question, 'How does an ecclesial context shape the theological apprehension and praxis of justice?' In particular, we have asked how, in view of its members having been admitted into God's restoring justice in Christ, the church might embody in the world this same justice of restoring right relationships. This ecclesial focus builds on Marshall's premise that, 'the first Christians experienced in Christ and lived out in their faith communities an understanding of justice as a power that heals, restores, and reconciles rather than hurts, punishes, and kills, and that this reality ought to shape and direct a Christian contribution to the criminal justice debate today'.[4]

1. Duncan B. Forrester, 'Working in the Quarry: A Response to the Colloquium', in *Public Theology for the 21st Century*, ed. William F. Storrar and Andrew R. Morton (London: T&T Clark International, 2004), 432.
2. Ibid., 436.
3. Ibid., 432–33.
4. Marshall, *Beyond Retribution*, 33.

Just as the early Christian communities exhibited a restorative understanding of justice within the ecclesia on account of how the justice of God was disclosed in Christ as a saving and peacemaking justice, so the church today should seek to embed practices of restorative justice as an outworking of its understanding of the justice of God. We have firmly established this claim by charting a direction through some of the challenges Forrester has identified. In particular, we have mined the long history of the Christian tradition to show how different conceptions of justice emerged from and shaped in turn their surrounding social and philosophical contexts, and with the sphere of corrective justice in particular. We have shown how some of these conceptions of justice owed more to the Greco-Roman intellectual tradition than to the biblical story of divine justice. These conceptions of justice tended to be interpreted in a legalistic and retributive sense rather than in terms of the relational reality of reconciliation and peace outlined in the biblical account of God's dealings with the world. This retributive logic imported from elsewhere was then read back into the divine nature, such that God's justice acquired a particularly harsh and retributive orientation. In order to recover resources within this tradition that accentuate the capacity for justice to contribute to human flourishing, I argued that an alternative conception of justice needs to emerge, one that is more anchored in the story of Scripture and lived out in the community that reads Scripture so that it might be embodied in life.

In Chapter 4 it was established that the biblical understanding of the justice of God is best understood as a saving, liberating, and restorative justice, rather than a purely retributive justice. The nature of divine justice is revealed in God's restoration of the covenantal relationship with his people when they had transgressed the law or were in need of deliverance. It was most decisively revealed in the death and resurrection of Jesus, through which humanity is delivered from the powers of Sin and Death and into a Spirit-filled and life-giving existence in Christ. Whatever retributive features of this story remain, they must be understood in light of an overall restorative trajectory, and must not be allowed to displace the predominant emphasis on the benevolent nature of divine justice.

Recognition of how justice is exemplified in God's own being and through his actions places a special obligation on the people of God to reflect this justice within their own communities. This was a consistent feature in our survey of the Christian tradition. However God's justice was understood, it always carried social and practical implications for the church and for wider society. It was only in the modern, increasingly secular era, with its confidence in the powers of human reason and the diminution of the traditional theological worldview, that the relative priority of divine and human justice was inverted. It must not be forgotten, however, that the established judicial systems for responding to crime and its victims emerged out of a confluence of theological ideas on the nature of justice, sin, and atonement. The question then is whether this judicial response is an adequate reflection of what it means to do justice as disclosed in the biblical story.

In addressing this question, we turned first to the recent trend in theological ethics that has emphasized the centrality of the 'ecclesia' as the place where the story of Scripture is being fulfilled. From the perspective of ecclesial ethics, the church is not just any community but one that cultivates its imagination and forms its character by engaging with the story of Scripture. The church is where the story of God's justice is being embodied in the common life of a people of faith. Ecclesial ethics is concerned to describe the nature of this embodied life and its significance for ethical considerations. This has spawned a series of significant reassessments, particularly of how the social and political nature of God's justice ought to be worked out in human affairs.

While ecclesial ethics has focused on nonviolent peacemaking as the primary witness of the church, curiously it has paid little attention to the place of justice in this vocation. Biblically there is a close relationship between the church as the embodiment of God's peace and as the embodiment of God's justice. However, this insight has not been prominent in ecclesial ethics. Its treatment of the church's relationship to justice has been slim at best, and often written for the purpose of combating problematic liberal conceptions of justice rather than developing the church's own distinctive way of understanding and enacting it.

In order to address this lacuna, I explored how one particular ecclesial tradition has developed a way of doing justice from an explicitly restorative angle. The Mennonite-Anabaptist community was largely responsible for the early theology and approach to conflict that came to be known as restorative justice. By uncovering the ecclesiological and theological influences on the Victim Offender Reconciliation Project, I argued that this practice of restorative justice should be understood as a concrete embodiment of the relational and restorative dimensions of the biblical story. We observed, however, that the restorative justice field has since eschewed its dependence on the theological insights that led to its conception. Much of what we have been doing has been an attempt to develop restorative justice in a more comprehensively theological direction, and through the life of the church in particular. By bringing an ecclesial approach to bear on restorative justice, we have proposed that the church's distinctive contribution to the wider restorative justice field must be informed by the ways in which the justice of God is taking shape in its own community.

Chapters 5 to 7 provided a series of reflections on how the church should center its life on the story of God's restoring justice. By attending to Jesus's parable of the Prodigal Son and Paul's instructions to the church in Corinth, I provided a theological reading of Scripture that attests to the ways in which the church might better embody a justice that restores. I also suggested that the church already performs, albeit imperfectly, the work of restorative justice through its liturgical life. By inviting sinners and victims to participate in the liturgical acts of confession, forgiveness, and especially the Eucharist, the church remembers and proclaims the restoring justice it has received in Christ. Having become practiced in the work of restorative justice, Christians might bring these actions performed in the Eucharistic liturgy to bear on other areas of the church's life and mission. The ministry provided to prison inmates through the Sycamore Tree Project was offered as a particular example of the church's practice of restorative justice in the wider community.

It is hoped that the present work has shown why a theological account of the theory and practice of restorative justice is fruitful for articulating and clarifying the witness of the church, especially in the face of conflict or wrongdoing. While the church already has resources within itself for responding peaceably to conflict, drawing upon the recent tradition of ecclesial ethics, this study has given expression to a largely unexplored tradition that combines the peace- and justice-making dimensions of the church's witness. By bringing an ecclesial perspective to the work of restorative justice, I have sought to extend the church's imagination as to how it might better become God's community of restoration.

This examination has drawn on diverse areas of research, from the history of criminal justice and the theological reflection upon it, through to the distinct approach of ecclesial ethics, the theory and practice of restorative justice, and the theological interpretation of Scripture. Such a far-ranging, boundary-crossing exercise has been necessary because of the complex nature of the church and its place in the world. The church is a historical institution, as well as a community of readers of Scripture. Throughout its long history it has produced a range of interpretations of, and practices for doing, corrective justice. The community of faith must continually test whether the manner in which it responds to conflict and wrongdoing, whether in the church or in society, is reflective of how God is bringing peace and healing to all of the constitutive relationships of its life.

Bibliography

Aladjem, Terry K. *The Culture of Vengeance and the Fate of American Justice*. New York: Cambridge University Press, 2008.

Allen, Danielle S. 'Democratic Dis-Ease: Of Anger and the Troubling Nature of Punishment'. Pages 191–214 in *The Passions of Law*. Edited by Susan A. Bandes. New York and London: New York University Press, 1999.

Allen, Francis. *The Decline of the Rehabilitative Ideal*. New Haven, CT: Yale University Press, 1981.

Anderson, Benedict. *Imagined Communities: Reflections on the Origin and Spread of Nationalism*. London: Verso, 1991.

Aristotle. *The Nicomachean Ethics*. Translated by David Ross. Oxford World's Classics. Oxford: Oxford University Press, 2009.

Augustine. *The City of God Against the Pagans*. Translated by R. W. Dyson. Cambridge: Cambridge University Press, 1998.

Ball, Jennifer, Wayne Caldwell and Kay Pranis. *Doing Democracy with Circles: Engaging Communities in Public Planning*. St Paul, MN: Living Justice Press, 2010.

Barth, Karl. *Church Dogmatics*. Translated by G. W. Bromiley and T. F. Torrance. Edinburgh: T. & T. Clark, 1957.

Bash, Anthony. *Forgiveness and Christian Ethics*. Cambridge: Cambridge University Press, 2007.

Beale, Greg. *We Become What We Worship: A Biblical Theology of Idolatry*. Downers Grove, IL: InterVarsity Press, 2008.

Beck, Jackson. 'The Elkhart County Victim Offender Reconciliation Program: A Story of Witness, 1978–1984'. Senior's dissertation, Goshen College, IN, 2013.

Beker, Johan Christiaan. *Suffering and Hope: The Biblical Vision and the Human Predicament*. Grand Rapids, MI: Eerdmans, 1994.

Bell Jr., Daniel. 'Deliberating: Justice and Liberation'. Pages 182–95 in *The Blackwell Companion to Christian Ethics*. Edited by Stanley Hauerwas and Samuel Wells. Oxford: Wiley-Blackwell, 2004.

———. 'Jesus, the Jews, and the Politics of God's Justice'. *Ex Auditu* 22 (2006): 87–112.

———. *Liberation Theology After the End of History: The Refusal to Cease Suffering*. London: Routledge, 2001.

———. 'What Gift Is Given? A Response to Volf'. *Modern Theology* 19, no. 2 (2003): 271–80.

Bell, Richard H. *Rethinking Justice: Restoring Our Humanity*. Lanham, MD: Lexington Books, 2007.

Belousek, Darrin W. Snyder. *Atonement, Justice, and Peace: The Message of the Cross and the Mission of the Church*. Grand Rapids, MI: Eerdmans, 2012.

Bender, John. 'Part I: Reconciliation Begins in Canada'. *Mennonite Central Committee Peace Section Newsletter* 16, no. 1 (1986): 1–2.

———. 'Part II: Reconciliation Spreads to the U.S.'. *Mennonite Central Committee Peace Section Newsletter* 16, no. 1 (1986): 3–5.

Berkman, John, and Michael Cartwright, ed. *The Hauerwas Reader*. Durham, NC: Duke University Press, 2001.

Berman, Harold J. *Law and Revolution: The Formation of the Western Legal Tradition*. Cambridge, MA: Harvard University Press, 1983.

Bianchi, Herman. 'A Biblical Vision of Justice'. *New Perspectives on Crime and Justice: Occasional Papers*, no. 2 (1984): n.p.

Birch, Bruce C. 'The Role of Scripture in Public Theology'. *Word and World* 4, no. 3 (1984): 260–68.

Blagg, H. 'A Just Measure of Shame: Aboriginal Youth and Conferencing in Australia'. *British Journal of Criminology* 37, no. 4 (1997): 481–501.

Boersma, Hans. *Violence, Hospitality, and the Cross: Reappropriating the Atonement Tradition*. Grand Rapids, MI: Baker Academic, 2004.

Bonhoeffer, Dietrich. *Letters and Papers from Prison*. Dietrich Bonhoeffer Works 8. Minneapolis, MN: Fortress Press, 2010.

Borton, Ian M., and Gregory D. Paul. 'Problematizing the Healing Metaphor of Restorative Justice'. *Contemporary Justice Review* 18, no. 3 (2015): 257–73.

Bottoms, Antony. 'The Philosophy and Politics of Punishment and Sentencing'. Pages 17–50 in *The Politics of Sentencing Reform*. Edited by C. Clarkson and R. Morgan. Oxford: Clarendon Press, 1995.

Bottoms, Anthony, and Joanna Shapland. 'Can Persistent Offenders Acquire Virtue?' *Studies in Christian Ethics* 27, no. 3 (2014): 318–33.

Boyes-Wilson, Carolyn, and Kay Pranis. *Circle Forward: Building a Restorative School Community*. St. Paul, MN: Living Justice Press, 2015.

Bradshaw, Paul F., and Maxwell E. Johnson. *The Eucharistic Liturgies: Their Evolution and Interpretation*. Collegeville, MN: Liturgical Press, 2012.

Braithwaite, John. *Crime, Shame and Reintegration*. Cambridge: Cambridge University Press, 1989.

———. *Restorative Justice and Responsive Regulation*. Oxford: Oxford University Press, 2002.

Braithwaite, J., and H. Strang, eds. *Restorative Justice and Civil Society*. Cambridge: Cambridge University Press, 2001.

Braithwaite, John, and Philip Pettit. *Not Just Deserts: A Republican Theory of Criminal Justice*. Oxford: Oxford University Press, 1990.

Bretherton, Luke. *Christianity and Contemporary Politics: The Conditions and Possibilities of Faithful Witness*. West Sussex, UK: Wiley-Blackwell, 2010.

Brock, Brian. *Christian Ethics in a Technological Age*. Grand Rapids, MI: Eerdmans, 2010.

———. *Singing the Ethos of God: On the Place of Christian Ethics in Scripture*. Grand Rapids, MI: Eerdmans, 2007.

Broughton, Geoff. 'Making Public Theology More Biblical or Biblical Theology More Public? Christopher Marshall's Interpretation of the Parable of the Prodigal Son in Luke 15'. Pages 72–87 in *The Bible, Justice and Public Theology*. Edited by David J. Neville. Sheffield: Sheffield Phoenix Press, 2014.

Campbell, Douglas A. 'An Apocalyptic Rereading of "Justification" in Paul: Or, an Overview of the Argument of Douglas Campbell's *The Deliverance of God*—by Douglas Campbell'. *The Expository Times* 123, no. 8 (2012): 382–93.
———. *The Deliverance of God: An Apocalyptic Rereading of Justification in Paul.* Grand Rapids, MI: Eerdmans, 2009.
———. *Framing Paul: An Epistolary Biography*. Grand Rapids, MI: Eerdmans, 2014.
———. 'Is Tom Right? An Extended Review of N.T. Wright's *Justification: God's Plan and Paul's Vision*'. *Scottish Journal of Theology* 65, no. 3 (2012): 323–45.
———. *The Quest for Paul's Gospel: A Suggested Strategy*. London: T&T Clark, 2005.
Campbell, John McLeod. *The Nature of Atonement*. 2nd ed. Grand Rapids, MI: Eerdmans, 1996 [1856].
Cavanaugh, William T. 'The Church in the Streets: Eucharist and Politics'. *Modern Theology* 30, no. 2 (2014): 384–402.
———. *Migrations of the Holy: God, State, and the Political Meaning of the Church.* Grand Rapids, MI: Eerdmans, 2011.
———. *Torture and Eucharist: Theology, Politics, and the Body of Christ.* Surrey, UK: Blackwell, 1998.
Cayley, David. *The Expanding Prison: The Crisis in Crime and Punishment and the Search for Alternatives*. Toronto: Anansi Press, 1998.
Chodorow, Stanley. *Christian Political Theory and Church Politics in the Mid-Twelfth Century*. Berkeley, CA: University of California Press, 1972.
Christie, Nils. 'Conflicts as Property'. *British Journal of Criminology* 17, no. 1 (1977): 1–15.
———. *Limits to Pain*. Oxford: Martin Robertson, 1982.
Chupp, Mark. 'Faith and VORP'. *Mennonite Central Committee Peace Section Newsletter* 16, no. 1 (1986): 5–6.
———. 'Reconciliation Procedures and Rationale'. Pages 56–68 in *Mediation and Criminal Justice*. Edited by Martin and Burt Galaway Wright. London: SAGE, 1989.
Classen, Ron, Howard Zehr and Duane Ruth-Heffelbower. *VORP Organizing: A Foundation in the Church*. Elkhart, IN: MCC U.S., 1989.
Consedine, Jim. *Restorative Justice: Healing the Effects of Crime*. Lyttelton, New Zealand: Ploughshares Publishers, 1995.
Corlett, J. Angelo. 'Punishment and the Socratic Roots of Retributivism'. Pages 1–15 in *Punishment and Ethics: New Perspectives*. Edited by Jesper Ryberg and J. Angelo Corlett. Hampshire, UK: Palgrave Macmillan, 2010.
Cornwell, David J. *Doing Justice Better: The Politics of Restorative Justice*. Hampshire, UK: Waterside Press, 2007.
Crossan, John Dominic. *The Historical Jesus: The Life of a Mediterranean Jewish Peasant*. San Francisco, CA: HarperCollins, 1991.
Cullen, Francis T., and Paul Gendreau. 'From Nothing Works to What Works: Changing Professional Ideology in the 21st Century'. *The Prison Journal* 81, no. 3 (2001): 313–38.
Daly, Kathleen. 'Restorative Justice—the Real Story'. *Punishment and Society* 4 (2002): 55–79.
———. 'A Tale of Two Studies: Restorative Justice from a Victims' Perspective'. Pages 153–74 in *New Directions in Restorative Justice: Issues, Practice, Evaluation*. Edited by Elizabeth Elliot and Robert M. Gordon. Cullompton, UK: Willan, 2005.

———. 'Revisiting the Relationship Between Retributive and Restorative Justice'. Pages 33–54 in *Restorative Justice: Philosophy to Practice*. Edited by John Braithwaite and Heather Strang. Aldershot, UK: Ashgate, 2000.

Deane, Herbert A. *The Political and Social Ideas of St. Augustine*. New York and London: Columbia University Press, 1963.

DeHart, Paul J. *The Trial of the Witnesses: The Rise and Decline of Postliberal Theology*. West Sussex, UK: Wiley-Blackwell, 2006.

Deme, Dániel. *The Christology of Anselm of Canterbury*. Hampshire, UK: Ashgate, 2003.

Department of Corrections, New Zealand. *Reconviction Patterns of Released Prisoners: A 60-Months Follow-up Analysis*. New Zealand: Department of Corrections, 2009.

Derrida, Jacques. 'Force of Law: The "Mystical Foundation of Authority"'. Pages 3–67 in *Deconstruction and the Possibility of Justice*. Edited by Drucilla Cornell, Michael Rosenfeld and David Gray Carlson. London: Routledge, 1992.

Dillenberger, John, ed. *Martin Luther: Selections from His Writings*. New York: Anchor Books, 1961.

Dodaro, Robert. *Christ and the Just Society in the Thought of Augustine*. Cambridge: Cambridge University Press, 2004.

Dreidger, Leo, and Donald B. Kraybill. *Mennonite Peacemaking: From Quietism to Activism*. Scottdale, PA: Herald Press, 1994.

Duff, R. A. 'Penance, Punishment and the Limits of Community'. *Punishment and Society* 5, no. 3 (2003): 295–312.

———. *Punishment, Communication and Community*. Oxford: Oxford University Press, 2001.

———. 'Responsibility, Restoration, and Retribution'. Pages 63–85 in *Retributivism Has a Past: Has It a Future?* Edited by Michael Tonry. Oxford: Oxford University Press, 2011.

Dunn, James D. G., and Alan M. Suggate. *The Justice of God: A Fresh Look at the Old Doctrine of Justification by Faith*. Grand Rapids, MI: Eerdmans, 1993.

Edgar, Kimmett, and Tim Newell. *Restorative Justice in Prisons: A Guide to Making It Happen*. Hampshire, UK: Waterside Press, 2006.

Elliot, Neil. *Liberating Paul: The Justice of God and the Politics of the Apostle*. Sheffield: Sheffield Academic Press, 1995.

Elshtain, Jean Bethke. 'Citizenship and Armed Civic Virtue: Some Questions on the Commitment to Public Life'. Pages 47–55 in *Community in America: The Challenges of Habits of the Heart*. Edited by Charles H. Reynolds and Ralph Norman. Berkeley, CA: University of California Press, 1988.

Epp, Edgar. 'Why Prisons Fail'. *Catalyst* (1982): 15.

Fee, Gordon D. *The First Epistle to the Corinthians*. Grand Rapids, MI: Eerdmans, 1987.

Feinberg, Joel. *Doing and Deserving*. Princeton, NJ: Princeton University Press, 1970.

Findlay, M. 'Decolonising Restoration and Justice: Restoration in Transitional Cultures'. *Howard Journal of Criminal Justice* 39, no. 4 (2000): 398–411.

Fletcher, Joseph F. *Situation Ethics: The New Morality*. Philadelphia, PA: Westminster Press, 1966.

Flood, Derek. *Healing the Gospel: A Radical Vision for Grace, Justice, and the Cross*. Eugene, OR: Wipf & Stock, 2012.

Fodor, Jim. 'Reading the Scriptures: Rehearsing Identity, Practicing Character'. Pages 141–55 in *The Blackwell Companion to Christian Ethics*. Edited by Stanley Hauerwas and Samuel Wells. Chichester, MA: Wiley-Blackwell, 2011.

Forrester, Duncan B. 'Working in the Quarry: A Response to the Colloquium'. Pages 431–38 in *Public Theology for the 21st Century*. Edited by William F. Storrar and Andrew R. Morton. Edinburgh: T. & T. Clark, 2004.

Fowl, Stephen E. *Engaging Scripture: A Model for Theological Interpretation*. Oxford: Blackwell Publishers, 1998.

Fowl, Stephen E., and L. Gregory Jones. *Reading in Communion: Scripture and Ethics in Christian Life*. London: SPCK, 1991.

Fox, Kathryn J. 'Restoring the Social: Offender Reintegration in a Risky World'. *International Journal of Comparative and Applied Criminal Justice* 38, no. 3 (2013): 235–56.

Freedman, David N., ed. *The Anchor Bible Dictionary*. 12 vols. New York: Doubleday, 1992.

Frei, Hans. *The Identity of Jesus Christ*. Philadelphia, PA: Fortress Press, 1975.

French, Peter. *The Virtues of Vengeance*. Lawrence, KS: University of Kansas Press, 2001.

Garland, David. *The Culture of Control: Crime and Social Order in Contemporary Society*. New York: Oxford University Press, 2001.

Garland, David, and Richard Sparks. 'Criminology, Social Theory and the Challenge of Our Times'. Pages 1–22 in *Criminology and Social Theory*. Edited by David Garland and Richard Sparks. Oxford: Oxford University Press, 2000.

Giddens, Anthony. *Modernity and Self-Identity: Self and Society in the Late Modern Age*. Stanford, CA: Stanford University Press, 1991.

Gorman, Michael J. *Becoming the Gospel: Paul, Participation, and Mission*. Grand Rapids, MI: Eerdmans, 2015.

———. *Inhabiting the Cruciform God: Kenosis, Justification, and Theosis in Paul's Narrative Soteriology*. Grand Rapids, MI: Eerdmans, 2009.

———. 'Justification and Justice in Paul, with Special Reference to the Corinthians'. *Journal for the Study of Paul and His Letters* 1, no. 1 (2011): 23–40.

Gorringe, Timothy. *God's Just Vengeance: Crime, Violence, and the Rhetoric of Salvation*. Cambridge: Cambridge University Press, 1996.

Gregory, Brad S. *The Unintended Reformation: How a Religious Revolution Secularized Society*. Cambridge, MA: Harvard University Press, 2012.

Grimsrud, Ted, and Howard Zehr. 'Rethinking God, Justice, and Treatment of Offenders'. *Journal of Offender Rehabilitation* 35, no. 3–4 (2002): 253–79.

Gunton, Colin E. *The Actuality of Atonement: A Study of Metaphor, Rationality and the Christian Tradition*. Edinburgh: T. & T. Clark, 1988.

Gustafson, James. 'The Sectarian Temptation: Reflections on Theology, the Church and the University'. *Proceedings of the Catholic Theological Society of America* 40 (1985): 83–94.

Hadley, Michael L., ed. *The Spiritual Roots of Restorative Justice*. Albany, NY: State University of New York Press, 2001.

Harink, Douglas. 'Romans: A Treatise on Justice?' *Direction: A Mennonite Brethren Forum* 44, no. 1 (2015): 30–42.

———. 'Setting It Right: Doing Justice to Justification'. *Christian Century* (2005): 20–25.

Hauerwas, Stanley. *After Christendom? How the Church Is to Behave If Freedom, Justice, and a Christian Nation Are Bad Ideas*. Nashville, TN: Abingdon Press, 1991.

———. *Against the Nations: War and Survival in a Liberal Society*. New York: Harper & Row, 1985.

———. *A Better Hope: Resources for a Church Confronting Capitalism, Democracy, and Postmodernity*. Grand Rapids, MI: Brazos Press, 2000.

———. *Character and the Christian Life: A Study in Theological Ethics*. San Antonio, TX: Trinity University Press, 1975.

———. *Christian Existence Today: Essays on Church, World, and Living in Between*. Grand Rapids, MI: Brazos Press, 1988.

———. 'Christian Practice of the Practice of Law in a World without Foundations'. *Mercer Law Review* 44 (1992): 743–51.

———. *A Community of Character: Towards a Constructive Christian Social Ethic*. Notre Dame, IN: Notre Dame University Press, 1981.

———. 'The Difference of Virtue and the Difference It Makes: Courage Exemplified'. *Modern Theology* 9, no. 3 (1993): 249–64.

———. *Dispatches from the Front: Theological Engagements with the Secular*. Durham, NC: Duke University Press, 1994.

———. 'On Doctrine and Ethics'. Pages 21–40 in *The Cambridge Companion to Christian Doctrine*. Edited by Colin Gunton. Cambridge: Cambridge University Press, 1997.

———. *The Peaceable Kingdom: A Primer in Christian Ethics*. Notre Dame, IN: University of Notre Dame, 1983.

———. *Unleashing the Scripture: Freeing the Bible from Captivity to America*. Nashville, TN: Abingdon Press, 1993.

———. *War and the American Difference: Theological Reflections on Violence and National Identity* Grand Rapids, MI: Baker Academic, 2011.

Hauerwas, Stanley, and Samuel Wells. *The Blackwell Companion to Christian Ethics*. Blackwell Companions to Religion. 2nd ed. Chichester, UK: Wiley-Blackwell, 2011.

Hauerwas, Stanley, and William H. Willimon. *Resident Aliens: A Provocative Christian Assessment of Culture and Ministry for People Who Know That Something Is Wrong*. Nashville, TN: Abingdon Press, 1989.

Havener, I. 'A Curse for Salvation—1 Corinthians 5:1–5'. Pages 334–44 in *Sin, Salvation and the Spirit*. Edited by D. Durken. Collegeville, MN: The Liturgical Press, 1979.

Hays, Richard B. *The Conversion of the Imagination: Paul as Interpreter of Israel's Scripture*. Grand Rapids, MI: Eerdmans, 2005.

———. *First Corinthians*. Louisville, KY: John Knox Press, 1997.

———. *The Moral Vision of the New Testament: Community, Cross, New Creation: A Contemporary Introduction to New Testament Ethics*. New York: HarperCollins Publishers, 1996.

Healy, Nicholas M. *Hauerwas: A (Very) Critical Introduction*. Grand Rapids, MI: Eerdmans, 2014.

Hegel, George Wilhelm Friedrich. *Outlines of the Philosophy of Right*. Translated by Stephen Houlgate. Oxford World's Classics. Oxford: Oxford University Press, 2008.

Hein, Kenneth. *Eucharist and Excommunication: A Study in Early Christian Doctrine and Discipline*. Bern, Switzerland: Herbert Lang, 1973.

Herzog II, William R. *Jesus, Justice and the Reign of God: A Ministry of Liberation*. Louisville, KY: John Knox Press, 1999.

Hirsch, Andreas von. 'Punishment Futures'. Pages 256–74 in *Retributivism Has a Past: Has It a Future?* Edited by Michael Tonry. Oxford: Oxford University Press, 2011.

Holmes, Stephen R. *The Holy Trinity: Understanding God's Life*. Milton Keynes, UK: Paternoster, 2012.

Hooker, Morna D. 'On Becoming the Righteousness of God: Another Look at 2 Cor 5:21'. *Novum Testamentum* 50 (2008): 358–75.

Horsley, Richard, ed. *Paul and Empire: Religion and Power in Roman Imperial Society*. Harrisburg, PA: Trinity Press International, 1997.

Hoyle, Carolyn, ed. *Restorative Justice*. Vol. 1. *The Rise of Restorative Justice*. London: Routledge, 2010.

Hudson, Barbara. *Justice Through Punishment: A Critique of the 'Justice' Model of Corrections*. Hampshire, UK: Macmillan Education, 1987.

Immarigeon, Russ. 'What Is the Place of Punishment and Imprisonment in Restorative Justice?'. Pages 143–53 in Zehr and toews, eds., *Critical Issues in Restorative Justice*.

Irenaeus. 'Against Heresies'. In *Ante-Nicene Fathers*. Edited by Alexander Roberts and James Donaldson. New York: Charles Scribner's Sons, 1907.

Johnstone, Gerry. *Restorative Justice: Ideas, Values, Debates*. 2nd ed. New York: Routledge, 2011.

Johnstone, Gerry, and Daniel W. Van Ness. 'The Meaning of Restorative Justice'. Pages 5–23 in *Handbook of Restorative Justice*. Edited by Gerry Johnstone and Daniel W. Van Ness. Devon, UK: Willan, 2007.

'Justice and the Christian Witness: A Summary Statement'. Adopted by General Conference Mennonite Church and Mennonite Church General Assembly. Newtown, KS: Faith and Life Press, 1985.

Justice, Ministry of. *Restorative Justice: Best Practice in New Zealand*. Wellington, New Zealand: Ministry of Justice, 2011.

The Kairos Document, Challenge to the Church: A Theological Comment on the Political Crisis in South Africa. Grand Rapids, MI: Eerdmans, 1986.

Kant, Immanuel. *The Philosophy of Law: An Exposition of the Fundamental Principles of Jurisprudence as the Science of Right*. Translated by W. Hastie. Edinburgh: T. & T. Clark, 1887.

———. 'Universal Practical Philosophy'. Translated by L. Infield. In *Lectures on Ethics 55*. Edited by L. Infield. New York: Harper & Row, 1978.

Keazirian, Edward M. *Peace and Peacemaking in Paul and the Greco-Roman World*. New York: Peter Land, 2014.

Kraybill, Ronald S. *Repairing the Breach: Ministering in Community Conflict*. Scottdale, PA: Herald Press, 1980.

Kreider, Eleanor. 'Let the Faithful Greet Each Other: The Kiss of Peace'. *The Conrad Grebel Review* 5 (1987): 29–49.

Krog, Antjie. *Country of My Skull: Guilt, Sorrow, and the Limits of Forgiveness in the New South Africa*. Johannesburg, South Africa: Random House, 1998.

Kuske, Martin. *The Old Testament as the Book of Christ: An Appraisal of Bonhoeffer's Interpretation*. Philadelphia, PA: Westminster Press, 1976.

Leithart, Peter J. *Defending Constantine: The Twilight of an Empire and the Dawn of Christendom*. Downers Grove, IL: InterVarsity Press, 2012.

Levad, Amy. *Redeeming a Prison Society: A Liturgical and Sacramental Response to Mass Incarceration*. Minneapolis, MN: Fortress Press, 2014.

Lewis, C. S. *God in the Dock: Essays on Theology and Ethics*. Edited by Walter Hooper. Grand Rapids, MI: Eerdmans, 1970.

Liebmann, Marian. *Restorative Justice: How It Works*. London: Jessica Kingsley Publishers, 2007.

Lind, Millard C. *Yahweh Is a Warrior: The Theology of Warfare in Ancient Israel*. Scottdale, PA: Herald Press, 1980.

Lindbeck, George. *The Nature of Doctrine*. Philadelphia, PA: Westminster Press, 1984.

Llewellyn, Jennifer J. 'Integrating Peace, Justice and Development in a Relational Approach to Peacebuilding'. *Ethics and Social Welfare* 6, no. 3 (2012): 290–302.

———. 'Truth Commissions and Restorative Justice'. Pages 351–71 in *Handbook of Restorative Justice*. Edited by Gerry Johnstone and Daniel W. Van Ness. Devon, UK: Willan, 2007.

Llewellyn, Jennifer J., and Daniel Philpott, eds. *Restorative Justice, Reconciliation, and Peacebuilding*, Studies in Strategic Peacebuilding. New York: Oxford University Press, 2014.

Logan, James S. *Good Punishment? Christian Moral Practice and U.S. Imprisonment*. Grand Rapids, MI: Eerdmans, 2008.

London, Ross. *Crime, Punishment, and Restorative Justice: From the Margins to the Mainstream*. Boulder, CO: Lynne Rienner Publishers, 2010.

Loughlin, Gerard. *Telling God's Story: Bible, Church, and Narrative Theology*. Cambridge: Cambridge University Press, 1996.

MacDonald, Arthur. *Criminology*. New York: Funk & Wagnalls, 1983.

MacIntyre, Alasdair. *After Virtue: A Study in Moral Theory*. Notre Dame, IN: University of Notre Dame Press, 1981.

———. *Whose Justice? Which Rationality?* Notre Dame, IN: University of Notre Dame Press, 1988.

Mansill, Douglas. 'Community Empowerment or Institutional Control: The Development of Restorative Justice in New Zealand's Adult Systems of Social Regulation, Control and Punishment'. PhD diss., Auckland University of Technology, New Zealand, 2013.

Markel, Dan. 'Bentham on Stilts: The Bare Relevance of Subjectivity to Retributive Justice'. *California Law Review* 98 (2010): 907–87.

Maruna, Shadd. 'The Role of Wounded Healing in Restorative Justice: An Appreciation of Albert Eglash'. *Restorative Justice: An International Journal* 2, no. 1 (2014): 9–23.

Marshall, Christopher D. *Beyond Retribution: A New Testament Vision for Justice, Crime, and Punishment*. Studies in Peace and Scripture. Grand Rapids, MI: Eerdmans, 2001.

———. *Compassionate Justice: An Interdisciplinary Dialogue with Two Gospel Parables on Law, Crime, and Restorative Justice*. Eugene, OR: Cascade Books, 2012.

———. 'A Gracious Legacy'. *Restorative Justice: An International Journal* 3, no. 3 (2015): 442–44.

———. '"I Have Sinned Against Heaven and Against You": Sin as Relational Rupture in the Teaching of Jesus'. Pages 65–73 in *A Thinker's Guide to Sin: Talking About Wrongdoing Today*. Edited by Neil Darragh. Auckland, New Zealand: Accent Publications, 2010.

———. *The Little Book of Biblical Justice: A Fresh Approach to the Bible's Teachings on Justice*. Intercourse, PA: Good Books, 2005.

———. '"Making Every Effort": Peacemaking and Ecclesiology in Ephesians 4:1–6'. Pages 256–66 in *Struggles for Shalom: Peace and Violence across the Testaments*. Edited by Laura L. Brenneman and Brad D. Schantz. Eugene, OR: Pickwick Publications, 2014.

———. 'Parables as Paradigms for Public Theology'. Pages 23–44 in *Bible, Justice, and Public Theology*. Edited by David Neville. Sheffield: Sheffield Phoenix Press, 2014.

———. 'Restoring What? The Practice, Promise, and Perils of Restorative Justice in New Zealand'. Paper presented at Rutherford House, Victoria University of Wellington, New Zealand, 25 March 2014.

Martinson, Robert. 'What Works? Questions and Answers About Prison Reform'. *The Public Interest* 35 (1974): 22–54.

Martyr, Justin. 'Dialogue with Trypho'. In *Ante-Nicene Fathers*. Edited by Alexander Roberts and James Donaldson. New York: Charles Scribner's Sons, 1907.

———. 'The First Apology'. In *Ante-Nicene Fathers*. Edited by Alexander Roberts and James Donaldson. New York: Charles Scribner's Sons, 1907.

Maruna, Shadd. *Making Good: How Ex-Convicts Reform and Rebuild Their Lives*. Washington DC: American Psychology Association, 2001.

Maruna, Shadd, Louise Wilson and Kathryn Curran. 'Why God Is Often Found Behind Bars: Prison Conversions and the Crisis of Self-Narrative'. *Research in Human Development* 3, no. 2–3 (2006): 161–84.

Mayo, Maria. *The Limits of Forgiveness: Case Studies in the Distortion of a Biblical Idea*. Minneapolis, MN: Fortress Press, 2015.

McClendon Jr., James Wm. *Biography as Theology: How Life Stories Can Remake Today's Theology*. Nashville, TN: Abingdon Press, 1974.

McCold, Paul. 'The Recent History of Restorative Justice: Mediation, Circles, and Conferencing'. Pages 136–75 in *Restorative Justice*. Vol. 1, *The Rise of Restorative Justice*. Edited by Carolyn Hoyle. London: Routledge, 2010.

McElrea, Judge Fred. 'A Christian Approach to Conflict Resolution'. Paper presented at *Australasian Christian Legal Convention*. Melbourne, Australia, 2001.

McGrath, Alister E. *Iustitia Dei: A History of the Christian Doctrine of Justification*. Cambridge: Cambridge University Press, 2005.

McMurray, Heather R., ed. *The New Interpreters Dictionary of the Bible*. Nashville, TN: Abingdon Press, 2009.

McIntyre, John. *St. Anselm and His Critics: A Re-Interpretation of the Cur Deus Homo*. Edinburgh: Oliver & Boyd, 1954.

Menninger, Karl. *Whatever Became of Sin?* London: Hodder & Stoughton, 1973.

'Mennonite Confession of Faith'. *Adopted by Mennonite General Conference*. Scottdale, PA: Herald Press, 1963.

Michael, Jerome, and Mortimer Adler, ed. *Crime, Law, and Social Science*. New York: Harcourt Brace, 1933.

Milbank, John. *Theology and Social Theory: Beyond Secular Reason*. Oxford: Basil Blackwell, 1990.

Moltmann, Jürgen. *The Church in the Power of the Spirit: A Contribution to Messianic Ecclesiology*. Translated by Margaret Kohl. London: SCM Press, 1977.

Moosa, Ebrahim. 'Truth and Reconciliation as Performance: Spectres of Eucharistic Redemption'. Pages 113–22 in *Looking Back, Reaching Forward: Reflections on the Truth and Reconciliation Commission of South Africa*. Edited by Charles Villa-Vicencio and Wilhelm Verwoerd. Cape Town, South Africa: University of Cape Town Press, 2000.

Murphy, Jeffrie G. 'Does Kant Have a Theory of Punishment?'. *Columbia Law Review* 87, no. 3 (1987): 509–32.

———. *Punishment and the Moral Emotions: Essays in Law, Morality, and Religion*. New York: Oxford University Press, 2012.

———. 'Some Second Thoughts on Retributivism'. Pages 93–106 in *Retributivism Has a Past: Has It a Future?* Edited by Michael Tonry. Oxford: Oxford University Press, 2011.

Neufeld, Thomas Yoder. '"In the Middle": Biblical Reflections on Restorative Justice'. Winnipeg, Canada: MCC Restorative Justice Network, 2003.

Neville, David J. 'The Bible, Justice and Public Theology: An Introductory Essay'. Pages 1–21 in *Bible, Justice, and Public Theology*. Edited by David J. Neville. The Bible in the Modern World. Sheffield: Sheffield Phoenix Press, 2014.

———. 'Justice and Divine Judgment: Scriptural Perspectives for Public Theology'. *International Journal of Public Theology* 3 (2009): 339–56.

Newbigin, Lesslie. 'Whose Justice?'. *The Ecumenical Review* 44, no. 3 (1992): 308–11.

Nussbaum, Martha Craven. *Sex and Social Justice*. New York: Oxford University Press, 1999.

O'Donovan, Oliver. *The Desire of the Nations: Rediscovering the Roots of Political Theology*. Cambridge: Cambridge University Press, 1996.

———. *The Ways of Judgment, Bampton Lectures 2003*. Grand Rapids, MI: Eerdmans, 2005.

Pavlich, G. *Governing Paradoxes of Restorative Justice*. London: Glasshouse Press, 2005.

Peachey, Dean E. 'The Kitchener Experiment'. Pages 14–26 in *Mediation and Criminal Justice*. Edited by Martin and Burt Galaway Wright. London: SAGE, 1989.

Penrod, Peter J., and Steven D. Van Koppen, ed. *Adversarial Versus Inquisitorial Justice: Psychological Perspectives on Criminal Justice Systems*. Perspectives in Law and Psychology Series 17. London: Springer, 2012.

Pincoffs, Edmund. *Quandaries and Virtues: Against Reductivism in Ethics*. Lawrence, KS: University of Kansas Press, 1986.

———. 'Quandry Ethics'. *Mind* (1971): 552–71.

Plato. *Gorgias*. Translated by Donald J. Zeyl. Indianapolis, IN: Hackett, 1986.

———. *The Laws*. Translated by Trevor J. Saunders. Harmondsworth, UK: Penguin, 1970.

Pogoloff, S. M. *Logos and Sophia: The Rhetorical Situation of 1 Corinthians*. Atlanta, GA: Scholars Press, 1992.

Porter, Thomas. *Conflict and Communion: Reconciliation and Restorative Justice at Christ's Table*. Nashville, TN: Discipleship Resources, 2006.

———, ed. *The Spirit and Art of Conflict Transformation: Creating a Culture of Justpeace*. Nashville, TN: Upper Room Books, 2010.

Power, David N. 'Eucharistic Justice'. *Theological Studies* 67 (2006): 856–79.

Pranis, Kay. *The Little Book of Circle Processes: A New/Old Approach to Peacemaking*. Intercourse, PA: Good Books, 2005.

———. 'Restorative Values'. Pages 59–74 in *Handbook of Restorative Justice*. Edited by Gerry Johnstone and Daniel W. Van Ness. Devon, UK: Willan, 2007.

Pranis, Kay, Barry Stuart and Mark Wedge. *Peacemaking Circles: From Crime to Community*. St. Paul, MN: Living Justice Press, 2003.

Price, Simon R. F. *Rituals and Power: The Roman Imperial Cult in Asia Minor*. Cambridge: Cambridge University Press, 1984.

Rae, Murray. 'Christ in/and the Old Testament'. *Journal of Theological Interpretation* 2, no. 1 (2008): 1–22.

Rawls, John. 'The Idea of Public Reason Revisited'. In *The Laws of Peoples*. Cambridge, MA: Harvard University Press, 2001.

Rea, Lisa M. 'Restorative Justice: The New Way Forward'. *Christian Reflection: A Series in Faith and Ethics: Prison*. Journal of the Center for Christian Ethics, Baylor University (2012): 29–35.

Robeck, C. M. Jr. 'Prophecy, Prophesying'. Pages 755–62 in *Dictionary of Paul and His Letters*. Edited by Gerald F. Hawthorne and Ralph P. Martin. Downers Grove, IL: InterVarsity Press, 1993.

Rome, Clement of. 'First Epistle to the Corinthians'. In *Ante-Nicene Fathers*. Edited by Alexander Roberts and James Donaldson. New York: Charles Scribner's Sons, 1907.

Ruth-Heffelbower, Duane. 'Toward a Christian Theology of Church and Society as It Relates to Restorative Justice'. Paper presented at the *4th Annual Restorative Justice Conference*. Fresno, CA, 25 October 1996.

Sampley, J. Paul. *Pauline Partnership in Christ: Christian Commitment and Community in Light of Roman Law*. Philadelphia, PA: Fortress Press, 1980.

Schleiermacher, Friedrich. *The Christian Faith*. Edinburgh: T. & T. Clark, 1976.

Schrey, H., H. Walz and W. Whitehouse. *The Biblical Doctrine of Justice and Law*. London: SCM Press, 1955.

Shapland, Joanna, Stephen Farrall and Anthony Bottoms. *Global Perspectives on Desistance: Reviewing What We Know and Looking to the Future*. London: Routledge, 2016.

Sharpe, Susan. 'How Large Should the Restorative Justice "Tent" Be?'. Pages 17–31 in Zehr and Toews, eds., *Critical Issues in Restorative Justice*.

Skotnicki, Andrew. *The Last Judgment: Christian Ethics in a Legal Culture*. Farnham, UK: Ashgate, 2012.

South, J. T. 'A Critique of the "Curse/Death" Interpretation of 1 Corinthians 5:1–8'. *New Testament Studies* 39 (1993): 539–61.

Southern, Richard. *Anselm: A Portrait in a Landscape*. Cambridge: Cambridge University Press, 1990.

Stout, Jeffrey. *Democracy and Tradition*. Princeton, NJ: Princeton University Press, 2004.

Strang, Heather. *Repair or Revenge: Victims and Restorative Justice*. Oxford: Clarendon Press, 2002.

Swartley, Willard M. 'The Relation of Justice/Righteousness to *Shalom/Eirênê*'. *Ex Auditu* 22 (2006): 29–53.

Tanner, Kathryn. 'Justification and Justice in a Theology of Grace'. *Theology Today* (1999): 510–23.

Tauri, J. 'Explaining Recent Innovations in New Zealand's Criminal Justice System: Empowering Maori or Biculturalising the State'. *Australian & New Zealand Journal of Criminology* 32, no. 2 (1999): 153–67.

Taylor, Charles. *A Secular Age*. Cambridge, MA: Belknap Press, 2007.

Temple, William. *Christianity and Social Order*. London: Penguin Special, 1942.

Theissen, Gerd. *The Social Setting of Pauline Christianity: Essays on Corinth*. Translated by John H. Schütz. Philadelphia, PA: Fortress Press, 1982.

Thiselton, Anthony C. *The First Epistle to the Corinthians: A Commentary on the Greek Text*. Grand Rapids, MI: Eerdmans, 2000.

Thorburn, Justice Stan. 'Restorative Justice: Some Biblical Perspectives'. Paper presented at *Prison Fellowship International: Toronto Convocation*. Toronto, Canada, 2003.

Toews, Barb. *The Little Book of Restorative Justice for People in Prison: Rebuilding the Web of Relationships*. Intercourse, PA: Good Books, 2006.

Tonry, Michael. 'Can Twenty-First Century Punishment Policies Be Justified in Principle'. Pages 3–29 in *Retributivism Has a Past: Has It a Future? Edited by* Michael Tonry. Oxford: Oxford University Press, 2011.

Torrance, Alan J. 'On Deriving "Ought" from "Is": Christology, Covenant and *Koinonia*'. Pages 167–90 in *The Doctrine of God and Theological Ethics*. Edited by Alan J. Torrance and Michael Banner. London: T&T Clark, 2006.

———. 'The Theological Grounds for Advocating Forgiveness and Reconciliation in the Sociopolitical Realm'. Pages 45–86 in *The Politics of Past Evil: Religion, Reconciliation, and the Dilemmas of Transitional Justice*. Edited by Daniel Philpott. Notre Dame, IN: University of Notre Dame, 2006.

Torrance, James B. 'Covenant or Contract? A Study of the Theological Background of Worship in Seventeenth-Century Scotland'. *Scottish Journal of Theology* 23 (1970): 51–76.

Truth and Reconciliation Commission of South Africa Report. Cape Town, South Africa: Truth and Reconciliation Commission, 1998.

Tutu, Desmond. *No Future without Forgiveness*. New York: Doubleday, 1999.

Umbreit, Mark, and Marilyn P. Armour. *Restorative Justice Dialogue: An Essential Guide for Research and Practice*. New York: Springer, 2010.

Umbreit, Mark, Jennifer Blevins and Ted Lewis. *The Energy of Forgiveness: Lessons from Those in Restorative Dialogue*. Eugene, OR: Cascade Books, 2015.

Umbreit, Mark S., Betty Vos, Robert B. Coates and Elizabeth Lightfoot. 'Restorative Justice in the Twenty-First Century: A Social Movement Full of Opportunities and Pitfalls'. *Marquette Law Review* 89 (2005/2006): 251–304.

Van Ness, Daniel W., and Karen Heetderks Strong. *Restoring Justice: An Introduction to Restorative Justice*. 4th ed. New Providence, NJ: LexisNexis/Anderson, 2010.

VanAntwerpen, Jonathan. 'Reconciliation as Heterodoxy'. Pages 77–117 in *Restorative Justice, Reconciliation, and Peacebuilding*. Edited by Jennifer J. Llewellyn and Daniel Philpott. New York: Oxford University Press, 2014.

Vanhoozer, Kevin, ed. *Dictionary for Theological Interpretation of the Bible*. Grand Rapids, MI: Baker Academic, 2005.

Vidu, Adonis. *Atonement, Law, and Justice: The Cross in Historical and Cultural Contexts*. Grand Rapids, MI: Baker Academic, 2014.

Volf, Miroslav. 'Against a Pretentious Church: A Rejoinder to Bell's Response'. *Modern Theology* 19, no. 2 (2003): 281–85.

———. *Captive to the Word of God: Engaging the Scriptures for Contemporary Theological Reflection*. Grand Rapids, MI: Eerdmans, 2010.

———. *Exclusion and Embrace: A Theological Exploration of Identity, Otherness, and Reconciliation*. Nashville, TN: Abingdon Press, 1996.

———. '*Liberation Theology After the End of History*: An Exchange'. *Modern Theology* 19, no. 2 (2003): 261–85.

Von Hirsch, Andreas. *Doing Justice*. New York: Hill & Wang, 1976.

Walgrave, Lode. *Restorative Justice, Self-Interest and Responsible Citizenship*. London: Routledge, 2012.

Wannenwetsch, Bernd. '"Members of One Another": *Charis*, Ministry and Representation: A Politico-Ecclesial Reading of Romans 12'. Pages 196–220 in *A Royal Priesthood? The Use of the Bible Ethically and Politically: A Dialogue with Oliver O'Donovan*. Edited by Craig Bartholomew, Jonathan Chaplin, Robert Song and Al Wolters. Grand Rapids, MI: Paternoster Press, 2002.

———. *Political Worship: Ethics for Christian Citizens*. Oxford: Oxford University Press, 2004. Originally Published as *Gottesdienst als Lebensform - Ethik für Christenbürger*. Berlin: W. Kohlhammer, 1997.

Ward, Graham. *The Politics of Discipleship*. Grand Rapids, MI: Baker Academic, 2009.

Ward, Tony, and Mark Brown. 'The Good Lives Model and Conceptual Issues in Offender Rehabilitation'. *Psychology, Crime & Law* 10, no. 3 (2004): 243–57.

Webster, John. *Barth's Ethics of Reconciliation*. Cambridge: Cambridge University Press, 1995.

Weitekamp, Elmar G. M., and Stephan Parmetier. 'Restorative Justice as Healing Justice: Looking Back to the Future of the Concept'. *Restorative Justice: An International Journal* 4, no. 2 (2016): 141–47.

Weitekamp, Elmar G. M., and Hans-Jurgen Kerner, ed. *Restorative Justice: Theoretical Foundations*. Devon, UK: Willan, 2002.

Wells, Samuel. *Improvisation: The Drama of Christian Ethics*. London: SPCK, 2004.

Wells, Samuel, and Ben Quash. *Introducing Christian Ethics*. West Sussex, UK: Wiley-Blackwell, 2010.

Wenzel, M., et al. 'Retributive and Restorative Justice'. *Law and Human Behavior* 32 (2008): 375–89.

Wheatley, Margaret J. *Turning to One Another: Simple Conversations to Restore Hope to the Future*. Los Angeles, CA: Berrett-Koehler Publishers, 2002.

Whitman, James Q. *The Origins of Reasonable Doubt: Theological Roots of the Criminal Trial*. New Haven, CT: Yale University Press, 2008.

———. *Harsh Justice: Criminal Punishment and the Widening Divide Between America and Europe*. New York: Oxford University Press, 2003.

Wiesenthal, Simon. *The Sunflower: On the Possibilities and Limits of Forgiveness*. New York: Schocken Books, 1998.

Will, Emily. '"Prophet" of Justice Visits New Zealand'. *Mennonite Weekly Review* (11 August 1994): 2.

Witte Jr., John. *God's Joust, God's Justice: Law and Religion in the Western Tradition*. Grand Rapids, MI: Eerdmans, 2006.

Witherington III, Ben W. *Conflict and Community in Corinth: A Socio-Rhetorical Commentary on 1 and 2 Corinthians*. Grand Rapids, MI: Eerdmans, 1995.

Wolterstorff, Nicholas. *Justice in Love*. Grand Rapids, MI: Eerdmans, 2011.

———. *Justice: Rights and Wrongs*. Princeton, NJ: Princeton University Press, 2008.

Woolford, Andrew. *The Politics of Restorative Justice: A Critical Introduction*. Winnipeg, MB: Fernwood, 2010.

Workman, Kim. 'Politics and Punitiveness: Limiting the Rush to Punish'. Paper presented at the The Rising Punitiveness, Wellington, New Zealand, 2011.

Wright, N. T. 'Translating δικαιοσύνη: A Response'. *The Expository Times* 125, no. 10 (2014): 487–90.

Yantzi, Mark, and Dave Worth. 'The Developmental Steps of the Victim/Offender Reconciliation Project'. Unpublished, 1977.

Yoder, John H. 'Binding and Loosing'. Pages 323–58 in *Royal Priesthood: Essays Ecclesiological and Ecumenical*. Edited by Michael Cartwright. Scottdale, PA: Herald Press, 1998.

———. *Body Politics: Five Practices of the Christian Community Before the Watching World*. Nashville, TN: Discipleship Resources, 1992.

———. *Christian Attitudes to War, Peace, and Revolution*. Edited by Theodore J. Koontz and Andy Alexis-Baker. Grand Rapids, MI: Brazos Press, 2009.

———. *Christian Witness to the State*. Newton, KS: Faith & Life Press, 1964.

———. 'The Hermeneutics of Peoplehood: A Protestant Perspective on Practical Moral Reasoning'. *The Journal of Religious Ethics* 10, no. 1 (1982): 40–67.

———. 'The Meaning of the Constantinian Shift'. Pages 57–74 in *Christian Attitudes to War, Peace, and Revolution*. Edited by Theodore J. Koontz and Andy Alexis-Baker. Grand Rapids, MI: Brazos Press, 2009.

———. *Nevertheless: A Meditation on the Varieties and Shortcomings of Religious Pacifism*. Scottdale, PA: Herald Press, 1971.

———. *The Original Revolution: Essays on Christian Pacifism*. Scottdale, PA: Herald Press, 1971.

———. *The Politics of Jesus*. Grand Rapids, MI: Eerdmans, 1972.

———. *The Politics of Jesus: Vicit Agnus Noster*. 2nd ed. Grand Rapids, MI: Eerdmans, 1994.

———. *The Priestly Kingdom: Social Ethics as Gospel*. Notre Dame, IN: University of Notre Dame, 1984.

Yoder, Perry B. *Shalom: The Bible's Word for Salvation, Justice, and Peace*. Newton, KS: Faith & Life Press, 1987.

———. 'Toward a Shalom Biblical Theology'. *Conrad Grebel Review* 1, no. 3 (1983): 39–49.

Zedner, L. 'Reparation and Retribution: Are They Reconcilable?'. *Modern Law Review* 57 (1994): 228–50.

Zehr, Howard. *Changing Lenses: A New Focus for Crime and Justice*. A Christian Peace Shelf Selection. Scottdale, PA: Herald Press, 1990.

———. *Changing Lenses: A New Focus for Crime and Justice*. 3rd ed. Scottdale, PA: Herald Press, 2005.

———. *Crime and the Development of Modern Society: Patterns of Criminality in Nineteenth Century Germany and France*. London: Croom Helm, 1976.

———. 'Justice Paradigm Shift? Values and Visions in the Reform Process'. *Mediation Quarterly* 12, no. 3 (1995): 207–16.

———. *The Little Book of Restorative Justice*. Intercourse, PA: Good Books, 2002.

———. *Mediating the Victim-Offender Conflict*. Elkhart, IN: Mennonite Central Committee, 1980.

———. 'Restoring Justice'. Pages 131–59 in *God and the Victim: Theological Reflections on Evil, Victimization, Justice, and Forgiveness*. Edited by Lisa Barnes Lampman and Michelle D. Shattuck. Grand Rapids, MI: Eerdmans, 1999.

———. 'Retributive Justice, Restorative Justice'. *New Perspectives on Crime and Justice: Occasional Papers*, no. 4 (1985): n.p.

———. *The VORP Book: An Organizational and Operations Manual*. Valparaiso, IN: Victim Offender Reconciliation Resource Center, 1984.

———. *Who Is My Neighbor? Learning to Care for Victims of Crime*. Elkhart, IN: Mennonite Central Committee, 1984.

Zehr, Howard, and Barb Toews, eds. *Critical Issues in Restorative Justice*. Devon, UK: Willan, 2004.

Zerbe, Gordon M. 'From Retributive to Restorative Justice in Romans'. *Direction: A Mennonite Brethren Forum* 44, no. 1 (2015): 43–58.

Zizioulas, John D. *Being as Communion: Studies in Personhood and the Church*. Crestwood, NY: St Vladimir's Seminary Press, 1985.

Index of References

Index of Authors

CPSIA information can be obtained
at www.ICGtesting.com
Printed in the USA
LVOW13*1917090518
576575LV00009B/130/P

9 780567 671530